# Travellers' Multilingual Phrase Book

D1337512

First published 1983 by Pan Books Ltd,
Cavaye Place, London SW10 9PG

The publishers would like to thank the various national tourist offices for their help during the preparation of this book

First published 1983 by Pan Books Ltd
Cavaye Place, London SW10 9PG
9 8 7 6
© A. Cheyne, F. Clark, D. L. Ellis, R. Ellis, D. van der Luit, C. Mariella,
K. Sandeman McLaughlin, H. Rapi, E. Spong 1983
Printed and bound in Great Britain by
Hazell Watson & Viney Limited,
Member of the BPCC Group,
Aylesbury, Bucks

ISBN 0 330 26976 3

# Contents

# Using the phrase book and a note on the pronunciation system

- This phrase book is designed to help you get by in eight languages, to get what you want or need. It concentrates on the simplest but most effective way you can express these needs in an unfamiliar language.

- The CONTENTS for each different language section gives you a good idea of which pages to consult for the phrase you need.

- The INDEX at the end of each language section gives more detailed information about where to look for your phrase. When you have found the right page you will be given:

  - either – the exact phrase
  - or – help in making up a suitable sentence
  - and – help in getting the pronunciation right

- The English sentences in **bold type** will be useful for you in a variety of different situations, so they are worth learning by heart.

- In some cases you will find help in understanding what people say to *you*, in reply to your questions.

- Note especially these two sections:
  Everyday expressions
  Shop talk
  You are sure to want to refer to them most frequently.

- When you arrive in the foreign country make good use of the tourist information offices.

- The pronunciation system in this book is founded on three assumptions: firstly, that it is not possible to describe in print the sounds of a foreign language in such a way that the English speaker with no phonetic training will produce them accurately, or even intelligibly; secondly, that perfect pronunciation is not essential for communication; and lastly that the average visitor abroad is more interested in achieving successful communication than in learning how to pronounce new speech sounds. Observation and experience have shown these assumptions to be justified. The most important characteristic of the present system, therefore, is that it makes no attempt whatsoever to teach the sounds of the other language, but uses instead the nearest English sounds to them. The sentences transcribed for pronunciation are designed to be read as naturally as possible, as if they were ordinary English (of a generally south-eastern variety) and with no attempt to make the words sound 'foreign'. In this way you will still sound quite English but you will at the same time be understood. Practice always helps performance and it is a good idea to rehearse out loud any of the sentences you know you are going to need. When you come to the point of using them, say them with conviction.

# Travellers' **Dutch**

D. L. Ellis, D. van der Luit

Pronunciation Dr J. Baldwin

*Useful addresses*

Netherlands National Tourist Office (NNTO)
Savory and Moore House
2nd Floor
143 New Bond Street
London W1Y 0QS

Belgian National Tourist Office
66 Haymarket
London SW1

# Contents

**Reference**

# Pronunciation hints

In Dutch it is important to stress or emphasize the syllables in italics, just as you would if we were to take as an English example: *Li*ttle Jack *Hor*ner *sat* in the *cor*ner. Here we have ten syllables but only four stresses.
*Succes!*

# Everyday expressions

*[See also 'Shop talk', p. 23]*

- Although you will find the correct greetings listed below, the Dutch commonly use **daag** (duk) to express all of these.

| | |
|---|---|
| Hello | **Hallo** <br> hull*o* |
| Good morning | **Goede morgen** <br> h*oo*-der m*o*r-hen |
| Good afternoon | **Goede middag** <br> h*oo*-der mid-d*u*k |
| Good day | **Goede dag** <br> h*oo*-der duk |
| Good evening | **Goede avond** <br> h*oo*-der *a*h-vent |
| Good night | **Goede nacht** <br> h*oo*-der nuk*t* |
| Goodbye | **Tot ziens** <br> tot z*ee*ns |
| Yes | **Ja** <br> yah |
| Please | **Alstublieft** <br> uls-too-bl*ee*ft |
| Thank you | **Dank u** <br> dunk oo |
| Thank you very much | **Dank u wel** <br> dunk oo wel |
| That's right | **Precies** <br> prer-s*ee*s |
| No | **Nee** <br> nay |
| No, thank you | **Nee, dank u** <br> nay dunk oo |
| I disagree | **Ik ben het er niet mee eens** <br> ik ben et er n*ee*t may ayns |
| Excuse me | **Pardon** <br> par-d*o*n |
| Don't mention it | **Geen dank** <br> hain dunk |

| | |
|---|---|
| It doesn't matter | **Het geeft niet** |
| | et ha*y*ft neet |
| Where's the toilet please? | **Waar is het toilet, alstublieft?** |
| | wahr is et twah-le*t* uls-too-bl*ee*ft |
| Do you speak English? | **Spreekt u engels?** |
| | spra*y*kt oo *e*ng-els |
| What's your name? | **Hoe heet u?** |
| | hoo hate oo |
| My name is . . . | **Ik heet . . .** |
| | ik hate . . . |

# Asking the way

## ESSENTIAL INFORMATION

- Keep a look out for all these place names as you will find them on shops, maps and notices.

## WHAT TO SAY

| | |
|---|---|
| Excuse me, please | **Neem me niet kwalijk . . .** |
| | name mer neet kw*a*h-lek . . . |
| How do I get . . . | **Hoe kom ik naar . . .** |
| | hoo kom ik nar . . . |
| to the airport? | **het vliegveld?** |
| | et vl*ee*k-velt |
| to Amsterdam? | **Amsterdam?** |
| | umster-d*u*m |
| to the beach? | **het strand?** |
| | et strunt |
| to the bus station? | **het bus station?** |
| | et b*u*s stats-see-on |
| to the Centraal hotel? | **het Centraal Hotel?** |
| | et cen-tr*a*hl hotel |
| to the Concertgebouw? | **het Concertgebouw?** |
| | et con-s*ai*rt-her-ba-oo |
| to the Delta Works? | **de Delta Werken?** |
| | der delta w*ai*rken |

**How do I get . . .**
Hoe kom ik naar . . .
hoo kom ik nar

to the market?
**de markt?**
der markt

to the police station?
**het politiebureau?**
et poh-*lee*-tsee-boo-ro

to the post office?
**het postkantoor?**
et posst-kun-tor

to the railway station?
**het spoorwegstation?**
et spor-wek-stats-see-on

to the Rijksmuseum?
**het Rijksmuseum?**
et reyks-moo-sayem

to the Rokin?
**het Rokin?**
et rok-kin

to the sports stadium?
**het stadion?**
et stah-dee-on

to the tourist information office?
**het VVV kantoor?**
et vay-vay-vay kun-tor

to Utrecht?
**Utrecht?**
oo-trekt

**Is there . . . near by?**
Is hier in de buurt . . .
is here in der boort . . .

a baker's
**een bakker?**
en bukker

a bank
**een bank?**
en bunk

a bar
**een bar?**
en bar

a bus stop
**een bushalte?**
en bus-hulter

a butcher's
**een slager?**
en slah-her

a café
**een café**
en cuf-fay

a cake shop
**een banketwinkel?**
en bunket-winkel

a campsite
**een camping?**
en camping

a car park
**een parkeerterrein?**
en par-kair-terreyn

a change bureau
**een wissel kantoor?**
en wissel kun-tor

| | |
|---|---|
| a chemist's | **een drogist?** |
| | en dro-*h*ist |
| a delicatessen | **een delicatessen winkel?** |
| | en day-lee-kah-*te*s-sen w*i*nkel |
| a dentist's | **een tandarts?** |
| | en t*u*nt-arts |
| a department store | **een warenhuis?** |
| | en w*a*h-ren-ho-ees |
| a disco | **een disco** |
| | en dis-ko |
| a doctor's surgery | **een dokter?** |
| | en d*o*k-ter |
| a dry-cleaner's | **een stomerij?** |
| | een stomer-r*e*y |
| a fishmonger's | **een viswinkel?** |
| | en v*i*s-winkel |
| a garage (for repairs) | **een garage?** |
| | en hah-*ra*h-zher |
| a hairdresser's | **een kapper?** |
| | en k*u*pper |
| a greengrocer's | **een groentewinkel?** |
| | en hroonter-w*i*nkel |
| a grocer's | **een kruidenierswinkel?** |
| | en kro-ee-der-n*ee*rs-w*i*nkel |
| a Health and Social Security Office | **een Kantoor Gezondheids en Sociale Zorg Dienst?** |
| | en kun-t*o*r her-*zo*nt-heyts en soh-see-*ah*-ler z*o*rk deenst |
| a hospital | **een ziekenhuis?** |
| | en z*ee*ken-ho-ees |
| a hotel | **een hotel?** |
| | en ho-t*e*l |
| an ice-cream parlour | **een ijs-salon?** |
| | en *e*ys-sah-lon |
| a laundry | **een wasserij?** |
| | en wusser-r*e*y |
| a night club | **een nacht club?** |
| | en n*u*kt cloop |
| a park | **een park?** |
| | en park |
| a petrol station | **een benzinepompstation?** |
| | en ben-zee-ner-p*o*mp-stats-see-on |

| | |
|---|---|
| **Is there . . . near by?** | **Is hier in de buurt . . .** |
| | is here in der boort . . . |
| a post box | **een brievenbus?** |
| | en br*ee*ven-bus |
| a public toilet | **een openbaar toilet?** |
| | en open-bar twah-let |
| a restaurant | **een restaurant?** |
| | en res-to-r*a*n |
| a supermarket | **een supermarkt?** |
| | en s*oo*per-markt |
| a telephone (booth) | **een telefoon cel?** |
| | en tele*f*one cel |
| a tobacconist's | **een sigarenwinkel?** |
| | en see-h*a*hren winkel |
| a travel agent's | **een reisbureau?** |
| | en r*ey*s-boo-r*o* |
| a youth hostel | **een jeugdherberg?** |
| | en y*e*rkt-hair-bairk |

## DIRECTIONS

- Asking where a place is, or if a place is near by, is one thing; making sense of the answer is another.

- Here are some of the most important key directions and replies.

| | |
|---|---|
| Left | **Links** |
| | links |
| Right | **Rechts** |
| | rekts |
| Straight on | **Rechtdoor** |
| | rekt-dor |
| There | **Daar** |
| | dar |
| First left/right | **Eerste links/rechts** |
| | *ai*r-ster links/rekts |

# Accommodation

## ESSENTIAL INFORMATION
### Hotel

- If you want hotel-type accommodation, all the following words in capital letters are worth looking for on name boards:
  **HOTEL   MOTEL**
  **PENSION** (boarding house)
  **JEUGDHERBERG** (youth hostel)
- A list of hotels in the town or district can usually be obtained at the local tourist office.
- All hotels are listed, the cheaper ones having no star rating, while the more luxurious and expensive having proportionally more stars.
- The cost is displayed in the room itself, so you can check it when having a look round before agreeing to stay.
- The displayed cost is for the room itself, per night and not per person. Breakfast is extra and therefore optional.
- Service and VAT (**BTW**) is always included in the cost of the room, so tipping is voluntary.
- Not all hotels provide meals, apart from breakfast. A breakfast will consist of coffee/tea, bread (usually rolls), cold meats, cheese, jam and fruit.
- An identity document is requested when registering at a hotel and will normally be kept overnight.

## WHAT TO SAY

| | |
|---|---|
| I have a booking | **Ik heb een gereserveerde kamer** |
| | ik hep en her-ray-ser-vair-der kah-mer |
| Have you any vacancies, please? | **Heeft u nog kamers?** |
| | hayft oo nok kah-mers |
| Can I book a room? | **Kan ik een kamer reserveren?** |
| | kun ik en kah-mer ray-ser-vairen |
| It's for . . . | **Het is voor . . .** |
| | et is vor . . . |
| one adult/person | **één volwassene/persoon** |
| | ayn vol-wusserner/pair-sohn |

| It's for . . . | **Het is voor . . .** |
| | et is vor . . . |
| two adults/people | **twee volwassenen/personen** |
| | tway vol-w*u*ssernen/pair-s*o*h-nen |
| and one child | **en één kind** |
| | en ayn kint |
| and two children | **en twee kinderen** |
| | en tway k*i*n-der-en |
| It's for . . . | **Het is voor . . .** |
| | et is vor . . . |
| one night | **één nacht** |
| | ayn nukt |
| two nights | **twee nachten** |
| | tway nukten |
| one week | **één week** |
| | ayn wake |
| two weeks | **twee weken** |
| | tway w*a*ken |
| I would like . . . | **Ik zou graag . . .** |
| | ik zow hrahk . . . |
| a room | **een kamer** |
| | en k*a*h-mer |
| two rooms | **twee kamers** |
| | tway k*a*hmers |
| with a single bed | **met een één-persoonsbed** |
| | met en *a*yn-pair-sohns-bet |
| with two single beds | **met twee één-persoonsbedden** |
| | met tway *a*yn-pair-sohns-bed-den |
| with a double bed | **met een tweepersoonsbed** |
| | met en tway-pair-sohns-bet |
| with a toilet | **met toilet** |
| | met twah-l*e*t |
| with a bathroom | **met badkamer** |
| | met b*u*t-kah-mer |
| with a shower | **met douche** |
| | met doosh |
| with a cot | **met een wieg** |
| | met en week |
| I'd like . . . | **Ik wil het graag met . . . hebben** |
| | ik wil et hrahk met . . . h*e*bben |
| full board | **vol pension** |
| | vol pun-see-*o*n |

| | |
|---|---|
| half board | **half (demi) pension** |
| | hulf (day-mee) pun-see-on |
| Do you serve meals? | **Kunnen we hier eten?** |
| | koonnen wer here ay-ten |
| Can I look at the room? | **Kan ik de kamer zien?** |
| | kun ik der kah-mer zeen |
| OK, I'll take it | **Goed, ik neem het** |
| | hoot ik name et |
| No thanks, I won't take it | **Nee dank u, deze niet** |
| | nay dunk oo dazer neet |
| The bill, please | **De rekening, alstublieft** |
| | der rayker-ning uls-too-bleeft |
| Is service included? | **Is het inclusief bediening?** |
| | is et in-cloo-seef ber-dee-ning |
| I think this is wrong | **Ik denk dat dit verkeerd is** |
| | ik denk dut dit ver-kairt is |
| May I have a receipt? | **Mag ik een kwitantie hebben?** |
| | muk ik en kwee-tun-tsee hebben |

## Camping

- Look for the words **CAMPING** or **KAMPEERTERREIN**.
- Be prepared to have to pay:
  per person
  for the car
  for the tent or caravan plot
  for electricity
  for hot showers
- You must provide proof of identity, such as your passport.
- Officially recognized campsites have a star rating: the more stars, the better equipped.
- Camping is regulated by local and provincial by-laws. Lists are available from the VVV.
- Off-site camping is not permitted.

## Youth hostels

- Look for the word: **JEUGDHERBERG**
- You must have a YHA card.
- The charge for the night is the same for all ages, but some hostels are dearer than others.

- You must bring your own sleeping bag lining.
- Accommodation is usually provided in small dormitories.
- Food and cooking facilities vary from place to place and you may also have to help with jobs.

## WHAT TO SAY

| | |
|---|---|
| Have you any vacancies? | **Heeft u nog iets vrij?** |
| | hayft oo nok eets vrey |
| **How much is it . . .** | **Hoeveel is het . . .** |
| | hoo-vale is et . . . |
| for the tent? | **voor de tent?** |
| | vor der tent |
| for the caravan? | **voor de caravan?** |
| | vor der caravan |
| for the car? | **voor de auto?** |
| | vor der owto |
| for the electricity? | **voor de elektriciteit?** |
| | vor der ay-lek-tree-see-tait |
| per person? | **per persoon?** |
| | pair pair-sohn |
| per day/night? | **per dag/nacht?** |
| | pair duk/nukt |
| May I look round? | **Mag ik even rondkijken?** |
| | muk ik ay-ven rond-kaiken |
| Do you provide anything . . . | **Serveert u iets . . .** |
| | sair-vairt oo eets . . . |
| to eat? | **te eten?** |
| | ter ay-ten |
| to drink? | **te drinken?** |
| | ter drinken |
| **Do you have . . .** | **Heeft u . . .** |
| | hayft oo . . . |
| a bar? | **een bar?** |
| | en bar |
| hot showers? | **warme douches?** |
| | warmer dooshes |
| a kitchen? | **een keuken?** |
| | en kerken |
| a laundry? | **een wasserij?** |
| | en wusser-rey |
| a restaurant? | **een restaurant?** |
| | en res-to-ran |

a shop? **een winkel?**
en winkel

a swimming pool? **een zwembad?**
en zwem-but

[*For food shopping, see p. 26, and for eating and drinking out, see p. 36*]

## Problems

The toilet **Het toilet**
et twah-let

The shower **De douche**
der doosh

The tap **De kraan**
der krahn

The razor point **Het scheer-contact**
et skair-contuct

The light **Het licht**
et likt

. . . is not working **. . . werkt niet**
. . . wairkt neet

My camping gas has run out **Ik heb geen kampgas meer**
ik hep hane kump-hus mair

## LIKELY REACTIONS

Have you an identity **Heeft u een identiteitsbewijs?**
document? hayft oo en ee-den-tee-taits-ber-
weys

Your membership card, please **Uw lidmaatschap-kaart, alstublieft**
oo lit-maht-skup-kart uls-too-bleeft

What's your name? **Wat is uw naam?**
[*see p. 11*] wut is oo nahm

Sorry, we're full **Het spijt me, we zijn vol**
et spate mer wer zane vol

How many people is it for? **Voor hoeveel personen is het?**
vor hoo-vale pair-soh-nen is et

How many nights is it for? **Voor hoeveel nachten is het?**
vor hoo-vale nukten is et

It's (12) guilders . . . **Het is (twaalf) gulden . . .**
et is (twahlf) hool-den . . .

per day/night **per dag/nacht**
[*For numbers, see p. 54*] pair duk/nukt

| | |
|---|---|
| I haven't any rooms left | **Ik heb geen kamers meer** |
| | ik hep hane k*a*h-mers mair |
| Do you want to have a look? | **Wilt u even kijken?** |
| | wilt oo *a*y-ven kai-ken |

# *General shopping*

## The chemist's

### ESSENTIAL INFORMATION

- Look for the words
  **APOTHEEK** and **DROGIST**.
  You may also see the following
  signs: a serpent on a staff denotes
  an **apotheek** and a bust of a **gaper**
  (yawner) a **drogist**.
- Medicines (drugs) are available
  only at the **apotheek**.
- Some non-drugs can be bought
  at the **drogist**, at department
  stores or supermarkets.
- Dispensing chemists are
  open Monday to Friday
  8.00 a.m. – 5.30 p.m.
  Chemists take it in turn to
  stay open over the weekend
  and at night.
- Some toiletries can also be
  bought at a **PARFUMERIE** and at hairdressing salons.

### WHAT TO SAY

| | |
|---|---|
| I'd like . . . | **Ik zou graag . . . hebben** |
| | ik zow hrahk . . . h*e*bben |
| some Alka Seltzer | **wat Alka Seltzer** |
| | wut alka seltzer |

| | |
|---|---|
| some antiseptic | **een antiseptisch middel** |
| | en *u*ntee-septees middel |
| some aspirin | **wat aspirine** |
| | wut uspee-r*ee*ner |
| some baby food | **wat baby voeding** |
| | wut b*a*by v*oo*ding |
| some contraceptives | **wat voorbehoedsmiddelen** |
| | wut v*o*r-ber-hoots-m*i*ddelen |
| some cotton wool | **wat watten** |
| | wut w*u*tten |
| some disposable nappies | **wat weggooi luiers** |
| | wut w*e*k-hoy lo-ee-ers |
| some eye drops | **wat oogdruppels** |
| | wut *oa*k-druppels |
| some inhalant | **een inhaleermiddel** |
| | en in-hah-l*air*-middel |
| some insect repellent | **een insecten afweermiddel** |
| | een insecten *u*f-wair-middel |
| some paper tissues | **wat papieren tissues** |
| | wut pah-p*ee*-ren t*i*s-sues |
| some sanitary towels | **wat damesverband** |
| | wut d*a*h-mer-ver-b*u*nt |
| some sticking plaster | **wat pleisters** |
| | wut pl*ey*-sters |
| some suntan oil/lotion | **wat zonnebrand olie/creme** |
| | wut z*o*nner-brunt *o*h-lee/crem |
| some Tampax | **wat Tampax** |
| | wut t*u*mpux |
| some throat pastilles | **wat keelpastilles** |
| | wut k*a*le-pus-til-yes |
| some (soft) toilet paper | **wat (zacht) toiletpapier** |
| | wut (zukt) twah-l*e*t-pah-peer |
| **I'd like something for . . .** | **Ik zou graag iets hebben voor . . .** |
| | ik zow hrahk eets h*e*bben vor . . . |
| bites | **beten** |
| | b*a*yten |
| burns | **brandwonden** |
| | br*u*nt-wonden |
| a cold | **verkoudheid** |
| | ver-k*o*wt-hate |
| constipation | **constipatie** |
| | con-stee-p*a*h-tsee |

| I'd like something for . . . | **Ik zou graag iets hebben voor . . .** |
| | ik zow hrahk eets hebben vor . . . |
| a cough | **hoest** |
| | hoost |
| diarrhoea | **diarree** |
| | dee-ar-ray |
| ear-ache | **oorpijn** |
| | or-pain |
| flu | **griep** |
| | hreep |
| sore gums | **zeer tandvlees** |
| | zair tunt-vlays |
| stings | **steken** |
| | stayken |
| sunburn | **zonnebrand** |
| | zonner-brunt |
| travel sickness | **reis ziekte** |
| | reys zeek-ter |

[*For other essential expressions, see 'Shop talk', p. 23*]

# Holiday items

## ESSENTIAL INFORMATION

- Places to shop at and signs to look for:
  **BOEKWINKEL** (bookshop, stationery)
  **FOTOGRAFIE**
  and of course department stores such as: **DE BIJENKORF**
  **HEMA     VROOM EN DREESMANN**

## WHAT TO SAY

| I'd like . . . | **Ik zou graag . . .** |
| | ik zow hrahk . . . |
| a bag | **een tas** |
| | en tus |

| a beach ball | **een strandbal** |
| | en str*u*nt-bul |
| a bucket | **een emmer** |
| | en *e*mmer |
| an English newspaper | **een engelse krant** |
| | en eng-el-ser kr*u*nt |
| some envelopes | **wat enveloppen** |
| | w*u*t enver-loppen |
| a guide book | **een reisgids** |
| | en r*e*ys-hits |
| a map (of the area) | **een kaart (van de omgeving)** |
| | en kart (v*u*n der om-h*a*yving) |
| some postcards | **wat ansichtkaarten** |
| | w*u*t uns*i*kt-karten |
| a spade | **een schop** |
| | en skop |
| a straw hat | **een stroohoed** |
| | en str*o*h-hoot |
| some sunglasses | **een zonnebril** |
| | en z*o*nner-bril |
| some writing paper | **wat schrijfpapier** |
| | w*u*t skr*e*yf-pah-peer |
| a colour film | **een kleurenfilm** |
| [*show camera*] | en kl*e*r-ren-film |
| a black and white film | **een zwart-wit film** |
| | en zwart-wit film |

# Shop talk

## ESSENTIAL INFORMATION

- Know how to say the important weights and measures. You will hear grams, ounces, kilos and pounds used in shops and markets. The metric Dutch pound **pond** (pont) is ten per cent more than the UK pound and there are exactly **2 pond** in 1 kilo. The metric

Dutch ounce **ons** (ons) is equivalent to 100 grams. Throughout the book you will find that we have used the colloquial Dutch expressions (i.e. ½ oz, 1 oz, 1 lb) to translate grams and kilograms, as they are both more widely used and simpler to say. [*For numbers, see p. 54*]

| | |
|---|---|
| 50 grams/½ oz | **vijftig gram/een half ons** |
| | ve*y*ftik hrum/en hulf ons |
| 100 grams/1 oz | **honderd gram/één ons** |
| | h*o*ndert hrum/ayn ons |
| 200 grams/2 oz | **tweehonderd gram/twee ons** |
| | tw*ay*-hondert hrum/tway ons |
| 250 grams/½ lb | **tweehonderdvijftig gram/een half pond** |
| | tw*ay*-hondert-ve*y*ftik hrum/en hulf pont |
| ½ kilo/l lb | **een halve kilo/één pond** |
| | en h*u*lver kilo/ayn pont |
| 1 kilo/2 lbs | **één kilo/twee pond** |
| | ayn kilo/tway pont |
| 2 kilos | **twee kilo** |
| | tway kilo |
| ½ litre | **een halve liter** |
| | een h*u*lver l*ee*ter |
| 1 litre | **één liter** |
| | ayn l*ee*ter |
| 2 litres | **twee liter** |
| | tway l*ee*ter |

● In small shops don't be surprised if customers, as well as the shop assistant say 'hello' and 'goodbye' to you.

## CUSTOMER

| | |
|---|---|
| I'm just looking | **Ik kijk even** |
| | ik keyk *a*y-ven |
| How much is this/that? | **Hoeveel is dit/dat?** |
| | h*oo*-vale is dit/dut |
| What's that? | **Wat is dat?** |
| | wut is dut |
| What are those? | **Wat zijn dat?** |
| | wut zane dut |
| Is there a discount? | **Is er korting op?** |
| | is er k*o*rting op |

| | |
|---|---|
| I'd like that, please | **Ik wil dat graag hebben, alstublieft** |
| | ik wil dut hrahk hebben uls-too- |
| | bleeft |
| Not that | **Dat niet** |
| | dut neet |
| Like that | **Zoals dat** |
| | zo-uls dut |
| That's enough, thank you | **Dat is genoeg, dank u** |
| | dut is her-nook dunk oo |
| More please | **Wat meer alstublieft** |
| | wut mair uls-too-bleeft |
| Less please | **Wat minder alstublieft** |
| | wut min-der uls-too-bleeft |
| That's fine | **Dat is fijn** |
| | dut is fane |
| OK | **Ok** |
| | okay |
| I won't take it, thank you | **Ik neem het niet, dank u** |
| | ik name et neet dunk oo |
| It's not right | **Het is niet goed** |
| | et is neet hoot |
| **Have you got something . . .** | **Heeft u iets . . .** |
| | heyft oo eets . . . |
| better? | **beters?** |
| | bayters |
| cheaper? | **goedkopers?** |
| | hoot-kopers |
| different? | **anders?** |
| | unders |
| larger? | **groters?** |
| | hroh-ters |
| smaller? | **kleiners?** |
| | kleyners |
| Can I have a bag, please? | **Mag ik een zak, alstublieft?** |
| | muk ik en zuk uls-too-bleeft |
| Can I have a receipt? | **Mag ik een kwitantie?** |
| | muk ik en kwee-tun-tsee |
| **Do you take . . .** | **Neemt u . . . aan?** |
| | naymt oo . . . ahn |
| English/American money? | **engels/amerikaans geld** |
| | eng-els/ah-may-ree-kahns helt |

| | |
|---|---|
| Do you take . . . | **Neemt u . . . aan?** |
| | naymt oo . . . ahn |
| travellers' cheques? | **reischeques** |
| | reys-sheks |
| credit cards? | **credietkaarten** |
| | credeet-karten |

## SHOP ASSISTANT

| | |
|---|---|
| Can I help you? | **Kan ik u helpen?** |
| | kun ik oo helpen |
| What would you like? | **Wat wilt u hebben?** |
| | wut wilt oo hebben |
| Will that be all? | **Is dat alles?** |
| | is dut ul-les |
| Anything else? | **Iets anders?** |
| | eets unders |
| Would you like it wrapped? | **Wilt u het ingepakt hebben?** |
| | wilt oo et in-her-pukt hebben |
| Sorry, none left | **Tot mijn spijt, uitverkocht** |
| | tot mane spate o-eet-ver-kokt |
| I haven't got any | **Ik heb geen** |
| | ik heb hane |
| I haven't got any more | **Ik heb geen meer** |
| | ik hep hane mair |
| How many do you want? ⎤<br>How much do you want? ⎦ | **Hoeveel wenst u?** |
| | hoo-vale wenst oo |
| Is this enough? | **Is dit genoeg?** |
| | is dit her-nook |

# Shopping for food

# Bread

## ESSENTIAL INFORMATION

- Key words to look for:
  **BAKKERIJ** (baker's)
  **BAKKER** (baker)
  **BROOD** (bread)

- Supermarkets of any size and general stores nearly always sell bread.
- Opening times are usually 8.30 a.m. – 5.30 p.m.; early closing time varies slightly locally.
- The most characteristic type of loaf is the 'French stick', which comes in two sizes: large and small.
- Most bread is sold unsliced in both bakeries and supermarkets. However, if you prefer your bread sliced **gesneden** (her-snayden), hand the loaf to the assistant and she will slice it for you. You will have to pay a small charge for this service.

**WHAT TO SAY**

| | |
|---|---|
| A loaf (like that) | **Een brood (zoals dat)**<br>en brote (zo-uls dut) |
| A white loaf | **Een wit brood**<br>en wit brote |
| A wholemeal loaf | **Een tarwe brood**<br>en tar-wer brote |
| A packet of pumpernickel | **Een pakje roggebrood**<br>en puk-yer rok-her-brote |
| A bread roll | **Een broodje**<br>een brote-yer |
| A currant bun | **Een krentenbol**<br>en krenter-bol |
| Two loaves | **Twee broden**<br>tway broden |
| A French stick | **Een stokbrood**<br>en stok-brote |

[*For other essential expressions, see 'Shop talk' p. 23*]

# Cakes and ice-creams

**ESSENTIAL INFORMATION**

- Key words to look for:
  **BANKETBAKKERIJ** (cake shop)
  **BANKETBAKKER** (cake/pastry maker)

**GEBAK** (pastries/cakes)
**IJS** (ice-cream)
**IJS-SALON** (ice-cream parlour)
**BONBONS en CHOCOLADE** (chocolates)
**SUIKERWERKEN** (sweet shop)

- **THEE-SALON**: a place to buy cakes and have a drink, usually in the afternoon. See also p. 36 'Ordering a drink and a snack'.

## WHAT TO SAY

The type of cakes you find in the shops may vary from region to region but the following are the most common; cake is *not* bought per slice, but gâteau is.

| | |
|---|---|
| **een cake** | a plain butter cake; size about |
| en cake | 300–700 grams |
| **een rozijnen cake** | a raisin cake |
| en roh-*zey*nen cake | |
| **een citroen cake** | a lemon cake |
| en citr*oo*n cake | |
| **een appeltaart** | an apple tart |
| en *u*ppel-tart | |
| **een slagroomtaart** | a cream tart/gâteau |
| en sl*u*k-rome-tart | |
| **een vruchtentaart** | a fruit tart/gâteau |
| en vr*u*kten-tart | |
| **een kwarktaart** | a cheese (cream) cake/gâteau |
| en kwark-tart | |
| **roomsoezen** | éclairs |
| r*o*me-soozen | |
| **slagroomgebakjes** | cream pastries |
| sl*u*k-rome-her-b*u*k-yers | |
| **vruchtengebakjes** | fruit pastries |
| vr*u*kten-her-b*u*k-yers | |
| **amandelbroodjes** | almond rolls |
| um-m*u*ndel-brote-yers | |
| | |
| A . . . ice, please | **Een . . . ijsje, alstublieft** |
| | en . . . *eys*-yer uls-too-bl*ee*ft |
| banana | **bananen** |
| | bah-*nah*-nen |
| chocolate | **chocolade** |
| | shocol*ah*-der |

| | |
|---|---|
| mocha | **mokka** |
| | mokka |
| pistachio | **pistache** |
| | peestush |
| strawberry | **aardbeien** |
| | ard-bey-yen |
| vanilla | **vanille** |
| | vun-il-yer |
| One (50 cent) cone | **Eén van (vijftig)** |
| | ayn vun (veyftik) |
| Two (F1.1) cones | **Twee van (één gulden)** |
| | tway vun (ayn hoolden) |

# Picnic food

## ESSENTIAL INFORMATION

- Key words to look for:
  **DELICATESSEN**
  **VLEESWAREN**   ⎤ delicatessen

## WHAT TO SAY

| Two slices of . . . | **Twee plakken . . .** |
|---|---|
| | tway plukken . . . |
| roast beef | **rosbief** |
| | ros-beef |
| roast pork | **varkens rollade** |
| | var-kens rollah-der |
| tongue | **tong** |
| | tong |
| ham | **ham** |
| | hum |
| liver sausage | **leverworst** |
| | layver-worst |
| garlic sausage | **knoflook worst** |
| | knof-loke worst |
| salami | **salami** |
| | sah-lah-mee |

You might also like to try some of these:

| | |
|---|---|
| **een stuk rookworst** | a piece of smoked sausage (best |
| en sterk roke-worst | eaten hot) |
| **een zoute nieuwe haring** | a salted fresh herring |
| en zowter nee-wer hahring | |
| **en gerookte paling** | a smoked eel |
| en her-roke-ter pah-ling | |
| **een Frankfurter** | a Frankfurter sausage |
| en frunk-foorter | |
| **een stuk boterhammenworst** | some luncheon meat |
| en sterk boter-hummer-worst | |
| **wat rookvlees** | some smoked beef (thin, salty |
| wut roke-vlays | slices) |
| **wat gerookte makreel** | some smoked mackerel |
| wut her-roke-ter mah-krayl | |
| **wat zult** | some brawn: pork (boar's flesh) |
| wut zult | pickled in vinegar |
| **wat vis-sla** | some fish salad |
| wut vis-slah | |
| **wat champignon-sla** | some mushroom salad |
| wut shum-peen-yon-slah | |
| **wat gehakt** | cold, spicy minced meat (pork or |
| wut her-hukt | beef) |
| **wat kippesla** | some chicken salad |
| wut kipper-slah | |
| **wat worstsla** | some sausage salad |
| wut worst-slah | |
| **wat kaassla** | some cheese salad |
| wut kahs-slah | |
| **Goudse kaas (belegen)** | Gouda cheese (mature) |
| howtser kahs (berlay-hen) | |
| **Edammer kaas** | Edam cheese |
| ay-dummer kahs | |
| **Leidse kaas** | Leiden cheese (cumin seed cheese) |
| leyt-ser kahs | |
| **nagelkaas** | clove cheese |
| nah-hel kahs | |
| **Limburgse kaas** | Limburger (piquant) cheese |
| limburg-ser kahs | |

# Fruit and vegetables

## ESSENTIAL INFORMATION

- Key words to look for:
  **FRUIT**
  **FRUITHANDELAAR** (fruiterer)
  **GROENTEN** (vegetables)
- It is customary for you to choose your own fruit and vegetables at the market and for the stallholder to weigh and price them. You must take your own shopping bag as paper and plastic bags are not normally provided.
  [*For further details of Dutch weights, see 'Shop talk', p. 23*]

## WHAT TO SAY

| 1 kilo of . . . | Eén kilo . . . |
|---|---|
| | ayn kilo . . . |
| apples | **appels** |
| | uppels |
| apricots | **abrikozen** |
| | ah-bree-kozen |
| bananas | **bananen** |
| | bah-nah-nen |
| bilberries | **bosbessen** |
| | bos-bessen |
| cherries | **kersen** |
| | kairsen |
| grapes (white/black) | **druiven (witte/zwarte)** |
| | dro-ee-ven (witter/zwarter) |
| greengages | **reine claudes** |
| | reyner-clowdes |
| mulberries | **moerbeien** |
| | moor-bey-en |
| oranges | **sinaasappels** |
| | see-nahs-uppels |
| pears | **peren** |
| | payren |
| peaches | **perziken** |
| | pairzi-ken |

| 1 kilo of . . . | Eén kilo . . . |
| --- | --- |
| | ayn kilo . . . |
| plums | pruimen |
| | pro-ee-men |
| raspberries | frambozen |
| | frum-bozen |
| strawberries | aardbeien |
| | ard-bey-yen |
| A pineapple, please | Een ananas, alstublieft |
| | en un-ah-nus uls-too-bleeft |
| A grapefruit | Een grapefruit |
| | en grape-fruit |
| A melon | Een meloen |
| | en mer-loon |
| A water melon | Een watermeloen |
| | en wah-ter-mer-loon |
| ½ kilo of . . . | Eén pond . . . |
| | ayn pont . . . |
| aubergines | aubergines |
| | oh-ber-sheens |
| broad beans | tuinbonen |
| | to-een-bonen |
| carrots | wortels |
| | wor-tels |
| green beans | slabonen |
| | slah-bonen |
| leeks | prei |
| | prey |
| mushrooms | champignons |
| | shum-peen-yons |
| onions | uien |
| | owe-yen |
| peas | doperwten |
| | dopair-ten |
| podded peas | peultjes |
| | perlt-yers |
| potatoes | aardappels |
| | ar-duppels |
| red cabbage | rode kool |
| | roder kohl |
| shallots | sjalotten |
| | shah-lot-ten |

| | |
|---|---|
| spinach | **spinazie** |
| | spee-n*ah*-zee |
| tomatoes | **tomaten** |
| | toh-m*ah*-ten |
| **A bunch of . . .** | **Een bosje . . .** |
| | en b*o*s-yer . . . |
| parsley | **peterselie** |
| | pa-ter-s*ay*lee |
| radishes | **radijs** |
| | rah-d*eys* |
| A garlic | **Een knoflook** |
| | en kn*o*f-loke |
| A lettuce | **Een krop sla** |
| | en kr*o*p slah |
| A stick of celery | **Een bleekselderij** |
| | en blake-sel-der-ray |
| A cucumber | **Een komkommer** |
| | en kom-k*o*mmer |
| A turnip | **Een witte raap** |
| | en w*i*tter rahp |
| Like that, please | **Zoals dat, alstublieft** |
| | zo-uls dut uls-too-bl*ee*ft |

[*For other essential expressions, see 'Shop talk' p. 23*]

---

# Meat and fish

## ESSENTIAL INFORMATION

- Key words to look for:
  **SLAGERIJ** (butcher's)
  **SLAGER** (butcher)
  **VISWINKEL** (fishmonger's)
- Lamb and mutton are expensive in Holland.
- Markets and large supermarkets usually have fresh fish stalls.

## WHAT TO SAY

For a joint, choose the type of meat and then say how many people it is for:

| | |
|---|---|
| Some beef, please | **Wat rundvlees, alstublieft**<br>wut runt-vlays uls-too-bleeft |
| Some lamb | **Wat lamsvlees**<br>wut lums-vlays |
| Some mutton | **Wat schapevlees**<br>wut skah-per-vlays |
| Some pork | **Wat varkensvlees**<br>wut varkens-vlays |
| Some veal | **Wat kalfsvlees**<br>wut kulfs-vlays |
| A joint . . . | **Groot stuk vlees . . .**<br>hrote sterk vlays . . . |
| for two people | **voor twee personen**<br>vor tway pair-sohnen |
| for four people | **voor vier personen**<br>vor veer pair-sohnen |
| for six people | **voor zes personen**<br>vor zes pair-sohnen |

For steak, liver and kidneys do as above:

| | |
|---|---|
| Some steak, please | **Wat biefstuk, alstublieft**<br>wut beef-sterk uls-too-bleeft |
| Some liver | **Wat lever**<br>wut layver |
| Some kidneys | **Wat nieren**<br>wut nee-ren |
| Some sausages | **Wat worst**<br>wut worst |
| for three people | **voor drie personen**<br>vor dree pair-sohnen |
| Two veal escalopes | **Twee kalfsoesters**<br>tway kulfs-oosters |
| Three pork chops | **Drie varkenskarbonaden**<br>dree varkens-karboh-nahden |

| | |
|---|---|
| Four mutton chops | **Vier schaapskarbonaden** |
| | veer sk*a*hps-karboh-nahden |
| Five lamb chops | **Vijf lamskarbonaden** |
| | veyf l*u*ms-karboh-nahden |
| A chicken | **Een kip** |
| | en kip |
| A rabbit | **Een konijn** |
| | en koh-n*ey*n |
| A tongue | **Een tong** |
| | en tong |

Purchase large fish and small shellfish by weight:

| | |
|---|---|
| ½ kilo of . . . | **Eén pond . . .** |
| | ayn pont . . . |
| cod | **kabeljauw** |
| | kahbel-y*ow* |
| eel | **paling** |
| | p*a*hling |
| haddock | **schelvis** |
| | sk*e*lvis |
| herring | **haring** |
| | h*a*h-ring |
| pike | **snoek** |
| | snook |
| plaice | **schol** |
| | skol |
| turbot | **tarbot** |
| | tarbot |
| mussels | **mosselen** |
| | m*o*ssel-en |
| prawns | **garnalen** |
| | har-n*a*hlen |
| shrimps | **kleine garnalen** |
| | kl*ey*ner har-n*a*hlen |
| salmon | **zalm** |
| | z*u*lm |
| tuna | **tonijn** |
| | toh-n*ey*n |

For some shellfish and 'frying pan' fish specify the number
you want:

| | |
|---|---|
| A crab, please | **Een krab, alstublieft**<br>en krup uls-too-bleeft |
| A lobster | **Een zeekreeft**<br>en zay-krayft |
| A scallop | **Een kammossel**<br>en kum-mossel |
| A whiting | **Een wijting**<br>en waiting |
| A trout | **Een forel**<br>en foh-rel |
| A sole | **Een tong**<br>en tong |
| A mackerel | **Een makreel**<br>en mah-krayl |

# Eating and drinking out

# Ordering a drink and a snack

## ESSENTIAL INFORMATION

- The places to ask for
  CAFÉ  SNELBUFFET  CAFETARIA
- By law, the price list of drinks (**TARIEF**) must be displayed
  outside or in the window.
- There is waiter service in all cafés, but you can drink at the bar
  or counter if you wish.
- When the bill is presented, the amount will be inclusive of service
  and VAT (**BTW**). Tipping: some additional small change is often
  given.
- Cafés serve both non-alcoholic drinks and alcoholic drinks and
  are normally open all day. Cream/milk is always served separately when ordering coffee or tea.
- Children are allowed into bars.

- If you want a sandwich lunch, look out for **KOFFIETAFEL**. You will be served a variety of breads, cold meats, cheeses -- possibly a hot dish -- and a bowl of soup or a salad. Coffee, milk or tea are also usually included.

## WHAT TO SAY

| I'll have . . . please | **Ik wil graag . . . alstublieft** |
| | ik wil hrahk . . . uls-too-bleeft |
| a cup of coffee | **een kop koffie** |
| | en kop koffee |
| a cup of tea | **een kop thee** |
| | en kop tay |
| with milk/lemon | **met melk/citroen** |
| | met melk/citroon |
| a glass of milk | **een glas melk** |
| | en hlus melk |
| a hot chocolate | **een kop chocolade** |
| | en kop shocolah-der |
| a chilled chocolate | **een glas chocomel** |
| | en hlus shoco-mel |
| a mineral water | **een mineral water** |
| | en mee-ne-rahl wah-ter |
| a lemonade | **een citroen limonade** |
| | en citroon leemo-nah-der |
| an orangeade | **een sinaasappel limonade** |
| | en seenahs-uppel leemo-nah-der |
| a Coca-Cola | **een Coca-Cola** |
| | en coca-cola |
| a fresh orange juice | **een sinaasappelsap** |
| | en seenahs-uppel-sup |
| a blackcurrant drink | **een cassis** |
| | en cussis |
| an apple juice | **een appelsap** |
| | en uppel-sup |
| a Pilsener beer (light ale) | **een Pils** |
| | en pils |
| a brown ale | **een donker bier** |
| | en donker beer |
| a bitter | **een bitter** |
| | en bitter |
| a draught beer | **een bier van het vat** |
| | en beer vun et vut |

| **I'll have . . . please** | **Ik zou graag . . . hebben** |
| | ik zow hrahk . . . hebben |
| a cheese roll | **een broodje kaas** |
| | en brote-yer kahs |
| a ham roll | **een broodje ham** |
| | en brote-yer hum |
| a hamburger | **een hamburger** |
| | en humbur-her |
| an omelet | **een omelet** |
| | en omerlet |
| with mushrooms | **met champignons** |
| | met shum-peen-yons |
| with ham | **met ham** |
| | met hum |
| with cheese | **met kaas** |
| | met kahs |

These are some other snacks you might like to try:

| **een boterham** | an open sandwich |
| en boter-rum | |
| **een dubbele boterham** | a sandwich with two pieces of |
| en dubay-lee boter-rum | bread, i.e. like our sandwiches |
| **een croquet** | a croquette |
| en croh-ket | |
| **een fricandel** | a minced meat roll |
| en free-cun-del | |
| **een saté** | cubed meat (mostly pork or |
| en sateh | chicken) on skewers with a spicy |
| | peanut sauce |
| **een pannekoek** | a pancake |
| en punner-kook | |
| **een saucijze broodje** | a sausage roll |
| en sow-seyzer-brote-yer | |
| **een broodje Tartaar** | a minced beef (raw) roll |
| en brote-yer tar-tar | |
| **een tosti** | a toastie (ham and cheese) |
| en tostee | |
| **een uitsmijter** | two slices of bread with ham, roast |
| en o-eet-smayter | beef or cheese, topped by two or |
| | three fried eggs |
| **hutspot met klapstuk** | carrots mashed with onions and |
| herts-pot met klup-sterk | potatoes, cooked with rib of |
| | pork |

| | |
|---|---|
| **een kop erwtensoep** | a cup of pea soup |
| en kop airten-soop | |
| **een kop tomatensoep** | a cup of tomato soup |
| en kop toh-*mah*ten-soop | |
| **een kop groentesoep** | a cup of vegetable soup |
| en kop hr*oon*ter-soop | |

# In a restaurant

## ESSENTIAL INFORMATION

- You can eat at the following places:
  **RESTAURANT**
  **HOTEL-RESTAURANT**
  **STATIONS-RESTAURATIE**
  **MOTEL**
  **CAFÉ-RESTAURANT**
- By law, the menus must be displayed outside or in the window – and that is the *only* way to judge if a place is right for your needs.
- Self-service restaurants are not unknown, but most places have waiter service.
- A service charge is always added to the bill. Tipping is therefore optional.
- Most restaurants have children's portions.
- Some 700 restaurants offer a *tourist menu* (three courses) at a set price throughout the Netherlands although the courses themselves will differ from region to region. Restaurants participating in this scheme display a sign with the words 'tourist menu'.
- Hot meals are served from 12.00 p.m. – 2.00 p.m. at lunchtime and from 6.00 p.m. – 9.00/10.00 p.m. at night. After that many restaurants offer snacks for latecomers (soups, sausages, salads etc.). Many cities have Indonesian restaurants, where you will find the best *rijsttafel* (lit. 'rice table') outside Indonesia. This speciality consists of nine to ten varying dishes of meats, vegetables, fruits.

## WHAT TO SAY

| | |
|---|---|
| May I book a table? | **Kan ik een tafel reserveren?** |
| | kun ik en *tah*-fel ray-ser-v*ai*ren |
| I have booked a table | **Ik heb een tafel gereserveerd** |
| | ik hep en *tah*-fel he-ray-ser-v*ai*rt |
| **A table . . .** | **Een tafel . . .** |
| | en *tah*-fel . . . |
| for one | **voor één persoon** |
| | vor ayn pair-s*oh*n |
| for three | **voor drie personen** |
| | vor dree pair-s*oh*nen |
| The à la carte menu, please | **Het à la carte menu, alstublieft** |
| | et ah la cart mer-n*oo* uls-too-bl*ee*ft |
| The fixed-price menu | **Het vastgestelde menu** |
| | et v*u*st-her-stelder mer-n*oo* |
| Today's special menu | **Het menu van de dag** |
| | et mer-n*oo* vun der d*u*k |
| The tourist menu | **Het touristen menu** |
| | et too-r*i*sten mer-n*oo* |
| What is this, please? | **Wat is dit, alstublieft?** |
| [*point to menu*] | wut is dit uls-too-bl*ee*ft |
| The wine list | **De wijnlijst** |
| | der weyn-leyst |
| A glass of wine | **Een glas wijn** |
| | en hlus weyn |
| A half-bottle | **Een halve fles** |
| | en h*u*lver fles |
| A bottle | **Een fles** |
| | en fles |
| Red/white/rosé/house wine | **Rode/witte/rosé/huis wijn** |
| | roder/witter/roh-s*ay*/ho-ees weyn |
| Some more bread, please | **Nog wat brood, alstublieft** |
| | nok wut brote uls-too-bl*ee*ft |
| Some more wine | **Nog wat wijn** |
| | nok wut weyn |
| Some oil | **Een beetje olie** |
| | en b*ay*t-yer *o*lee |
| Some vinegar | **Een beetje azijn** |
| | en b*ay*t-yer ah-z*ey*n |
| Some salt/pepper | **Een beetje zout/peper** |
| | en b*ay*t-yer zowt/p*a*per |

| Some water | **Een beetje water** |
| | en bayt-yer wah-ter |
| With/without garlic | **Met/zonder knoflook** |
| | met/zonder knof-loke |
| How much does that come to? | **Hoeveel is dat?** |
| | hoo-vale is dut |
| Is service included? | **Is het inclusief bediening?** |
| | is et in-cloo-seef ber-deening |
| Where is the toilet? | **Waar is het toilet?** |
| | wahr is et twah-let |
| Miss! [*This does not sound abrupt in Dutch*[ | **Juffrouw!** |
| | yer-frow |
| Waiter! | **Ober!** |
| | ober |
| The bill, please | **De rekening, alstublieft** |
| | der rayker-ning uls-too-bleeft |

**Key words for courses, as seen on some menus**

[*Only ask this question if you want the waiter to remind you of the choice*]

| What have you got in the way of . . . | **Wat voor . . . heeft u?** |
| | wut vor . . . hayft oo |
| STARTERS? | **VOORGERECHTEN** |
| | vor-her-rekten |
| SOUP? | **SOEP** |
| | soop |
| EGG DISHES? | **EIERGERECHTEN** |
| | ey-er-her-rekten |
| FISH? | **VIS** |
| | vis |
| MEAT? | **VLEES** |
| | vlays |
| GAME? | **WILD** |
| | wilt |
| FOWL? | **GEVOGELTE** |
| | her-voh-helter |
| VEGETABLES? | **GROENTE** |
| | hroonter |
| CHEESE? | **KAAS** |
| | kahs |
| FRUIT? | **FRUIT** |
| | fro-eet |

| | |
|---|---|
| What have you got in the way of . . . | Wat voor . . . heeft u? |
| | wut vor . . . hayft oo |
| ICE-CREAM? | **IJS** |
| | eys |
| DESSERT? | **DESSERT** |
| | des-sairt |

## UNDERSTANDING THE MENU

- You will find the names of the principal ingredients of most dishes on these pages:

| | |
|---|---|
| Starters p. 29 | Fruit p. 31 |
| Meat p. 33 | Cheese p. 30 |
| Fish p. 35 | Ice-cream p. 28 |
| Vegetables p. 32 | Dessert p. 28 |

  Used together with the following lists of cooking and menu terms, they should help you decode the menu.
- These cooking and menu terms are for understanding – not for speaking.

### Cooking and menu terms

| | |
|---|---|
| aangemaakt | dressed |
| aspic | aspic |
| bouillon | broth, clear soup |
| doorgebakken | well-done |
| gebakken | fried, baked |
| gebraden | roasted |
| gefileerd | filleted |
| gegarneerd | garnished |
| geglazeerd | glazed |
| gegratineerd | au gratin |
| gegrilleerd | grilled |
| gekookt | boiled |
| gekruid | spiced |
| gelardeerd | larded |
| gemarineerd | marinated |
| gemengd | mixed |
| gepaneerd | dressed with eggs and breadcrumbs |
| gepocheerd | poached |
| geraapt | grated |
| gerookt | smoked |

| | |
|---|---|
| geroosterd | toasted |
| gesmoord | braised |
| gestoomd | steamed |
| gevulde | filled |
| gezouten | salted |
| in gelei | jellied |
| jus | gravy |
| kaasgerechten | cheese dishes |
| koude schotels | cold dishes |
| pikant | savoury |
| puree | mashed |
| ragout | ragout |
| rauw | raw |
| room | cream |
| salade/sla | salad |
| saté/sateh | meat cubes on sticks with peanut sauce |
| slagroom | whipped cream (with sugar) |
| soufflé | soufflé |
| wild en gevogelte | game and poultry |
| zoet | sweet |
| zuur | sour |

**Further words to help you understand the menu**

| | |
|---|---|
| aalbessen; rode, witte, zwarte | currants; red, white, black |
| aalbessen gelei | currant jelly |
| artisjok | artichoke |
| asperge | asparagus |
| augurken | pickled gherkins |
| bami | Indonesian noodle dish with diced pork and often shrimps |
| blinde vinken | veal fillet, filled with spiced minced veal, fried in butter |
| bloemkool | cauliflower |
| boerenkool (stamppot) | kale (hotchpotch) |
| borst | breast |
| bruine bonensoep | brown bean soup |
| brussels lof met ham en kaas | chicory with ham and cheese (oven dish) |
| chantilly crème met kastanje puree | whipped cream with chestnut purée |

| | |
|---|---|
| chinese kool | chinese cabbage |
| compote | stewed fruit |
| doperwten | peas |
| duitse biefstuk | hamburger steak |
| eend | duck |
| fazant | pheasant |
| flensjes | very thin pancakes |
| fondue | fondue |
| gebakken aardappels | fried potatoes |
| gebakken ananas | fried pineapple |
| gehakt | minced meat |
| gewelde boter | creamed butter |
| haantje | young cock |
| haas | hare |
| hachee | braised steak with onions, spices and vinegar |
| jachtschotel | hot-pot |
| kalfsvlees | veal |
| kappertjes saus | caper sauce |
| kapucijners | marrowfat peas |
| karbonade | chops |
| kervel | chervil |
| kip (gebraden) | chicken (roasted) |
| kotelet | cutlet |
| koude schotels | cold dishes |
| leverworst | liver sausage |
| loempia | Indonesian deep-fried pancake, filled with bamboo shoots, meat and vegetables |
| nasi goreng | Indonesian spicy rice dish |
| ossestaart soep | oxtail soup |
| paprika (gevulde) | green/red peppers (stuffed) |
| peterselie | parsley |
| prei | leeks |
| reebout | haunch of venison |
| roerei | scrambled egg |
| rolmop | rolled-up pickled herring filled with onion |
| russische eieren | hard boiled eggs with mayonnaise and caper sauce |
| schildpadsoep | turtle soup |

| snijbonen | green beans |
| sperciebonen | french beans |
| spruitjes | sprouts |
| taugé soup | bean sprouts soup |
| tonijn | tuna fish |
| zuukool met spek | sauerkraut with boiled bacon |

# Health

## ESSENTIAL INFORMATION

- For details of reciprocal health agreements between the UK and the Netherlands or Belgium ask for leaflet SA 30 at your local Department of Health and Social Security a month before leaving, or ask at your travel agent.
- For minor disorders and treatment at a chemist's, see p. 20.
- For finding your own way to a doctor, dentist, chemist or Health and Social Security Office (for reimbursement), see p. 13.
- The cost of the medical care of the tourist must be settled directly with the doctor, chemist, dentist, hospital, etc.
- The name of the medical practitioner on duty at weekends and nights can be found in the local papers.

**What's the matter?**

| I have a pain here [*point*] | **Ik heb hier pijn** |
| | ik hep here pain |
| I have toothache | **Ik heb kiespijn** |
| | ik hep kees-pain |
| **I have broken . . .** | **Ik heb . . . gebroken** |
| | ik hep . . . herbroken |
| my dentures | **mijn kunstgebit** |
| | mane koonst-her-bit |
| my glasses | **mijn bril** |
| | mane bril |

| | |
|---|---|
| **I have lost . . .** | **Ik heb . . . verloren**<br>ik hep . . . ver-loren |
| my contact lenses | **mijn contact lenzen**<br>mane contuct lenzen |
| a filling | **een vulling**<br>en verling |
| My child is ill | **Mijn kind is ziek**<br>mane kint is zeek |

**Already under treatment for something else?**

| | |
|---|---|
| **I take . . . regularly** [*show*] | **Ik neem geregeld . . .**<br>ik name her-ray-helt . . . |
| this medicine | **dit medicijn**<br>dit may-dee-seyn |
| these pills | **deze pillen**<br>dazer pillen |
| **I have . . .** | **Ik heb . . .**<br>ik hep . . . |
| a heart condition | **een hart conditie**<br>en hart con-dee-tsee |
| haemorrhoids | **aambeien**<br>ahm-bey-yen |
| rheumatism | **reumatiek**<br>rer-mah-teek |
| **I think I have . . .** | **Ik geloof dak ik . . . heb**<br>ik her-lohf dut ik . . . hep |
| food poisoning | **voedselvergiftiging**<br>vootsel-ver-hiftee-hing |
| sunstroke | **een zonnesteak**<br>en zonner-stake |
| **I'm . . .** | **Ik lijd aan . . .**<br>ik leyt ahn . . . |
| diabetic | **diabetes**<br>dee-ah-bay-tes |
| asthmatic | **asthma**<br>ust-mah |
| I'm pregnant | **Ik ben zwanger**<br>ik ben zwung-er |
| I'm allergic to penicillin | **Ik ben gevoelig voor penicilline**<br>ik ben her-voolik vor penicilleener |

# Problems: loss, theft

## ESSENTIAL INFORMATION

- If the worst comes to the worst, find a police station. To ask the way, see p. 12.
- Look for: **POLITIE**
- If you lose your passport report the loss to the nearest police station and go to the British Consulate.

## LOSS
[See also 'Theft' below: the lists are interchangeable]

| | |
|---|---|
| I have lost . . . | **Ik heb . . . verloren** |
| | ik hep . . . verloren |
| my camera | **mijn camera** |
| | mane cahmer-rah |
| my car keys | **mijn autosleutels** |
| | mane owto-slertels |
| my car logbook | **mijn auto papieren** |
| | mane owto pah-pee-ren |
| my driving licence | **mijn rijbewijs** |
| | mane rey-ber-weys |
| my insurance certificate | **mijn verzekeringsbewijs** |
| | mane ver-zaykerrings-ber-weys |

## THEFT
[See also 'Loss' above: the lists are interchangeable]

| | |
|---|---|
| Someone has stolen . . . | **Iemand heeft . . . gestolen** |
| | ee-munt hayft . . . her-stolen |
| my car | **mijn auto** |
| | mane ow-to |
| my money | **mijn geld** |
| | mane helt |
| my purse | **mijn portemonnaie** |
| | mane porter-monay |
| my tickets | **mijn kaartjes** |
| | mane kart-yers |

| Someone has stolen . . . | Iemand heeft . . . gestolen |
| | *ee*-munt hayft . . . her-st*o*len |
| my travellers' cheques | mijn reischeques |
| | mane r*e*ys-sheks |
| my wallet | mijn portefeuille |
| | mane porter-f*o*y-yer |
| my luggage | mijn bagage |
| | maine bah-*h*ah-sher |

---

# The post office and phoning home

---

## ESSENTIAL INFORMATION

- Key words to look for:
  **POSTKANTOOR**
  **POSTERIJEN**
  **POST EN SPAARBANK**
- Look for the following sign:
- For stamps look for the word **POSTZEGELS** on a machine, or **ZEGELVERKOOP** or **FRANKEERZEGELS** at a post office counter.
- Stamps may be obtained at a stationer's, provided postcards are also bought there.
- Unless you read and speak Dutch well, it is best not to make phone calls by yourself. Go to a post office and write the town and number you want on a piece of paper.
- The code for the UK is 0944, and for the USA 091; then dial the number you want (less any initial 0).

## WHAT TO SAY

| To England, please | **Naar Engeland, alstublieft** |
| | nar *e*ng-er-lunt uls-too-bl*ee*ft |

[*Hand letters, cards or parcels over the counter*]

| To Australia | **Naar Australië** |
| | nar ah-oostr*ah*-lee-yer |

| | |
|---|---|
| To the United States | **Naar de Verenigde Staten** |
| | nar der very-*ay*-nik-der st*ah*-ten |
| I'd like to send a telegram | **Ik zou graag een telegram sturen** |
| | ik zow hrahk en telehr*u*m st*oo*-ren |
| Where can I make a telephone call? | **Waar kan ik telefoneren?** |
| | wahr kun ik telefon*ay*-ren |
| Local/abroad | **Lokaal/buitenland** |
| | l*o*kahl/b*o*-ee-ten-lunt |
| I'd like this number . . . | **Ik wou dit nummer . . .** |
| [*show number*] | ik wow dit n*oo*mmer . . . |
| in England | **in Engeland** |
| | in *e*ng-er-lunt |
| in Canada | **in Canada** |
| | in c*ah*nada |
| Can you dial it for me, please? | **Kunt u het voor me draaien, alstublieft?** |
| | koont oo et vor mer dr*ah*-yen uls-too-bl*ee*ft |

# Changing cheques and money

## ESSENTIAL INFORMATION

- Look for these words on buildings:
  **BANK**
  **GRENSWISSELKANTOREN NV**
  (more commonly given as **GWK**: these are to be found in stations
  and at the borders only)
  **BUREAU DE CHANGE**
- Banks are open weekdays 9.00 a.m. – 4.00 p.m. The exchange
  offices (**WISSELKANTOREN**) are open Monday to Saturday and
  often in the evenings and on Sundays.
- To cash your own cheques, exactly as at home, use your banker's
  card where you see the Eurocheque sign. Write in English, in
  pounds.
- Exchange rate information might show the pound as: **£,
  LONDEN, ENGELAND (GR BR)** or the British flag.
- Have your passport ready.

**WHAT TO SAY**

| | |
|---|---|
| I'd like to cash . . . | **Ik wou . . . wisselen**<br>ik wow . . . w*i*sselen |
| this travellers' cheque | **deze reischeque**<br>d*a*zer r*eys*-shek |
| these travellers' cheques | **deze reischeques**<br>d*a*zer r*eys*-sheks |
| this cheque | **deze cheque**<br>d*a*zer shek |
| I'd like to change this . . . | **Ik wou dit graag omwisselen . . .**<br>ik wow dit hrahk *o*m-wisselen . . . |
| into guilders | **in guldens**<br>in h*oo*ldens |
| into Belgian francs | **in belgische franken**<br>in b*e*l-hee-ser fr*u*nken |
| into French francs | **in franse franken**<br>in fr*u*n-ser fr*u*nken |
| into German marks | **in duitse marken**<br>in d*o*-eet-ser m*a*rken |
| What is the rate of exchange? | **Wat is de koers?**<br>wut is der koors |

# Car travel

**ESSENTIAL INFORMATION**

- Is it a self-service station? Look out for: **ZELFBEDIENING**
  Grades of petrol:
  **NORMAAL** (standard)
  **SUPER** (premium)
  **DIESEL OLIE** (diesel)
- 1 gallon is about 4½ litres (accurate enough for up to 6 gallons).
- The minimum sale is often 5 litres (less at self-service pumps).
- Filling stations may be able to deal with minor mechanical problems during the day only. For major repairs you have to go to a garage.

● All main roads are patrolled by the yellow cars of the Royal Dutch Touring Club (**ANWB**) between 7.00 a.m. and 12.00 p.m. Telephones have been installed along Holland's main roads to be used to obtain information from the local **ANWB** station. They will assist tourists whose cars break down. If you are not a member of an automobile club affiliated with the **AIT**, roadside service will be available if you become a temporary member of the **ANWB**.

## WHAT TO SAY

[*For numbers, see p. 54*]

| | |
|---|---|
| (Nine) litres of . . . | (Negen) liter . . . |
| | (n*a*yhen) leeter . . . |
| (20) guilders of . . . | Voor (twintig) gulden . . . |
| | vor (tw*i*ntik) h*oo*lden . . . |
| Fill it up, please | **Vol alstublieft** |
| | vol uls-too-bl*ee*ft |
| standard/premium/diesel | **normaal/super/diesel** |
| | norm*ah*l/s*oo*per/diesel |
| Will you check . . . | **Wilt u . . . nakijken?** |
| | wilt oo . . . n*ah*-kayken |
| the oil? | **de olie** |
| | der *o*lee |
| the battery? | **de accu** |
| | der *u*ccoo |
| the radiator? | **de radiator** |
| | der rah-d*ee*-ah-tor |
| the tyres? | **de banden** |
| | der b*u*nden |
| I have run out of petrol | **Ik zit zonder benzine** |
| | ik zit z*o*nder ben-z*ee*ner |
| Can you help me, please? | **Kunt u me helpen, alstublieft?** |
| | koont oo mer h*e*lpen uls-too-bl*ee*ft |
| Do you do repairs? | **Doet u reparaties?** |
| | doot oo ray-pah-r*ah*tsees |
| I have a puncture | **Ik heb een lekke band** |
| | ik hep en l*e*kker b*u*nt |
| I have a broken windscreen | **Ik heb een kapotte voorruit** |
| | ik hep en kah-p*o*tter vor-ro-eet |

| | |
|---|---|
| I think the problem is here ... [point] | **Ik denk dat het probleem hier is . . .** |
| | ik denk dut et pro-blame here is . . . |

## LIKELY REACTIONS

| | |
|---|---|
| I don't do repairs | **Ik repareer niet** |
| | ik ray-pah-rair neet |
| Where is your car? | **Waar is uw auto?** |
| | wahr is oo owto |
| What make is it? | **Welk merk is het?** |
| | welk mairk is et |
| Come back tomorrow/on Wednesday [For days of the week, see p. 56] | **Kom morgen/woensdag terug** kom mor-hen/woons-duk ter-rerk |

# Public transport

## ESSENTIAL INFORMATION

- Key words on signs:
  **TREINKAARTJES** (tickets)
  **LOKET** (ticket office)
  **INGANG** (entrance)
  **UITGANG** (exit)
  **VERBODEN** (forbidden)
  **PERRON** (platform)
  **DOORGAAND VERKEER** (transit passengers)
  **WACHTKAMER** (waiting room)
  **INLICHTINGEN** (information)
  **BAGAGE DEPOT** (left luggage)
  **AANKOMST** (arrivals)
  **VERTREK** (departures)
  **NS** (initials of Dutch railways)
  **BUSHALTE** (bus stop)
  **DIENSTREGELING** (timetable)

- Buying a ticket: train tickets are available at the station ticket office, in some main post offices and in some tobacconists'.
- When travelling by bus or tram you usually pay as you enter. A bus and tram **STRIPPENKAART** can be bought at post offices.
- There is a 'rover ticket' allowing unlimited travel through Holland for 3–7 days.
- A **GROEP KAART** permits unlimited travel by train for 2–6 persons for one day at a reduced rate.
- In some towns you can purchase a tram ticket which allows you to interchange between trams in the one direction.

## WHAT TO SAY

| | |
|---|---|
| Where does the train for (Rotterdam) leave from? | **Van waar vertrekt de trein naar (Rotterdam)?** |
| | vun wahr ver-trekt der train nar (rotter-dum) |
| Is this the train for (Rotterdam)? | **Is dit de trein naar (Rotterdam)?** |
| | is dit der train nar (rotter-dum) |
| Where does the bus for (Edam) leave from? | **Van waar vertrekt de bus naar (Edam)?** |
| | vun wahr ver-trekt der bus nar (ay-dum) |
| Is this the bus for (Edam)? | **Is dit de bus naar (Edam)?** |
| | is dit der bus nar (ay-dum) |
| Do I have to change? | **Moet ik overstappen?** |
| | moot ik over-stuppen |
| Can you put me off at the right stop, please? | **Kunt u mij op de juiste plaats afzetten, alstublieft?** |
| | koont oo mey op der yo-ees-ter plahts uf-zetten uls-too-bleeft |
| Where can I get a taxi? | **Waar kan ik een taxi krijgen?** |
| | wahr kun ik en tuk-see kray-hen |
| Can I book a seat? | **Kan ik een plaats bespreken?** |
| | kun ik en plahts ber-sprayken |
| A single | **Een enkele** |
| | en enkerler |
| A return | **Een retour** |
| | en rer-toor |
| First class | **Eerste klas** |
| | airster klus |
| Second class | **Tweede klas** |
| | tway-der klus |

| One adult | **Eén volwassene** |
| | ayn vol-wusserner |
| Two adults | **Twee volwassenen** |
| | tway vol-wussernen |
| and one child | **en één kind** |
| | en ayn kint |
| and two children | **en twee kinderen** |
| | en tway kin-der-ren |
| How much is it? | **Hoeveel is het?** |
| | hoo-vale is et |

# Reference

## NUMBERS

| 0 | **nul** | nerl |
|---|---|---|
| 1 | **één** | ayn |
| 2 | **twee** | tway |
| 3 | **drie** | dree |
| 4 | **vier** | veer |
| 5 | **vijf** | veyf |
| 6 | **zes** | zes |
| 7 | **zeven** | zayven |
| 8 | **acht** | ukt |
| 9 | **negen** | nayhen |
| 10 | **tien** | teen |
| 11 | **elf** | elf |
| 12 | **twaalf** | twahlf |
| 13 | **dertien** | dairteen |
| 14 | **veertien** | vairteen |
| 15 | **vijftien** | veyfteen |
| 16 | **zestien** | zesteen |
| 17 | **zeventien** | zayventeen |
| 18 | **achttien** | ukteen |
| 19 | **negentien** | nayhenteen |
| 20 | **twintig** | twintik |

| | | |
|---|---|---|
| 21 | **éénentwintig** | *ayn*-en-tw*i*ntik |
| 22 | **tweeëntwintig** | tw*ay*-en-tw*i*ntik |
| 23 | **drieëntwintig** | dr*ee*-en-tw*i*ntik |
| 24 | **vierentwintig** | v*ee*r-en-tw*i*ntik |
| 25 | **vijfentwintig** | v*ey*f-en-tw*i*ntik |
| 26 | **zesentwintig** | z*e*s-en-tw*i*ntik |
| 27 | **zevenentwintig** | z*ay*ven-en-tw*i*ntik |
| 28 | **achtentwintig** | *u*kt-en-tw*i*ntik |
| 29 | **negenentwintig** | n*ay*hen-en-tw*i*ntik |
| 30 | **dertig** | d*ai*rtik |
| 31 | **éénendertig** | ayn-en-d*ai*rtik |
| 35 | **vijfendertig** | v*ey*f-en-d*ai*rtik |
| 40 | **veertig** | v*ai*rtik |
| 41 | **éénenveertig** | *ayn*-en-v*ai*rtik |
| 50 | **vijftig** | v*ey*ftik |
| 51 | **éénenvijftig** | *ayn*-en-v*ey*ftik |
| 60 | **zestig** | z*e*stik |
| 70 | **zeventig** | z*ay*ventik |
| 80 | **tachtig** | t*u*ktik |
| 81 | **éénentachtig** | *ayn*-en-t*u*ktik |
| 90 | **negentig** | n*ay*hentik |
| 95 | **vijfennegentig** | v*ey*f-en-n*ay*hentik |
| 100 | **honderd** | h*o*ndert |
| 101 | **honderdéén** | h*o*ndert-*ayn* |
| 102 | **honderdtwee** | h*o*ndert-tw*ay* |
| 125 | **hondervijfentwintig** | h*o*ndert-v*ey*f-en-tw*i*ntik |
| 150 | **honderdvijftig** | h*o*ndert-v*ey*ftik |
| 175 | **honderdvijfenzeventig** | h*o*ndert-v*ey*f-en-z*ay*ventik |
| 200 | **tweehonderd** | tw*ay*-h*o*ndert |
| 300 | **driehonderd** | dr*ee*h*o*ndert |
| 400 | **vierhonderd** | v*ee*r-h*o*ndert |
| 500 | **vijfhonderd** | v*ey*f-h*o*ndert |
| 1000 | **duizend** | d*o*-ee-zent |
| 1100 | **elfhonderd** | *e*lf-h*o*ndert |
| 3000 | **drieduizend** | dr*ee*-d*o*-ee-zent |
| 5000 | **vijfduizend** | v*ey*f-d*o*-ee-zent |
| 10,000 | **tienduizend** | t*ee*n-d*o*-ee-zent |
| 100,000 | **honderdduizend** | h*o*ndert-d*o*-ee-zent |
| 1,000,000 | **één miljoen** | *ayn* mil-y*oo*n |

## TIME

| What time is it? | **Hoe laat is het?** |
|---|---|
| | hoo laht is et |
| It's . . . | **Het is . . .** |
| | et is . . . |
| one o'clock | **één uur** |
| | ayn oor |
| two o'clock | **twee uur** |
| | tway oor |
| three o'clock | **drie uhr** |
| | dree oor |
| four o'clock | **vier uur** |
| | veer oor |
| noon | **middag** |
| | mid-duk |
| midnight | **middernacht** |
| | midder-nukt |
| a quarter past five | **kwart over vijf** |
| | kwart over veyf |
| half past five | **half zes** |
| | hulf zes |
| a quarter to six | **kwart vóór zes** |
| | kwart vor zes |

## DAYS AND MONTHS

| Monday | **maandag** |
|---|---|
| | mahn-duk |
| Tuesday | **dinsdag** |
| | dins-duk |
| Wednesday | **woensdag** |
| | woons-duk |
| Thursday | **donderdag** |
| | donder-duk |
| Friday | **vrijdag** |
| | vrey-duk |
| Sunday | **zondag** |
| | zon-duk |
| January | **januari** |
| | yun-oo-ah-ree |

| February | **februari** | |
| | fay-broo-*ah*-ree | |
| March | **maart** | |
| | mart | |
| April | **april** | |
| | ah-pr*i*l | |
| May | **mei** | |
| | may | |
| June | **juni** | |
| | y*oo*-nee | |
| July | **juli** | |
| | y*oo*-lee | |
| August | **augustus** | |
| | ow-h*er*s-tes | |
| September | **september** | |
| | sept*e*mber | |
| October | **oktober** | |
| | okt*o*ber | |
| November | **november** | |
| | nov*e*mber | |
| December | **december** | |
| | day-sember | |

## Public holidays

• Shops, schools and offices are closed on the following dates:

| 1 January | **Nieuwjaarsdag** | New Year's Day |
| ... | **Paasmaandag** | Easter Monday |
| | **Pinkstermaandag** | Whitsun Monday |
| | **Hemelvaartsdag** | Ascension Day |
| 30 April | **Koninginnedag** | The Queen's birthday |
| 25 December | **Eerste Kerstdag** | Christmas Day |
| 26 December | **Tweede Kerstdag** | Boxing Day |
| 5 May | **Bevrijdingsdag** | Liberation Day (once every 5 years) |

# Index

# Travellers' French

**D. L. Ellis, F. Clark**

Pronunciation **Dr J. Baldwin**

*Useful addresses*
French Tourist Office
178 Piccadilly, London W1

Swiss National Tourist Office
The Swiss Centre
1 New Coventry Street, London W1

# Contents

# Pronunciation hints

In French it is important to read each syllable with equal emphasis.
For instance, in the following English example we have ten syllables
and ten stresses: *Little Jack Horner sat in the corner*. Though this
will probably sound rather mechanical to an English ear, it will help
the French speaker to understand you.
**Bon courage!**

# Everyday expressions

[*See also 'Shop talk' p. 77*]

| | |
|---|---|
| Hello | **Bonjour** |
| Good morning | bonshoor |
| Good day | **Salut** (friends only) |
| Good afternoon | saloo |
| Good evening | **Bonsoir** |
| | bonswah |
| Good night | **Bonne nuit** |
| | bon nwee |
| Goodbye | **Au revoir** |
| | o-revwah |
| Yes | **Oui** |
| | wee |
| Please | **S'il vous plaît** |
| | sil voo pleh |
| Yes, please | **Oui, s'il vous plaît** |
| | wee sil voo pleh |
| Thank you | **Merci** |
| | mair-see |
| Thank you very much | **Merci beaucoup** |
| | mair-see bo-coo |
| That's right | **C'est exact** |
| | set exah |
| No | **Non** |
| | non |
| No, thank you | **Non, merci** |
| | non mair-see |
| ('Merci' by itself can also mean 'No thank you.') | |
| I disagree | **Je ne suis pas d'accord** |
| | sher ner swee pah dah-cor |
| Excuse me ⎤ | **Pardon** |
| Sorry ⎦ | par-don |
| Don't mention it ⎤ | **De rien** |
| That's OK ⎦ | der ree-an |
| It doesn't matter | **Ça ne fait rien** |
| | sah ner feh ree-an |
| Where's the toilet, please? | **Où sont les WC, s'il vous plaît?** |
| | oo son leh veh-seh sil voo pleh |

Do you speak English? **Parlez-vous anglais?**
parleh-voo ahngleh

What is your name? **Comment vous appelez-vous?**
commahn vooz appleh-voo

My name is . . . **Je m'appelle . . .**
shmappel . . .

# Asking the way

## ESSENTIAL INFORMATION

● Keep a look out for all these place names as you will find them on shops, maps and notices.

## WHAT TO SAY

Excuse me, please **Pardonnez-moi, s'il vous plaît**
par-do-neh mwah sil voo pleh

How do I get . . . **Pour aller . . .**
poor alleh . . .

to Paris? **à Paris?**
ah pahree

to rue St Pierre? **à la rue Saint-Pierre?**
ah lah roo san-pee-air

to the hotel Metropole? **à l'hôtel Métropole?**
ah lotel meh-tro-pol

to the airport? **à l'aéroport?**
ah lah-eh-ropor

to the beach? **à la plage?**
ah lah plash

to the bus station? **à la gare d'autobus?**
ah lah gar dotoboos

to the market? **au marché?**
o marsheh

to the police station? **au commissariat?**
o commissaree-ah

| | |
|---|---|
| to the port? | **au port?** |
| | o por |
| to the post office? | **à la poste?** |
| | ah lah post |
| to the railway station? | **à la gare?** |
| | ah lah gar |
| to the sports stadium? | **au stade?** |
| | o stad |
| to the tourist information office? | **au syndicat d'initiative?** |
| | o sandeecah dinisee-ativ |
| to the town centre? | **au centre de la ville?** |
| | o sahnt der lah veel |
| to the town hall? | **à la mairie?** |
| | ah lah mai-ree |
| Excuse me, please | **Pardonnez-moi, s'il vous plaît** |
| | par-do-neh mwah sil voo pleh |
| **Is there . . . near by?** | **Est-ce qu'il y a . . . près d'ici?** |
| | eskil yah . . . preh dee-see |
| a baker's | **une boulangerie** |
| | oon boolahn-shree |
| a bank | **une banque** |
| | oon bahnk |
| a bar | **un bar** |
| | an bar |
| a bus stop | **un arrêt d'autobus** |
| | an ahreh dotoboos |
| a butcher's | **une boucherie** |
| | oon booshree |
| a café | **un café** |
| | an cahfeh |
| a campsite | **un camping** |
| | an camping |
| a car park | **un parking** |
| | an parking |
| a change bureau | **un bureau de change** |
| | an buro der shahnsh |
| a chemist's | **une pharmacie** |
| | oon pharmacy |
| a delicatessen | **une charcuterie** |
| | oon sharcootree |
| a dentist's | **un dentiste** |
| | an dahnteest |

| Is there . . . near by? | Est-ce qu'il y a . . . près d'ici? |
| --- | --- |
| | eskil yah . . . preh dee-see |
| a department store | **un grand magasin** |
| | an grahn mahgahzan |
| a disco | **une discothèque** |
| | oon discotek |
| a doctor's surgery | **un docteur** |
| | an doc-ter |
| a dry cleaner's | **un pressing** |
| | an pressing |
| a fishmonger's | **une poissonnerie** |
| | oon pwah-son-ree |
| a garage (for repairs) | **un garage** |
| | an gahrash |
| a hairdresser's | **un coiffeur** |
| | an kwah-fer |
| a greengrocer's | **un marchand de légumes** |
| | an marshahn der lehgoom |
| a grocer's | **une épicerie** |
| | oon ehpeess-ree |
| a Health and Social Security Office | **un bureau de la Sécurité Sociale** |
| | an buro der lah sehcooreeteh sossee-al |
| a hospital | **un hôpital** |
| | an opeetal |
| a hotel | **un hôtel** |
| | an otel |
| a hypermarket | **un hypermarché** |
| | an eepair-marsheh |
| a laundry | **une laverie** |
| | oon lav-ree |
| a newsagent's | **un marchand de journaux** |
| | an marshahn der shoorno |
| a night club | **une boîte de nuit** |
| | oon bwaht der nwee |
| a petrol station | **une station service** |
| | oon stah-see-on sairvees |
| a post box | **une boîte à lettres** |
| | oon bwaht ah let |
| a public telephone | **un téléphone** |
| | an telefon |

| a public toilet | **des WC publics** |
| | deh veh-seh poobleek |
| a restaurant | **un restaurant** |
| | an restorahn |
| a supermarket | **un supermarché** |
| | an soopair-marsheh |
| a taxi stand | **une station de taxis** |
| | oon stah-see-on der taxee |
| a tobacconist's | **un bureau de tabac** |
| | an buro der tahbah |
| a travel agent's | **une agence de voyage** |
| | oon ashahns der vwah-yash |
| a youth hostel | **une auberge de jeunesse** |
| | oon obairsh der sher-ness |

## DIRECTIONS

- Asking where a place is, or if a place is nearby, is one thing; making sense of the answer is another.
- Here are some of the most important key directions and replies.

| Left | **Gauche** |
| | goshe |
| Right | **Droite** |
| | drwaht |
| Straight on | **Tout droit** |
| | too drwah |
| There | **Là** |
| | lah |
| First left/right | **La première rue à gauche/droite** |
| | lah prem-yair roo ah goshe/drwaht |
| Second left/right | **La deuxième rue à gauche/droite** |
| | lah der-zee-em roo ah goshe/ |
| | drwaht |

# Accommodation

## ESSENTIAL INFORMATION
### Hotel

- If you want hotel-type accommodation, all the following words in capital letters are worth looking for on name boards:
  HÔTEL
  MOTEL
  PENSION (a small, privately run hotel)
  AUBERGE (often picturesque type of hotel situated in the countryside)
- Lists of hotels and **pensions** can be obtained from local tourist offices or the French Tourist Office in London.
- The cost is displayed in the room itself, so you can check it when having a look round before agreeing to stay.
- The displayed cost is for the room itself, per night and not per person. Breakfast is extra, and therefore optional.
- Not all hotels provide meals, apart from breakfast. A **pension** always provides meals. Breakfast is continental style: coffee or tea with rolls/croissants, butter and jam.
- An identity document is requested when registering at a hotel and will normally be kept overnight. Passports or driving licences are accepted.
- Tipping: Look for the words **service compris/non compris** (service included/not included) on your bill. Tip porters.

## WHAT TO SAY

| | |
|---|---|
| I have a booking | **J'ai une réservation**<br>sheh oon rehzairvah-see-on |
| Have you any vacancies, please? | **Avez-vous des chambres libres, s'il vous plaît**<br>ahveh-voo deh shahmb leeb sil voo pleh |
| Can I book a room? | **Puis-je réserver une chambre?**<br>pweesh rehzairveh oon shahmb |
| It's for . . . | **C'est pour . . .**<br>seh poor . . . |
| one adult/one person | **un adulte/une personne**<br>an ahdoolt/oon pairson |

| | |
|---|---|
| two adults/two people | **deux adultes/deux personnes** |
| | der zahdoolt/der pairson |
| and one child | **et un enfant** |
| | eh an ahnfahn |
| and two children | **et deux enfants** |
| | eh der zahnfahn |

[*For numbers, see p. 106*]

| | |
|---|---|
| It's for . . . | **C'est pour . . .** |
| | seh poor . . . |
| one night | **une nuit** |
| | oon nwee |
| two nights | **deux nuits** |
| | der nwee |
| one week/two weeks | **une semaine/deux semaines** |
| | oon ser-men/der ser-men |
| I would like . . . | **Je voudrais . . .** |
| | sher voodreh . . . |
| a (quiet) room | **une chambre (tranquille)** |
| | oon shahmb (trahnkeel) |
| two rooms | **deux chambres** |
| | der shahmb |
| with a single bed | **à un lit** |
| | ah an lee |
| with two single beds | **à deux lits** |
| | ah der lee |
| with a double bed | **avec un grand lit** |
| | ahvec an grahn lee |
| with a toilet | **avec WC** |
| | ahvec veh-seh |
| with a bathroom | **avec salle de bains** |
| | ahvec sal der ban |
| with a shower | **avec douche** |
| | ahvec doosh |
| with a cot | **avec un lit d'enfant** |
| | ahvec an lee dahnfahn |
| with a balcony | **avec balcon** |
| | ahvec bal-con |
| I would like . . . | **Je voudrais . . .** |
| | sher voodreh |
| full board | **pension complète** |
| | pahn-see-on complet |

| | |
|---|---|
| **I would like . . .** | **Je voudrais . . .**<br>sher voodreh . . . |
| half board | **demi-pension**<br>der-me pahn-see-on |
| bed and breakfast<br>[see *essential information*] | **chambre et petit déjeuner**<br>shahmb eh ptee desh-neh |
| Do you serve meals? | **Est-ce que vous faites restaurant?**<br>esk voo fet restorahn |
| Can I look at the room? | **Puis-je voir la chambre?**<br>pweesh vwah lah shahmb |
| OK, I'll take it | **D'accord, je la prends**<br>daccor sher lah prahn |
| No thanks, I won't take it | **Non merci, je ne la prends pas**<br>non mair-see sher ner lah prahn pah |
| The bill, please | **La note, s'il vous plaît**<br>lah not sil voo pleh |
| Is service included? | **Est-ce que le service est compris?**<br>esk ler sairvees eh compree |
| I think this is wrong | **Je crois qu'il y a une erreur**<br>sher crwah kil yah oon error |
| May I have a receipt? | **Puis-je avoir un reçu?**<br>pweesh ahvwah oon rer-soo |

#### Camping

- Look for the word **CAMPING**
- Be prepared to have to pay:
  per person
  for the car (if applicable)
  for the tent or caravan plot
  for electricity
  for hot showers
- You must provide proof of identity such as your passport.
- You can obtain lists of campsites from local tourist offices or from the French Tourist Office in London.
- Some campsites offer discounts to campers with the International Camping Carnet and some offer weekly, fortnightly or monthly rates.
- Officially recognized campsites have a star rating (like hotels).

- Municipal-run campsites are often reasonably priced and well-run.
- Off-site camping (**le camping sauvage**) is prohibited in many areas. As a rule it is better and safer to use recognized sites.

**Youth hostels**

- Look for the words: **AUBERGE DE JEUNESSE**.
- You will be asked for a YHA card and your passport on arrival.
- Food and cooking facilities vary from hostel to hostel and you may have to help with the domestic chores.
- You must take your own sleeping bag lining but sheets can usually be hired on arrival.
- In the high season it is advisable to book beds in advance, and your stay will be limited to a maximum of three consecutive nights per hostel.
- Apply to the French Tourist Office in London or local tourist offices in France for lists of youth hostels and details of regulations for hostellers.

**WHAT TO SAY**

| | |
|---|---|
| I have a booking | **J'ai une réservation**<br>sheh oon rehzairvah-see-on |
| Have you any vacancies? | **Avez-vous de la place?**<br>ahveh-voo der lah plass |
| How much is it . . . | **C'est combien . . .**<br>seh combee-an . . . |
| for the tent? | **pour la tente?**<br>poor lah tahnt |
| for the caravan? | **pour la caravane?**<br>poor lah caravan |
| for the car? | **pour la voiture?**<br>poor lah vwah-toor |
| for the electricity? | **pour l'électricité?**<br>poor leh-lectriciteh |
| per person? | **par personne?**<br>par pairson |
| per day/night? | **par jour/nuit?**<br>par shoor/nwee |
| May I look round? | **Puis-je voir?**<br>pweesh vwah |

| | |
|---|---|
| Do you provide anything . . . | **Est-ce qu'on peut avoir . . .** |
| | eskon per ahvwah . . . |
| to eat? | **de la nourriture?** |
| | der lah nooreetoor |
| to drink? | **des boissons?** |
| | deh bwah-son |
| **Is there/are there . . .** | **Est-ce qu'il y a . . .** |
| | eskil yah . . . |
| a bar? | **un bar?** |
| | an bar |
| hot showers? | **des douches chaudes?** |
| | deh doosh shod |
| a kitchen? | **une cuisine?** |
| | oon kweezeen |
| a laundry? | **une laverie?** |
| | oon lav-ree |
| a restaurant? | **un restaurant?** |
| | an restorahn |
| a shop? | **un magasin?** |
| | an mahgah-zan |
| a swimming pool? | **une piscine?** |
| | oon pee-seen |
| a takeaway? | **des plats à emporter?** |
| | deh plah ah ahmporteh |

[*For food shopping, see p. 80, and for eating and drinking out, see p. 90.*]

| | |
|---|---|
| I would like a counter for the shower | **Je voudrais un jeton pour la douche** |
| | sher voodreh an sher-ton poor lah doosh |

**Problems**

| | |
|---|---|
| The toilet | **Le WC** |
| | ler veh-seh |
| The shower | **La douche** |
| | lah doosh |
| The tap | **Le robinet** |
| | ler robbeeneh |
| The razor point | **La prise pour le rasoir** |
| | lah preez poor ler rah-zwah |

| | |
|---|---|
| The light | **La lumière** |
| | lah loom-yair |
| **. . . is not working** | **. . . ne marche pas** |
| | . . . ner marsh pah |
| My camping gas has run out | **Je n'ai plus de gaz** |
| | sher neh ploo der gaz |

## LIKELY REACTIONS

| | |
|---|---|
| Have you an identity document? | **Avez-vous une pièce d'identité?** |
| | ahveh-voo oon pee-ess deedahnteeteh |
| Your membership card, please | **Votre carte, s'il vous plaît** |
| | vot cart sil voo pleh |
| What's your name? | **Votre nom, s'il vous plaît** |
| | vot nom sil voo pleh |
| Sorry, we're full | **Je regrette, c'est complet** |
| | sher rer-gret seh compleh |
| How many people is it for? | **C'est pour combien de personnes?** |
| | seh poor combee-an der pairson |
| I haven't any rooms left | **Je n'ai plus de chambres** |
| | sher neh ploo der shahmb |
| Do you want to have a look? | **Vous voulez voir?** |
| | voo vooleh vwah |
| How many nights is it for? | **C'est pour combien de nuits?** |
| | seh poor combee-an der nwee |
| It's (5) francs . . . | **C'est (cinq) francs . . .** |
| | seh (san) frahn . . . |
| per day/per night | **par jour/par nuit** |
| | par shoor/par nwee |

[*For numbers, see p. 106*]

# General shopping

## ESSENTIAL INFORMATION
### The chemist's

- Look for the word **PHARMACIE**.
- Medicines (drugs) are only available at a chemist's.

- Some non-drugs can be bought at a supermarket or department store.
- Try the chemist *before* going to a doctor: they are usually qualified to treat minor injuries.
- To claim money back on prescriptions, remove price labels from medicines, and stick them on the prescription sheet.
- Chemists take it in turns to stay open all night and on Sundays. A notice on the door headed **PHARMACIE DE GARDE** or **PHARMACIE DE SERVICE** gives the address of the nearest chemist on duty.
- Some toiletries can also be bought at a **PARFUMERIE** but these will be more expensive.
- Finding a chemist, see p. 65.

## WHAT TO SAY

| I'd like . . . | **Je voudrais . . .** |
|---|---|
| | sher voodreh . . . |
| some Alka Seltzer | **de l'Alka Seltzer** |
| | der lalka seltzer |
| some antiseptic | **un antiseptique** |
| | an anti-septeek |
| some aspirin | **de l'aspirine** |
| | der laspeereen |
| some baby food | **de la nourriture pour bébés** |
| | der lah nooreetoor poor behbeh |
| some contraceptives | **des contraceptifs** |
| | deh contraceptif |
| some cotton wool | **du coton** |
| | doo cotton |
| some deodorant | **un déodorant** |
| | an deh-odorahn |
| some disposable nappies | **des couches en cellulose** |
| | deh coosh ahn celluloz |
| some handcream | **de la crème pour les mains** |
| | der lah crem poor leh man |
| some eye drops | **des gouttes pour les yeux** |
| | deh goot poor leh zee-er |
| some inhalant | **un inhalateur** |
| | an eenahlah-ter |
| some insect repellent | **une crème anti-moustiques** |
| | oon crem anti-moosteek |

| | |
|---|---|
| some lipstick | **du rouge à lèvres** |
| | doo roosh ah lev |
| some make-up remover | **un démaquillant** |
| | an dehmahkee-yahn |
| some paper tissues | **des Kleenex** |
| | deh kleenex |
| some razor blades | **des lames de rasoir** |
| | deh lam der rahzwah |
| some safety pins | **des épingles de sûreté** |
| | dez ehpang der soor-teh |
| some sanitary towels | **des serviettes périodiques** |
| | deh sairv-yet pehree-odeek |
| some shaving cream | **de la crème à raser** |
| | der lah crem ah rahzeh |
| some soap | **du savon** |
| | doo sav-on |
| some suntan lotion/oil | **une crème/huile solaire** |
| | oon crem/weel solair |
| some toilet paper | **du papier hygiénique** |
| | doo pap-yeh eeshee-ehneek |
| I'd like something for . . . | **Je voudrais un produit pour . . .** |
| | sher voodreh an prodwee poor . . . |
| bites/stings (insect) | **les piqûres (d'insectes)** |
| | leh peek-oor (dan-sect) |
| burns/scalds | **les brûlures** |
| | leh brool-yoor |
| a cold | **le rhume** |
| | ler room |
| constipation | **la constipation** |
| | lah consteepah-see-on |
| a cough | **la toux** |
| | lah too |
| diarrhoea | **la diarrhée** |
| | lah dee-ah-reh |
| ear-ache | **le mal d'oreille** |
| | ler mal doray |
| flu | **la grippe** |
| | lah greep |
| sore gums | **la gingivite** |
| | lah shanshee-veet |
| sunburn | **les coups de soleil** |
| | leh coo der solay |

| I'd like something for . . . | **Je voudrais un produit pour . . .** |
|---|---|
| | sher voodreh an prodwee poor . . . |
| travel sickness | **le mal de mer** |
| | ler mal der mair |

[*For other essential expressions, see 'Shop Talk', opposite.*]

# Holiday items

## ESSENTIAL INFORMATION

- Places to shop at and signs to look for:
  **LIBRAIRIE-PAPÈTERIE** (stationer's)
  **BUREAU DE TABAC** (tobacconist's)
  **CARTES POSTALES – SOUVENIRS** (postcards – souvenirs)
  **PHOTOGRAPHIE** (films and photographic equipment)
- and the main department stores:
  **MONOPRIX  PRISUNIC  INNO**

## WHAT TO SAY

| I'd like . . . | **Je voudrais . . .** |
|---|---|
| | sher voodreh . . . |
| a bag | **un sac** |
| | an sac |
| a beach ball | **un ballon pour la plage** |
| | an bah-lon poor lah plash |
| a bucket | **un seau** |
| | an so |
| an English newspaper | **un journal anglais** |
| | an shoornahl ahngleh |
| some envelopes | **des enveloppes** |
| | deh zahnv-lop |
| a guide book | **un guide** |
| | an gheed |
| a map (of the area) | **une carte (de la région)** |
| | oon cart (der lah resh-yon) |

| | |
|---|---|
| some postcards | **des cartes postales** |
| | deh cart postahl |
| a spade | **une pelle** |
| | oon pel |
| a straw hat | **un chapeau de paille** |
| | an shahpo der pie |
| some sunglasses | **des lunettes de soleil** |
| | deh loonet der solay |
| some writing paper | **du papier à lettres** |
| | doo pap-yeh ah let |
| a colour film | **un rouleau de pellicules couleur** |
| [*show camera*] | an roolo der pelleecool cooler |
| a black and white film | **un rouleau de pellicules noir et blanc** |
| | an roolo der pelleecool nwah eh blahn |

# Shop talk

## ESSENTIAL INFORMATION

* Know how to say the important weights and measures:

| | |
|---|---|
| 50 grams | **cinquante grammes** |
| | sankahnt gram |
| 100 grams | **cent grammes** |
| | sahn gram |
| 200 grams | **deux cents grammes** |
| | der sahn gram |
| ½ kilo | **un demi-kilo** |
| | an der-me keelo |

| | |
|---|---|
| 1 kilo | **un kilo**<br>an keelo |
| 2 kilos | **deux kilos**<br>der keelo |
| ½ litre | **un demi-litre**<br>an der-me leet |
| 1 litre | **un litre**<br>an leet |
| 2 litres | **deux litres**<br>der leet |

- In small shops don't be surprised if customers, as well as the shop assistant, say 'hello' and 'goodbye' to you.

## CUSTOMER

| | |
|---|---|
| I'm just looking | **Je regarde**<br>sher rer-gard |
| How much is this/that? | **C'est combien ça?**<br>seh combee-an sah |
| What is that/what are those? | **Qu'est-ce que c'est ça?**<br>kesk seh sah |
| Is there a discount? | **Est-ce que vous faites une remise?**<br>esk voo fet oon rer-meez |
| I'd like that, please | **Je voudrais ça, s'il vous plaît**<br>sher voodreh sah sil voo pleh |
| Not that | **Pas ça**<br>pah sah |
| Like that | **Comme ça**<br>com sah |
| That's enough, thank you | **Ça suffit, merci**<br>sah soofee mair-see |
| More please | **Encore un peu, s'il vous plaît**<br>ahncor an per sil voo pleh |
| Less please | **Moins, s'il vous plaît**<br>mwen sil voo pleh |
| That's fine ⎤<br>OK     ⎦ | **Ça va**<br>sah vah |
| I won't take it, thank you | **Merci je ne le prends pas**<br>mair-see sher ner ler prahn pah |
| It's not right | **Ça ne va pas**<br>sah ner vah pah |

| | |
|---|---|
| **Have you got something . . .** | **Avez-vous quelque chose . . .** |
| | ahveh-voo kelk shoz . . . |
| better? | **de mieux?** |
| | der me-er |
| cheaper? | **de moins cher?** |
| | der mwen shair |
| different? | **de différent?** |
| | der dee-fay-rahn |
| larger? | **de plus grand?** |
| | der ploo grahn |
| smaller? | **de plus petit?** |
| | der ploo ptee |
| Can I have a bag, please? | **Puis-je avoir un sac, s'il vous plaît?** |
| | pweesh ahvwah an sac sil voo pleh |
| Can I have a receipt? | **Puis-je avoir un reçu?** |
| | pweesh ahvwah an rer-soo |
| **Do you take . . .** | **Acceptez-vous . . .** |
| | accepteh-voo . . . |
| English/American money? | **l'argent anglais/américain?** |
| | larshahn ahngleh/american |
| travellers' cheques? | **les traveller chèques?** |
| | leh traveller sheck |
| credit cards? | **la carte bleue?** |
| | lah cart bler |

## SHOP ASSISTANT

| | |
|---|---|
| Can I help you? | **Qu'y a-t-il pour votre service?** |
| | kee ah-til poor vot sairvees |
| What would you like? | **Vous désirez?** |
| | voo dehzeereh |
| Will that be all? | **Ce sera tout?** |
| | ser ser-rah too |
| Is that all? | **C'est tout?** |
| | seh too |
| Anything else? | **Vous désirez autre chose?** |
| | voo dehzeereh ot shoz |
| Would you like it wrapped? | **Je vous l'enveloppe?** |
| | sher voo lahnv-lop |
| Sorry, none left | **Je regrette, il n'y en a plus** |
| | sher rer-gret il nee ahn-nah ploo |

| | |
|---|---|
| I haven't got any | **Je n'en ai pas**<br>sher nahn-neh pah |
| I haven't got any more | **Je n'en ai plus**<br>sher nahn-neh ploo |
| How many do you want? ⎤<br>How much do you want? ⎦ | **Vous en voulez combien?**<br>voo-zahn vooleh combee-an |
| Is that enough? | **Ça suffit?**<br>sah soofee |

# Shopping for food

# Bread

## ESSENTIAL INFORMATION

- Finding a baker's, see p. 65.
- Key words to look for:
  **BOULANGERIE** (baker's)
  **BOULANGER** (baker)
  **PAIN** (bread)
- Small bakers are usually open between 7.30 a.m. and 7/8 p.m. Most close on Mondays and public holidays but open on Sunday mornings.
- For types of loaf other than a 'French stick' say **'un pain'** (an pan) and point.

## WHAT TO SAY

| | |
|---|---|
| Some bread, please | **Du pain, s'il vous plaît**<br>doo pan sil voo pleh |
| A loaf (like that) | **Un pain (comme ça)**<br>an pan (com sah) |
| A French stick | **Une baguette**<br>oon bah-get |
| A large one | **Une grande**<br>oon grahnd |
| A long, thin one | **Une ficelle**<br>oon feesel |

| | |
|---|---|
| Half a French stick | **Une demi-baguette** |
| | oon der-me bah-get |
| A brown loaf | **Un pain intégral** |
| | an pan an-tay-gral |
| A bread roll | **Un petit pain** |
| | an ptee pan |

---

# Cakes and ice-creams

---

## ESSENTIAL INFORMATION

- Key words to look for:
  **PÂTISSERIE** (cake shop)
  **PÂTISSIER** (cake/pastry maker)
  **PÂTISSERIES** (pastries/cakes)
  **GLACES** (ice-creams)
  **GLACIER** (ice-cream maker/seller)
  **CONFISERIE** (sweet shop)
  **CONFISEUR** (sweet maker/seller)
- **SALON DE THÉ**: a room, usually off a pâtisserie, where customers sit at tables and are served with cakes, ices, soft drinks, tea, coffee or chocolate. See p. 90, 'Ordering a drink and a snack'.
- Pâtisseries are open on Sundays, but not on Mondays.

## WHAT TO SAY

The types of cakes you find in the shops vary from region to region, but the following are some of the most common.

| | |
|---|---|
| **un éclair** | an éclair |
| an eclair | |
| **un chou à la crème** | choux pastry filled with vanilla |
| an shoo ah lah crem | cream |
| **une religieuse** | choux pastry in the shape of a |
| oon rer-leeshee-erz | small cottage loaf with coffee |
| | cream filling (literally: a nun) |
| **un baba au rhum** | a rum baba |
| an bahbah o rom | |

| | |
|---|---|
| **un millefeuille** | alternate layers of puff pastry and |
| an meelfey |   almond cream |
| **un chausson aux pommes** | an apple turnover |
| an sho-son o pom | |
| **un pet de nonne** | a doughnut |
| an peh der non | |
| **une tartelette aux pommes** | a small apple tart |
| oon tartlet o pom | |
| **. . . aux fraises** | . . . strawberry . . . |
| . . . o frez | |
| **. . . aux abricots** | . . . apricot . . . |
| . . . o-zahbreeco | |
| A . . . ice, please | **Une glace . . . s'il vous plaît** |
| | oon glass . . . sil voo pleh |
| banana | **à la banane** |
| | ah lah bah-nan |
| chocolate | **au chocolat** |
| | o shocolah |
| coffee | **au moka** |
| | o makah |
| pistachio | **à la pistache** |
| | ah lah pee-stash |
| raspberry | **à la framboise** |
| | ah lah frahm-bwahz |
| strawberry | **à la fraise** |
| | ah lah frez |
| vanilla | **à la vanille** |
| | ah lah vahneel |
| Two francs worth | **Deux francs** |
| | der frahn |
| A single cone [*specify flavour, as above*] | **Un cornet simple** |
| | an corneh samp |

# Picnic food

## ESSENTIAL INFORMATION

- Key words to look for:
  **CHARCUTERIE** (pork butcher's, delicatessen)
  **TRAITEUR** (delicatessen)
  **CHARCUTIER** (pork butcher)
- In these shops you can buy a wide variety of food such as ham, salami, cheese, olives, appetizers, sausages and freshly made takeaway dishes. Specialities differ from region to region.

## WHAT TO SAY

| Two slices of . . . | Deux tranches de . . . |
|---|---|
| | der trahnsh der . . . |
| garlic sausage | **saucisson à l'ail** |
| | so-see-son ah lie |
| ham (cooked) | **jambon cuit** |
| | shahmbon kwee |
| ham (cured) | **jambon cru** |
| | shahmbon croo |
| pâté | **pâté** |
| | pahteh |
| roast beef | **rôti de bœuf** |
| | rotee der berf |
| roast pork | **rôti de porc** |
| | rotee der por |
| salami | **saucisson** |
| | so-see-son |

You might also like to try some of these:

| **andouille** | tripe sausage |
|---|---|
| ahn-dooy | |
| **barquette de crevettes** | boat-shaped pastry case with |
| barket der crer-vet | prawn filling |
| **bœuf aux champignons** | diced beef cooked with wine and |
| berf o shahmpeen-yon | mushrooms |
| **. . . aux olives** | sliced beef cooked with wine and |
| . . . o zoleev | olives |

| | |
|---|---|
| **. . . en daube** | diced beef in a thick wine sauce |
| . . . ahn dobe | |
| **bouchée à la reine** | vol-au-vent case filled with sweet- |
| boo-shay ah lah rain | breads and mushrooms in cream |
| | sauce |
| **boudin** | black pudding |
| boo-dain | |
| **brandade de morue** | salt cod, crushed and mixed with |
| brahn-dad der moroo | oil, cream and garlic |
| **champignons à la grecque** | mushrooms cooked in wine, |
| shahmpeen-yon ah lah grec | tomatoes and spices |
| **cœurs d'artichaux** | artichoke hearts |
| ker dar-tee-sho | |
| **macédoine de légumes** | diced vegetables in mayonnaise |
| masshe-dwan der lehgoom | |
| **œufs mayonnaise** | hard boiled eggs with mayonnaise |
| er my-onez | |
| **quiche lorraine** | egg and ham/bacon pie |
| keesh lorren | |
| **rillettes** | minced pork (goose or duck) |
| ree-yet | baked in fat |
| **rouleau au fromage** | pastry roll with creamy cheese |
| roolo o fromash | filling |
| **salade niçoise** | tomato, potato, egg, anchovy, |
| sal-ad nee-swahz | tunny fish and olive salad in oil |
| | and vinegar |
| **saucisse de Strasbourg** | frankfurter |
| so-seess der strasboor | |
| **saucisson sec** | smoked garlic sausage |
| so-see-son sec | |
| **tarte à l'oignon** | onion pie |
| tart ah lonion | |
| **tarte au fromage** | cheese pie |
| tart o fromash | |
| **tomates farcies** | stuffed tomatoes |
| tomaht far-see | |
| **Brie** | creamy white cheese |
| bree | |
| **Camembert** | full fat soft white cheese |
| cahmahmbair | |
| **Emmental** | Swiss cheese with big holes |
| emmentahl | |

| | |
|---|---|
| **fromage de chèvre** | goat's cheese |
| fromash der shev | |
| **Gruyère** | Swiss cheese, rich in flavour, |
| gru-yair | smooth in texture |
| **Pont l'Évêque** | soft, runny cheese with holes, |
| pon leh-vek | strong flavour |
| **Roquefort** | resembles Stilton |
| rockfor | |

[*For other essential expressions, see 'Shop talk', p. 77.*]

# Fruit and vegetables

## ESSENTIAL INFORMATION

- Key words to look for:
  **FRUITS** (fruit)
  **LÉGUMES** (vegetables)
  **PRIMEURS** (fresh fruit and vegetables)
  **FRUITIER** (fruit seller)
  **MARCHÉ** (market)
- It is customary for you to choose your own fruit and vegetables at the market (and in some shops) and for the stallholder to weigh and price them. You must take your own shopping bag: paper and plastic bags are not normally provided.

## WHAT TO SAY

| | |
|---|---|
| 1 kilo of . . . | **Un kilo de\* . . .** |
| | an keelo der . . . |
| apples | **pommes** |
| | pom |
| bananas | **bananes** |
| | bah-nan |
| cherries | **cerises** |
| | ser-eez |
| grapes (white/black) | **raisins (blancs/noirs)** |
| | rehzan (blahn/nwah) |

\*Use d' in front of words beginning with a vowel.

| 1 kilo of . . . | **Un kilo de\* . . .**<br>an keelo der . . . |
| oranges | **oranges**<br>orahnsh |
| peaches | **pêches**<br>pesh |
| pears | **poires**<br>pwah |
| plums | **prunes**<br>proon |
| strawberries | **fraises**<br>frez |
| A grapefruit, please | **Un pamplemousse, s'il vous plaît**<br>an pahmp-mousse sil voo pleh |
| A melon | **Un melon**<br>an mer-lon |
| A pineapple | **Un ananas**<br>an ahnahnah |
| A water melon | **Une pastèque**<br>oon passtek |
| ½ kilo of . . . | **Un demi-kilo de\* . . .**<br>an der-me keelo der . . . |
| asparagus | **asperges**<br>aspersh |
| carrots | **carottes**<br>car-rot |
| green beans | **haricots verts**<br>ahreeco vair |
| leeks | **poireaux**<br>pwah-ro |
| mushrooms | **champignons**<br>shahmpeen-yon |
| onions | **oignons**<br>onion |
| peas | **petits pois**<br>ptee pwah |
| peppers (green/red) | **poivrons (verts/rouges)**<br>pwah-vron (vair/roosh) |
| potatoes | **pommes de terre**<br>pom der tair |

\*Use d' in front of words beginning with a vowel.

| shallots | **échalotes** |
| | eh-shallot |
| spinach | **épinards** |
| | ehpeenar |
| tomatoes | **tomates** |
| | tomaht |
| A bunch of parsley | **Un bouquet de persil** |
| | an bookeh der pair-see |
| A bunch of radishes | **Une botte de radis** |
| | oon bot der rahdee |
| A head of garlic | **Une tête d'ail** |
| | oon tet die |
| A lettuce | **Une salade** |
| | oon sal-ad |
| A stick of celery | **Un pied de céleri** |
| | an pee-eh der seleree |
| A cucumber | **Un concombre** |
| | an concomb |
| Like that, please | **Comme ça, s'il vous plaît** |
| | com sah sil voo pleh |

# Meat and fish

### ESSENTIAL INFORMATION

- Key words to look for:
  **BOUCHERIE** (butcher's)
  **BOUCHER** (butcher)
  **UNE POISSONNERIE** (fishmonger's)
  **FRUITS DE MER** (seafood)
- Markets and large supermarkets usually have a fresh fish stall.

### WHAT TO SAY

For a joint, choose the type of meat and then say how many people it is for:

| Some beef, please | **Du bœuf, s'il vous plaît** |
| | doo berf sil voo pleh |

| | |
|---|---|
| Some lamb | **De l'agneau**<br>der lan-yo |
| Some mutton | **Du mouton**<br>doo mooton |
| Some pork | **Du porc**<br>doo por |
| Some veal | **Du veau**<br>doo vo |
| **A joint . . .** | **Un rôti . . .**<br>an rotee . . . |
| for two people | **pour deux personnes**<br>poor der pair-son |
| for four people | **pour quatre personnes**<br>poor kat pair-son |
| for six people | **pour six personnes**<br>poor see pair-son |
| Some steak, please | **Du biftek, s'il vous plaît**<br>doo beeftek sil voo pleh |
| Some liver | **Du foie**<br>doo fwah |
| Some kidneys | **Des rognons**<br>deh ron-yon |
| Some heart | **Du cœur**<br>doo ker |
| Some sausages | **Des saucisses**<br>deh so-seess |
| Some mince | **De la viande hachée**<br>der lah vee-ahnd asheh |
| Two veal escalopes | **Deux escalopes de veau**<br>der escalop der vo |
| Three pork chops | **Trois côtelettes de porc**<br>trwah cotlet der por |
| Four lamb chops | **Quatre côtelettes d'agneau**<br>kat cotlet dan-yo |
| Five mutton chops | **Cinq côtelettes de mouton**<br>san cotlet der mooton |
| A chicken | **Un poulet**<br>an pooleh |
| A rabbit | **Un lapin**<br>an lah-pan |
| A tongue | **Une langue**<br>oon lahng |

Purchase large fish and small shellfish by weight:

| ½ kilo of . . . | **Un demi-kilo de\*** . . . |
|---|---|
| | an der-me keelo der . . . |
| anchovies | **anchois** |
| | ahn-shwah |
| cod | **morue** |
| | moroo |
| eel | **anguille** |
| | ahn-gweel |
| mussels | **moules** |
| | mool |
| oysters | **huîtres** |
| | weet |
| prawns | **crevettes roses** |
| | crer-vet rose |
| red mullet | **rougets** |
| | roosheh |
| sardines | **sardines** |
| | sardeen |
| shrimps | **crevettes grises** |
| | crer-vet greez |
| turbot | **turbot** |
| | toorbo |
| whiting | **merlans** |
| | mairlahn |
| salmon | **saumon** |
| | somon |
| tuna (fresh) | **thon** |
| | ton |

For some shellfish and 'frying pan' fish, specify the number you want:

| A crab, please | **Un crabe, s'il vous plaît** |
|---|---|
| | an crab sil voo pleh |
| A herring | **Un hareng** |
| | an ah-rahn |
| A lobster | **Une langouste/un homard** |
| | oon lahngoost/an omar |
| A mackerel | **Un maquereau** |
| | an mackro |

\*Use **d'** in front of words beginning with a vowel.

| | |
|---|---|
| A scallop | **Une coquille de Saint-Jacques** |
| | oon cokee der san shack |
| A sole | **Une sole** |
| | oon sol |
| A trout | **Une truite** |
| | oon trweet |
| A whiting | **Un merlan** |
| | an mairlahn |

# *Eating and drinking out*

## Ordering a drink and a snack

### ESSENTIAL INFORMATION

- The places to ask for:
  BAR
  CAFÉ
- The price list of drinks (**TARIF DES CONSOMMATIONS**) must, by law, be displayed outside or in the window.
- There is a waiter service in all cafés and bars, but you can drink at the bar or counter if you wish (cheaper).
- Always leave a tip of 10% or 15% of the bill unless you see **SERVICE COMPRIS** or **PRIX NETS** (service included) printed on the bill or on a notice.
- Bars and cafés serve both alcoholic and non-alcoholic drinks. There are no licensing laws and children are allowed in.

### WHAT TO SAY

| | |
|---|---|
| I'd like . . . please | **Je voudrais . . . s'il vous plaît** |
| | sher voodreh . . . sil voo pleh |
| a black coffee | **un café nature/un café noir** |
| | an cahfeh nahtoor/an cahfeh nwah |

| | |
|---|---|
| a coffee with cream | **un café crème** |
| | an cahfeh crem |
| a hot chocolate | **un chocolat chaud** |
| | an shocolah sho |
| a tea | **un thé** |
| | an teh |
| with milk | **au lait** |
| | o leh |
| with lemon | **au citron** |
| | o seetron |
| a Coca-Cola | **un Coca-Cola** |
| | an coca-cola |
| a glass of milk | **un verre de lait** |
| | an vair der leh |
| a lemonade | **une limonade** |
| | oon leemonad |
| a lemon squash | **une citronnade** |
| | oon seetronad |
| a mineral water | **un Perrier** |
| | an pair-yeh |
| an orangeade | **une orangeade** |
| | oon orahn-shad |
| an orange juice | **un jus d'orange** |
| | an shoo dorahnsh |
| a grape juice | **un jus de raisin** |
| | an shoo der rehzan |
| a pineapple juice | **un jus d'ananas** |
| | an shoo dahnahnah |
| a beer | **une bière** |
| | oon be-air |
| a draught beer | **une bière pression** |
| | oon be-air pressee-on |
| a half | **un demi** |
| | an der-me |
| **I'd like . . . please** | **Je voudrais . . . s'il vous plaît** |
| | sher voodreh . . . sil voo pleh |
| a cheese sandwich | **un sandwich au fromage** |
| | an sandwich o fromash |
| a ham sandwich | **un sandwich au jambon** |
| | an sandwich o shahmbon |
| a pancake | **une crêpe** |
| | oon crep |

These are some other snacks you may like to try:

| | |
|---|---|
| **une choucroûte garnie** | sauerkraut usually served with |
| oon shoo-croot gahrnee | ham, smoked bacon and sausage |
| **un croque-monsieur** | toasted ham and cheese sandwich |
| an crok-mer-see-er | |
| **des frites** | chips |
| deh freet | |
| **un hot-dog** | a hot dog |
| an ot-dog | |
| **un sandwich au saucisson** | a salami sandwich |
| an sandwich o so-see-son | |
| **un sandwich au pâté** | a pâté sandwich |
| an sandwich o pah-teh | |

# In a restaurant

## ESSENTIAL INFORMATION

- The place to ask for: UN RESTAURANT
- You can eat at these places:
  RESTAURANT
  CAFÉ
  BUFFET (at stations)
  ROUTIERS (transport cafés)
  BRASSERIE (limited choice here)
  RELAIS
  AUBERGE
  RÔTISSERIE
  DRUGSTORE
  BISTRO
  LIBRE-SERVICE (self-service cafeterias)
- By law, the menus must be displayed outside or in the window
  – and that is the *only* way to judge if a place is right for your
  needs.
- Self-service restaurants are not unknown (see above), but all
  other places have waiter service.

- Leave a tip unless you see **SERVICE COMPRIS** on the bill or on the menu.
- Children's portions are not usually available.
- Eating times: usually from 11.30–2, and from 7–10, but these vary a great deal according to the type of establishment.

## WHAT TO SAY

| | |
|---|---|
| May I book a table? | **Puis-je réserver une table?**<br>pweesh reh-zairveh oon tab |
| I've booked a table | **J'ai réservé une table**<br>sheh reh-zairveh oon tab |
| A table . . . | **Une table . . .**<br>oon tab . . . |
| for one | **pour une personne**<br>poor oon pair-son |
| for three | **pour trois personnes**<br>poor trwah pair-son |
| The à la carte menu, please | **La carte, s'il vous plaît**<br>la cart sil voo pleh |
| The fixed price menu | **Le menu à prix fixe**<br>ler mer-noo ah pree fix |
| The 25 franc menu | **Le menu à vingt-cinq francs**<br>ler mer-noo ah vant-san frahn |
| The tourist menu | **Le menu touristique**<br>ler mer-noo touristeek |
| Today's special menu | **Le menu du jour**<br>ler mer-noo doo shoor |
| The wine list | **La carte des vins**<br>lah cart deh van |
| What's this, please? [*point to menu*] | **Qu'est ce que c'est ça, s'il vous plaît?**<br>kesk seh sah sil voo pleh |
| A carafe of wine, please | **Une carafe de vin, s'il vous plaît**<br>oon car-af der van sil voo pleh |
| A quarter (25 cc) | **Un quart**<br>an car |
| A half (50 cc) | **Une demi-carafe**<br>oon der-me car-af |
| A glass | **Un verre**<br>an vair |

| | |
|---|---|
| A bottle/a litre | **Une bouteille/un litre** |
| | oon bootay/an leet |
| A half-bottle | **Une demi-bouteille** |
| | oon der-me bootay |
| Red/white/rosé/house wine | **Du vin rouge/blanc/rosé/maison** |
| | doo van roosh/blahn/roseh/mehzon |
| Some more bread, please | **Encore du pain, s'il vous plaît** |
| | ahncor doo pan sil voo pleh |
| Some more wine | **Encore du vin** |
| | ahncor doo van |
| Some oil | **De l'huile** |
| | der lweel |
| Some vinegar | **Du vinaigre** |
| | doo veeneg |
| Some salt | **Du sel** |
| | doo sel |
| Some pepper | **Du poivre** |
| | doo pwahv |
| Some water | **De l'eau** |
| | der lo |
| With/without (garlic) | **Avec de/sans (l'ail)** |
| | ahvec der/sahn (lie) |
| How much does that come to? | **Ça fait combien?** |
| | sah feh combee-an |
| Is service included? | **Est-ce que le service est compris?** |
| | esk ler sairvees eh compree |
| Where is the toilet, please? | **Où sont les WC s'il vous plaît?** |
| | oon son leh veh-seh sil voo pleh |
| Miss! [this does not sound 'abrupt in French] | **Mademoiselle!** |
| | mad-mwahzel |
| Waiter! | **Garçon!** |
| | gar-son |
| The bill, please | **L'addition, s'il vous plaît** |
| | laddisee-on sil voo pleh |

**Key words for courses, as seen on some menus:** [Only ask this question if you want the waiter to remind you of the choice.]

| | |
|---|---|
| What have you got in the way of . . . | Qu'est-ce que vous avez comme . . . |
| | kesk voozahveh com |
| starters? | **hors d'œuvre?** |
| | or derv |

| | |
|---|---|
| soup? | **soupe?** |
| | soup |
| egg dishes? | **œufs?** |
| | er |
| fish? | **poisson?** |
| | pwah-son |
| meat? | **viande?** |
| | vee-ahnd |
| game? | **gibier?** |
| | sheeb-yeh |
| fowl? | **volaille?** |
| | vol-eye |
| vegetables? | **légumes?** |
| | lehgoom |
| cheese? | **fromages?** |
| | fromash |
| fruit? | **fruits?** |
| | frwee |
| ice-cream? | **glaces?** |
| | glass |
| dessert? | **dessert?** |
| | deh-sair |

## UNDERSTANDING THE MENU

- You will find the names of the principal ingredients of most dishes on these pages:

  Starters p. 83        Fruit p. 85
  Meat p. 87            Cheese p. 84
  Fish p. 89            Ice-cream p. 81
  Vegetables p. 86      Dessert p. 81

  Used together with the following lists of cooking and menu terms, they should help you to decode the menu.
- These cooking and menu terms are for understanding only – not for speaking.

### Cooking and menu terms

| | |
|---|---|
| **à l'anglaise** | boiled |
| **au beurre** | with butter |
| **au beurre noir** | fried in sizzling butter |
| **bien cuit** | well done |

| | |
|---|---|
| bisque | shellfish soup |
| blanquette | cooked in a creamy sauce |
| au bleu | boiled in water, oil and thyme (fish) very rare (meat) |
| bonne femme | baked with wine and vegetables |
| bouilli | boiled |
| braisé | braised |
| en broche | spit-roasted |
| en cocotte | stewed |
| coquilles | cooked in a white sauce and browned under the grill |
| en croûte | in a pastry case |
| en daube | braised in a wine stock |
| à l'étouffée | stewed |
| farci | stuffed |
| au four | baked |
| à la française | cooked with lettuce and onion |
| frit | fried |
| froid | cold |
| fumé | smoked |
| garni | served with vegetables or chips |
| au gratin | sprinkled with breadcrumbs and browned under the grill |
| grillé | grilled |
| haché | minced |
| maître d'hôtel | served with butter mixed with parsley and lemon juice |
| Marengo | cooked in oil, tomatoes and white wine |
| mousseline | mousse |
| Parmentier | containing potatoes |
| poché | poached |
| à point | medium |
| à la provençale | cooked with garlic, tomatoes, olive oil, olives, onions and herbs |
| rôti | roasted |
| saignant | rare |
| salade | served with oil and vinegar dressing |
| sauce béarnaise | vinegar, egg yolks, white wine, butter, shallots and tarragon |
| sauce béchamel | flour, butter and milk |

| | |
|---|---|
| sauce bourguignonne | red wine sauce with herbs, onions and spices |
| sauce madère | cooked in Madeira wine |
| sauce Mornay | cheese sauce |
| sauce piquante | sharp vinegar sauce with chopped gherkins and herbs |
| sauté | fried slowly in butter |
| en terrine | preparation of meat, game or fowl baked in a terrine (casserole) and served cold |
| à la vapeur | steamed |
| Vichy | garnished with carrots |
| vinaigrette | with oil and vinegar dressing |

**Further words to help you understand the menu**

| | |
|---|---|
| assiette anglaise | cold meat and salad |
| boudin | black pudding |
| bouillabaisse | rich fish soup in which a variety of fish and shell fish have been cooked. Soup and fish are served in separate dishes |
| champignons | mushrooms |
| chantilly | cream whipped with icing sugar |
| choucroûte | sauerkraut |
| compote | stewed fruit |
| consommé | clear broth |
| crudités | raw vegetables and salads served as starters |
| cuisses de grenouilles | frogs' legs |
| escalopes panées | veal escalopes fried in egg and breadcrumbs |
| escargots | snails |
| flan | egg custard |
| moules | mussels |
| potage | vegetable soup |
| quenelles | fish or meat fingers cooked in a white sauce |
| ragoût | stew |
| ratatouille | a vegetable stew |
| ris de veau | veal sweetbreads |
| sorbet | water ice |
| tournedos | fillet steak |

# Health

## ESSENTIAL INFORMATION

- For details of reciprocal health agreements between the UK and France, ask for leaflet SA30 at your local Department of Health and Social Security a month before leaving, or ask your travel agent.
- For minor disorders and treatment at a chemist's, see p. 73.
- For finding your way to a doctor, dentist, chemist or Health and Social Security Office (for reimbursement), see p. 66.
- To find a doctor in an emergency, look for:
  Médecins (in the Yellow Pages of the telephone directory)
  Les Urgences (casualty department)
  H
  Hôpital ⏌ (hospital)

**What's the matter?**

| | |
|---|---|
| I have a pain here [*point*] | **J'ai mal ici** |
| | sheh mal ee-see |
| I have a toothache | **J'ai mal aux dents** |
| | sheh mal o dahn |
| **I have broken . . .** | **J'ai cassé . . .** |
| | sheh casseh . . . |
| my dentures | **mon dentier** |
| | moon dahnt-yeh |
| my glasses | **mes lunettes** |
| | meh loonet |
| I have lost . . . | **J'ai perdu . . .** |
| | sheh pairdoo . . . |
| my contact lenses | **mes verres de contact** |
| | meh vair der contact |
| a filling | **un plombage** |
| | an plombash |
| My child is ill | **Mon enfant est malade** |
| | mon ahnfahn eh mal-ad |

**Already under treatment for something else?**

| | |
|---|---|
| I take . . . regularly [*show*] | **Je prends . . . régulièrement** |
| | sher prahn . . . rehgool-yair-mahn |
| this medicine | **ce médicament** |
| | ser meh-deecah-mahn |
| these pills | **ces pilules** |
| | seh peelool |
| I have . . . | **J'ai . . .** |
| | sheh . . . |
| a heart condition | **le cœur malade** |
| | ler ker mal-ad |
| haemorrhoids | **des hémorroïdes** |
| | deh zeh-moro-eed |
| rheumatism | **des rhumatismes** |
| | deh rheumateesm |
| I am . . . | **Je suis . . .** |
| | sher swee . . . |
| diabetic | **diabétique** |
| | dee-ah-beh-teek |
| asthmatic | **asthmatique** |
| | asthmateek |
| pregnant | **enceinte** |
| | ahn-sant |
| allergic to (penicillin) | **allergique à (la pénicilline)** |
| | allersheek ah (lah penicillin) |

# Problems: loss, theft

## ESSENTIAL INFORMATION

- If the worst comes to the worst, find the police station. To ask the way, see p. 64.
- Look for:
  **GENDARMERIE** (police)
  **COMMISSARIAT DE POLICE** (police station)

- If you lose your passport report the loss to the police and go to the nearest British Consulate.
- In an emergency, dial 17 for police/ambulance and 18 for the fire brigade.

## LOSS
[*See also 'Theft' below: the lists are interchangeable*]

| I have lost . . . | J'ai perdu . . . |
|---|---|
| | sheh pairdoo . . . |
| my camera | mon appareil photo |
| | mon appah-ray photo |
| my car keys | les clés de ma voiture |
| | leh cleh der mah vwahtoor |
| my car logbook | ma carte grise |
| | mah cart greez |
| my driving licence | mon permis de conduire |
| | mon pairmee der condweer |
| my insurance certificate | mon assurance |
| | mon assoorahns |

## THEFT

| Someone has stolen . . . | On m'a volé . . . |
|---|---|
| | on mah voleh . . . |
| my car | ma voiture |
| | mah vwahtoor |
| my money | mon argent |
| | mon arshahn |
| my tickets | mes billets |
| | meh bee-yeh |
| my travellers' cheques | mes traveller chèques |
| | meh traveller shek |
| my wallet | mon portefeuille |
| | mon port-fey |
| my luggage | mes bagages |
| | meh baggash |

# The post office and phoning home

## ESSENTIAL INFORMATION

- To find a post office, see p. 65.
- Key words to look for:
  **POSTES**
  **POSTE, TÉLÉGRAPHE,**
  **TÉLÉPHONE (PTT)**
  **POSTES ET TÉLÉCOMMUNICATIONS (PT)**

**POSTES TELECOMMUNICATIONS**

- It is best to buy stamps at the tobacconist's.
- Unless you read and speak French well, it's best not to make phone calls by yourself. Go to the main post office and write the town and number you want on a piece of paper.
- For international calls dial 19. Wait for second buzzing noise and then dial 44 for Great Britain. Then dial the town/area code number and the subscriber's number.

## WHAT TO SAY

| | |
|---|---|
| To England, please | **Pour l'Angleterre, s'il vous plaît**<br>poor lahng-tair sil voo pleh |
| [*Hand letters, cards or parcels over the counter*] | |
| To Australia | **Pour l'Australie**<br>poor lostrah-lee |
| To the United States | **Pour les États-Unis**<br>poor leh zehtah-zoonee |
| I'd like to send a telegram | **Je voudrais envoyer un télégramme**<br>sher voodreh ahn-vwah-yeh an telegram |
| I'd like this number . . . | **Je voudrais ce numéro . . .**<br>sher voodreh ser noomehro . . . |
| [*show number*] | |
| in England | **en Angleterre**<br>ahn ahng-tair |
| in Canada | **au Canada**<br>o canada |
| Can you dial it for me, please? | **Pouvez-vous me l'appeler, s'il vous plaît?**<br>pooveh-voo mer lap-leh sil voo pleh |

# Changing cheques and money

## ESSENTIAL INFORMATION

- Finding your way to a bank or change bureau, see p. 65.
- Look for these words on buildings:
  **BANQUE**
  **CRÉDIT**
  **SOCIÉTÉ GÉNÉRALE**
  **BUREAU DE CHANGE**
  **CHANGE**
- To cash your normal cheques, exactly as at home, use your banker's card where you see the Eurocheque sign. Write in English, in pounds.
- Exchange rate information might show the pound as:
  **£, L, Livre Sterling, L St**, or even **GB**.
- Have your passport handy.

## WHAT TO SAY

| | |
|---|---|
| I'd like to cash . . . | **Je voudrais encaisser . . .** |
| | sher voodreh ahn-kesseh . . . |
| these travellers' cheques | **ces traveller chèques** |
| | seh traveller shek |
| this cheque | **ce chèque** |
| | ser shek |
| I'd like to change this . . . | **Je voudrais changer ceci . . .** |
| | sher voodreh shan-sheh ser-see . . . |
| into French francs | **en francs français** |
| | ahn frahn frahn-seh |
| into schillings | **en schillings autrichiens** |
| | ahn shilling otreesh-yan |
| into Belgian francs | **en francs belges** |
| | ahn frahn belsh |
| into marks | **en marks** |
| | ahn mark |
| into lire | **en lires** |
| | ahn leer |
| into pesetas | **en pesetas** |
| | ahn pesetas |
| into Swiss francs | **en francs suisses** |
| | ahn frahn sweess |

# Car travel

## ESSENTIAL INFORMATION

- Finding a filling station or garage, see p. 66.
- Is it a self-service station? Look out for **LIBRE SERVICE** or **SERVEZ-VOUS**.
- Grades of petrol:
  **NORMALE**
  **ORDINAIRE** (2 star, standard)
  **SUPER (CARBURANT)** (3 star and above, premium)
  **GAS-OIL** (diesel)
- 1 gallon is about 4½ litres (accurate enough up to 6 gallons).
- For car repairs, look for:
  **DÉPANNAGE** (repairs)
  **GARAGE** (garage)
  **MÉCANICIEN** (mechanic)
  **CARROSSERIE** (for body work)
- Petrol stations outside towns will sometimes close from 12–3.
- In the case of a breakdown or an emergency look for the **TCF** (French Touring Club) sign, or dial 6969 (**Touring Secours**) from any telephone box.

## WHAT TO SAY

[*For numbers, see p. 106*]

| | |
|---|---|
| (Nine) litres | **(Neuf) litres** |
| | (nerf) leet |
| (Two hundred) francs . . . | **(Deux cents) francs . . .** |
| | (der sahn) frahn . . . |
| of standard | **d'ordinaire** |
| | dordeenair |
| of premium | **de super** |
| | der soopair |
| of diesel | **de gas-oil** |
| | der gazwahl |
| Fill it up, please | **Faites le plein, s'il vous plaît** |
| | fet ler plan sil voo pleh |
| Can you check . . . | **Pouvez-vous vérifier . . .** |
| | pooveh voo vehrif-yeh . . . |
| the oil? | **l'huile?** |
| | lweel |

| | |
|---|---|
| Can you check . . . | **Pouvez-vous vérifier . . .**<br>pooveh voo vehrif-yeh . . . |
| the battery? | **la batterie?**<br>lah battree |
| the radiator? | **le radiateur?**<br>ler raddee-atter |
| the tyres? | **les pneus?**<br>leh pner |
| I've run out of petrol | **Je suis en panne d'essence**<br>sher swee ahn pan dessahns |
| Can you help me, please? | **Pouvez-vous m'aider, s'il vous plaît?**<br>pooveh voo med-eh sil voo pleh |
| Do you do repairs? | **Est-ce que vous faites les réparations?**<br>esk voo fet leh rehpahrah-see-on |
| I have a puncture | **J'ai une crevaison**<br>sheh oon crer-veh-zon |
| I have a broken windscreen | **Mon pare-brise est cassé**<br>mon par-breez eh casseh |
| I think the problem is here . . . [point] | **Je crois que c'est ça qui ne va pas . . .**<br>sher crwah ker seh sah kee ner vah pah . . . |

## LIKELY REACTIONS

| | |
|---|---|
| I don't do repairs | **Je ne fais pas les réparations**<br>sher ner feh-pah leh rehpahrah-see-on |
| Where's your car? | **Où est votre voiture?**<br>oo eh vot vwahtoor |
| What make is it? | **C'est quelle marque?**<br>seh kel mark |
| Come back tomorrow/on Monday | **Revenez demain/lundi**<br>rer-venneh der-man/lerndee |
| [For days of the week, see p. 109] | |
| We don't hire cars | **On ne fait pas la location**<br>on ner feh pah lah locah-see-on |
| Your driving licence, please | **Votre permis, s'il vous plaît**<br>vot pairmee sil voo pleh |
| The mileage is unlimited | **Le kilométrage n'est pas limité**<br>ler keelomeh-trash neh pah limiteh |

# Public transport

## ESSENTIAL INFORMATION

- Key words on signs:
  **ACCÈS AUX QUAIS** (to the trains)
  **ARRÊT D'AUTOBUS** (bus stop)
  **BILLETS** (tickets, ticket office)
  **CONSIGNE** (left luggage)
  **ENTRÉE** (entrance)
  **HORAIRE** (timetable)
  **INTERDIT(E)** (forbidden)
  **LOCATIONS** (bookings)
  **MONTÉE** (entrance for buses)
  **N'OUBLIEZ PAS DE COMPOSTER** (don't forget to validate)
  **RENSEIGNEMENTS** (information)
  **QUAI** (platform)
  **SORTIE** (exit)
  **VOIE** (platform)
- As French Railways have abolished ticket control at platform barriers, *you* must validate your ticket by using one of the orange-coloured date stamping machines provided at platform entrances *before* departure. If you fail to do so, you will be liable to a fine of up to 20% of your fare. However, these regulations do not apply to international tickets purchased outside France.
- There is a flat rate for underground tickets and it is cheaper to buy a **carnet** (a book of ten tickets). In Paris, bus and underground tickets are interchangeable.

## WHAT TO SAY

| | |
|---|---|
| Where does the train for (Paris) leave from? | **De quelle voie part le train de (Paris)?** der kel vwah par ler tran der (pahree) |
| Is this the train for (Paris)? | **Est-ce le train de (Paris)?** ess ler tran der (pahree) |
| Where does the bus for (Toulouse) leave from? | **D'où part l'autobus de (Toulouse)?** doo par lotoboos der (too-looz) |

| | | |
|---|---|---|
| Is this the bus for (Toulouse)? | **Est-ce l'autobus de (Toulouse)?** | |
| | ess lotoboos der (too-looz) | |
| Do I have to change? | **Faut-il changer?** | |
| | fo-til shahn-sheh | |
| Where can I get a taxi? | **Où puis-je trouver un taxi?** | |
| | oo pweesh trooveh an taxee | |
| Can you put me off at the right stop, please? | **Pouvez-vous me dire où je dois descendre?** | |
| | pooveh-voo mer deer oo sher dwah dessahnd | |
| Can I book a seat? | **Puis-je réserver une place?** | |
| | pweesh reh-zairveh oon plass | |
| A single | **Un aller** | |
| | an alleh | |
| A return | **Un aller-retour** | |
| | an alleh rer-toor | |
| First class | **Première classe** | |
| | prem-yair class | |
| Second class | **Deuxième classe** | |
| | der-zee-em class | |
| One adult | **Un adulte** | |
| | an ahdoolt | |
| Two adults | **Deux adultes** | |
| | der zahdoolt | |
| and one child | **et un enfant** | |
| | eh an ahnfahn | |
| and two children | **et deux enfants** | |
| | eh der zahnfahn | |
| How much is it? | **C'est combien?** | |
| | seh combee-an | |

# Reference

**NUMBERS**

| | | |
|---|---|---|
| 0 | **zéro** | zehro |
| 1 | **un** | an |
| 2 | **deux** | der |
| 3 | **trois** | trwah |

| 4 | quatre | kat |
|---|---|---|
| 5 | cinq | sank |
| 6 | six | seess |
| 7 | sept | set |
| 8 | huit | weet |
| 9 | neuf | nerf |
| 10 | dix | deess |
| 11 | onze | onz |
| 12 | douze | dooz |
| 13 | treize | trez |
| 14 | quatorze | kattorz |
| 15 | quinze | kanz |
| 16 | seize | sez |
| 17 | dix-sept | dee-set |
| 18 | dix-huit | deezweet |
| 19 | dix-neuf | deez-nerf |
| 20 | vingt | van |
| 21 | vingt et un | vanteh an |
| 22 | vingt-deux | vant-der |
| 23 | vingt-trois | vant-trwah |
| 24 | vingt-quatre | vant-kat |
| 25 | vingt-cinq | vant-sank |
| 26 | vingt-six | vant-seess |
| 27 | vingt-sept | vant-set |
| 28 | vingt-huit | vant-weet |
| 29 | vingt-neuf | vant-nerf |
| 30 | trente | trahnt |
| 31 | trente et un | trahnteh an |
| 35 | trente-cinq | trahnt sank |
| 38 | trente-huit | trahnt weet |
| 40 | quarante | kah-rahnt |
| 41 | quarante et un | kahrahnteh an |
| 45 | quarante-cinq | kah-rahnt sank |
| 48 | quarante-huit | kah-rahnt weet |
| 50 | cinquante | sankahnt |
| 55 | cinquante-cinq | sankahnt sank |
| 60 | soixante | swah-sahnt |
| 65 | soixante-cinq | swah-sahnt sank |
| 70 | soixante-dix | swah-sahnt deess |
| 75 | soixante-quinze | swah-sahnt kanz |
| 80 | quatre-vingts | kat van |
| 85 | quatre-vingt-cinq | kat van sank |

| 90 | **quatre-vingt-dix** | kat van deess |
|---|---|---|
| 95 | **quatre-vingt-quinze** | kat van kanz |
| 100 | **cent** | sahn |
| 101 | **cent un** | sahn an |
| 102 | **cent deux** | sahn der |
| 125 | **cent vingt-cinq** | sahn vant sank |
| 150 | **cent cinquante** | sahn sankahnt |
| 175 | **cent soixante-quinze** | sahn swah-sahnt kanz |
| 200 | **deux cents** | der sahn |
| 300 | **trois cents** | trwah sahn |
| 400 | **quatre cents** | kat sahn |
| 500 | **cinq cents** | san sahn |
| 1,000 | **mille** | meel |
| 1,500 | **mille cinq cents** | meel san sahn |
| 2,000 | **deux mille** | der meel |
| 5,000 | **cinq mille** | san meel |
| 10,000 | **dix mille** | dee meel |
| 100,000 | **cent mille** | sahn meel |
| 1,000,000 | **un million** | an meel-yon |

## TIME

| **What time is it?** | **Quelle heure est-il?** |
|---|---|
| | keller eh-til |
| It's one o'clock | **Il est une heure** |
| | il eh ooner |
| It's . . . | **Il est . . .** |
| | il eh . . . |
| two o'clock | **deux heures** |
| | der-zer |
| three o'clock | **trois heures** |
| | trwah-zer |
| noon | **midi** |
| | meedee |
| midnight | **minuit** |
| | meenwee |
| a quarter past five | **cinq heures et quart** |
| | sanker eh kar |
| half past five | **cinq heures et demie** |
| | sanker eh der-me |
| a quarter to six | **six heures moins le quart** |
| | seezer mwen ler kar |

# DAYS AND MONTHS

| Monday | **lundi** |
|---|---|
| | lerndee |
| Tuesday | **mardi** |
| | mardee |
| Wednesday | **mercredi** |
| | mairk-dee |
| Thursday | **jeudi** |
| | sher-dee |
| Friday | **vendredi** |
| | vahnd-dee |
| Saturday | **samedi** |
| | samdee |
| Sunday | **dimanche** |
| | deemahnsh |
| January | **janvier** |
| | shahnv-yeh |
| February | **février** |
| | fehvree-eh |
| March | **mars** |
| | marss |
| April | **avril** |
| | avreel |
| May | **mai** |
| | meh |
| June | **juin** |
| | shoo-an |
| July | **juillet** |
| | shwee-yeh |
| August | **août** |
| | oot |
| September | **septembre** |
| | septahmb |
| October | **octobre** |
| | octob |
| November | **novembre** |
| | novahmb |
| December | **décembre** |
| | dessahmb |

# Index

# Travellers' German

**D. L. Ellis, A. Cheyne**

Pronunciation **Dr J. Baldwin**

*Useful addresses*

Austrian National Tourist Office
30 St George Street, London W1

German National Tourist Office
61 Conduit Street, London W1

Swiss National Tourist Office
The Swiss Centre,
1 New Coventry Street, London W1

# Contents

**Reference**

# Pronunciation hints

In German it is important to stress or emphasize the syllables in italics, just as you would if we were to take as an English example: *li*ttle Jack *Hor*ner *sat* in the *cor*ner. Here we have ten syllables, but only four stresses. German will pose no problems as there is an obvious and consistent relationship between pronunciation and spelling.
**Viel Spass!**

# Everyday expressions

[*See also 'Shop talk', p. 128*]

| | |
|---|---|
| Hello | **Guten Tag** |
| | goo-ten tahk |
| Hello (Austria) | **Grüss Gott** |
| | grooss got |
| Good morning | **Guten Morgen** |
| | goo-ten morgen |
| Good day | **Guten Tag** |
| Good afternoon ] | goo-ten tahk |
| Good evening | **Guten Abend** |
| | goo-ten ah-bent |
| Good night | **Gute Nacht** |
| | goo-teh nakt |
| Good-bye | **Auf Wiedersehn** |
| | owf veeder-zain |
| Yes | **Ja** |
| | yah |
| Please | **Bitte** |
| | bitteh |
| Yes, please | **Ja, bitte** |
| | yah bitteh |
| Thank you | **Danke** |
| | dankeh |
| That's right | **Das stimmt** |
| | das shtimmt |
| No | **Nein** |
| | nine |
| I disagree | **Das stimmt nicht** |
| | das shtimmt nisht |
| Excuse me ] | **Entschuldigen Sie** |
| Sorry ] | ent-shool-dig-en zee |
| It doesn't matter | **Es macht nichts** |
| | es makt nishts |
| Where's the toilet, please? | **Wo sind die Toiletten?** |
| | vo zint dee twa-letten |
| Do you speak English? | **Sprechen Sie Englisch?** |
| | shpreshen zee eng-lish |
| What's your name? | **Wie ist Ihr Name?** |
| | vee ist eer nahmeh |
| My name is . . . | **Mein Name ist . . .** |
| | mine nahmeh ist . . . |

# Asking the way

## ESSENTIAL INFORMATION

- Keep a look out for all these place names as you will find them on shops, maps and notices.

## WHAT TO SAY

| | |
|---|---|
| Excuse me, please | **Entschuldigen Sie, bitte**<br>ent-shool-dig-en zee bitteh |
| How do I get . . . | **Wie komme ich . . .**<br>vee kommeh ish . . . |
| to Hamburg? | **nach Hamburg?**<br>nahk hum-boork |
| to (Station) Road? | **zur (Bahnhof) strasse?**<br>tsoor (bahn-hof-)shtrahsseh |
| to the hotel (Krone)? | **zum Hotel (Krone)?**<br>tsoom hotel (krone-eh) |
| to the airport? | **zum Flughafen?**<br>tsoom flook-hahfen |
| to the beach? | **zum Strand?**<br>tsoom shtrant |
| to the bus station? | **zum Busbahnhof?**<br>tsoom boos-bahn-hof |
| to the market? | **zum Markt?**<br>tsoom markt |
| to the police station? | **zur Polizeiwache**<br>tsoor poli-tsy-vakkeh |
| to the port? | **zum Hafen?**<br>tsoom hahfen |
| to the post office? | **zum Postamt?**<br>tsoom post-amt |
| to the railway station? | **zum Bahnhof?**<br>tsoom bahn-hof |
| to the sports stadium? | **zum Stadion?**<br>tsoom shtah-dee-on |
| to the tourist information office? | **zum Fremdenverkehrsbüro?**<br>tsoom fremden-ferkairs-buro |
| to the town centre? | **zum Stadtzentrum?**<br>tsoom shtatt-tsent-room |

| | |
|---|---|
| to the town hall? | **zum Rathaus?** |
| | tsoom r*a*ht-house |
| **Is there . . . near by?** | **Gibt es . . . in der Nähe?** |
| | geept es . . . in der n*a*y-eh |
| a baker's | **eine Bäckerei** |
| | *i*neh becker-ry |
| a bank | **eine Bank** |
| | *i*neh b*a*nk |
| a bar | **eine Bar** |
| | *i*neh bar |
| a bus stop | **eine Bushaltestelle** |
| | *i*neh b*oo*s-halteh-shtelleh |
| a butcher's | **eine Metzgerei** |
| | *i*neh mets-ga-ry |
| a café | **ein Café** |
| | ine caff*a*y |
| a cake shop | **eine Konditorei** |
| | *i*neh con-dee-to-ry |
| a campsite | **eine Campingplatz** |
| | *i*nen camping-plats |
| a car park | **einen Parkplatz** |
| | *i*nen p*a*rk-plats |
| a change bureau | **eine Wechselstube** |
| | *i*neh v*e*ksel-shtoobeh |
| a chemist's | **eine Apotheke** |
| | *i*neh ah-pot*a*ke-eh |
| a delicatessen | **ein Feinkostgeschäft** |
| | ine f*i*ne-kost-gash*e*ft |
| a dentist's | **einen Zahnarzt** |
| | *i*nen ts*a*hn-artst |
| a department store | **ein Kaufhaus** |
| | ine k*o*wf-house |
| a disco | **eine Diskothek** |
| | *i*neh disco-t*a*ke |
| a doctor's surgery | **eine Arztpraxis** |
| | *i*neh artst-prak-sis |
| a dry cleaner's | **eine Reinigung** |
| | *i*neh ry-nee-goong |
| a fishmonger's | **ein Fischgeschäft** |
| | ine fish-gash*e*ft |
| a garage (for repairs) | **eine Autowerkstatt** |
| | *i*neh *o*wto-vairk-shtatt |

**Is there . . . near by?**     **Gibt es . . . in der Nähe?**
*geept es . . . in der nay-eh*

a hairdresser's     **einen Frisör**
*inen free-zer*

a greengrocer's     **eine Gemüsehandlung**
*ineh ga-moozeh-hant-loong*

a grocer's     **ein Lebensmittelgeschäft**
*ine labens-mittel-gasheft*

a hospital     **ein Krankenhaus**
*ine kranken-house*

a hotel     **ein Hotel**
*ine hotel*

an ice-cream parlour     **eine Eisdiele**
*ineh ice-deeleh*

a local sickness insurance office     **eine Krankenkasse**
*ineh kranken-kasseh*

a laundry     **eine Wäscherei**
*ineh vesheh-ry*

a newsagent's     **einen Zeitungshändler**
*inen tsy-toongs-hentler*

a night club     **einen Nachtklub**
*inen nakt-kloop*

a park     **einen Park**
*inen park*

a petrol station     **eine Tankstelle**
*ineh tank-shtelleh*

a post box     **einen Briefkasten**
*inen breef-kasten*

a public telephone     **eine Telefonzelle**
*ineh telefone-tselleh*

a public toilet     **öffentliche Toiletten**
*erffent-lish-eh twa-letten*

a restaurant     **ein Restaurant**
*ine rest-o-rung*

a supermarket     **einen Supermarkt**
*inen zooper-markt*

a taxi stand     **einen Taxistand**
*inen taxi-shtant*

a tobacconist's     **einen Zigarettenladen**
*inen tsee-garetten-lahden*

a travel agent's     **ein Reisebüro**
*ine ryzeh-buro*

| | |
|---|---|
| a youth hostel | **eine Jugendherberge** |
| | ineh y*oo*gent-hair-bairgeh |

## DIRECTIONS

| | |
|---|---|
| Left | **Links** |
| | links |
| Right | **Rechts** |
| | reshts |
| Straight on | **Geradeaus** |
| | grahdeh-*ows* |
| There | **Dort** |
| | dort |
| First left/right | **Erste Strasse links/rechts** |
| | *ai*rsteh shtr*a*hsseh l*i*nks/*re*shts |
| Second left/right | **Zweite Strasse links/rechts** |
| | twvy-teh shtr*a*hsseh l*i*nks/*re*shts |

---

# Accommodation

---

## ESSENTIAL INFORMATION
### Hotel

- If you want hotel-type accommodation, all the following words
  in capital letters are worth looking for on name boards:
  **HOTEL**
  **HOTEL GARNI** (room and breakfast, no other meals provided)
  **MOTEL**
  **PENSION** (boarding house)
  **GASTHOF** (inexpensive type of inn with a limited number of
  rooms)
  **ZIMMER FREI** (rooms to let in private houses, bed and
  breakfast)
- A list of hotels in the town or district can usually be obtained at
  the local tourist information office.
- Not all hotels and boarding-houses provide meals apart from
  breakfast; inquire about this, on arrival, at the reception.

- The cost is displayed in the room itself, so you can check it when having a look round before agreeing to stay.
- The displayed cost is for the room itself, per night and not per person. It usually includes service charges and taxes, but quite often does not include breakfast.
- Breakfast is continental style, with rolls, butter and jam; boiled eggs, cheese and cold meats are usually available on request. Some larger hotels also offer a **FRÜHSTÜCKS-BUFFET** where you can help yourself to cereals, yoghurt, fresh fruit etc.
- It is customary to tip the porter and leave a tip for the chambermaid in the hotel room.

## WHAT TO SAY

| | |
|---|---|
| I have a booking | **Ich habe reserviert** |
| | ish hahbeh reserveert |
| Have you any vacancies, please? | **Haben Sie noch Zimmer frei?** |
| | hahben zee nok tsimmer fry |
| Can I book a room? | **Kann ich ein Zimmer reservieren lassen?** |
| | kan ish ine tsimmer reser-veeren lassen |
| It's for . . . | **Es ist für . . .** |
| | es ist foor . . . |
| one adult/one person | **einen Erwachsenen/eine Person** |
| | inen er-vaksen-en/ineh per-zone |
| two adults/two people | **zwei Erwachsene/zwei Personen** |
| | tsvy er-vaksen-eh/tsvy per-zonen |
| and one child | **und ein Kind** |
| | oont ine kint |
| and two children | **und zwei Kinder** |
| | oont tsvy kin-der |
| It's for . . . | **Es ist für . . .** |
| | es ist foor . . . |
| one night | **eine Nacht** |
| | ineh nakt |
| two nights | **zwei Nächte** |
| | tsvy nesh-teh |
| one week | **eine Woche** |
| | ineh vok-eh |
| two weeks | **zwei Wochen** |
| | tsvy vokken |

| I would like . . . | **Ich möchte . . .** |
| | ish mershteh . . . |
| a room | **ein Zimmer** |
| | ine tsimmer |
| two rooms | **zwei Zimmer** |
| | tsvy tsimmer |
| a room with a single bed | **ein Einzelzimmer** |
| | ine ine-tsel-tsimmer |
| a room with two single beds | **ein Zweibettzimmer** |
| | ine tsvy-bett-tsimmer |
| a room with a double bed | **ein Doppelzimmer** |
| | ine doppel-tsimmer |
| I would like a room . . . | **Ich möchte ein Zimmer . . .** |
| | ish mershteh ine tsimmer . . . |
| with a toilet | **mit Toilette** |
| | mit twa-letteh |
| with a bathroom | **mit Bad** |
| | mit baht |
| with a shower | **mit Dusche** |
| | mit doo-sheh |
| with a cot | **mit einem Kinderbett** |
| | mit inem kin-der-bett |
| with a balcony | **mit Balkon** |
| | mit bal-kone |
| I would like . . . | **Ich möchte . . .** |
| | ish mershteh . . . |
| full board | **Vollpension** |
| | foll-penzee-on |
| half board | **Halbpension** |
| | hal-penzee-on |
| bed and breakfast [see essential information] | **Übernachtung mit Frühstück** |
| | oober-naktoong mit froo-shtok |
| Do you serve meals? | **Kann man bei Ihnen essen?** |
| | kan man by eenen essen |
| Can I look at the room? | **Kann ich mir das Zimmer ansehen?** |
| | kan ish meer das tsimmer un-zay-en |
| OK, I'll take it | **Gut, ich nehme es** |
| | goot ish nay-meh es |
| No thanks, I won't take it | **Nein, danke, ich nehme es nicht** |
| | nine dankeh ish nay-meh es nisht |

| | |
|---|---|
| The bill, please | **Die Rechnung, bitte** |
| | dee resh-noong bitteh |
| Is service included? | **Ist Bedienung inbegriffen?** |
| | ist bedee-noong in-begriffen |
| I think this is wrong | **Ich glaube, hier ist ein Fehler** |
| | ish gla-oobeh here ist ine failer |
| May I have a receipt? | **Kann ich eine Quittung haben?** |
| | kan ish ineh kvit-oong hahben |

## Camping

- Look for: **CAMPINGPLATZ** or **ZELTPLATZ**
- Be prepared for the following charges:
  per person
  for the car (if applicable)
  for the tent or caravan plot
  for electricity
  for hot showers
- You must provide proof of identity, such as your passport.
- If you cannot find an official camping site and want to camp elsewhere, get the permission of the farmer/landowner or the local police first.
- It is usually not possible to make advance reservations on camping sites. Try and secure a site in mid-afternoon if you are travelling during the high season.
- Owners of camping sites in Germany are not liable for losses. You should make your own insurance arrangements in advance.

## Youth hostels

- Look for the word **JUGENDHERBERGE**.
- You must have a YHA card with a photograph.
- There is no upper age limit at German youth hostels, except in Bavaria where the age limit is twenty-seven.
- Accommodation is usually in small dormitories.
- Many German youth hostels do *not* provide a kitchen in which visitors can prepare their own meals; but usually meals at a reasonable price are provided by the house-parents.
- You may have to help with domestic chores in some hostels.

## WHAT TO SAY

| | |
|---|---|
| Have you any vacancies? | **Haben Sie noch etwas frei?** |
| | hahben zee nok etvas fry |
| How much is it . . . | **Wie hoch ist die Gebühr . . .** |
| | vee hoke ist dée gaboor . . . |
| for the tent? | **für das Zelt?** |
| | foor das tselt |
| for the caravan? | **für den Wohnwagen?** |
| | foor den vone-vahgen |
| for the car? | **für das Auto?** |
| | foor das owto |
| for the electricity? | **für Elektrizität** |
| | foor elektri-tsee-tate |
| per person? | **pro Person?** |
| | pro per-zone |
| per day/night? | **pro Tag/Nacht?** |
| | pro tahk/naht |
| May I look round? | **Kann ich mich etwas umsehen?** |
| | kan ish mish etvas oom-zay-en |
| Do you provide anything . . . | **Kann man bei Ihnen etwas . . . bekommen?** |
| | kan man by eenen etvas . . . bekommen |
| to eat? | **zu essen** |
| | tsoo essen |
| to drink? | **zu trinken** |
| | tsoo trinken |
| Do you have . . . | **Haben Sie . . .** |
| | hahben zee . . . |
| a bar? | **eine Bar?** |
| | ineh bar |
| hot showers? | **heisse Duschen?** |
| | hysseh doo-shen |
| a kitchen? | **eine Küche?** |
| | ineh koo-sheh |
| a launderette? | **einen Waschsalon?** |
| | inen vash-zalong |
| a restaurant? | **ein Restaurant?** |
| | ine resto-rung |
| a shop? | **ein Geschäft?** |
| | ine gasheft |

**Do you have . . .**　　　　　**Haben Sie . . .**
　　　　　　　　　　　　　　hahben zee . . .

　a swimming pool?　　　　**ein Schwimmbad?**
　　　　　　　　　　　　　　ine shvimm-baht

　a snack-bar?　　　　　　**eine Imbisstube?**
　　　　　　　　　　　　　　ineh im-bis-shtoobeh

[*For food shopping, see p. 131, and for eating and drinking out, see
　p. 141*]

## Problems

The toilet　　　　　　　**Die Toilette**
　　　　　　　　　　　　　dee twa-letteh

The shower　　　　　　　**Die Dusche**
　　　　　　　　　　　　　dee doosheh

The tap　　　　　　　　　**Der Wasserhahn**
　　　　　　　　　　　　　der vasser-hahn

The razor point　　　　　**Die Steckdose für den
　　　　　　　　　　　　　　Rasierapparat**
　　　　　　　　　　　　　dee shteck-doze-eh foor den
　　　　　　　　　　　　　razeer-apparaht

The light　　　　　　　　**Das Licht**
　　　　　　　　　　　　　das lisht

. . . is not working　　　　**. . . funktioniert nicht**
　　　　　　　　　　　　　. . . foonk-tsee-o-neert nisht

My camping gas has run out　**Ich habe kein Camping-Gas mehr**
　　　　　　　　　　　　　ish hahbeh kine camping-gahs mair

## LIKELY REACTIONS

Have you an identity　　　　**Haben Sie einen Pass oder
　document?　　　　　　　　Personalausweis?**
　　　　　　　　　　　　　hahben zee inen pass oder
　　　　　　　　　　　　　per-zonahl-ows-vice

Your membership card, please　**Ihre Mitgliedskarte, bitte**
　　　　　　　　　　　　　eereh mit-gleets-karteh bitteh

What's your name [*see p. 115*]　**Wie ist Ihr Name?**
　　　　　　　　　　　　　vee ist eer nahmeh

Sorry, we're full　　　　　**Est tut mir leid, wir sind voll
　　　　　　　　　　　　　　besetzt**
　　　　　　　　　　　　　es toot meer lite veer zint foll
　　　　　　　　　　　　　bezetst

How many people is it for?　**Für wieviele Personen?**
　　　　　　　　　　　　　foor vee-feeleh per-zonen

| | |
|---|---|
| How many nights is it for? | **Für wieviele Nächte?**<br>foor vee-feeleh nesh-teh |
| It's (4) marks . . . | **Es kostet (vier) Mark . . .**<br>es kostet (feer) mark . . . |
| per day/per night | **pro Tag/pro Nacht**<br>pro tahk/pro nakt |
| I haven't any rooms left | **Ich habe keine Zimmer mehr frei**<br>ish hahbeh kineh tsimmer mair fry |
| Do you want to have a look? | **Wollen Sie es sich ansehen?**<br>vollen zee es zish un-zay-en |

## *General shopping*

## The chemist's

### ESSENTIAL INFORMATION

- Look for the word **APOTHEKE** (chemist's) or this sign:
- There are two kinds of chemist in Germany. The **APOTHEKE** (dispensing chemist's) is the place to go for prescriptions, medicines etc.; toilet and household articles, as well as patent medicines, are sold at the **DROGERIE** (chemist's shop).
- Try the chemist *before* going to a doctor: they are usually qualified to treat minor injuries.
- Chemists are open during normal business hours, i.e. from 8.30 a.m. to 12.30 p.m., and from 2.30 to 6.30 p.m. on weekdays. On Saturdays they close at 2.00 p.m.
- Chemists take it in turns to stay open all night and on Sundays. If the chemist is shut, a notice on the door will give the address of the nearest night (**NACHTDIENST**) and Sunday service (**SONNTAGSDIENST**).
- Some toiletries can be bought at a **PARFÜMERIE** but they will be more expensive.

**WHAT TO SAY**

| I'd like . . . | **Ich möchte . . .** |
|---|---|
| | ish mershteh . . . |
| some Alka Seltzer | **Alka Seltzer** |
| | alka zeltser |
| some antiseptic | **ein antiseptisches Mittel** |
| | ine anti-zeptishes mittel |
| some aspirin | **Aspirin** |
| | ahs-pee-reen |
| some baby food | **Babynahrung** |
| | baby-nah-roong |
| some contraceptives | **ein Verhütungsmittel** |
| | ine fer-hootoongs-mittel |
| some cotton wool | **Watte** |
| | vatteh |
| some disposable nappies | **Papierwindeln** |
| | papeer-vin-deln |
| some eye drops | **Augentropfen** |
| | owghen-tropfen |
| some inhalant | **ein Inhaliermittel** |
| | ine in-hahleer-mittel |
| some insect repellent | **ein Insektenschutzmittel** |
| | ine in-zekten-shoots-mittel |
| some paper tissues | **Papiertücher** |
| | papeer-toosher |
| some sanitary towels | **Monatsbinden** |
| | monahts-bin-den |
| some sticking plaster | **Heftpflaster** |
| | heft-pflaster |
| some suntan lotion/oil | **Sonnenmilch/öl** |
| | zonnen-milsh/erl |
| some Tampax | **eine Packung Tampax** |
| | ineh pack-oong tampax |
| some throat pastilles | **Halspastillen** |
| | hals-past-ill-en |
| some toilet paper | **Toilettenpapier** |
| | twa-letten-papeer |
| I'd like something for . . . | **Ich möchte etwas gegen . . .** |
| | ish mershteh etvas gay-ghen . . . |
| bites (snakes, dogs) | **Bisswunden** |
| | bis-voon-den |

| | |
|---|---|
| burns | **Verbrennungen** |
| | fer-bren-oong-en |
| a cold | **Erkältung** |
| | er-kelt-oong |
| constipation | **Verstopfung** |
| | fer-shtopf-oong |
| a cough | **Husten** |
| | hoosten |
| diarrhoea | **Durchfall** |
| | doorsh-fahl |
| ear-ache | **Ohrenschmerzen** |
| | or-en-shmairts-en |
| flu | **Grippe** |
| | grippeh |
| scalds | **Verbrühung** |
| | fer-broo-oong |
| sore gums | **wundes Zahnfleisch** |
| | voondes tsahn-flysh |
| stings (mosquitos, bees) | **Insektenstiche** |
| | in-zekten-shtee-sheh |
| sunburn | **Sonnenbrand** |
| | zonnen-brant |
| car (air)/sea sickness | **Reisekrankheit/Seekrankheit** |
| | ryzeh-krank-hite/zeh-krank-hite |

[*For other essential expressions, see 'Shop talk', p. 128*]

---

# Holiday items

### ESSENTIAL INFORMATION

- Places to shop at and signs to look for:
  **SCHREIBWARENGESCHÄFT** (stationery)
  **PHOTOGESCHÄFT** (films)
  **KUNSTGEWERBE** (arts and crafts)
  **GESCHENKARTIKEL** (gifts)
- and the main department stores:

| | |
|---|---|
| **KARSTADT** | **HERTIE** |
| **HORTEN** | **KAUHOF** |

## WHAT TO SAY

| I'd like . . . | Ich möchte . . . |
|---|---|
| | ish mershteh . . . |
| a bag | eine Tasche |
| | ineh tasheh |
| a beach ball | einen Strandball |
| | inen shtrant-bal |
| a bucket | einen Eimer |
| | inen imer |
| an English newspaper | eine englische Zeitung |
| | ineh eng-lisheh tsy-toong |
| some envelopes | Briefumschläge |
| | breef-oom-shlaig-eh |
| a guide book | einen Reiseführer |
| | inen ryzeh-foorer |
| some postcards | Ansichtskarten |
| | un-zishts-karten |
| a spade | eine Schaufel |
| | ineh sha-oofel |
| a straw hat | einen Strohhut |
| | inen shtro-hoot |
| some sunglasses | eine Sonnenbrille |
| | ineh zonnen-brilleh |
| some writing paper | Schreibpapier |
| | shripe-papeer |
| a colour film | einen Farbfilm |
| [show the camera] | inen farp-film |
| a black and white film | einen Schwarzweiss-Film |
| | inen shvarts-vice film |

# Shop talk

## ESSENTIAL INFORMATION

- Know how to say the important weights and measures: note that though Germany is metric, people still use the word **Pfund** (pound).

| | |
|---|---|
| 50 grams | **fünfzig Gramm** |
| | foonf-tsik gramm |
| 100 grams | **einhundert Gramm** |
| | ine-hoondert gramm |
| 200 grams | **zweihundert Gramm** |
| | tsvy-hoondert gramm |
| ½ lb (250 grams) | **ein halbes Pfund** |
| | ine halbes pfoont |
| 1 lb | **ein Pfund** |
| | ine pfoont |
| 1 kilo | **ein Kilo** |
| | ine kilo |
| 2 kilos | **zwei Kilo** |
| | tsvy kilo |
| ½ litre | **einen halben Liter** |
| | inen halben litre |
| 1 litre | **einen Liter** |
| | inen litre |
| 2 litres | **zwei Liter** |
| | tsvy litre |

[*For numbers, see* p. 159]

## CUSTOMER

| | |
|---|---|
| I'm just looking | **Ich sehe mich nur um** |
| | ish zay-eh mish noor oom |
| How much is this/that? | **Wieviel kostet dies/das?** |
| | vee-feel kostet dees/das |
| What is that?/What are those? | **Was ist das?** |
| | vas ist das |
| Is there a discount? | **Gibt es einen Rabatt?** |
| | geept es inen rah-batt |
| I'd like that, please | **Ich möchte das da, bitte** |
| | ish mershteh das dah bitteh |
| Not that | **Nicht das** |
| | nisht das |
| Like that | **Wie das da** |
| | vee das dah |
| That's enough, thank you | **Das ist genug, danke** |
| | das ist ganook dankeh |
| More, please | **Mehr, bitte** |
| | mair bitteh |

| | |
|---|---|
| Less than that | **Etwas weniger**<br>etvas vay-neeg-er |
| That's fine | **Das ist gut so**<br>das ist goot zo |
| I won't take it, thank you | **Ich nehme es nicht, danke**<br>ish nay-meh es nisht dankeh |
| It's not right | **Es ist nicht das Richtige**<br>es ist nisht das rish-teeg-eh |
| **Have you got something . . .** | **Haben Sie etwas . . .**<br>hahben zee etvas . . . |
| better? | **Besseres?**<br>besser-es |
| cheaper? | **Billigeres?**<br>billig-er-es |
| different? | **anderes?**<br>ander-es |
| larger?/smaller? | **Grösseres?/Kleineres?**<br>grersser-es/kliner-es |
| Can I have a bag, please? | **Kann ich bitte eine Tragetasche haben?**<br>kan ish bitteh ineh trahg-eh-tasheh hahben |
| Can I have a receipt? | **Kann ich eine Quittung haben?**<br>kan ish ineh kvitt-oong hahben |
| **Do you take . . .** | **Nehmen Sie . . .**<br>nay-men zee . . . |
| English/American money? | **englisches/amerikanisches Geld?**<br>eng-lishes/ameri-kah-nishes ghelt |
| travellers' cheques? | **Reiseschecks?**<br>ryzeh-shecks |
| credit cards? | **Kreditkarten?**<br>kredeet-karten |

## SHOP ASSISTANT

| | |
|---|---|
| Can I help you? | **Kann ich Ihnen behilflich sein?**<br>kan ish eenen behilf-lish zine |
| What would you like? | **Was darf es sein**<br>vas darf es zine |
| Will that be all? | **Kommt noch etwas dazu?**<br>komt nok etvas dah-tsoo |

| | |
|---|---|
| Is that all? | **Ist das alles?**<br>ist das *a*lles |
| Anything else? | **Sonst noch etwas?**<br>*zo*nst nok *e*tvas |
| Would you like it wrapped? | **Soll ich es einwickeln?**<br>zoll ish es *i*ne-vickeln |
| Sorry, none left | **Leider ausverkauft**<br>*li*der *o*ws-fer-kowft |
| I haven't got any | **Wir haben keine**<br>veer h*a*hben k*i*neh |
| I haven't got any more | **Wir haben keine mehr**<br>veer h*a*hben k*i*neh mair |
| How many do you want? | **Wieviele möchten Sie?**<br>*ve*e-feeleh m*e*rshten zee |
| How much do you want? | **Wieviel möchten Sie?**<br>*ve*e-feel m*e*rshten zee |
| Is that enough? | **Ist das genug?**<br>ist das gan*oo*k |

# *Shopping for food*

## Bread

### ESSENTIAL INFORMATION

- Key words to look for:<br>
**BÄCKEREI** (baker's)<br>
**BÄCKER** (baker)<br>
**BROT** (bread)
- Bakers are open from 7.30 a.m. to 12.30 p.m. and from 2.30 to 6.30 p.m. on weekdays. On Saturdays they close at lunchtime. Many bakers will open on Sunday mornings from 10 a.m. to noon and close one afternoon during the week, usually on Wednesdays.

**WHAT TO SAY**

| | |
|---|---|
| A loaf (like that) | **Ein Brot (wie das da)**<br>ine br*o*te (vee d*a*s dah) |
| A bread roll | **Ein Brötchen**<br>ine br*e*rt-shen |
| A bread roll (Bavaria, Austria) | **Eine Semmel**<br>*i*neh z*e*mmel |
| A crescent roll | **Ein Hörnchen**<br>ine h*e*rn-shen |
| Sliced bread | **Geschnittenes Brot**<br>ga-shn*i*tten-es br*o*te |
| White bread | **Weissbrot**<br>v*i*ce-brote |
| Rye bread | **Graubrot**<br>gr*a*-oo-brote |
| (Black) rye bread | **Schwarzbrot**<br>shv*a*rts-brote |
| Wholemeal bread | **Vollkornbrot**<br>f*o*ll-korn-brote |

[*For other essential expressions, see 'Shop talk', p. 128*]

# Cakes and ice-creams

**ESSENTIAL INFORMATION**

- Key words to look for:
  **BÄCKEREI** (bread and cake shop)
  **KONDITOREI** (cake shop, often with a tea-room in the back)
  **EIS** (ice-cream)
  **EISDIELE** (ice-cream parlour)
  **EISCAFÉ** (ice-cream parlour/tea room)
  **SÜSSWARENLADEN** (sweet shop)
- **CAFÉ** or **KAFFEEHAUS** in Austria: a place to buy cakes and have a drink at a table, usually in the afternoon. See also p. 141, 'Ordering a drink and a snack'.

## WHAT TO SAY

The type of cakes you find in the shops varies slightly from region to region but the following are some of the most common.

| | |
|---|---|
| **der Berliner** | jam filled doughnut |
| der ber-*lee*ner | |
| **der Florentiner** | almond flakes on a thin cake and |
| der flor-en-*tee*ner | chocolate base |
| **die Schwarzwälder Kirschtorte** | Black Forest gâteau |
| dee shv*a*rts-velder *kee*rsh-torteh | |
| **die Obsttorte** | fruit on a sponge base with glazing |
| dee *o*bst-torteh | over |
| **der Apfelstrudel** | flaky pastry filled with apple, nuts, |
| der *a*pfel-shtroodel | and raisins |
| **der Mohrenkopf** | ball-shaped pastry filled with |
| der *mo*ren-kopf | pudding, covered with chocolate |
| **der Käsekuchen** | cheesecake |
| der *ka*izeh-kooken | |
| **die Sachertorte** | rich Viennese chocolate cake with |
| dee *za*hker-torteh | jam |
| **der Sandkuchen** | Madeira cake |
| der *za*nt-kooken | |
| **die Sahnetorte** | cream cake |
| dee *za*h-neh-torteh | |
| **der Bienenstich** | cream cake sprinkled with flaky |
| der *bee*nen-shtish | almonds and honey |
| **A . . . ice, please** | **Ein . . . Eis, bitte** |
| | *i*ne . . . *i*ce b*i*tteh |
| strawberry | **Erdbeer** |
| | *ai*rt-bear |
| chocolate | **Schokoladen** |
| | shoko-*la*hden |
| vanilla | **Vanille** |
| | van*i*lyeh |
| lemon | **Zitronen** |
| | tsee-tr*o*nen |
| caramel | **Karamel** |
| | kara-m*e*l |
| raspberry | **Himbeer** |
| | h*i*m-bear |

| | |
|---|---|
| A cone . . . | **Ein Hörnchen . . .**<br>ine hern-shen . . . |
| a tub . . . | **Einen Becher . . .**<br>inen besher . . . |
| (60 Pfennig's) worth of ice-cream | **Ein Eis zu (sechzig)**<br>ine ice tsoo (zek-tsig) |

---

# Picnic food

## ESSENTIAL INFORMATION

- Key words to look for:
  **DELIKATESSENGESCHÄFT**
  **FEINKOSTGESCHÄFT** } (delicatessen)
  **METZGEREI**
  **SCHLACHTEREI** } (butcher's)

## WHAT TO SAY

| Two slices of . . . | **Zwei Scheiben . . .**<br>tsvy shy-ben . . . |
|---|---|
| roast beef | **Rostbraten**<br>rost-brahten |
| tongue sausage | **Zungenwurst**<br>tsoongen-voorst |
| Saveloy sausage | **Zervelatwurst**<br>zervelaht-voorst |
| raw cured ham | **rohen Schinken**<br>ro-en shinken |
| cooked ham | **gekochten Schinken**<br>gakokten shinken |
| garlic sausage | **Knoblauchwurst**<br>knop-lowk-voorst |
| salami | **Salami**<br>zalah-mi |

You might also like to try some of these:

| **eine Pizza** | a pizza |
|---|---|
| ineh pizza | |

| | |
|---|---|
| **ein Stück Gänseleberpastete**<br>ine shtook ghen-zeh-laber-<br>past*ai*teh | some goose liver pâté |
| **ein Stück Fleischwurst**<br>ine shtook flysh-voorst | some luncheon sausage |
| **einen Matjeshering**<br>*i*nen m*a*t-yes-hering | white salted herring |
| **eine Frikadelle**<br>*i*neh frikah-d*e*lleh | a spicy thick hamburger (often<br>eaten cold) |
| **einen Räucheraal**<br>*i*nen roy-sher-ahl | a smoked eel |
| **ein paar Frankfurter**<br>ine par fr*a*nk-foorter | two Frankfurter sausages |
| **eine Weisswurst**<br>*i*neh v*i*ce-voorst | a Bavarian sausage |
| **eine Thüringer Bratwurst**<br>*i*neh t*oo*ring-er br*a*ht-voorst | a spicy sausage from Thuringia |
| **einen Elsässer Wurstsalat**<br>*i*nen *e*l-zesser v*o*orst-zalaht | shredded meat and cheese salad |
| **ein Stück Leberkäse**<br>ine shtook l*a*ber-kay-zeh | some meatloaf |
| **eine Wurstpastete**<br>*i*neh v*o*orst-past*ai*teh | a sausage roll |
| **eine Königin-Pastete**<br>*i*neh k*e*rneeg-in past*ai*teh | a vol-au-vent |
| **eine Geflügelpastete**<br>*i*neh gafl*oo*g-el-past*ai*teh | a chicken vol-au-vent |
| **einen Kräuterquark**<br>*i*nen kr*o*yter-kwark | soft cream cheese with herbs |
| **Tilsiter**<br>t*i*l-zit-er | mild cheese |
| **Kümmelkäse**<br>k*oo*mmel-kaizeh | cheese with caraway seeds |
| **einen Harzer Roller**<br>*i*nen h*a*rtser r*o*ller | sharp roll-shaped cheese |
| **Emmentaler**<br>emmen-tahler | Swiss cheese |
| **Gouda**<br>g*o*wdah | Dutch cheese |
| **Camembert/Brie**<br>c*a*men-bair/br*ee* | Camembert/Brie |

[*For other essential expressions, see 'Shop talk', p. 128*]

# Fruit and vegetables

## ESSENTIAL INFORMATION

- Key words to look for:
  **OBST** (fruit)
  **GEMÜSE** (vegetables)
  **OBST-UND GEMÜSEHÄNDLER** (greengrocer)

## WHAT TO SAY

| 1 kilo of . . . | **Ein Kilo . . .** |
|---|---|
| | *ine kilo . . .* |
| apples | **Äpfel** |
| | *epfel* |
| bananas | **Bananen** |
| | *banah-nen* |
| cherries | **Kirschen** |
| | *keer-shen* |
| grapes | **Weintrauben** |
| | *vine-tra-ooben* |
| oranges | **Apfelsinen** |
| | *apfel-zeenen* |
| pears | **Birnen** |
| | *beer-nen* |
| peaches | **Pfirsiche** |
| | *pfeer-zisheh* |
| plums | **Pflaumen** |
| | *pfla-oomen* |
| strawberries | **Erdbeeren** |
| | *aird-bairen* |
| A pineapple, please | **Eine Ananas, bitte** |
| | *ineh ah-nanas bitteh* |
| A grapefruit | **Eine Pampelmuse** |
| | *ineh pampel-moozeh* |
| A melon | **Eine Melone** |
| | *ineh melone-eh* |
| A water melon | **Eine Wassermelone** |
| | *ineh vasser-melone-eh* |

| 1lb of . . . | **Ein Pfund . . .** |
| --- | --- |
| | *i*ne pfoont . . . |
| artichokes | **Artischocken** |
| | arti-sho*k*en |
| aubergines | **Auberginen** |
| | ober-g*ee*nen |
| avocado pears | **Avokados** |
| | ahvo-*k*ahdos |
| carrots | **Karotten** |
| | karo*t*ten |
| courgettes | **Zucchini** |
| | tsoo-*k*ini |
| green beans | **grüne Bohnen** |
| | gr*oo*neh bone-en |
| leeks | **Lauch/Porree** |
| | lowk/*por*-ray |
| mushrooms | **Pilze** |
| | p*i*l-tseh |
| onions | **Zwiebeln** |
| | tsv*ee*-beln |
| peas | **Erbsen** |
| | *air*psen |
| potatoes | **Kartoffeln** |
| | kar-*to*ffeln |
| red cabbage | **Rotkohl** |
| | r*o*te-kole |
| spinach | **Spinat** |
| | shpee-n*a*ht |
| tomatoes | **Tomaten** |
| | tom*a*hten |
| A bunch of . . . | **Ein Bund . . .** |
| | *i*ne boont . . . |
| parsley | **Petersilie** |
| | pater-z*ee*l-yeh |
| radishes | **Radieschen** |
| | rah-d*ee*s-shen |
| shallots | **Schalotten** |
| | shah-l*o*tten |
| A head of garlic | **Knoblauch** |
| | kn*o*pe-la-ook |
| A lettuce | **Einen Kopfsalat** |
| | *i*nen k*o*pf-zalaht |

| A cucumber | **Eine Salatgurke** |
| | *i*neh zal*a*ht-goorkeh |
| Like that, please | **So eine, bitte** |
| | zo *i*neh b*i*tteh |

# Meat and fish

## ESSENTIAL INFORMATION

- Key words to look for:

| METZGEREI | | METZGER | |
| FLEISCHEREI | (butcher's) | FLEISCHER | (butcher) |
| SCHLACHTEREI | | SCHLACHTER | |

- When buying fish look for:
  **FISCHGESCHÄFT** (fishmonger's)
  **FISCHABTEILUNG** (fish section in store)
  **NORDSEE** (fish shop chain selling fresh fish as well as smoked and marinated specialities)

## WHAT TO SAY

For a joint, choose the type of meat and then say how many people it is for:

| Some beef, please | **Rindfleisch, bitte** |
| | r*i*nt-flysh b*i*tteh |
| Some lamb | **Lamm** |
| | l*a*mm |
| Some mutton | **Hammelfleisch** |
| | h*a*mmel-flysh |
| Some pork | **Schweinefleisch** |
| | shv*i*ne-eh-flysh |

| | |
|---|---|
| Some veal | **Kalbfleisch** |
| | kalp-flysh |
| A joint . . . | **Einen Braten . . .** |
| | inen brahten . . . |
|   for two people | **für zwei Personen** |
| | foor tsvy per-zonen |
|   for four people | **für vier Personen** |
| | foor feer per-zonen |
| Some steak, please | **Steak, bitte** |
| | steak bitteh |
| Some liver | **Leber** |
| | laber |
| Some kidneys | **Nieren** |
| | neeren |
| Some sausages | **Würstchen** |
| | voorst-shen |
| Some minced meat | **Hackfleisch** |
| | hack-flysh |
| Two veal escalopes, please | **Zwei Kalbsschnitzel, bitte** |
| | tsvy kalps-shnitsel bitteh |
| Three pork chops | **Drei Schweinekoteletts** |
| | dry shvine-eh-kotelts |
| Five lamb chops | **Fünf Lammkoteletts** |
| | foonf lamm-kotelts |

You may also want:

| | |
|---|---|
| A chicken | **Ein Huhn** |
| | ine hoon |
| A tongue | **Eine Zunge** |
| | ineh tsoong-eh |

Purchase large fish and small shellfish by the weight:

| | |
|---|---|
| 1lb (½ kilo) of . . . | **Ein Pfund . . .** |
| | ine pfoont . . . |
|   cod | **Kabeljau** |
| | kahbel-yow |
|   haddock | **Schellfisch** |
| | shell-fish |
|   turbot | **Steinbutt** |
| | shtine-boott |
|   carp | **Karpfen** |
| | karp-fen |

| **1 lb (½ kilo) of . . .** | **Ein Pfund . . .** |
| --- | --- |
| | *i*ne pfoont . . . |
| red sea-bass | **Rotbarsch** |
| | r*o*te-barsh |
| halibut | **Heilbutt** |
| | h*i*le-boott |
| pike | **Hecht** |
| | hesht |
| shrimps | **Garnelen** |
| | gar-n*a*y-len |
| shrimps (N. Germany) | **Granat** |
| | grah-n*a*ht |
| prawns | **Krabben** |
| | kr*a*bben |
| mussels | **Muscheln** |
| | m*oo*sheln |
| salmon | **Lachs** |
| | laks |

For some shellfish and 'frying pan' fish, specify the number you want:

| A crab, please | **Einen Krebs, bitte** |
| --- | --- |
| | *i*nen kr*e*ps b*i*tteh |
| A lobster | **Einen Hummer** |
| | *i*nen h*oo*mmer |
| A spiny lobster | **Eine Languste** |
| | *i*neh lang*oo*st-eh |
| A plaice | **Eine Scholle** |
| | *i*neh sh*o*ll-eh |
| A trout | **Eine Forelle** |
| | *i*neh for*e*ll-eh |
| A sole | **Eine Seezunge** |
| | *i*neh z*a*y-tsoong-eh |
| A mackerel | **Eine Makrele** |
| | *i*neh mak-r*a*ileh |
| A herring | **Einen Hering** |
| | *i*nen h*ai*r-ing |

# *Eating and drinking out*

## Ordering a drink and a snack

**ESSENTIAL INFORMATION**

- The places to ask for: **EIN CAFÉ.**
  **EINE WIRTSCHAFT** (a type of pub)
  **EINE WEINSTUBE** (a wine bar)
- By law, the price list of drinks (**GETRÄNKEKARTE**) must be displayed outside or in the window.
- There is always waiter service in cafés, pubs and wine bars. In a pub you can also drink at the bar if you wish (cheaper).
- A service charge of 10–15% is almost always included on the bill (**BEDIENUNG INBEGRIFFEN**), but it is customary to leave some additional small change.
- Cafés serve non-alcoholic and alcoholic drinks, and are normally open all day.

**WHAT TO SAY**

| | |
|---|---|
| I'll have . . . please | **Ich hätte gern . . . bitte** |
| | ish hetteh gairn . . . bitteh |
| a black coffee | **einen schwarzen Kaffee** |
| | *i*nen shv*a*r-tsen k*a*ffeh |
| a coffee with cream | **einen Kaffee mit Sahne** |
| | *i*nen k*a*ffeh mit z*a*hneh |
| a tea | **einen Tee** |
| | *i*nen t*a*y |
| with milk/lemon | **mit Milch/Zitrone** |
| | mit m*i*lsh/tsee-tr*o*ne-eh |
| a glass of milk | **ein Glas Milch** |
| | ine glass m*i*lsh |
| a hot chocolate | **eine heisse Schokolade** |
| | *i*neh h*y*sseh shoko-l*a*hdeh |
| a mineral water | **ein Mineralwasser** |
| | ine miner*a*hl-vasser |
| a lemonade | **eine Limonade** |
| | *i*neh lim-o-n*a*hdeh |

| **I'll have . . . please** | **Ich hätte gern . . . bitte** |
|---|---|
| | ish hetteh gairn . . . bitteh |
| an orangeade | **einen Orangensprudel** |
| | inen o-rung-shen-shproodel |
| a fresh orange juice | **einen frischen Orangensaft** |
| | inen frishen o-rung-shen-zaft |
| a grape juice | **einen Traubensaft** |
| | inen tra-ooben-zaft |
| an apple juice | **einen Apfelsaft** |
| | inen apfel-zaft |
| a beer | **ein Bier** |
| | ine beer |
| a draught beer | **ein Bier vom Fass** |
| | ine beer fom fass |
| a bitter | **ein Altbier** |
| | ine alt-beer |
| a brown ale | **ein dunkles Bier** |
| | ine doonk-les beer |
| a half | **ein Kleines** |
| | ine kly-nes |
| **I'll have . . . please** | **Ich hätte gern . . . bitte** |
| | ish hetteh gairn . . . bitteh |
| a cheese sandwich/roll | **ein Käsebrot/Käsebrötchen** |
| | ine kaizeh-brote/kaizeh-brertshen |
| a ham sandwich/roll | **ein Schinkenbrot/ Schinkenbrötchen** |
| | ine shinken-brote/shinken-brertshen |
| a roll with fish | **ein Fischbrötchen** |
| | ine fish-brertshen |
| an omelet | **ein Omelett** |
| | ine omelet |
| with mushrooms | **mit Pilzen** |
| | mit pil-tsen |
| with diced ham | **mit Schinken** |
| | mit shinken |

These are some other snacks you may like to try:

| | |
|---|---|
| **eine Bratwurst** | a fried spicy pork sausage |
| ineh braht-voorst | |
| **eine Bockwurst** | a large Frankfurter |
| ineh bock-voorst | |

| | |
|---|---|
| **eine Currywurst** | a grilled sausage topped with curry |
| *i*neh c*u*rry-voorst | and ketchup |
| **ein halbes Hähnchen** | half a (roast) chicken |
| *i*ne h*a*lbes h*ai*n-shen | |
| **ein Deutsches Beefsteak** | a hamburger steak |
| ine d*o*yt-shes b*ee*fsteak | |
| **ein paar Spiegeleier** | two fried eggs |
| ine par shp*ee*g-el-eye-er | |
| **eine Gulaschsuppe** | spicy beef soup |
| *i*neh g*oo*lash-z*oo*ppeh | |

# In a restaurant

## ESSENTIAL INFORMATION

- You can eat at these places:
  **RESTAURANT**
  **HOTEL-RESTAURANT**
  **GASTSTÄTTE/GASTHOF**
  **RASTHOF** (motorway restaurant)
  **GASTWIRTSCHAFT**
  **BAHNHOFSBÜFETT** (at stations)
  **GRILLSTUBE**
  **CAFÉ** (limited choice here)
- By law, the menus must be displayed outside or in the window
  – and that is the *only* way to judge if a place is right for you.
- Self-service restaurants are not unknown, but most places have
  waiter service.
- A service charge of 10–15% is usually included in restaurant
  bills, but if satisfied with the service you should always leave
  some small change.
- Most restaurants offer small portions for children. Look for
  **KINDER-TELLER** (children's portions) on the menu.
- Hot meals are served from 12.00 to 2.00 p.m. at lunchtime and
  from 6.00 to 9.00–10.00 p.m. at night. After that many res-
  taurants offer snacks for latecomers (soups, sausages, salads etc.)
  Ask for the 'small menu': **die kleine Karte** (dee kly-neh k*a*rteh).

**WHAT TO SAY**

| | |
|---|---|
| May I book a table? | **Kann ich einen Tisch reservieren lassen?** |
| | kan ish *i*nen tish reser-v*ee*ren lassen |
| I've booked a table | **Ich habe einen Tisch reservieren lassen** |
| | ish h*a*hbeh inen tish reser-v*ee*ren lassen |
| A table . . . | **Einen Tisch . . .** |
| | *i*nen tish . . . |
| for one | **für eine Person** |
| | foor *i*neh per-z*o*ne |
| for three | **für drei Personen** |
| | foor dry per-z*o*nen |
| The à la carte menu, please | **Die Speisekarte, bitte** |
| | dee shp*y*zeh-karteh b*i*tteh |
| The fixed-price menu | **Die Gedeck-Karte** |
| | dee gad*e*ck-karteh |
| The tourist menu | **Das Touristen-Menü** |
| | das tour*i*sten-men*oo* |
| Today's special menu | **Die Karte mit Tagesgedecken** |
| | dee k*a*rteh mit t*a*hg-es-gad*e*cken |
| What's this, please [*point to menu*] | **Was ist dies, bitte?** |
| | vas ist d*ee*s b*i*tteh |
| The wine list | **Die Weinkarte** |
| | dee v*i*ne-karteh |
| A carafe of wine, please | **Eine Karaffe Wein, bitte** |
| | *i*neh ka-r*a*ffeh v*i*ne b*i*tteh |
| A quarter (250cc) | **Einen Viertelliter** |
| | *i*nen f*ee*r-tel-litre |
| A half (500cc) | **Einen halben Liter** |
| | *i*nen h*a*lben l*i*tre |
| A glass | **Ein Glas** |
| | ine glass |
| A (half) bottle | **Eine (halbe) Flasche** |
| | *i*neh (h*a*lbeh) fl*a*sheh |
| A litre | **Einen Liter** |
| | *i*nen l*i*tre |
| Red/white/rosé/house wine | **Rotwein/Weisswein/Rosé/Hauswein** |
| | r*o*te-vine/v*i*ce-vine/roz*ay*/house-vine |

| | |
|---|---|
| Some more bread, please | **Noch etwas Brot, bitte** |
| | nok etvas brote bitteh |
| Some more wine | **Noch etwas Wein** |
| | nok etvas vine |
| Some oil | **Etwas Öl** |
| | etvas erl |
| Some vinegar | **Etwas Essig** |
| | etvas essick |
| Some salt/pepper | **Etwas Salz/Pfeffer** |
| | etvas zalts/pfeffer |
| Some water | **Etwas Wasser** |
| | etvas vasser |
| With/without garlic | **Mit/ohne Knoblauch** |
| | mit/o-neh knope-la-ook |
| How much does that come to? | **Wieviel macht das insgesamt?** |
| | vee-feel makt das ins-gazamt |
| Is service included? | **Ist Bedienung inbegriffen?** |
| | ist be-deen-ong in-begriffen |
| Where is the toilet, please? | **Wo sind die Toiletten?** |
| | vo zint dee twa-letten |
| Miss!/Waiter! | **Fräulein!/Herr Ober!** |
| | froy-line/hair o-ber |
| The bill, please | **Die Rechnung, bitte** |
| | dee resh-noong bitteh |

**Key words for courses, as seen on some menus**

[*Only ask this question if you want the waiter to remind you of the choice.*]

| | |
|---|---|
| What have you got in the way of . . . | **Was für . . . haben Sie?** |
| | vas foor . . . hahben zee |
| STARTERS? | **VORSPEISEN** |
| | for-shpyzen |
| SOUP? | **SUPPEN** |
| | zooppen |
| EGG DISHES? | **EIERSPEISEN** |
| | eye-er-shpyzen |
| FISH? | **FISCHGERICHTE** |
| | fish-garisht-eh |
| MEAT? | **FLEISCHGERICHTE** |
| | flysh-garisht-eh |

| | |
|---|---|
| What have you got in the way of . . . | **Was für . . . haben Sie?** *vas foor . . . hahben zee* |
| GAME? | **WILDGERICHTE** *vilt-garisht-eh* |
| FOWL? | **GEFLÜGELGERICHTE** *ga-floogel-garisht-eh* |
| VEGETABLES? | **GEMÜSE** *ga-moozeh* |
| CHEESE? | **KÄSE** *kay-zeh* |
| FRUIT? | **OBST** *opst* |
| ICE-CREAM? | **EIS** *ice* |
| DESSERT? | **NACHSPEISEN** *nahk-shpyzen* |

## UNDERSTANDING THE MENU

You will find the names of the principal ingredients of most dishes on these pages:

Starters, see p. 134          Fruit, see p. 136
Meat, see p. 138             Dessert, see p. 133
Fish, see p. 139              Cheese, see p. 135
Vegetables, see p. 137       Ice-cream, see p. 133

Used together with the following lists of cooking and menu terms, they should help you to decode the menu.

**Cooking and menu terms**

| | |
|---|---|
| **angemacht** | in a special dressing |
| **Auflauf** | soufflé |
| **blau** | steamed and served with butter |
| **blutig** | rare |
| **Bouillon** | broth, clear soup |
| **Brat-** | fried |
| **-braten** | roast, joint |
| **-brühe** | broth |
| **-brust** | breast |
| **Butter-** | buttered |
| **durchgebraten** | well done |
| **gebacken** | baked |

| | |
|---|---|
| gedämpft | steamed |
| gedünstet (Austria) | steamed, stewed |
| gefüllt | stuffed |
| gegrillt | grilled |
| gekocht | boiled |
| in Gelee | jellied |
| gemischt | mixed |
| gepökelt | salted, pickled |
| geräuchert | smoked |
| gerieben | grated |
| geschmort | braised, stewed |
| gespickt | larded, smoked |
| halbdurch | medium |
| Hausfrauenart | with apple, sour cream and onions |
| hausgemacht | homemade |
| Holländisch | with mayonnaise |
| Holstein | topped with fried egg, garnished with anchovies and vegetables |
| Jägerart | served in red wine sauce with mushrooms |
| -Kaltschale | chilled fruit soup |
| -Kompott | stewed fruit |
| Kraftbrühe | broth, beef consommé |
| Kräuter- | with herbs |
| mariniert | marinated |
| Meerrettich- | with horse radish |
| Müllerin | baked in butter, dressed with breadcrumbs and egg |
| paniert | dressed with egg and breadcrumbs |
| Pell- | boiled in the jacket |
| Petersilien- | parsleyed |
| -püree | mashed |
| Rahm- | with cream |
| roh | raw |
| Röst- | fried |
| Sahne- | creamed |
| sauer | sour |
| Schlemmer- | for the gourmet |
| Schnitzel | escalope (of veal) |
| Senf- | with mustard |
| Sosse | sauce |
| Sülz- | in aspic |

| | |
|---|---|
| süss | sweet |
| überbacken | au gratin |
| Zwiebel- | with onions |

**Further words to help you understand the menu**

| | |
|---|---|
| Aalsuppe | eel soup, a speciality of Hamburg |
| Aufschnitt | sliced cold meat and sausages |
| Austern | oysters |
| Bauernomelett | bacon and onion omelette |
| Bierwurst | beer sausage |
| Birne Helene | vanilla ice-cream with pear and hot chocolate sauce |
| Bismarckhering | soused herring with onions |
| Blutwurst | black pudding |
| Bockwurst | large Frankfurter sausage |
| Bratkartoffeln | fried potatoes |
| Bratwurst | fried sausage (with herbs) |
| Deutsches Beefsteak | Hamburger steak |
| Eisbein | pig's knuckle |
| Ente | duck |
| Erbsensuppe | thick pea soup |
| Fasan | pheasant |
| Fleischkäse | type of meatloaf, sliced and fried |
| Forelle | trout |
| Frühlingssuppe | fresh vegetable soup |
| Gänseleberpastete | goose liver pâté |
| Gefrorenes | ice-cream specialities |
| Grünkohl | kale |
| Hackbraten | hamburger steak |
| Kaiserschmarren | shredded pancake with raisins and almonds |
| Kartoffelpuffer | small potato and onion pancakes |
| Kasseler Rippenspeer | cured pork chops with mustard sauce |
| Klösse ⎤ Knödel ⎦ | dumplings |
| Königsberger Klopse | meat balls in a white caper sauce |
| Kohlrouladen | cabbage stuffed with minced meat |
| Labskaus | pork and potato stew served with fried eggs and gherkins |
| Lachs | salmon |

| | |
|---|---|
| Leberknödelsuppe | soup with liver dumplings |
| Leberwurst | liver pâté |
| Linsensuppe | lentil soup |
| Matjeshering | young salted herring |
| Ochsenschwanzsuppe | oxtail soup |
| Ölsardinen | tinned sardines |
| Paprikaschoten | green peppers |
| Pfannkuchen | pancake |
| Pfirsich Melba | peach with vanilla ice-cream, whipped cream, raspberry syrup |
| Räucheraal | smoked eel |
| Rauchwurst | smoked sausage |
| Rehrücken | saddle of deer |
| Rollmops | pickled herring fillet, rolled around onion slices |
| Rosenkohl | Brussels sprouts |
| Rösti | hashed brown potatoes |
| Röstkartoffeln | roast potatoes |
| Rote Beete | beetroot |
| Rotkraut | red cabbage |
| Rouladen | thin slices of meat, rolled up and braised in rich brown sauce |
| Russische Eier | hard-boiled eggs, with caper and mayonnaise dressing |
| Sardellen | anchovies |
| Sauerkraut | pickled white cabbage |
| Sauerbraten | beef marinated in vinegar, sugar and spices, and then braised |
| Schildkrötensuppe | turtle soup |
| Schinkenwurst | ham sausage |
| Schlachtplatte | assorted cold meat and sausages |
| Schweinshaxe | pig's knuckle |
| Serbische Bohnensuppe | spicy Serbian bean soup |
| Spargel | asparagus |
| Spätzle | South German variety of pasta |
| Speck | bacon |
| Strammer Max | raw ham and fried eggs, served on rye-bread |
| Truthahn | turkey |
| Weinbergschnecken | snails with garlic, herbs and butter |
| Wienerschnitzel | veal escalope in breadcrumbs |

# Health

## ESSENTIAL INFORMATION

- For details of reciprocal health agreements between the UK and Germany, Austria and Switzerland, ask for leaflet SA 30 at your local Department of Health and Social Security a month before leaving or ask your travel agent.
- For minor disorders, and treatment at a chemist's, see p. 125.
- For finding your way to a doctor, dentist, chemist or Health and Social Security Office (for reimbursement), see p. 118.
- In an emergency dial 110 for an ambulance service.
- If you need a doctor look for:
  ÄRZTE (in the telephone directory) or these signs:
  PRAXIS (surgery)
  ERSTE HILFE (first aid)
  KRANKENHAUS ⎤
  HOSPITAL        ⎦ (hospital)
  UNFALLSTATION (casualty department of a hospital)

**What's the matter?**

| | |
|---|---|
| I have a pain here [*point*] | **Ich habe hier Schmerzen**<br>ish hahbeh here shmairts-en |
| I have a toothache | **Ich habe Zahnschmerzen**<br>ish hahbeh tsahn-shmairts-en |
| I have broken my dentures | **Mein Gebiss ist zerbrochen**<br>mine gabis ist tsair-brocken |
| I have broken my glasses | **Meine Brille ist zerbrochen**<br>mineh brilleh ist tsair-brocken |
| **I have lost . . .** | **Ich habe . . . verloren**<br>ish hahbeh . . . fer-loren |
| my contact lenses | **meine Kontaktlinsen**<br>mineh kontakt-lin-zen |
| a filling | **eine Füllung**<br>ineh foolloong |
| My child is ill | **Mein Kind ist krank**<br>mine kint ist krank |

**Already under treatment for something else?**

| | |
|---|---|
| I take . . . regularly [*show*] | **Ich nehme regelmässig . . .**<br>ish nay-meh raig-el-masik . . . |
| this medicine | **dieses Medikament**<br>deezes medikament |
| these tablets | **diese Tabletten**<br>deezeh tabletten |
| I have . . . | **Ich habe . . .**<br>ish hahbeh . . . |
| a heart condition | **ein Herzleiden**<br>ine hairts-ly-den |
| haemorrhoids | **Hämorrhoiden**<br>hemorro-ee-den |
| rheumatism | **Rheuma**<br>roymah |
| I'm . . . | **Ich bin . . .**<br>ish bin . . . |
| diabetic | **Diabetiker**<br>dee-ah-beticker |
| asthmatic | **Asthmatiker**<br>ast-mah-ticker |
| pregnant | **schwanger**<br>shvanger |
| allergic to (penicillin) | **allergisch gegen (Penicillin)**<br>allair-gish gay-ghen (peni-tsee-leen) |

# Problems: loss, theft

### ESSENTIAL INFORMATION

- If the worst comes to the worst, find the police station. To ask the way, see p. 116.
- Look for:
**POLIZEI** (police)
**POLIZEIWACHE** (police station)

- Ask for:
  **FUNDBÜRO** (lost property)
- If you lose your passport go to the nearest British Consulate.
- In an emergency dial 110 (for police) or 112 (if there's a fire).

## LOSS
[*See also 'Theft' below: the lists are interchangeable*]

| I have lost . . . | Ich habe . . . verloren |
|---|---|
| | ish hahbeh . . . fer-loren |
| my camera | meine Kamera |
| | mineh kamerah |
| my car keys | meine Autoschlüssel |
| | mineh owto-shloossel |
| my car logbook | meinen Kraftfahrzeugschein |
| | minen kraft-far-tsoyk-shine |
| my driving licence | meinen Führerschein |
| | minen foorer-shine |
| my insurance certificate | meine Versicherungskarte |
| | mineh fer-zisheroongs-karteh |

## THEFT

| Someone has stolen . . . | Man hat . . . gestohlen |
|---|---|
| | man hat . . . ga-shtolen |
| my car | mein Auto |
| | mine owto |
| my money | mein Geld |
| | mine ghelt |
| my tickets | meine Fahrkarten |
| | mineh far-karten |
| my travellers' cheques | meine Reiseschecks |
| | mineh ryzeh-shecks |
| my wallet | meine Brieftasche |
| | mineh breef-tasheh |
| my luggage | mein Gepäck |
| | mine gapeck |

# The post office and phoning home

## ESSENTIAL INFORMATION

- Key words to look for:
  **POST**
  **POSTAMT**
  **BUNDESPOST** or this sign .
- For stamps look for the words **BRIEFMARKEN** or **POSTWERTZEICHEN** on a post office counter.
- Some stationers' and kiosks which sell postcards, also sell stamps.
- Unless you read and write German well, it's best not to make phone calls by yourself. Go to the main post office and write the town and number you want on a piece of paper and then hand it to the operator.

## WHAT TO SAY

To England, please

**Nach England, bitte**
nahk eng-lant bitteh

[*Hand letters, cards or parcels over the counter*]

To Australia

**Nach Australien**
nahk owstrah-lee-en

To the United States

**In die Vereinigten Staaten**
in dee ferine-nik-ten shtahten

I'd like this number . . .
[*show number*]

**Ich möchte diese Nummer . . .**
ish mershteh deezeh noommer . . .

in England

**in England**
in eng-lant

in Canada

**in Kanada**
in kanadah

Can you dial it for me, please?

**Können Sie für mich wählen?**
kernnen zee foor mish vay-len

# Changing cheques and money

## ESSENTIAL INFORMATION

- Look for these words on buildings:
  **BANK** (bank)
  **SPARKASSE** (bank, savings-bank)
  **WECHSELSTUBE** ⎤
  **GELDWECHSEL** ⎦ (change bureau)
- Changing money or travellers' cheques is usually a two-stage process. The formalities are completed at a desk called **DEVISEN**; you will then be sent to the cashier (**KASSE**) to get your money.
- To cash your own normal cheques, exactly as at home, use your banker's card where you see the Eurocheque sign. Write in English, in pounds.
- Exchange rate information might show the pound as: **£, £ Sterling**, or even **GB**.
- Have your passport handy.

## WHAT TO SAY

| | |
|---|---|
| I'd like to cash . . . | **Ich möchte . . . einlösen** |
| | ish m*e*rshteh . . . *i*ne-lerzen |
| these travellers' cheques | **diese Reiseschecks** |
| | d*ee*zeh ryzeh-shecks |
| this cheque | **diesen Scheck** |
| | d*ee*zen sheck |
| I'd like to change this . . . | **Ich möchte dies . . . wechseln** |
| | ish m*e*rshteh dees . . . v*e*xeln |
| into German marks | **in deutsche Mark** |
| | in d*oy*tsheh mark |
| into Austrian schillings | **in österreichische Schillinge** |
| | in *e*rster-ry-kisheh sh*i*lling-eh |
| into Belgian francs | **in belgische Franken** |
| | in b*e*l-ghish-eh fr*a*nken |
| into Danish kroner | **in dänische Kronen** |
| | in d*a*-nisheh kr*o*-nen |
| into Dutch guilders | **in holländische Gulden** |
| | in h*o*llendisheh g*oo*l-den |

| | |
|---|---|
| into French francs | **in französische Franken** |
| | in fran-tser-zisheh franken |
| into Swiss francs | **in Schweizer Franken** |
| | in shvyster franken |

---

# Car travel

---

## ESSENTIAL INFORMATION

- Is it a self-service station? Look out for:
  **SELBSTBEDIENUNG** or **SB**.
- Grades of petrol:
  **BENZIN**
  **NORMAL** ⎤ (standard)
  **SUPER** (premium)
  **DIESEL**
  **MOTORRADÖL**
  **MEHRBEREICHSÖL** ⎤ (two-stroke)
- 1 gallon is about 4½ litres (accurate enough up to 6 gallons).
- The minimum sale is often 5 litres (often less at self-service pumps).
- Filling stations are usually able to deal with minor mechanical problems. For major repairs you have to find a garage (**REPARATURWERKSTATT**).

## WHAT TO SAY

| | |
|---|---|
| (9) litres of . . . | **(Neun) Liter . . .** |
| | (noyn) litre . . . |
| (20) marks of . . . | **Für (zwanzig) Mark . . .** |
| | foor (tsvan-tsik) mark . . . |
| standard/premium/diesel | **Normal/Super/Diesel** |
| | nor-mahl/zooper/deezel |
| Fill it up, please | **Volltanken, bitte** |
| | folltanken bitteh |

| | |
|---|---|
| Will you check . . . | **Bitte prüfen Sie . . .**<br>*bitteh proofen zee . . .* |
| the oil | **das Öl**<br>*das erl* |
| the battery | **die Batterie**<br>*dee batteree* |
| the radiator | **das Kühlwasser**<br>*das kool-vasser* |
| the tyres | **die Reifen**<br>*dee ryfen* |
| I've run out of petrol | **Ich habe kein Benzin mehr**<br>*ish hahbeh kine ben-tseen mair* |
| Can you help me, please? | **Können Sie mir bitte helfen?**<br>*kernnen zee meer bitteh helf-en* |
| Do you do repairs? | **Machen Sie Reparaturen?**<br>*mak-en zee repara-tooren* |
| I have a puncture | **Ich habe eine Reifenpanne**<br>*ish hahbeh ineh ryfen-panneh* |
| I have a broken windscreen | **Die Windschutzscheibe ist<br>zerbrochen**<br>*dee vint-shoots-shybeh ist<br>tsair-brocken* |
| I don't know what's wrong | **Ich weiss nicht, woran es liegt**<br>*ish vice nisht voran es leekt* |
| I think the problem is<br>here . . . [point] | **Ich glaube, es liegt hieran . . .**<br>*ish gla-oobeh es leekt here-un . . .* |

## LIKELY REACTIONS

| | |
|---|---|
| I don't do repairs | **Wir machen keine Reparaturen**<br>*veer mak-en kineh repara-tooren* |
| Where's your car? | **Wo steht Ihr Wagen?**<br>*vo shtait eer vahg-en* |
| What make is it? | **Was für ein Wagen ist es?**<br>*vas foor ine vahg-en ist es* |
| Come back tomorrow/on<br>Monday | **Kommen Sie morgen/Montag<br>wieder**<br>*kommen zee morgen/mone-tahk<br>veeder* |

[*For days of the week, see p. 161*]

# Public transport

## ESSENTIAL INFORMATION

- Finding the way to the bus station, a bus stop, a tram stop, the railway station and a taxi rank, see p. 116.
- Remember that queuing for buses is unheard of!
- To get a taxi you usually have to telephone the local **TAXIZENTRALE** (taxi centre) or go to a taxi rank. Hailing a taxi is less common and doesn't always work.
- Types of trains:
  **Tee** (Trans-Europe-Express; luxury high-speed train with first class only)
  **INTER CITY**
  **EXPRESS** ⎱
  **SCHNELLZUG** ⎰ (long distance trains, often between countries, stopping only at principal stations)
  **D-ZUG**
  **EILZUG** (medium-distance, internal train, stopping only at bigger towns)
  **PERSONENZUG** (slow local train, stopping at all stations)
  **NAHVERKEHRSZUG** (short distance train, often to suburbs)
- Key words on signs:
  **FAHRKARTEN** (tickets, ticket office)
  **EINGANG** (entrance)
  **AUSGANG** (exit)
  **VERBOTEN** (forbidden)
  **GLEIS** (platform, literally: track)
  **BAHNSTEIG** (platform)
  **BAHNHOFSMISSION** (Travellers' Aid Office)
  **AUSKUNFT** (information, information office)
  **DB** (initials for German railways)
  **GEPÄCKAUFBEWAHRUNG** (left-luggage)
  **BUSHALTESTELLE** (bus stop)
  **ABFAHRT** (timetable, departures)
  **ANKUNFT** (timetable, arrivals)
  **GEPÄCKABFERTIGUNG** ⎱ (luggage office/forwarding office)
  **GEPÄCKANNAHME** ⎰

- Buying a ticket:
  Buy your train ticket at the ticket office inside the station.
  When travelling by bus or tram you usually pay as you enter.
  When travelling by underground (U-BAHN) you buy your
  ticket from an automatic machine at the station. This also
  applies to trams in the larger cities where there is a ticket
  machine at each tram stop.

  In most German cities you can purchase a ticket which
  allows you to interchange between trams, underground and
  buses, in the one direction. (These can often be bought at
  tobacconists.) You can also buy a 'Rover' ticket for a specified
  number of days; ask for a **TOURISTEN-FAHRKARTE**
  (tooristen-far-karteh) at a main station ticket office.

## WHAT TO SAY

Where does the train for
(Bonn) leave from?

**Auf welchem Gleis fährt der Zug
nach (Bonn) ab?**
owf velshem glyss fairt der tsook
nahk (bonn) up

Is this the train for (Bonn)?

**Ist dies der Zug nach (Bonn)?**
ist dees der tsook nahk (bonn)

Where does the bus for (Köln)
leave from?

**Wo fährt des Bus nach (Köln) ab?**
vo fairt der boos nahk (kerln) up

Is this the bus for (Köln)?

**Ist dies der Bus nach (Köln)?**
ist dees der boos nahk (kerln)

Do I have to change?

**Muss ich umsteigen?**
moos ish oom-shtyg-en

Can you put me off at the
right stop, please?

**Können Sie mir bitte sagen, wann
ich aussteigen muss?**
kernnen zee meer bitteh zahg-en
vann ish ows-shtyg-en-moos

Where can I get a taxi?

**Wo Kann ich ein Taxi bekommen?**
vo kan ish ine taxi bekommen

Can I book a seat?

**Kann ich einen Sitzplatz
reservieren?**
kann ish inen zits-plats reserveeren

A single

**Eine einfache Fahrt**
ineh ine-fak-eh fart

A return

**Eine Rückfahrkarte**
ineh rook-far-karteh

| First class | **Erster Klasse** |
| | *ai*rster kl*a*sseh |
| Second class | **Zweiter Klasse** |
| | tsvy-ter kl*a*sseh |
| One adult | **Ein Erwachsener** |
| | ine er-v*a*ksen-er |
| Two adults | **Zwei Erwachsene** |
| | tsvy er-v*a*ksen-eh |
| and one child | **und ein Kind** |
| | oont ine k*i*nt |
| and two children | **und zwei Kinder** |
| | oont tsvy k*i*n-der |
| How much is it? | **Wieviel kostet das?** |
| | *vee*-feel k*o*stet das |

# Reference

## NUMBERS

| 0  | **null**      | nool       |
|----|---------------|------------|
| 1  | **eins**      | ines       |
| 2  | **zwei**      | tsvy       |
| 3  | **drei**      | dry        |
| 4  | **vier**      | feer       |
| 5  | **fünf**      | foonf      |
| 6  | **sechs**     | zex        |
| 7  | **sieben**    | z*ee*ben   |
| 8  | **acht**      | ahkt       |
| 9  | **neun**      | noyn       |
| 10 | **zehn**      | tsain      |
| 11 | **elf**       | elf        |
| 12 | **zwölf**     | tsverlf    |
| 13 | **dreizehn**  | dry-tsain  |
| 14 | **vierzehn**  | feer-tsain |
| 15 | **fünfzehn**  | foonf-tsain|
| 16 | **sechzehn**  | zek-tsain  |
| 17 | **siebzehn**  | zeep-tsain |
| 18 | **achtzehn**  | *a*hk-tsain|

| | | |
|---|---|---|
| 19 | **neunzehn** | noyn-tsain |
| 20 | **zwanzig** | tsvan-tsik |
| 21 | **einundzwanzig** | ine-oont-tsvan-tsik |
| 22 | **zweiundzwanzig** | tsvy-oont-tsvan-tsik |
| 23 | **dreiundzwanzig** | dry-oont-tsvan-tsik |
| 24 | **vierundzwanzig** | feer-oont-tsvan-tsik |
| 25 | **fünfundzwanzig** | foonf-oont-tsvan-tsik |
| 30 | **dreissig** | dry-sik |
| 35 | **fünfunddreissig** | foonf-oont-dry-sik |
| 36 | **sechsunddreissig** | zex-oont-dry-sik |
| 37 | **siebenunddreissig** | zeeben-oont-dry-sik |
| 38 | **achtunddreissig** | akt-oont-dry-sik |
| 39 | **neununddreissig** | noyn-oont-dry-sik |
| 40 | **vierzig** | feer-tsik |
| 41 | **einundvierzig** | ine-oont-feer-tsik |
| 50 | **fünfzig** | foonf-tsik |
| 51 | **einundfünfzig** | ine-oont-foonf-tsik |
| 60 | **sechzig** | zek-tsik |
| 61 | **einundsechzig** | ine-oont-zek-tsik |
| 70 | **siebzig** | zeep-tsik |
| 71 | **einundsiebzig** | ine-oont-zeep-tsik |
| 80 | **achtzig** | ahk-tsik |
| 81 | **einundachtzig** | ine-oont-ahk-tsik |
| 90 | **neunzig** | noyn-tsik |
| 91 | **einundneunzig** | ine-oont-noyn-tsik |
| 100 | **hundert** | hoondert |
| 101 | **hunderteins** | hoondert-ines |
| 102 | **hundertzwei** | hoondert-tsvy |
| 125 | **hundertfünfundzwanzig** | hoondert-foonf-oont-tsvan-tsik |
| 150 | **hundertfünfzig** | hoondert-foonf-tsik |
| 175 | **hundertfünfundsiebzig** | hoondert-foonf-oont-zeep-tsik |
| 200 | **zweihundert** | tsvy-hoondert |
| 250 | **zweihundertfünfzig** | tsvy-hoondert-foonf-tsik |
| 300 | **dreihundert** | dry-hoondert |
| 400 | **vierhundert** | feer-hoondert |
| 500 | **fünfhundert** | foonf-hoondert |
| 700 | **siebenhundert** | zeeben-hoondert |
| 1,000 | **tausend** | towzent |
| 1,100 | **tausendeinhundert** | towzent-ine-hoondert |
| 2,000 | **zweitausend** | tsvy-towzent |
| 5,000 | **fünftausend** | foonf-towzent |
| 10,000 | **zehntausend** | fsain-towzent |

| | | |
|---|---|---|
| 100,000 | **hunderttausend** | h*oo*ndert-t*ow*zent |
| 1,000,000 | **eine Million** | *i*neh mill-*y*on |

## TIME

| | |
|---|---|
| What time is it? | **Wie spät ist es?** |
| | vee shp*ai*t ist es |
| It's . . . | **Es ist . . .** |
| | es ist . . . |
| one o'clock | **ein Uhr** |
| | *i*ne oor |
| two o'clock | **zwei Uhr** |
| | tsvy oor |
| noon | **zwölf Uhr mittags** |
| | tsverlf oor m*i*ttahks |
| midnight | **Mitternacht** |
| | mitter-nakt |
| a quarter past five | **viertel nach fünf** |
| | f*ee*rtel nahk foonf |
| half past five | **halb sechs** |
| | halp z*e*x |
| a quarter to six | **viertel vor sechs** |
| | f*ee*rtel for zex |

## DAYS AND MONTHS

| | |
|---|---|
| Monday | **Montag** |
| | m*o*ne-tahk |
| Tuesday | **Dienstag** |
| | d*ee*ns-tahk |
| Wednesday | **Mittwoch** |
| | m*i*tt-vok |
| Thursday | **Donnerstag** |
| | d*o*nners-tahk |
| Friday | **Freitag** |
| | fry-tahk |
| Saturday | **Samstag/Sonnabend** |
| | z*a*ms-tahk/z*o*nn-ahbent |
| Sunday | **Sonntag** |
| | z*o*nn-tahk |

| January | **Januar** |
| | yah-noo-ahr |
| February | **Februar** |
| | fay-broo-ahr |
| March | **März** |
| | mairts |
| April | **April** |
| | ah-pril |
| May | **Mai** |
| | my |
| June | **Juni** |
| | yoo-nee |
| July | **Juli** |
| | yoo-lee |
| August | **August** |
| | ow-goost |
| September | **September** |
| | zeptember |
| October | **Oktober** |
| | oktober |
| November | **November** |
| | november |
| December | **Dezember** |
| | detsember |

## Public holidays

Unless otherwise specified, offices, shops and schools are closed on these days in Austria, Germany and Switzerland.

| 1 January | **Neujahrstag** | New Year's Day |
| . . . | **Himmelfahrt** | Ascension |
| . . . | **Pfingstmontag** | Whit Monday |
| 24 December | **Heiligabend** | Christmas Eve (half day) |
| 25 December | **erster Weihnachtstag** | Christmas Day |
| 26 December | **zweiter Weihnachtstag** | Boxing Day |
| 26 December | **Stephanstag** | St Stephen's Day (Austria and Switzerland) |

# Index

# Travellers' **Greek**

D. L. Ellis, H. Rapi

Pronunciation **Dr J. Baldwin**

*Useful address*

The National Tourist Organization of Greece
195 Regent Street
London W1

# Contents

# Pronunciation hints

In Greek it is important to stress or emphasize the syllables in *italics*, just as you would if we were to take as an English example: *Li*ttle *Jack Hor*ner *sat* in the *cor*ner. Here we have ten syllables, but only four stresses. This is particularly important in Greek, as meaning can be dependent on stress and many words will be completely unintelligible to a Greek unless the stress is put in the correct place.

καλή επιτυχί!

# Everyday expressions

[*See also 'Shop talk', p. 181*]

| | |
|---|---|
| Hello | Γειά σας<br>yassas |
| Good morning ⎤<br>Good day ⎦ | Καλημέρα<br>kal-eemehra |
| Good afternoon (after siesta) ⎤<br>Good evening ⎦ | Καλησπέρα<br>kaleespera |
| Good night | Καληνύχτα<br>kal-eeneehta |
| Goodbye | Γειά σας<br>yassas |
| Yes | Ναί<br>neh |
| Please | Παρακαλῶ<br>parakalo |
| Yes, please | Ναί, παρακαλῶ<br>neh, parakalo |
| Thank you | Εὐχαριστῶ<br>ef-har-eesto |
| Thank you very much | Ευ'χαριστῶ πάρα πολύ<br>ef-har-eesto para pol-ee |
| That's right | Σωςτά<br>sosta |
| No | Όχι<br>o-hee |
| No, thank you | Όχι, ευ'χαριστῶ<br>o-hee ef-har-eesto |
| I disagree | Διαφωνῶ<br>thee-af-on-o |
| Excuse me ⎤<br>Sorry ⎦ | Συγγνώμη<br>seeg-nom-ee |
| Where's the toilet, please? | Ποῦ ειναι ή τουαλέτα, παρακαλῶ;<br>poo een-eh ee too-aleh-ta parakalo |
| Do you speak English? | Μιλᾶπε 'Αγγλικά;<br>meelat-eh angleeka |
| What's your name? | Πῶς λεγεσται;<br>poss leg-es-teh |
| My name is . . . | Μέ λένε . . .<br>meh len-eh . . . |

# Asking the way

## ESSENTIAL INFORMATION

- Keep a look out for all these place names as you will find them on shops, maps and notices.

## WHAT TO SAY

| | |
|---|---|
| Excuse me, please | Μέ συγχωρείτε, παρακαλῶ |
| | meh seenhor-*eet*-eh parakal*o* |
| How do I get . . . | Πῶς μπορῶ νά πάω . . . |
| | p*o*ss bor*o* na p*a*-o . . . |
| to Athens? | στήν 'Αθήνα; |
| | steen ath*ee*na |
| To Ermou Street? | στήν ὁδό Ἑρμοῦ; |
| | steen oth*o* ehrm*oo* |
| to the Hotel Caravel? | στό ξενοδοχεῖο Κάραβελ; |
| | sto ksen-otho-h*ee*-o karavel |
| to the airport? | στό ἀεροδρόμιο; |
| | sto ehr-othrom-yo |
| to the beach? | στή παραλία; |
| | stee paral*ee*a |
| to the bus station? | στή στάση λεωφορείου; |
| | stee st*a*ssee leh-oforee-oo |
| to the market? | στήν ἀγορά; |
| | steen agor*a* |
| to the police station? | στήν ἀστυνομία; |
| | steen asteen-om*ee*-a |
| to the port? | στό Λιμάνι; |
| | sto leeman-ee |
| to the post office? | στό ταχυδρομεῖο; |
| | sto ta-hee-throm*ee*-o |
| to the railway station? | στό σιδηροδρομικό σταθμό; |
| | sto see-theerothrom-eek*o* stathm*o* |
| to the sports stadium? | στό στάδιο; |
| | sto st*a*thio |
| to the tourist information office? | στό γραφεῖο πληροφοριῶν γιά τουρίστες; |
| | sto graf*ee*-o pleerof-oree-on ya toor*ee*st-ess |

**How do I get . . .**   Πῶς μπορῶ νά πάω . . .
poss boro na pa-o . . .

  to the town centre?   στό κέντρο τῆς πόλης;
sto kendro teess pol-eess

  to the town hall?   στό δημαρχεῖο;
sto theem-ar-hee-o

**Is there . . . near by?**   Ὑπάρχει ἐδῶ κοντά . . .
eepar-hee eth-o konda . . .

  a baker's   ἀρτοποιεῖο;
artop-ee-ee-o

  a bank   τράπεζα;
trap-ez-a

  a bar   μπάρ;
bar

  a bus stop   στάση λεωφορείου;
stassee leh-oforee-oo

  a butcher's   κρεοπωλεῖο;
kreh-opolee-o

  a café   καφενεῖο;
kafen-eeo

  a cake and coffee shop   ζαχαροπλαστεῖο;
za-har-oplastee-o

  a campsite   κατασκήνωση;
kata-skeenossee

  a car park   πάρκιγκ;
parking

  a change bureau   γραφεῖο συναλλάγματος;
grafee-o seenal-agmat-oss

  a chemist's   φαρμακεῖο;
farma-kee-o

  a concert hall   αἴθουσα συναυλιῶν;
eh-thoossa seen-avli-on

  a delicatessen   ἐ᾽δωδιμοπωλεῖο;
eth-oth-eemopolee-o

  a dentist's   ὀδοντιατρεῖο;
othondi-atree-o

  a department store   μεγάλο ἐμπορικό κατάστημα;
meh-gal-o emboreeko katasteema

  a disco   ντισκοτέκ;
discotek

  a doctor's surgery   ἰατρεῖο;
ee-atree-o

| | |
|---|---|
| a dry-cleaner's | στεγνοκαθαριστήριο;<br>stegno-kathar-eest*eer*io |
| a fishmonger's | ψαράδικο;<br>psar*a*th-eeko |
| a garage (for repairs) | συνεργείο;<br>seenehr-g*ee*o |
| a hairdresser's | κομμωτήριο;<br>kommot-*ee*rio |
| a greengrocer's | μανάβικο;<br>man*a*v-eeko |
| a grocer's | μπακάλικο;<br>bak*a*l-eeko |
| a hospital | νοσοκομείο;<br>nosokom*ee*-o |
| a hotel | ξενοδοχείο;<br>ksen-otho-h*ee*-o |
| a laundry | καθαριστήριο;<br>kathar-eest*ee*rio |
| a newsagent's | περίπτερο;<br>peh-r*ee*ptero |
| a nightclub | νάϊτ κλάμπ;<br>night club |
| a petrol station | βενζινάδικο;<br>venzeen-*a*theeko |
| a postbox | γραμματοκιβώτιο;<br>grammatok-eevot-yo |
| a toilet | τουαλέτα;<br>too-al-*eh*-ta |
| a restaurant | έστιατόριο;<br>estee-atorio |
| a supermarket | σούπερ μαρκέτ;<br>supermarket |
| a sweet shop (kiosk) | περίπτερο;<br>peh-r*ee*ptero |
| a taxi stand | πιάτσα γιά ταξί;<br>pee-*a*tsa ya taks*ee* |
| a public telephone | τηλέφωνο;<br>teelef-ono |
| a tobacconist's kiosk | περίπτερο;<br>peh-r*ee*ptero |
| a travel agent's | πρακτορείο ταξιδιών;<br>praktor*ee*-o takseethee-*o*n |

| | |
|---|---|
| **Is there . . . near by?** | Ὑπάρχει ἐδῶ κοντά . . . |
| | eep*ar*-hee eth-*o* kond*a* . . . |
| a youth hostel | ξενών νεότητος; |
| | ksen-*on* neh-*ot*-eetoss |

## DIRECTIONS

| | |
|---|---|
| Left | 'Αριστερά |
| | areesteh-r*a* |
| Right | Δεξιά |
| | theksy*a* |
| Straight on | 'Ίσια |
| | *ee*sia |
| There | 'Εκεῖ |
| | ek-*ee* |
| First left/right | Ὁ πρῶτος δρόμος ἀριστερά/δεξιά |
| | o pr*ot*-oss thr*o*m-oss areesteh-r*a*/ |
| | theksy*a* |
| Second left/right | Ὁ δεύτερος δρόμος ἀριστερά/δεξιά |
| | o thefteross thr*o*m-oss areesteh-r*a*/ |
| | theksy*a* |

# Accommodation

## ESSENTIAL INFORMATION
### Hotel

- If you want hotel-type accommodation, all the following words in capital letters are worth looking for on name boards:
  ΞΕΝΟΔΟΧΕΙΟ (hotel)
  ΜΟΤΕΛ (motel)
  ΕΝΟΙΚΙΑΖΟΝΤΑΙ ΔΩΜΑΤΙΑ (rooms to let)
  ΞΕΝΙΑ (luxurious hotels and usually more expensive than ordinary hotels)
- A list of hotels in the town or district can usually be obtained at the local tourist office or at the local Tourist Police or police station. These lists are also available from the National Tourist Organization of Greece in London.

- Recommended hotels are classified into six categories: De luxe or AA and 1st to 5th class or A to E.
- The cost is displayed in the room itself; so you can check it when having a look around before agreeing to stay.
- The displayed cost is for the room itself, per night and not per person. Breakfast is extra and therefore optional.
- In small hotels and village rooms breakfast is paid for separately, if available.
- A Greek breakfast will usually consist of a cup of coffee or tea with bread, butter and jam or honey.
- A service charge of 15% is usually included in the bill but tipping is optional.
- Your passport is requested when registering at a hotel and will normally be kept overnight.

## WHAT TO SAY

| | |
|---|---|
| I have a booking | Ἔχω κλείσει ἕνα δωμάτιο |
| | eh-ho kleessee enna thomat-yo |
| Have you any vacancies, please? | Ἔχετε δωμάτια, παρακαλῶ; |
| | eh-het-eh thomat-ya parakalo |
| Can I book a room? | Μπορῶ νά κλείω ἕνα δωμάτιο; |
| | boro na kleeso enna thomat-yo |
| It's for . . . | Εἶναι γιά . . . |
| | eeneh ya . . . |
|    one adult/one person | ἕναν ενηλικο/ἕνα ἄτομο |
| | ennan en-eeleeko/enna atomo |
|    two adults/two people | δύο ἐνήλικες/δύο ἄτομα |
| | thee-o en-eeleekess/thee-o atoma |
|    and one child | και' ἕνα παιδί |
| | keh enna peth-ee |
|    and two children | καί δύο παιδιά |
| | keh theeo peth-ya |
| It's for . . . | Εἶναι γιά . . . |
| | eeneh ya . . . |
|    one night | μία βραδιά |
| | mee-a vrath-ya |
|    two nights | δύο βραδιές |
| | thee-o vrath-yes |
|    one week | μία βδομάδα |
| | mee-a vthoma-tha |
|    two weeks | δύο βδομάδες |
| | thee-o vthomath-ess |

| | |
|---|---|
| **I would like . . .** | Θά ἤθελα . . . |
| | tha *ee*thella . . . |
| a (quiet) room | ἕνα (ἥσυχο) δωμάτιο |
| | enna (*ee*-seeho) thom*a*t-yo |
| two rooms | δύο δωμάτια |
| | th*ee*-o thom*a*t-ya |
| with a single bed | μέ ἕνα μονό κρεββάτι |
| | meh enna mono krevv*a*t-ee |
| with two single beds | μέ δύο μονά κρεββάτια |
| | meh th*ee*-o mona krevv*a*t-ya |
| with a double bed | μέ ἕνα διπλό κρεββάτι |
| | meh enna theepl*o* krevv*a*t-ee |
| with a toilet | μέ τουαλέτα |
| | meh too-al-*eh*-ta |
| with a bathroom | μέ μπάνιο |
| | meh ban-yo |
| with a shower | μέ ντούς |
| | meh d*oo*ss |
| with a cot | μέ παιδικό κρεββάτι |
| | meh peh-theek*o* krevv*a*t-ee |
| with a balcony | μέ μπαλκόνι |
| | meh balk*o*n-ee |
| Do you serve meals? | Σερβίρετε γεύματα; |
| | sehrv*ee*r-et-eh g*e*vmata |
| Can I look at the room? | Μπορῶ νά δῶ τό δωμάτιο; |
| | bor*o* na th*o* toh thom*a*t-yo |
| OK, I'll take it | Ἐντάξει, θά τό πάρω |
| | end*a*ksee tha toh p*a*r-o |
| No thanks, I won't take it | Οχι εὐχαριστῶ, δέν θά τό πάρω |
| | *o*-hee ef-har-*ee*sto then tha toh p*a*r-o |
| The bill, please | Τό λογαριασμό, παρακαλῶ |
| | toh logaree-*a*zmo parakal*o* |
| Is service included? | Εἶναι μέ τό σερβίς; |
| | *ee*neh meh toh serv*ee*ss |
| I think this is wrong | Νομίζω πώς αυ'τό εἶναι λάθος |
| | nom-*ee*zo poss afto *ee*neh lath-oss |
| May I have a receipt? | Μπορῶ νά ἔχω μία ἀπόδειξη; |
| | bor*o* na *e*hho m*ee*-a ap*o*th-eeksee |

### Camping

- Look for the word: KAMΠINΓK (camping) or this sign.
  Note μ = metres.

- Be prepared for the following charges:
  per person
  for the car (if applicable)
  for the tent or caravan plot
  for electricity
  for hot showers
- A reduction of 10% is made to the holders of AIT or FIA
  membership cards.
- You must provide proof of identity, such as your passport.
- Passports or identity cards can be returned to their holders only
  on settlement of the account.
- For the NTOG camping sites, which are better organized, advance booking is strongly recommended.
- Camping is tolerated almost anywhere outside built-up areas but
  it is always best to get the landowner's permission beforehand.
  The police have the right to forbid you camping off-site in case
  of overcrowding, poor hygiene etc.

### Youth hostels

- Look for the word: ΞΕΝΩΝ ΝΕΟΤΗΤΟΣ (youth hostel).
- The charge per night is the same everywhere.
- You must have a YHA card.
- Accommodation is in dormitories.
- In most youth hostels there are cafeterias where light meals and
  drinks can be bought at reasonable prices.

## WHAT TO SAY

| | |
|---|---|
| Have you any vacancies? | Έχετε θέσεις;<br>eh-het-eh thesseess |
| How much is it . . . | Πόσο κάνει . . .<br>posso kan-ee . . . |
| for the tent? | ή σκηνή;<br>ee skeenee |
| for the caravan? | τό κάραβαν;<br>toh karavan |
| for the car? | τό αὐτοκίνητο;<br>toh aftokeen-eeto |
| for the electricity? | τό ἠλεκτρικό;<br>toh eelek-treeko |
| per person? | τό ἄτομο;<br>toh atomo |
| per day/night? | τή μέρα/βραδιά;<br>tee-meh-ra/vrath-ya |
| May I look round? | Μπορῶ νά ρίξω μία ματιά;<br>boro na reekso mee-a mat-ya |
| Do you provide anything . . . | Σερβίρετε . . .<br>sehr-veer-et-eh . . . |
| to eat? | φαγητό;<br>fag-eeto |
| to drink? | ποτά;<br>pota |
| Is there/are there . . . | Έχετε . . .<br>eh-het-eh . . . |
| a bar? | μπάρ;<br>bar |
| hot showers? | ζεστά ντούς;<br>zesta dooss |
| a kitchen? | κουζίνα;<br>koozeena |
| a laundry? | πλυντήριο;<br>pleendeerio |
| a restaurant? | ἐστιατόριο;<br>estee-atorio |
| a shop? | μαγαζί;<br>magaz-ee |
| a swimming pool? | πισίνα;<br>peeseena |

[*For food shopping, see p. 184, and for eating and drinking out, see p. 192*]

**Problems**

| | |
|---|---|
| The toilet | Ἡ τουαλέτα |
| | ee too-al-*et*-a |
| The shower | Τό ντούς |
| | toh d*oo*ss |
| The tap | Ἡ βρύση |
| | ee vr*ee*ssee |
| The razor point | Ἡ πρίζα γιά τή ξυριστική μηχανή |
| | ee pr*ee*za ya tee kseer-eesteek-*ee* mee-han-*ee* |
| The light | Τό φῶς |
| | toh f*o*ss |
| . . . is not working | . . . χάλασε |
| | . . . h*a*l-ass-eh |
| My camping gas has run out | Ἡ φιάλη υ᾿γραερίου τελείωσε |
| | ee fee-*a*l-ee eegra-ehr-*ee*-oo telee-osseh |
| The bill, please | Τό λογαριασμό, παρακαλῶ |
| | toh logaree-azm*o* parakal*o* |

**LIKELY REACTIONS**

| | |
|---|---|
| Have you an identity document? | Ἔχετε ταυτότητα; |
| | eh-h*e*t-eh taft*o*t-eeta |
| Your membership card, please | Τήν κάρτα σας, παρακαλῶ |
| | teen k*a*rta sas parakal*o* |
| What's your name? | Πῶς ὀνομάζεστε; |
| | poss on-omaz-es-teh |
| Sorry, we're full | Λυπᾶμαι, ἀλλά δέν ἔχουμε θέση |
| | leepam-eh all*a* then eh*oo*meh th*e*ssee |
| How many people is it for? | Γιά πόσα ἄτομα εἶναι; |
| | ya p*o*ssa *a*toma *ee*neh |
| How many nights is it for? | Γιά πόσες βραδιές εἶναι; |
| | ya p*o*sess vrath-yes *ee*neh |
| It's (80) drachmas . . . | (᾿Ογδόντα) δραχμές . . . |
| | (ogth*o*nda) thra-hm*e*ss . . . |
| per day/per night | τή μέρα/τή βραδιά |
| | tee m*e*h-ra/tee vrath-y*a* |

| | |
|---|---|
| I haven't any rooms left | Δέν ἔχουμε δωμάτια |
| | then eh-hoomeh thomat-ya |
| Do you want to have a look? | Θέλετε νά ρίξετε μία ματιά; |
| | thel-et-eh na reekset-eh mee-a mat-ya |

# *General shopping*

# The chemist's

## ESSENTIAL INFORMATION

**ΦΑΡΜΑΚΕΙΟΝ**

**PHARMACIE**

- Look for the word ΦΑΡΜΑΚΕΙΟΝ (chemist's) or this sign.
- Medicines (drugs) are only available at a chemist's. Some non-drugs can be bought at a supermarket or department store.
- Try the chemist before going to a doctor: they are usually qualified to treat minor injuries.
- Chemists take it in turns to stay open all night and on Sundays. A chemist's will display an illuminated list of all-night chemists (ΔΙΑΝΥΚΤΕΡΥΟΝΤΑ ΦΑΡΜΑΚΕΙΑ).
- Normal opening times are: 8.00 a.m. to 1.00 p.m. and 5.30 p.m. to 8.30 p.m. Chemists are closed on Monday, Wednesday afternoon and all day Saturday.

## WHAT TO SAY

| | |
|---|---|
| I'd like . . . | Θά ἤθελα . . . |
| | tha eethella . . . |
| some Alka Seltzer | αλκασέλτζερ |
| | alka seltzer |
| some antiseptic | ἔνα ἀντισηπτικό |
| | enna antee-seepteeko |
| some aspirin | ἔνα κουτί ἀσπιρίνες |
| | enna kootee aspeer-eeness |
| some baby food | βρεφική τροφή |
| | vrefeekee trof-ee |

| | |
|---|---|
| some contraceptives | προφυλακτικά |
| | prof-eelak-teek*a* |
| some cotton wool | ἕνα βαμβάκι |
| | *e*nna vamv*a*k-ee |
| some disposable nappies | πάνες μίας χρήσεως |
| | pan-ess mee-ass hr*ee*ss-eh-oss |
| some eye drops | σταγόνες γιά τά μάτια |
| | stagon-ess ya ta m*a*t-ya |
| some gauze dressing | μερικές γάζες |
| | mehr-eekess g*a*z-ess |
| some inhalant | κάτι γιά εἰσπνοές |
| | kat-ee ya eess-pno-*e*ss |
| some insect repellent | ἕνα ἐντομοκτόνο |
| | *e*nna endomokton-o |
| some paper tissues | χαρτομάνδηλα |
| | hart-oman-theela |
| some sanitary towels | σερβιέτες ὑγείας |
| | sehr-vee-et-ess eeg-*ee*-ass |
| some sticking plaster | ἕνα λευκοπλάστη |
| | *e*nna lefkoplastee |
| some suntan lotion/oil | μία ἀντιηλιακή κρέμα/λάδι |
| | mee-a antee-eelee-ak-*ee* krem-a/lathee |
| some Tampax | ἕνα ταμπάξ |
| | *e*nna tampax |
| some throat pastilles | παστίλλιες γιά τό λαιμό |
| | past*ee*l-ee-ess ya toh lem-*o* |
| some toilet paper | ἕνα χαρτί ὑγείας |
| | *e*nna hartee ee-y*e*e-ass |
| **I'd like something for . . .** | Θά ἤθελα κάτι γιά . . . |
| | tha *ee*thella kat-ee ya . . . |
| bites | τσίμπημα |
| | ts*ee*m-beema |
| burns | ἔγκαυμα |
| | engavma |
| a cold | ἕνα κρύωμα |
| | *e*nna kr*ee*oma |
| constipation | δυσκοιλιότητα |
| | theeskeelee-*o*t-eeta |
| a cough | τόν βῆχα |
| | ton v*ee*-ha |

| | |
|---|---|
| **I'd like something for . . .** | Θά ἤθελα κάτι γιά . . . |
| | tha *ee*thella kat-ee ya . . . |
| diarrhoea | διάρροια |
| | thee-*arria* |
| earache | πόνο στό αὐτί |
| | pon-o sto aft*ee* |
| flu | γρίππη |
| | gr*ee*pee |
| scalds | κάψιμο |
| | *kap*seemo |
| sore gums | σπυράκια |
| | speer*ak*-ya |
| stings | κεντρίσματα |
| | ken-dr*ee*zmata |
| sunburn | ἔγκαυμα η'λίου |
| | engavma eelee-oo |
| sea/travel sickness | ναυτία |
| | naft*ee*-a |

[*For other essential expressions, see 'Shop talk', opposite*]

---

# Holiday items

---

## ESSENTIAL INFORMATION

- Places to shop at and signs to look for:
  ΒΙΒΛΙΟΠΩΛΕΙΟ (bookshop)
  ΧΑΡΤΟΠΩΛΕΙΟ (stationery)
  ΦΩΤΟΓΡΑΦΙΚΑ ΕΙΔΗ (photographic items)
- and the main department stores:
  MARINOPOULOS – PRISUNIC
  MINION, ATHENÈE, TSITSOPOULOS, LAMBROPOULOS
- The pavement kiosks (ΠΕΡΙΠΤΕΡΑ) are particularly useful as
  they are open late at night and sell a variety of goods such as
  aspirins, razor blades, playing cards, pens, soft drinks etc.

## WHAT TO SAY

| | |
|---|---|
| **I'd like . . .** | Θά ἤθελα . . . |
| | tha *ee*thella . . . |

| a bag | μία τσάντα |
| | mee-a tsanda |
| a beach ball | μία μπάλλα |
| | mee-a balla |
| a bucket | ἕνα κουβᾶ |
| | enna koova |
| an English newspaper | μία ἀγγλική ἐφημερίδα |
| | mee-a ang-leekee ef-eemehr-eetha |
| some envelopes | μερικούς φακέλους |
| | mehr-eek-oos fak-el-ooss |
| some postcards | μερικές κάρτες |
| | mehr-eek-ess kartess |
| a spade | ἕνα φτιάρι |
| | enna ftee-ar-ee |
| a straw hat | ἕνα ψάθινο καπέλλο |
| | enna psathee-no kapello |
| some sunglasses | γυαλιά ἡλίου |
| | yal-ya eelee-oo |
| some writing paper | χαρτί ἀλληλογραφίας |
| | hartee alleel-ograf-ee-ass |
| a colour film [show the camera] | ἕνα ἔγχρωμο φίλμ |
| | enna en-hrom-o film |
| a black and white film | ἕνα ἀσπρόμαυρο φίλμ |
| | enna assprom-avro film |

[For other essential expressions, see 'Shop talk', below]

# Shop talk

## ESSENTIAL INFORMATION

- Know how to say the important weights and measures:

| 50 grams | πενῆντα γραμμάρια |
| | pen-eenda gramma-ria |
| 100 grams | ἑκατό γραμμάρια |
| | ek-at-o gramma-ria |
| 200 grams | διακόσια γραμμάρια |
| | thee-akoss-ya gramma-ria |

| ½ kilo | μισό κιλό |
| | meesso keelo |
| 1 kilo | ἔνα κιλό |
| | enna keelo |
| 2 kilos | δύο κιλά |
| | thee-o keela |
| ½ litre | μισό λίτρο |
| | meesso leetro |
| 1 litre | ἔνα λίτρο |
| | enna leetro |
| 2 litres | δύο λίτρα |
| | thee-o leetra |

[For numbers, see p. 209]

## CUSTOMER

| I'm just looking | Ρίχνω μία ματιά |
| | reehno mee-a mat-ya |
| How much is this/that? | Πόσο κάνει αὐτό/ἐκεῖνο; |
| | posso kan-ee afto/ek-eeno |
| What is that? | Τί εἶναι ἐκεῖνο; |
| | tee eeneh ek-eeno |
| What are those? | Τί εἶναι ἐκεῖνα; |
| | tee eeneh ek-eena |
| Is there a discount? | Κάνετε ἔκπτωση; |
| | kan-et-eh ekptoss-ee |
| I'd like that, please | Θά ἤθελα ἐκεῖνο, παρακαλῶ |
| | tha eethella ek-eeno parakalo |
| Not that | Οχι ἐκεῖνο |
| | o-hee ek-eeno |
| Like that | Σάν ἐκεῖνο |
| | san ek-eeno |
| That's enough, thank you | Φτάνει, εὐχαριστῶ |
| | ftan-ee ef-har-eesto |
| More, please | Περισσότερο, παρακαλῶ |
| | perissot-ehro parakalo |
| Less than that, please | Λιγότερο ἀπό αὐτό, παρακαλῶ |
| | leegot-ehro apo afto parakalo |
| I won't take it, thank you | Δέν θά τό πάρω, εὐχαριστῶ |
| | then tha toh par-o ef-har-eesto |
| It's not right | Δέν εἶναι σωστό |
| | then eeneh sosto |

| | |
|---|---|
| Thank you very much | Εὐχαριστῶ πάρα πολύ |
| | ef-har-eesto para pol-ee |
| **Have you got something . . .** | Ἔχετε κάτι . . . |
| | eh-het-eh kat-ee . . . |
| better? | καλύτερο; |
| | kal-eet-ehro |
| cheaper? | φθηνότερο; |
| | ftheenot-ehro |
| different? | διαφορετικό; |
| | thee-afor-et-eeko |
| larger?/smaller? | μεγαλύτερο;/μικρότερο; |
| | meg-aleet-ehro/meekrot-ehro |
| Can I have a bag, please? | Μπορῶ νά ἔχω μία τσάντα, παρακαλῶ; |
| | boro na eh-ho mee-a tsanda parakalo |
| Can I have a receipt? | Μπορῶ νά ἔχω μία ἀπόδειξη; |
| | boro na eh-ho mee-a apoth-eeksee |
| **Do you take . . .** | Παίρνετε . . . |
| | pehr-net-eh . . . |
| English/American money? | ἐγγλέζικα/ἀμερικάνικα λεφτά; |
| | englez-eeka/amerikan-eeka lefta |
| travellers cheques? | τράβελερς τσέκς; |
| | travelers tseks |
| credit cards? | πιστωτικές κάρτες; |
| | peestohteekess kartess |

## SHOP ASSISTANT

| | |
|---|---|
| Can I help you? | Μπορῶ νά σᾶς βοηθήσω; |
| | boro na sas vo-eeth-eeso |
| What would you like? | Τί θά θέλατε; |
| | tee tha thellat-eh |
| Will that be all? <br> Is that all? <br> Anything else? | Τίποτα ἄλλο; |
| | teepota allo |
| Would you like it wrapped? | Θέλετε νά σᾶς τό τυλίξω; |
| | thellet-eh na sas toh teeleek-so |
| Sorry, none left | Λυπᾶμαι, δέν ἔχει μείνε\ τίποτα |
| | leepam-eh then eh-hee meenee teepota |

| | |
|---|---|
| I haven't got any | Δέν ἔχω |
| | then eh-ho |
| I haven't got any more | Δέν μοῦ ἔχει μείνει τίποτα |
| | then moo eh-hee meenee teepota |
| How many do you want? ⎤ | Πόσα θέλετε; |
| How much do you want? ⎦ | possa thellet-eh |
| Is that enough? | Φτάνει αυ'τό; |
| | ftan-ee afto |

# Shopping for food

# Bread

## ESSENTIAL INFORMATION

- Key words to look for:
  ΑΡΤΟΠΟΙΕΙΟΝ (baker's)
  ΨΩΜΙ (bread)
- Some supermarkets sell bread.
- All loaves are sold by weight, rolls by item.

## WHAT TO SAY

| | |
|---|---|
| A loaf (like that) | Ἕνα ψωμί (σάν ἐκείνο) |
| | enna psom-ee (san ek-een-o) |
| A large one | Ἕνα μεγάλο ψωμί |
| | enna megalo psom-ee |
| A small one | Ἕνα μικρό ψωμί |
| | enna meekro psom-ee |
| A bread roll | Ἕνα ψωμάκι |
| | enna psomak-ee |
| Two French-type loaves | Δύο φραντζόλες |
| | thee-o frant-zol-ess |
| ½ kilo of white bread | Μισό κιλό ασπρο ψωμί |
| | meesso keelo aspro psom-ee |
| 1 kilo of brown bread | Ἕνα κιλό ψωμί μαῦρο |
| | enna keelo psom-ee mavr-o |

# Cakes and ice-creams

## ESSENTIAL INFORMATION

- Key words to look for:
  ΖΑΧΑΡΟΠΛΑΣΤΕΙΟΝ (a place to buy cakes and have a drink)
  ΓΑΛΑΚΤΟΠΩΛΕΙΟΝ (milk bars specializing in dairy produce,
  e.g. rice puddings, yoghurt, ice-creams etc., but which also serve
  cakes.
  ΠΑΓΩΤΑ (ice-cream)
  [See p. 192 for 'Ordering a drink and a snack'.]

## WHAT TO SAY

The types of cake you find in the shops vary from region to region
but the following are some of the most common.

| | |
|---|---|
| μπακλαβᾶ<br>baklava | mille feuilles pastry with nuts and<br>honey |
| καταΐφι<br>kata-eefee | fine shredded pastry with walnuts<br>and honey |
| γαλακτομπούρεκο<br>galakto-boorek-o | custard pudding with mille feuilles<br>pastry |
| λουκουμάδες<br>lookoomath-ess | small doughnuts fried in oil and<br>served with honey |
| σοκολατίνα<br>sokolateena | chocolate cake |
| πάστα ἀμυγδάλου<br>pasta ameegthal-oo | almond cake |
| μπουγάρσα<br>boogatsa | flaky pastry filled with custard |
| ριζόγαλο<br>reezogalo | rice pudding |
| γιαούρτι<br>ya-oortee | yoghurt |
| **A . . . ice, please** | Ἕνα παγωτό . . . παρακαλῶ<br>enna pagoto . . . parakalo |
| vanilla | βανίλα<br>vanilla |
| chocolate | σοκολάτα<br>sokola-ta |

| | |
|---|---|
| A . . . ice, please | Ένα παγωτό . . . παρακαλῶ |
| | enna pago*to* . . . parakal*o* |
| cream | κρέμα |
| | krem-a |
| cassata | κασσάτα |
| | kass*a*t-a |
| lemon | λεμόνι |
| | lem*o*n-ee |
| strawberry | φράουλα |
| | fra-oola |
| cherry | βύσσινο |
| | veessino |

# Picnic food

## ESSENTIAL INFORMATION

- Key words to look for:
  ΠΑΝΤΟΠΩΛΕΙΟΝ (grocer's)
  ΣΟΥΠΕΡΜΑΡΚΕΤ (supermarket)
  ΣΕ ΠΑΚΕΤΟ (take-away)
- Hot food to take away can be bought in restaurants and pizza houses.

## WHAT TO SAY

| | |
|---|---|
| Two slices of . . . | Δύο φέτες . . . |
| | th*ee*-o fet-ess . . . |
| ham | ζαμπόν |
| | zamb*o*n |
| garlic sausage | λονκάνικο μέ σκόρδο |
| | lookan-eeko meh sk*o*rtho |
| salami | σαλάμι |
| | sal*a*m-ee |
| mortadella | μορταδέλλα |
| | mortath*e*lla |

You may also like to try some of these:

| | |
|---|---|
| ταραμοσαλάτα<br>taramo-sala-ta | cod's roe mixed with oil and lemon |
| φέτα<br>fet-a | white cheese made of goat's milk |
| κασέρι<br>kassehr-ee | yellow cheese, rich in cream |
| κεφαλοτύρι<br>kef-aloteer-ee | very salty yellow cheese |
| μανούρι<br>manooree | very creamy white cheese |
| μυτζήθρα<br>meetzeethra | white soft cheese made from ewe's milk |
| χαλβάς<br>halv-ass | sweet made from sesame seeds or semolina, and honey |

[*For other essential expressions see 'Shop talk', p. 181*]

# Fruit and vegetables

## ESSENTIAL INFORMATION

- Key words to look for:
  ΦΡΟΥΤΑ (fruit)
  ΛΑΧΑΝΙΚΑ (vegetables)
  ΟΠΟΡΟΠΩΛΕΙΟΝ (greengrocer's)
- It is customary for you to choose your own fruit and vegetables at the market and for the stallholder to weigh and price them. You must take your own shopping bag – paper and plastic bags are not normally provided.

## WHAT TO SAY

| | |
|---|---|
| **1 kilo of . . .** | Ἔνα κιλό . . .<br>enna keelo . . . |
| apples | μῆλα<br>meela |
| apricots | βερύκοκκα<br>vehr-eekoka |

| | |
|---|---|
| **1 kilo of . . .** | Ἕνα κιλό<br>enna keelo . . . |
| bananas | μπανάνες<br>banan-ess |
| cherries | κεράσια<br>kehr-ass-ya |
| figs | σῦκα<br>seeka |
| grapes (white/black) | σταφύλια (ἄσπρα/μαῦρα)<br>staf-eel-ya (aspra/mavra) |
| oranges | πορτοκάλια<br>portokal-ya |
| peaches | ροδάκινα<br>rothak-eena |
| pears | ἀχλάδια<br>a-hlath-ya |
| plums | δαμάσκηνα<br>thamask-eena |
| strawberries | φράουλες<br>fra-ool-ess |
| A pineapple, please | Ἕναν α'νανά, παρακαλῶ<br>ennan anana parakalo |
| A grapefruit | Μία φράπα<br>mee-a frap-a |
| A melon/water melon | Ἕνα πεπόνι/καρπούζι<br>enna pep-on-ee/karpoozee |
| **½ kilo of . . .** | Μισό κιλό . . .<br>meesso keelo . . . |
| aubergines | μελιτζάνες<br>mel-eetzan-ess |
| beetroot | παντζάρια<br>pannzar-ya |
| carrots | καρότα<br>karota |
| courgettes | κολοκυθάκια<br>kolokee-thak-ya |
| green beans | φασολάκια<br>fassolak-ya |
| leeks | πράσσα<br>prassa |
| mushrooms | μανιτάρια<br>maneeta-ria |

| | |
|---|---|
| onions | κρεμμύδια |
| | kremmeeth-ya |
| **2 kilos of . . .** | Δύο κιλά . . . |
| | thee-o keela . . . |
| peas | μπιζέλια |
| | beezel-ya |
| peppers (green/red) | πιπεριές (πράσινες/κόκκινες) |
| | pee-peh-ree-ess (prasseen-ess/ |
| | kokeen-ess) |
| potatoes | πατάτες |
| | patat-ess |
| spinach | σπανάκι |
| | spanak-ee |
| tomatoes | ντομάτες |
| | domat-ess |
| **A bunch of . . .** | Ένα ματσάκι . . . |
| | enna matsak-ee . . . |
| parsley | μαϊντανό |
| | ma-ee-dan-o |
| radishes | ραπανάκια |
| | rapanak-ya |
| **A head of garlic** | Ένα σκόρδο |
| | enna skortho |
| **A lettuce** | Ένα μαρούλι |
| | enna maroolee |
| **A cucumber** | Ένα αγγούρι |
| | enna angooree |
| Like that, please | Όπως εκείνο, παρακαλώ |
| | op-oss ek-eeno parakalo |

# Meat and fish

## ESSENTIAL INFORMATION

- Key words to look for:
  ΚΡΕΟΠΩΛΕΙΟΝ (butcher's)
  ΚΡΕΟΠΩΛΗΣ (butcher)
  ΨΑΡΑΔΙΚΟ (fishmonger's)
  ΘΑΛΑΣΣΙΝΑ (seafood)

- There are no labels on counters and supermarket displays in Greece which could help you in deciding what cut or joint to have, so you will have to ask or simply point. Do not expect, however, to find the same cuts of meat you would find at home.
- Pork in Greece is of a very high quality.
- Markets usually have fresh fish stalls.
- You will find that cod and herring are sold dried and salted: they simply require soaking in water overnight.

## WHAT TO SAY

For a joint, choose the type of meat and then say how many people it is for:

| | |
|---|---|
| Some beef, please | Βοδινό, παρακαλῶ |
| | vothee-no parakalo |
| Some lamb | 'Αρνάκι |
| | arnak-ee |
| Some pork | Χοιρινό |
| | heereeno |
| Some veal | Μοσχαρίσιο |
| | moss-har-ees-yo |
| A joint . . . | Ἔνα κομμάτι . . . |
| | enna kommat-ee . . . |
| for two people | γιά δύο ἄτομα |
| | ya thee-o atoma |
| for four people | γιά τέσσερα ἄτομα |
| | ya tessera atoma |
| Some steak, please | Μπόν φιλέ, παρακαλῶ |
| | bon feeleh parakalo |
| Some liver | Συκωτάκια |
| | seekotak-ya |
| Some kidneys | Νεφρά |
| | nefra |
| Some sausages | Λουκάνικα |
| | lookan-eeka |
| Some mince | Κιμά |
| | keema |
| Two veal escalopes, please | Δύο μοσχαρίσιες μπριζόλες, παρακαλῶ |
| | thee-o moss-ha-rees-yess breezol-ess parakalo |
| Three pork chops | Τρεῖς χοιρινές μπριζολες |
| | treess heereen-ess breezol-ess |

Five lamb chops
Πέντε ἀρνίσιες μπριζόλες
pendeh arneess-yess breezol-ess

You may also want:
A chicken
Ἕνα κοτόπουλο
enna kotop-oolo

A rabbit
Ἕνα κουνέλι
enna koonel-ee

A tongue
Μία γλῶσσα
mee-a glossa

Purchase most fish by weight:
½ kilo of . . .
Μισό κιλό . . .
meesso keelo . . .

anchovies
ἀντσούγες
ants-oog-ess

grey mullet
λυθρίνια
lee-threen-eea

mussels
μύδια
meeth-ya

octopus
χταπόδια
htapoth-ya

oysters
στρείδια
streeth-ya

prawns
γαρίδες
ga-reethess

red mullet
μπαρμπούνια
barboon-ya

sardines
σαρδέλες
sar-thel-ess

smelt (fried)
μαρίδες (τηγανιτές)
ma-reethess (teeganeetess)

squid
καλαμάρια
kalama-ria

shrimps
γαρίδες
ga-reethess

sea bream
συναγρίδες
seen-agreeth-ess

trout
πέστροφες
pestrof-ess

cod
μπακαλιάρο
bakal-ya-ro

For some shellfish and 'frying pan' fish; specify the number:

| | |
|---|---|
| A crab, please | Ἕνα καβούρι, παρακαλῶ |
| | enna kavoo-ree parakalo |
| A lobster | Ἕναν ἀστακό |
| | ennan astako |
| A sole | Μία γλῶσσα |
| | mee-a glossa |
| A mackerel | Ἕνα σκουμπρί |
| | enna skoombree |
| A herring | Μία ρέγγα |
| | mee-a renga |

# Eating and drinking out

## Ordering a drink and a snack

### ESSENTIAL INFORMATION

- The places to ask for: ΜΠΑΡ (bar), ΣΝΑΚ-ΜΠΑΡ (snack bar),
  ΟΥΖΕΡΙ (bar which serves hors d'oeuvres)
  ΖΑΧΑΡΟΠΛΑΣΤΕΙΟ (pastry shop which serves drinks as well)
  ΚΑΦΕΝΕΙΟ (coffee house, where Greek women are rarely seen)
- By law the price list (ΤΙΜΟΛΟΓΙΟΝ) must be on display. Service
  is usually included.
- Bars open late in the afternoon and close at 2.00 a.m. All other
  establishments are normally open all day.
- Bars and cafés serve both non-alcoholic and alcoholic drinks.
  Children are allowed in.
- Greek beer comes in small bottles of 350 g (about ½ pint) and
  500 g (about 1 pint).
- Greek coffee is made by heating water, mixing in the ground
  coffee and sugar, and bringing it to the boil – it is very strong.

### WHAT TO SAY

| | |
|---|---|
| **I'll have . . . please** | Θέλω . . . παρακαλῶ |
| | thello . . . parakalo |
| a black coffee | ἕνα νέσκαφε σκέτο |
| | enna nescafe sket-o |

| | |
|---|---|
| a coffee with milk | ἕνα καφέ μέ γάλα |
| | enna kaf-eh meh ga-la |
| a Greek coffee | ἕνα Ἑλληνικό καφέ |
| | enna elleen-eeko kaf-eh |
| without sugar | σκέτο |
| | sket-o |
| medium sweet | μέτριο |
| | metrio |
| sweet | γλυκό |
| | gleeko |
| a tea | ἕνα τσάϊ |
| | enna tsa-ee |
| with milk | μέ γάλα |
| | meh ga-la |
| with lemon | μέ λεμόνι |
| | meh lem-on-ee |
| a glass of milk | ἕνα ποτήρι γάλα |
| | enna poteeree ga-la |
| a hot chocolate | μία ζεστή σοκολάτα |
| | mee-a zestee sokola-ta |
| an iced coffee | ἕνα νέσκαφε φραπέ |
| | enna nescafe frap-eh |
| a mineral water | ἐμφιαλωμένο νερό |
| | emfee-alomen-o nehro |
| a lemonade | μία λεμονάδα |
| | mee-a lem-on-atha |
| a lemon squash | μία λεμονάδα χυμό |
| | mee-a lem-on-atha heemo |
| a Coca-Cola | μία κόκα κόλα |
| | mee-a koka kola |
| an orangeade | μία πορτοκαλάδα |
| | mee-a portokal-atha |
| an orange juice | μία πορτοκαλάδα χυμό |
| | mee-a portokal-atha heemo |
| a pineapple juice | ἕναν ἀνανᾶ χυμό |
| | ennan anana heemo |
| a beer | μία μπύρα |
| | mee-a bee-ra |
| a large bottle | ἕνα μεγάλο μπουκάλι |
| | enna megalo bookalee |
| a small bottle | ἕνα μικρό μπουκάλι |
| | enna meekro bookal-ee |

| **I'll have . . . please** | Θέλω . . . παρακαλῶ |
| --- | --- |
| | thello . . . parakalo |
| a cheese sandwich | ἔνα σάντουϊτς μέ τθρί |
| | enna sandwits meh teeree |
| a ham sandwich | ἔνα σάντουϊτς μέ ζαμπόν |
| | enna sandwits meh zambon |
| a meat pie | μία κρεατόπιττα |
| | mee-a kreh-at-op-ita |
| a spinach pie | μία σπανακόπιττα |
| | meea-a spanak-op-ita |
| a cheese pie | μία τυρόπιττα |
| | mee-a teer-op-ita |
| a hot dog | ενα χότ ντόγκ |
| | enna hot dog |

This is another snack you may like to try:

| ἔνα σουβλάκι | pieces of grilled meat wrapped in |
| --- | --- |
| enna soovlak-ee | pitta bread; doner kebab |

# In a restaurant

## ESSENTIAL INFORMATION

- You can eat at the following places:
  ΕΣΤΙΑΤΟΡΙΟΝ (restaurant)
  ΤΑΒΕΡΝΑ (typical Greek restaurant)
  ΨΑΡΟΤΑΒΕΡΝΑ (restaurant specialising in seafood)
  ΨΗΣΤΑΡΙΑ (restaurant specialising in charcoal-grilled food)
- In smaller restaurants there may be no printed menu, so you will either have to ask what is available or look at the food displayed and point. The Greeks themselves often go into the kitchen to choose their meal.
- If the menu lists two prices for each item, the second price includes a 10% service charge, but an extra tip is always welcome.
- If there is a wine waiter (he will also serve the water and bread), a small tip should be left for him on the table (not on the plate with the bill).

- Times when restaurants stay open depend on the area and the season. However, they are normally open from midday to 4.00 p.m. and 8.00 p.m. to midnight. Although Greeks tend to eat late in the summer, all restaurants, bars and cafés are obliged by law to close at 2.00 a.m.
- In most tavernas and many restaurants draught wine is available. It is served in small cans and sold by weight. Order 1 kilo (1 litre), ½ kilo (½ litre) or ¼ kilo (a large glass).

## WHAT TO SAY

| | |
|---|---|
| May I book a table? | Μπορῶ νά κλείσω ἕνα τραπέζι; |
| | boro na kleeso enna trap-ez-ee |
| I've booked a table | Ἔχω κλείσει τραπέζι |
| | eh-ho kleessee trap-ez-ee |
| **A table . . .** | Ἕνα τραπέζι . . . |
| | enna trap-ez-ee . . . |
| for one | γιά ἕναν |
| | ya ennan |
| for three | γιά τρεῖς |
| | ya treess |
| The menu, please | Τόν κατάλογο παρακαλῶ |
| | ton katalogo parakalo |
| What's this please? [point to the menu] | Τί εἶναι αὐτό παρακαλῶ; |
| | tee eeneh afto parakalo |
| 1 kilo of wine | Ἕνα κιλό κρασί |
| | enna keelo krassee |
| ½ kilo of wine | Μισό κιλό κρασί |
| | meeso keelo krassee |
| ¼ kilo of wine | Τέταρτο κρασί |
| | tetartoh krassee |
| A glass | Ἕνα ποτήρι |
| | enna poteeree |
| A bottle | Ἕνα μπουκάλι |
| | enna bookal-ee |
| A half bottle | Ἕνα μικρό μπουκάλι |
| | enna meekro bookal-ee |
| Red/white/rosé | Κόκκινο/ἄσπρο/ροζέ |
| | kokino/aspro/roz-eh |
| Some more bread, please | Καί ἄλλο/ἀκόμα ψωμί, ηαρακαλῶ |
| | keh allo/akoma psom-ee parakalo |

| | |
|---|---|
| Some more wine | Καί άλλο/ἀκόμα κρασί |
| | keh allo/akoma krassee |
| Some oil | Λίγο λάδι |
| | leego la-thee |
| Some vinegar | Λίγο ξύδι |
| | leego ksee-thee |
| Some salt/pepper | Λίγο α'λάτι/πιπέρι |
| | leego alat-ee/peepeh-ree |
| Some water | Λίγο νερό |
| | leego nehro |
| With/without garlic | με/χωρίς σκόρδο |
| | meh/horeess skortho |
| How much does that come to? | Πόσο κάνει; |
| | posso kan-ee |
| Is service included? | Ει'ναι μέ τό σερβὶς; |
| | eeneh meh toh serveess |
| Where is the toilet, please? | Ποῦ ει'ναι ἡ τουαλέτα, παρακαλῶ; |
| | poo eeneh ee too-al-et-a parakalo |
| Miss!/Waiter! | Δεσποινίς!/Γκαρσόν! |
| | thespeen-eess/garson |
| The bill, please | Τό λογαριασμό, παρακαλῶ |
| | toh logaree-azmo parakalo |

**Key words for courses, as seen on some menus**

[*Only ask if you want the waiter to remind you of the choice.*]

| | |
|---|---|
| **What have you got in the way of . . .** | Τί . . . ἔχετε; |
| | tee . . . eh-het-eh |
| starters? | ορεκτικα |
| | orekteeka |
| soup? | σογιιες |
| | soopess |
| egg? | αγγα |
| | avgah |
| fish? | ψατια |
| | psareea |
| meat? | κπεας |
| | kreass |
| game? | κωνηγι |
| | keeneegee |

| | |
|---|---|
| fowl? | πουλερικα |
| | poolereeka |
| vegetables? | λαχαρικα |
| | lahaneeka |
| cheese? | τυρια |
| | teereea |
| fruit? | φρουτα |
| | froota |
| ice-cream? | παγωτα |
| | pagota |
| dessert? | γλυκα |
| | gleeka |

## UNDERSTANDING THE MENU

You will find the names of the principal ingredients of most dishes on these pages:

| | |
|---|---|
| Starters p. 186 | Fruit p. 187 |
| Meat p. 190 | Cheese p. 187 |
| Fish p. 191 | Ice-cream p. 185 |
| Vegetables p. 188 | Dessert p. 185 |

### Cooking and menu terms

| | |
|---|---|
| Βραστό | boiled, poached, stewed |
| vrasto | |
| γεμιστό | stuffed |
| ghemeesto | |
| ζεστό | hot |
| zesto | |
| καπνιστό | smoked |
| kapneesto | |
| στά κάρβουνα | charcoal-grilled |
| sta karvoona | |
| τῆς κατσαρόλας | en casserole |
| teess katsar-olass | |
| κοκκινιστό | cooked with oil and tomatoes |
| kokkin-eesto | |
| σενιάν (κρέας) | rare (meat) |
| sen-yan (kreh-ass) | |
| μέτρια ψημένο | medium |
| metria pseemen-o | |

| | |
|---|---|
| καμοψημένο | well-done |
| kalops-eemen-o | |
| κρύο | cold |
| kree-o | |
| μέ μαϊνταυό | with parsley |
| meh my-dan-o | |
| μαρινάτο | marinated |
| mareenat-o | |
| παστό | cured |
| pasto | |
| πουρέ | mashed (potatoes) |
| poo-reh | |
| μέ σάλτσα | with sauce |
| meh saltsa | |
| στή σχάρα | grilled |
| stee skar-a | |
| τηγανισμένο σέ πολύ λάδι | deep fried |
| teegan-eesmen-o seh pol-ee la-thee | |
| τηγανητό | fried |
| teegan-eeto | |
| τριμμένο | grated |
| trimmen-o | |
| στό φοῦρνο | baked |
| sto foorno | |
| ψητό | roasted, baked |
| pseeto | |
| ψητό τῆς κατσαρόλας | pot-roasted |
| pseeto teess katsar-olass | |
| ψηλοκομμένο | finely chopped |
| psee-lokommen-o | |
| ὠμό | raw |
| om-o | |

## Further words to help you understand the menu

| | |
|---|---|
| ἀγγούρι | cucumber |
| angooree | |
| αὐγολέμονο | rice, egg and lemon soup |
| avgol-em-ono | |
| γαριδοσαλάτα | shrimps in oil and lemon sauce |
| gareeth-osala-ta | |

| | |
|---|---|
| γιουβαρλάκια | minced meat and rice balls |
| yoo-varlak-ya | |
| γιουβέτσι | meat with noodles baked in the |
| yoo-vet-see | oven |
| κεφτέδες | meatballs made with bread and |
| kefteth-ess | herbs |
| κοκορέτσι | lamb innards roasted on a spit |
| kokoret-see | |
| κρεμμύδι | onion |
| kremmeethee | |
| μελιτζάνες γεμιστές | stuffed aubergines |
| mel-eetzan-ess ghe-meess-tess | |
| μουσακά | layers of baked aubergines and |
| moossaka | minced meat |
| μπιζέλια | peas |
| beezel-ya | |
| μπιφτέκια | grilled meatballs |
| beeftekya | |
| ντολμάδες | vine or cabbage leaves stuffed with |
| dolmath-ess | rice and/or meat |
| ντοσάτες γεμιστές | stuffed tomatoes with rice and/or |
| domat-ess ghemeess-tess | minced meat |
| παστίτσιο | minced meat and macaroni baked |
| pasteetsio | and completed by a sauce |
| παστρουμάς | heavily spiced, dried or smoked |
| pastroom-ass | meat |
| πατσάς | tripe soup |
| patsass | |
| πιπεριές γεμιστές | stuffed peppers |
| peepeh-ree-ess ghemeess-tess | |
| ρεβύθια | chick-peas |
| reh-veethia | |
| σκορδαλιά | garlic sauce |
| skor-thal-ya | |
| σκόρδο | garlic |
| skortho | |
| σουβλάκι | cubes of meat grilled on a spit |
| soovlak-ee | |
| σουτζουκάκια | spicy meatballs in sauce |
| soot-zookak-ya | |
| ταραμοσαλάτα | dip of fish roe blended with bread, |
| taramo-sala-ta | oil and lemon |

| | |
|---|---|
| τζατζίκι<br>tsat-zeekee | dip of yoghurt, cucumber, garlic,<br>   olive oil and mint |
| φακιές<br>fak-yess | lentils |
| φασολάδα<br>fassol-atha | kidney bean soup with tomatoes |
| χόρτα σαλάτα<br>horta sala-ta | made from greens resembling<br>   spinach |
| χθλόπιττες<br>heelop-eet-ess | noodles |
| χωριάτικη σαλάτα<br>horeeat-eekee sala-ta | mixed salad, (tomatoes, cucumber,<br>   green peppers, cheese, onion) |
| ψαρόσουπα<br>psaross-oopa | fish soup |

# Health

## ESSENTIAL INFORMATION

- For details of reciprocal health agreements between the UK and Greece, ask for leaflet SA30 at your local Department of Health and Social Security a month before leaving, or ask your travel agent. However, the public health sector offers an extremely limited service. It is *essential* to have proper medical insurance.
- Take your own 'first line' first aid kit with you.
- See p. 178 for minor disorders and treatment at a chemist's.
- See p. 170 for asking the way to a doctor, dentist, or chemist.
- To find a doctor in an emergency look for: ΝΟΣΟΚΟΜΕΙΟΝ (hospital) or contact the police.
- Because of the limited ambulance service in Greece, taxis are frequently used to take people to hospital.

## What's the matter?

| | |
|---|---|
| I have a pain here [*point*] | Ἔχω ἕνα πόνο ἐδῶ<br>eh-ho enna pon-o eth-o |
| I have toothache | Ἔχω πονόδοντο<br>eh-ho pon-othondo |

| | |
|---|---|
| I have broken . . . | Έσπασα . . . |
| | *espassa* . . . |
| my dentures | τή μασέλα μου |
| | tee mass*e*la moo |
| my glasses | τά γυαλιά μου |
| | ta yal-*y*a moo |
| I have lost . . . | Έχασα . . . |
| | eh-h*a*ssa . . . |
| my contact lenses | τούς φακούς ἐπαφῆς μου |
| | tooss fak-*oo*ss ep-af*ee*ss moo |
| a filling | ἕνα σφράγισμα |
| | enna sfr*a*g-eesma |
| My child is ill | Τό παιδί μου εἶναι αρρωστο |
| | toh peth-*ee* moo *ee*neh *a*rrosto |

**Already under treatment for something else?**

| | |
|---|---|
| I take . . . regularly [*show*] | Παίρνω συνήθως . . . |
| | pehr-no seen*ee*th-oss . . . |
| this medicine | αὐτό τό φάρμακο |
| | aft*o* toh f*a*rmako |
| these pills | αὐτά τά χάπια |
| | aft*a*ta h*a*p-ya |
| I have . . . | Έχω . . . |
| | eh-ho . . . |
| haemorrhoids | αἱμορροΐδες |
| | em-orro-*ee*thess |
| rheumatism | ρευματισμούς |
| | revma-teezm*oo*ss |
| I'm . . . | Εἶμαι . . . |
| | *ee*meh . . . |
| diabetic | διαβητικός/διαβητική* |
| | thee-av-eeteek-*o*ss/thee-av-eeteek-*ee** |
| asthmatic | ἀσθματικός/ἀσθματικύ* |
| | as-thmat-eek-*o*ss/as-thmat-eek-*ee** |
| pregnant | ἔγκυος |
| | engee-oss |
| I have a heart condition | Εἶμαι καρδιακός/καρδιακή* |
| | *ee*meh karthee-akoss/karthee-ak*ee** |

*For men use the first alternative, for women the second.

| | |
|---|---|
| I am allergic to (pencillin) | Εἶμαι ἀλλεργικός/α'λλεργική*<br>στή (πενικιλλίνη)<br>*ee*meh allehr-geek-*oss*/allehr-geek-<br>*ee* stee (pen-eekeel-*ee*nee) |

# Problems: loss, theft

## ESSENTIAL INFORMATION

- If the worst comes to the worst, find the police station; to ask the way, see p. 169.
- Look for:
  ΑΣΤΥΝΟΜΙΑ (police in towns) or ΧΩΡΟΦΥΛΑΚΗ (gendarmerie, i.e. rural police)
- If you loose your passport go to the nearest British Consulate.
- In an emergency, dial 100 for the police.

**LOSS**

[*See also 'Theft' below; the lists are interchangeable*]

| | |
|---|---|
| **I have lost . . .** | Ἔχασα . . .<br>*eh*-hassa . . . |
| my camera | τήν φωτογραφική μηχανή μου<br>teen fotograffee*kee* meehan*ee* moo |
| my car logbook | τήν ἄδεια κθκλοφορίας<br>teen *ath*-eya keek-lofor*ee*-ass |
| my driving licence | τήν αδεια ὁδηωῆσεφς<br>teen *ath*ee-a othee-*gees*-eh-oss |
| my insurance certificate | τήν ἀσφαλεια τοῦ αυ'τοκινήτου<br>μου<br>teen asf*alee*-a too aftokeen-*ee*too<br>moo |

**THEFT**

| | |
|---|---|
| **Someone has stolen . . .** | Κάποιος μοῦ ἔκλεψε . . . |
| | kap-ee-oss moo eklepseh . . . |
| my car | τό αὐτοκίνητο μου |
| | toh aftokeen-eeto moo |
| my keys | τά κλειδιά μου |
| | ta kleeth-ya moo |
| my money | τά χρήματα μου |
| | ta hreem-ata moo |
| my tickets | τά εἰσιτήρια μου |
| | ta eess-eeteeree-a moo |
| my travellers cheques | τά τράβελερς τσέκς μου |
| | ta travelers' tseks moo |
| my wallet | τό πορτοφόλι μου |
| | toh portofol-ee moo |
| my luggage | τά πράγματα μου |
| | ta pragmata moo |

# The post office and phoning home

## ESSENTIAL INFORMATION

- Key words to look for:
  ΤΑΧΥΔΡΟΜΕΙΟΝ (post office)
  ΕΛ.ΤΑ, (abbreviation for Greek post office:
  look out for this symbol)
  ΟΤΕ (telecommunications)
- For stamps, look for the word ΓΡΑΜΜΑΤΟΣΗΜΑ.
- Telegrams are not sent from post offices, but from the offices of the OTE.
- Unless you read and speak Greek well, it's best not to make phone calls by yourself. Go to OTE (Telecommunications Organization of Greece, look out for this symbol) – and not to the post office – and write the town and number you want on a piece of paper.

- To phone the UK from Greece, dial 0044 and then the number you want.

## WHAT TO SAY

| | |
|---|---|
| To England, please | Γιά τήν 'Αγγλία, παρακαλῶ<br>ya teen anglee-a parakalo |

[*Hand letters, cards or parcels over the counter*]

| | |
|---|---|
| To Australia | Γιά τήν Αὐστραλία<br>ya teen af-straleea |
| To the United States | Γιά τήν 'Αμερική<br>ya teen amerik-ee |
| I'd like this number . . . | Θέλω αὐτό τόν ἀριθμό . . .<br>thello afto ton a-reethmo . . . |
| in England | στήν 'Αγγλία<br>steen angleea |
| in Canada | στόν Καναδᾶ<br>ston kana-tha |
| Can you dial it for me, please? | Μπορεῖτε νά μοῦ πάρετε τόν ἀριθμό, σᾶς παρακαλῶ;<br>boreeteh na moo par-et-eh ton a-reethmo sas parakalo |
| I'd like to send a telegram | Θέλω νά στείλω ενα τηλεγράφημα<br>thello na steelo enna teelegraf-eema |

---

# Changing cheques and money

---

## ESSENTIAL INFORMATION

- Look for these signs:
  ΤΡΑΠΕΖΑ (bank)
  BUREAU DE CHANGE (change bureau)
- To cash your normal cheques, exactly as at home, use your banker's card where you see the Eurocheque sign. Write in English, in pounds.
- Exchange rate information shows the pound as: £. It is also quite often simply shown by the British flag.

- Have your passport handy.
- Banks are open between 8.00 a.m. and 2.00 p.m. except on Saturdays, Sundays and public holidays. However, during the high season some banks will remain open during the afternoons.

## WHAT TO SAY

| | |
|---|---|
| **I'd like to cash . .** | Θέλω νά ἐξαργυρώσω . . . |
| | thello na ek-sarg-eerosso . . . |
| these travellers' cheques | αὐτά τά τράβελερς τσέκ |
| | afta ta travelers tseks |
| this cheque | αὐτό τό τσέκ |
| | afto toh tsek |
| **I'd like to change this . . .** | Θά ἤθελα νά αλλάξω αὐτό . . . |
| | tha eethella na allakso afto . . . |
| into Italian lira | σέ Ἰταλικές λιρέττες |
| | seh eetal-eekess leeret-ess |
| into Turkish pounds | σέ τούρκικες λίρες |
| | seh toor-keekess leeress |
| into Yugoslav dinar | σέ γιουγκοσλαυικά δηνάρια |
| | seh yoogoslavika deenareeya |

# Car travel

## ESSENTIAL INFORMATION

- Is it a self-service filling station? Look out for:
  ΣΕΛΦ-ΣΕΡΒΙΣ
- Grades of petrol:
  ΒΕΝΖΙΝΗ (petrol)          ΣΟΥΠΕΡ (premium)
  ΑΠΛΗ (standard)           ΔΙΧΡΟΝΟ (two stroke)
  ΝΤΗΖΕΛ (diesel)
- One gallon is about 4½ litres (accurate enough up to 6 gallons).
- Most filling stations in Greece (ΓΚΑΡΑΖ) do not do major repairs. The place to go to for repairs is ΣΥΝΕΡΓΕΙΟΝ.
- Holders of British driving licences do not need an international driving licence.

- The Greek Automobile and Touring Club (ELPA) offers assistance to foreign motorists free of charge.
- Dial 104 for assistance in Athens and Thessaloniki (up to a radius of 60 km) and Larissa, Patras, Herakleion, Volos, Lamia, Kalamata and Yannina (up to a radius of 25 km).

## WHAT TO SAY

[*For numbers, see p. 209*]

| | |
|---|---|
| (Nine) litres of . . . | (Ἐννέα) νίτρα . . . |
| | (enneh-a) leetra . . . |
| (150) drachmas of . . . | (ἑκατό πενῆντα) δραχμές . . . |
| | (ek-at-o pen-eenda) thra-hmess . . . |
| standard | ἁπλή |
| | aplee |
| premium | σοῦπερ |
| | soopehr |
| diesel | ντῆζελ |
| | diesel |
| Fill it up, please | Νά τό γεμίσετε, παρακαλω8 |
| | na toh gemeesset-eh parakalo |
| Will you check . . . | Μπορεῖτε νά κοιτάξετε . . . |
| | boreeteh na keetak-set-eh . . . |
| the oil? | τό λάδι; |
| | toh la-thee |
| the battery? | τήν μπαταρία; |
| | teen bataree-a |
| the radiator? | τό ψυγεῖο; |
| | toh pseeg-ee-o |
| the tyres? | τά λάστιχα; |
| | ta lastee-ha |
| I've run out of petrol | Ἔμεινα ἀπό πετρέλαιο |
| | em-eena apo petrel-eh-o |
| Can you help me, please? | Μπορεῖτε νά μέ βοηθήσετε, σᾶς παρακαλῶ; |
| | boreeteh na meh vo-eeth-eeset-eh sas parakalo |
| Do you do repairs? | Κάνετε ἐπισκευές; |
| | kan-et-eh ep-eeskev-ess |
| I have a puncture | Τρύπησε τό λάστιχο |
| | treepees-eh toh lastee-ho |

| | |
|---|---|
| I have a broken windscreen | Έσπασε τό μπροστινό τζάμι |
| | espas-eh toh brosteeno tzam-ee |
| I think the problem is here . . . [point] | Νομίζω ὅτι τό πρόβλημα εἶναι ἐδῶ . . . |
| | nomeezo otee toh prov-leema eeneh eth-o |

## LIKELY REACTIONS

| | |
|---|---|
| I don't do repairs | Δέν κάνω ἐπισκευές |
| | then kan-o ep-eeskev-ess |
| Where's your car? | Ποῦ εἰναι τό αὐτοκίνητο σας; |
| | poo eeneh toh aftokeen-eeto sas |
| What make is it? | Τί μάρκα εἶναι; |
| | tee marka eeneh |
| Come back tomorrow/on Monday | Ἐλᾶτε αὔριο/τή Δευτέρα |
| | ellat-eh anrio/tee thef-tehra |

[*For days of the week, see p. 212*]

# Public transport

## ESSENTIAL INFORMATION

- Finding the way to the bus station, a bus stop, a trolley stop, the railway station and a taxi rank, see p. 169.
- If you flag down a taxi, there's a flat rate of 15 drs.
- Remember that queuing for buses is not strictly followed.
- The railway network in Greece is not very extensive. The national railways connect Athens with the most important regions of the country. Buses are more frequent (much faster than trains).
- The underground in Athens is called Ὁ ΗΛΕΚΤΡΙΚΟΣ, and joins Piraeus with Athens and Kifissia.
- There are frequent ferry-boats to most islands from Piraeus.
- In Athens there are electric trolleys in addition to the bus services. For urban buses and trolleys there is a flat rate which you pay to the conductor. Some of these have no conductors, so no

change is available and you drop the fare into a box. They have a large sign on the front: ΧΩΡΙΣ ΕΙΣΠΡΑΚΤΟΡΑ (without conductor) and you get in and pay at the front and get out at the back.

● Key words on signs:
ΓΡΑΦΕΙΟΝ ΕΙΣΤΗΡΙΩΝ (ticket office)
ΕΙΣΟΔΟΣ (entrance)
ΑΠΑΓΟΡΕΥΕΤΑΙ Η ΕΙΣΟΔΟΣ (no entrance)
ΑΝΟΔΟΣ (entrance, for buses)
ΚΑΘΟΔΟΣ (exit, for buses)
ΠΡΟΣ ΤΑΣ ΑΠΟΒΑΘΡΑΣ (to the platforms)
ΓΡΑΦΕΙΟΝ ΠΛΗΡΟΦΟΡΙΩΝ (information office)
ΟΣΕ (initials for Greek railways)
ΚΤΕΛ (initials for Greek coach services)
ΕΞΟΔΟΣ (exit)
ΘΥΡΙΔΕΣ ΑΠΟΣΚΕΥΩΝ (left luggage)
ΣΤΑΣΙΣ stop: in Athens the stops are yellow for trolleys and blue for buses. The sign shows a bus stop.
ΔΡΟΜΟΛΟΓΙΟΝ (timetable)

## WHAT TO SAY

| | |
|---|---|
| Where does the ferry-boat for (Piraeus) leave from? | ᾿Από ποῦ φεύγει τό φέρυ μπότ γιά (τόν Πειραιᾶ); |
| | apo poo fev-ghee toh feh-ree-bot ya (ton peereya) |
| Is this the ferry-boat for (Piraeus)? | Εἶναι αὐτό τό φέρυ μπότ γιά (τόν Πειραιᾶ); |
| | eeneh afto toh feh-ree-bot ya (ton peereya) |
| Where does the bus for (Delphi) leave from? | ᾿Από ποῦ φεύγει τό λεωφορεῖο γιά (τούς Δελφούς); |
| | apo poo fev-ghee toh leh-oforee-o ya (tooss thelfooss) |
| Is this the bus for (Delphi)? | Αὐτό εἶναι τό λεωφορεῖο γιά (τούς Δελφούς); |
| | afto eeneh toh leh-oforee-o ya (tooss thelfooss) |
| Do I have to change? | Πρέπει νά ἀλλάξω; |
| | prep-ee na allak-so |

| | |
|---|---|
| Can you put me off at the right stop, please? | Μπορεῖτε νά μέ κατεβάσετε στή σωστή στάση, παρακαλῶ;<br>boreeteh na meh kat-ev-asset-eh stee sostee stassee parakalo |
| Where can I get a taxi? | Ποῦ μπορῶ νά βρῶ ἕνα ταξί;<br>poo boro na vro enna taksee |
| Can I book a seat? | Μπορῶ νά κλείσω μιά θέση;<br>boro na kleeso mee-a thessee |
| A single | Ἕνα ἁπλό εἰσιτήριο<br>enna aplo eess-eeteerio |
| A return | Ἕνα εἰσιτήριο μετ'ἐπιστροφῆς<br>enna eess-eeteerio met-ep-eestr-of-eess |
| First class | Πρώτη θέση<br>prot-ee thess-ee |
| Second class | Δεύτερη θέση<br>thef-tehree thessee |
| One adult | Ἕνας ἐνήλικας<br>ennas en-eeleek-ass |
| Two adults | Δύο ἐνήλικες<br>thee-o en-eeleek-ess |
| and one child | καί ενα παιδί<br>keh enna peth-ee |
| and two children | καί δύο παιδιά<br>keh thee-o peth-ya |
| How much is it? | Πόσο κάνει;<br>posso kan-ee |

# Reference

## NUMBERS

| | | |
|---|---|---|
| 0 | μηδέν | meethen |
| 1 | ἕνας, μία, ἕνα | ennas mee-a enna |
| 2 | δύο | thee-o |
| 3 | τρία | tree-a |
| 4 | τέσσερα | tessera |
| 5 | πέντε | pendeh |

| | | |
|---|---|---|
| 6 | ἕξη | eksee |
| 7 | ἑπτά | epta |
| 8 | ὀκιὼ | okto |
| 9 | ἐννέα | enneh-a |
| 10 | δέκα | theh-ka |
| 11 | ἕντεκα | endek-a |
| 12 | δώδεκα | thothek-a |
| 13 | δεκατρία | thek-atree-a |
| 14 | δεκατέσσεπα | thek-atesser-a |
| 15 | δεκαπέντε | thek-apendeh |
| 16 | δεκαέξη | theh-ka-eksee |
| 17 | δεκαεπτά | theh-ka-epta |
| 18 | δεκαοκτώ | theh-ka-okto |
| 19 | δεκαεννέα | theh-ka-enneh-a |
| 20 | εἴκοσι | eekossee |
| 21 | εἴκοσι ἕνα | eekossee enna |
| 22 | εἴκοσι δύο | eekossee thee-o |
| 23 | εἴκοσι τρία | eekossee tree-a |
| 24 | εἴκοσι τέσσερα | eekossee tessera |
| 25 | εἴκοσι πέντε | eekossee pendeh |
| 26 | εἴκοσι ἕξη | eekosse eksee |
| 27 | εἴκοσι ἑπτά | eekossee epta |
| 28 | εἴκοσι ὀκτώ | eekossee okto |
| 29 | εἴκοσι ἐννέα | eekossee enneh-a |
| 30 | τριάντα | tree-anda |
| 35 | τριάντα πέντε | tree-anda pendeh |
| 38 | τριάντα ὀκτώ | tree-anda okto |
| 40 | σαράντα | saranda |
| 41 | σαράντα ἕνα | saranda enna |
| 45 | σαράντα πέντε | saranda pendeh |
| 48 | σαράντα ὀκτώ | saranda okto |
| 50 | πενῆντα | pen-eenda |
| 55 | πενῆντα πέντε | pen-eenda pendeh |
| 56 | πενῆντα εξη | pen-eenda eksee |
| 60 | ἑξῆντα | ekseenda |
| 65 | ἑξῆντα πέντε | ekseenda pendeh |
| 70 | ἑβδομῆντα | ev-thomeenda |
| 75 | ἑβδομῆντα πέντε | ev-thomeenda pendeh |
| 80 | ὀγδόντα | ogthonda |
| 85 | ὀγδόντα πέντε | ogthonda pendeh |
| 90 | ἐνενῆντα | enneh-neenda |
| 95 | ἐνενῆντα πέντε | enneh-neenda pendeh |

| 100 | ἑκατό | ek-at-o |
|---|---|---|
| 101 | ἑκατόν ἕνα | ek-at-on enna |
| 102 | ἑκατόν δύο | ek-at-on thee-o |
| 125 | ἑκατόν εἴκοσι πέντε | ek-at-on eekossee pendeh |
| 150 | ἑκατόν πενῆντα | ek-at-on pen-eenda |
| 175 | ἑκατόν ἑβδομῆντα πέντε | ek-at-on ev-thomeenda pendeh |
| 200 | διακόσια | thee-akoss-ya |
| 300 | τριακόσια | tree-akoss-ya |
| 400 | τετρακόσια | tetra-koss-ya |
| 500 | πεντακόσια | pend-akoss-ya |
| 1,000 | χίλια | heel-ya |
| 1,500 | χίλια πεντακόσια | heel-ya pend-akoss-ya |
| 2,000 | δύο χιλιάδες | thee-o heel-yathess |
| 5,000 | πέντε χιλιάδες | pendeh heel-yathess |
| 10,000 | δέκα χιλιάδες | theh-ka heel-yathess |
| 100,000 | ἑκατόν χιλιάδες | ek-at-on heel-yathess |
| 1,000,000 | ἕνα ἑκατομμύριο | enna ekatomeereeo |

## TIME

| What time is it? | Τί ὥνα εἶναι; |
|---|---|
| | tee ora eeneh |
| It's . . . | Εἶναι . . . |
| | eeneh . . . |
| one o'clock | μία |
| | mee-a |
| two o'clock | δύο |
| | thee-o |
| three o'clock | τρεῖς |
| | treess |
| noon | μεσημέρι |
| | mess-eemehree |
| midnight | μεσάνυχτα |
| | messan-ee-hta |
| a quarter past five | πέντε καί τέταρτο |
| | pendeh keh tet-arto |
| half past five | πέντε καί μισή |
| | pendeh keh meessee |
| a quarter to six | ἕξη παρά τέταρτο |
| | eksee para tet-arto |

## DAYS AND MONTHS

| | |
|---|---|
| Monday | Δευτέρα |
| | thef-tehra |
| Tuesday | Τρίτη |
| | treetee |
| Wednesday | Τετάρτη |
| | tet-artee |
| Thursday | Πέμπτη |
| | pemp-tee |
| Friday | Παρασκευή |
| | paraskev-ee |
| Saturday | Σάββατο |
| | savvato |
| Sunday | Κυριακή |
| | keeree-ak-ee |
| January | Ίανουάριος |
| | yanoo-ar-ee-oss |
| February | Φεβρουάριος |
| | fevroo-ar-ee-oss |
| March | Μάρτιος |
| | martee-oss |
| April | Ἀπρίλος |
| | apreelee-oss |
| May | Μάιος |
| | ma-ee-oss |
| June | Ἰούνιος |
| | ee-ounee-oss |
| July | Ἰούλιος |
| | ee-oulee-oss |
| August | Αύγουστος |
| | avgoost-oss |
| September | Σεπτέμβριος |
| | septem-vree-oss |
| October | Ὀκτώβριος |
| | oktovree-oss |
| November | Νοέμβριος |
| | no-em-vree-oss |
| December | Δεκέμβριος |
| | thek-em-vree-oss |

# Index

# Travellers' Italian

D. L. Ellis, C. Mariella

Pronunciation Dr J. Baldwin

*Useful addresses*

Italian State Tourist Office (ENIT)
201 Regent Street, London W1R 8AY
47 Merrion Square, Dublin 2.

# Contents

# Pronunciation hints

In Italian it is important to stress, or emphasize the syllables in *italics*, just as you would if we were to take as an English example: little Jack Horner sat in the corner. Here we have ten syllables, but only four stresses. This Italian sentence also has ten syllables but only four stresses: questa macchina è rumorosa (this car is noisy). **Divertitevi!**

# Everyday expressions

[*See also 'Shop talk', p. 231*]

| | |
|---|---|
| Hello ⎤ | **Buon giorno** |
| | boo-*on* j*o*rno |
| Good morning | **Ciao** (friends only) |
| Good day (before lunch) ⎦ | chow |
| Good afternoon (after lunch) | **Buona sera** |
| Good evening | boo-*o*na s*e*h-ra |
| Good night | **Buona notte** |
| | boo-*o*na n*o*t-teh |
| Good-bye | **A rivederci** |
| | ah reeveh-d*ai*rchee |
| Yes | **Sí** |
| | see |
| Please | **Per favore** |
| | pair fav-*o*reh |
| Yes, please | **Sí, grazie** |
| | see gr*a*tzee-eh |
| Thank you | **Grazie** |
| | gr*a*tzee-eh |
| Thank you very much | **Molte grazie** |
| | m*o*lteh gr*a*tzee-eh |
| That's right | **Esatto** |
| | ez*a*t-to |
| No | **No** |
| | noh |
| I disagree | **Non sono d'accordo** |
| | non s*o*nno dak-k*o*rdo |
| Excuse me ⎤ | **Scusi** |
| Sorry ⎦ | sc*oo*zee |
| It doesn't matter | **Non importa** |
| | non imp*o*rta |
| Where's the toilet, please? | **Dov'è il bagno, per favore?** |
| | dov-*e*h il b*a*n-yo pair fav-*o*reh |
| Do you speak English? | **Parla inglese?** |
| | p*a*rla ingl*ai*zeh |
| What's your name? | **Come si chiama?** |
| | c*o*m-eh see kee-*a*m-ah |
| My name is . . . | **Mi chiamo . . .** |
| | mee kee-*a*m-o . . . |

# Asking the way

## ESSENTIAL INFORMATION

- Keep a look-out for all these place names as you will find them on shops, maps and notices.

## WHAT TO SAY

| | |
|---|---|
| Excuse me, please | **Scusi, per favore** |
| | sc*oo*zee pair fav-*o*reh |
| **How do I get . . .** | **Per andare . . .** |
| | pair and*a*r-eh . . . |
| to Rome? | **a Roma?** |
| | ah *r*oma |
| to the Via Nomentana? | **in via Nomentana?** |
| | in vee-ah nomentan-ah |
| to the Hotel Torino? | **all'hotel Torino?** |
| | al-lot-*e*l tor*ee*no |
| to the airport? | **all'aeroporto?** |
| | al-la-airop*o*rto |
| to the beach? | **alla spiaggia?** |
| | al-la spee-*a*d-ja |
| to the bus station? | **alla stazione degli autobus?** |
| | al-la statzi*o*neh del-yee ah-*oo*tobus |
| to the market? | **al mercato?** |
| | al mairc*a*t-o |
| to the police station? | **alla stazione di polizia?** |
| | al-la statzi*o*neh dee politz*ee*-ah |
| to the port? | **al porto?** |
| | al p*o*rto |
| to the post office? | **all'ufficio postale?** |
| | al-loof-f*ee*cho post*a*l-eh |
| to the railway station? | **alla stazione ferroviaria?** |
| | al-la statzi*o*neh ferrovee-*a*r-ee-ah |
| to the sports stadium? | **allo stadio?** |
| | al-lo st*a*d-eeo |
| to the tourist information office? | **all'ufficio informazioni turistiche?** |
| | al-loof-f*ee*cho informatzi*o*nee toor*i*stikeh |

| | |
|---|---|
| **How do I get . . .** | **Per andare . . .** |
| | pair and*ar*-eh . . . |
| to the town centre? | **in centro?** |
| | in ch*en*tro |
| to the town hall? | **al Municipio?** |
| | al moonich*ee*-peeo |
| Excuse me, please | **Scusi, per favore** |
| | sc*oo*zee pair fav-*or*eh |
| **Is there . . . near by?** | **C'è . . . qui vicino?** |
| | cheh . . . quee veech*ee*no |
| a baker's | **una panetteria** |
| | oona panet-ter*ee*-ah |
| a bank | **una banca** |
| | oona b*a*nca |
| a bar | **un bar** |
| | oon bar |
| a bus stop | **una fermata d'autobus** |
| | oona fairm*at*-ah d*a-oo*tobus |
| a butcher's | **una macelleria** |
| | oona machel-ler*ee*-ah |
| a café | **un caffè** |
| | oon caf-f*eh* |
| a cake shop | **una pasticceria?** |
| | oona pasteet-chair*ee*-ah |
| a campsite | **un campeggio** |
| | oon camped-jo |
| a car park | **un parcheggio** |
| | oon parked-jo |
| a change bureau | **un ufficio del cambio** |
| | oon oof-f*ee*cho del c*a*mbeeo |
| a chemist's | **una farmacia** |
| | oona farmach*ee*-ah |
| a delicatessen | **una salumeria** |
| | oona saloomer*ee*-ah |
| a dentist's | **un dentista** |
| | oon dent*ee*sta |
| a department store | **un grande magazzino** |
| | oon gr*a*ndeh magad-dz*ee*no |
| a disco | **una discoteca** |
| | oona discot*ec*-ah |
| a doctor's surgery | **una sala medica** |
| | oona s*al*-ah m*e*d-eeca |

| | |
|---|---|
| a dry-cleaner's | **una lavanderia a secco** |
| | oona lavander*ee*-ah ah sec-co |
| a fishmonger's | **una pescheria** |
| | oona pesker*ee*-ah |
| a garage (for repairs) | **un' autoriparazioni** |
| | oon a-ootoriparatzi-*o*nee |
| a hairdresser's | **un parrucchiere** |
| | oon par-rooc-kee-*ai*reh |
| a greengrocer's | **un verduriere** |
| | oon vairdoo-ree-*ai*reh |
| a grocer's | **un alimentari** |
| | oon alimen-t*a*r-ee |
| a Health and Social Security Office | **una sezione dell'INAM** |
| | oona setzi*o*neh del-l*ee*nam |
| a hospital | **un ospedale** |
| | oon osped*a*l-eh |
| a hotel | **un hotel** |
| | oon otel |
| an ice-cream parlour | **una gelateria** |
| | oona jelat-er*ee*-ah |
| a laundry | **una lavanderia** |
| | oona lavander*ee*-ah |
| a newsagent's | **un'edicola** |
| | ooned*ee*cola |
| a night club | **un night** |
| | oon night |
| a petrol station | **un distributore** |
| | oon distriboot*o*reh |
| a post box | **una buca per lettere** |
| | oona booca pair let-tereh |
| a public toilet | **un gabinetto pubblico** |
| | oon gabin*e*t-to p*oo*b-blico |
| a restaurant | **un ristorante** |
| | oon ristor*a*nteh |
| a supermarket | **un supermercato** |
| | oon sooper-mairc*a*t-o |
| a taxi stand | **una stazione taxi** |
| | oona statzi*o*neh t*a*xi |
| a telephone | **un telefono** |
| | oon tel*e*phono |
| a tobacconist's | **un tabaccaio** |
| | oon tabac-c*a*h-yo |

| | |
|---|---|
| **Is there . . . near by?** | **C'è . . . qui vicino?** |
| | cheh . . . quee veech*ee*no |
| a travel agent's | **un'agenzia di viaggi** |
| | oonajentz*ee*-ah dee vee-*a*d-jee |
| a youth hostel | **un ostello per la gioventú** |
| | oon ost*el*-lo pair la jovent*oo* |

## DIRECTIONS

| | |
|---|---|
| Left | **Sinistra** |
| | sin*ee*stra |
| Right | **Destra** |
| | d*e*stra |
| Straight on | **Sempre diritto** |
| | sempreh deer*ee*t-to |
| There | **Là** |
| | la |
| First left/right | **La prima a sinistra/destra** |
| | la pr*ee*ma ah sin*ee*stra/d*e*stra |
| Second left/right | **La seconda a sinistra/destra** |
| | la sec*o*nda ah sin*ee*stra/d*e*stra |

# Accommodation

## ESSENTIAL INFORMATION
### Hotel

- If you want hotel-type accommodation, all the following words in capital letters are worth looking for on name boards:
  HOTEL
  ALBERGO ⎤ (hotel)
  MOTEL (two main chains are run by **ACI** and **Agip**)
  PENSIONE (boarding house)
- Hotels are divided into five classes (from luxury to tourist class) and **pensioni** into three.
- Lists of hotels and **pensioni** can be obtained from local tourist offices or ENIT in London.
- The cost is displayed in the room itself, so you can check it when having a look round before agreeing to stay.

- The displayed cost is for the room itself, per night and not per person. Breakfast is extra and therefore optional.
- Service and VAT are always included in the cost of the room, so tipping is voluntary.
- Not all hotels provide meals, apart from breakfast. A **pensione** always provides meals. Breakfast is continental-style: coffee or tea, with rolls and jam.
- An identity document is requested when registering at a hotel and will normally be kept overnight. Passports or driving licences are accepted.

## WHAT TO SAY

| | |
|---|---|
| I have a booking | **Ho una prenotazione** |
| | o oona prenotatzi-oneh |
| Have you any vacancies, please? | **Avete delle camere libere, per favore?** |
| | avet-eh del-leh camereh leebereh pair fav-oreh |
| Can I book a room? | **Potrei prenotare una camera?** |
| | potray prenot-ar-eh oona camera |
| It's for . . . | **È per . . .** |
| | eh pair . . . |
| one adult/one person | **un adulto/una persona** |
| | oon adoolto/oona pairsona |
| two adults/two people | **due adulti/due persone** |
| | dooeh adooltee/dooeh pairsoneh |
| and one child | **e un bambino** |
| | eh oon bambeeno |
| and two children | **e due bambini** |
| | eh dooeh bambeenee |
| It's for . . . | **È per . . .** |
| | eh pair . . . |
| one night | **una notte** |
| | oona not-teh |
| two nights | **due notti** |
| | dooeh not-tee |
| one week | **una settimana** |
| | oona set-timan-ah |
| two weeks | **due settimane** |
| | dooeh set-timan-eh |

| | |
|---|---|
| I would like . . . | **Vorrei . . .** |
| | vor*ray* . . . |
| a (quiet) room | **una camera (tranquilla)** |
| | *oo*na *c*amera (tran*quee*l-la) |
| two rooms | **due camere** |
| | *doo*eh *c*amereh |
| with a single bed | **singola/e\*** |
| | *sin*gola/eh |
| with two single beds | **a due letti** |
| | ah *doo*eh *l*et-tee |
| with a double bed | **con un letto matrimoniale** |
| | con oon *l*et-to matrimon-y*al*-eh |
| with a toilet | **con bagno** |
| with a bathroom | con b*a*n-yo |
| with a shower | **con doccia** |
| | con *d*ot-cha |
| with a cot | **con una culla** |
| | con *oo*na *c*ool-la |
| with a balcony | **con terrazza** |
| | con terr*a*t-tza |
| I would like . . . | **Vorrei . . .** |
| | vor*ray* |
| full board | **pensione completa** |
| | pen-see*o*neh complet-ah |
| half board | **mezza pensione** |
| | med-dza pen-see*o*neh |
| bed and breakfast | **solo colazione** |
| [see essential information] | solo colatz*io*neh |
| Do you serve meals? | **Servite i pasti?** |
| | sair*vee*teh ee *p*astee |
| Can I look at the room? | **Potrei vedere la stanza?** |
| | pot*ray* ved-*ai*reh la st*a*ntza |
| OK, I'll take it | **Va bene, la prendo** |
| | va ben-eh la pr*e*ndo |
| No thanks, I won't take it | **No grazie, non la prendo** |
| | noh gr*a*tzee-eh non la pr*e*ndo |
| The bill, please | **Il conto, per favore** |
| | il *c*onto pair fav-*o*reh |
| Is service included? | **Il servizio è compreso?** |
| | il sair*v*itzio eh compr*ai*zo |

\*Use 'a' for one single bed, 'e' for two single beds.

| | |
|---|---|
| I think this is wrong | **Penso che questo sia sbagliato** |
| | penso keh questo see-ah sbal-*yat*-o |
| May I have a receipt? | **Potrei avere una ricevuta?** |
| | pot*ray* av*ai*reh oona reechev*oo*ta |

## Camping

- Look for the words: **CAMPING** or **CAMPEGGIO**.
- Be prepared to have to pay:
  per person
  for the car (if applicable)
  for the tent or caravan plot
  for electricity
  for hot showers
- You must provide proof of identity, such as your passport.
- You can obtain lists of campsites from local tourist offices and from ENIT in London.
- To book plots in advance (particularly recommended in July and August) write to the **Centro Internazionale Prenotazioni Campeggio, Casella Postale 649, 1-50100 Firenze, Italy**.
- Some campsites offer discounts to campers with the International Camping Carnet.
- Camping off-site is allowed except in state forests and national parks. It is always best to ask permission from the landowner.

## Youth hostels

- Look for the words:
  **OSTELLO PER LA GIOVENTÙ**
- You will be asked for a YHA card and your passport on arrival.
- Food and cooking facilities vary from hostel to hostel and you may have to help with domestic chores.
- You will have to hire sheets on arrival.
- In the high season it is advisable to book beds in advance, and your stay will be limited to a maximum of three consecutive nights per hostel.
- Apply to ENIT or local tourist offices in Italy for lists of youth hostels and details of regulations for hostellers.

**WHAT TO SAY**

| | |
|---|---|
| Have you any vacancies? | **Avete dei posti liberi?** |
| | avet-eh day postee leeberee |
| **How much is it . . .** | **Quant'è . . .** |
| | quanteh . . . |
| for the tent? | **per la tenda?** |
| | pair la tenda |
| for the caravan? | **per la roulotte?** |
| | pair la roolot |
| for the car? | **per la macchina?** |
| | pair la mac-keena |
| for the electricity? | **per l'elettricità?** |
| | pair lelet-treechita |
| per person? | **per persona?** |
| | pair pairsona |
| per day/night? | **per giorno/notte?** |
| | pair jorno/not-teh |
| May I look round? | **Potrei dare uno sguardo?** |
| | potray dar-eh oono zgoo-ardo |
| Do you provide anything . . . | **È possibile . . .** |
| | eh posseebeeleh . . . |
| to eat? | **mangiare qui?** |
| | manjar-eh quee |
| to drink? | **bere qui?** |
| | baireh quee |
| **Do you have . . .** | **Avete . . .** |
| | avet-eh . . . |
| a bar? | **un bar?** |
| | oon bar |
| hot showers? | **docce con acqua calda?** |
| | dot-cheh con acqua calda |
| a kitchen? | **una cucina?** |
| | oona coocheena |
| a laundry? | **una lavanderia?** |
| | oona lavanderee-ah |
| a restaurant? | **un ristorante?** |
| | oon ristoranteh |
| a shop? | **un negozio?** |
| | oon negotzi-o |
| a swimming pool? | **una piscina?** |
| | oona pisheena |

[*For food shopping see p. 234, and for eating and drinking out see p. 244.*]

**Problems**

| | |
|---|---|
| The toilet | **Il gabinetto**<br>il gabinet-to |
| The shower | **La doccia**<br>la dot-cha |
| The tap | **Il rubinetto**<br>il roobinet-to |
| The razor point | **La spina per il rasoio**<br>la speena pair il razoyo |
| The light | **La luce**<br>la loocheh |
| . . . is not working | **. . . non funziona**<br>. . . non foontzi-ona |
| My camping gas has run out | **La bombola del gas è finita**<br>la bombola del gaz eh feeneeta |

**LIKELY REACTIONS**

| | |
|---|---|
| Have you an identity document? | **Ha un documento di riconoscimento?**<br>ah oon docoomento dee riconosheemento |
| Your membership card, please | **La sua tessera, per favore**<br>la soo-ah tes-saira pair fav-oreh |
| What's your name? [*see p. 218*] | **Come si chiama?**<br>com-eh see kee-am-ah |
| Sorry, we're full | **Spiacente, siamo al completo**<br>spee-achenteh see-am-o al complet-o |
| How many people is it for? | **Per quante persone?**<br>pair quanteh pairsoneh |
| How many nights is it for? | **Per quante notti?**<br>pair quanteh not-tee |
| It's (8,000) lira . . . | **Fa (ottomila) lire . . .**<br>fa (ot-tomeela) leereh . . . |
| per day/per night | **al giorno/per notte**<br>al jorno/pair not-teh |

| | |
|---|---|
| I haven't any rooms left | **Non ci sono piú camere** |
| | non chee sonno pew camereh |
| Do you want to have a look? | **Vuole vederla?** |
| | voo-oleh ved-airia |

# General shopping

## The chemist's

### ESSENTIAL INFORMATION

- Look for the word **FARMACIA** (chemist's).
- Medicines (drugs) are only available at a chemist's.
- Some non-drugs can be bought at a supermarket or department store.
- Try the chemist *before* going to a doctor: they are usually qualified to treat minor injuries.
- Chemists take it in turns to stay open all night and on Sundays. A notice on the door headed **FARMACIE DI TURNO** or **SERVIZIO NOTTURNO** gives details of opening times.
- Some toiletries can also be bought at a **PROFUMERIA**, but they will be more expensive.

### WHAT TO SAY

| | |
|---|---|
| I'd like . . . | **Vorrei . . .** |
| | vorray . . . |
| some Alka Seltzer | **dell'Alka Seltzer** |
| | del-lalka seltzer |
| some antiseptic | **dell'antisettico** |
| | del-lantiset-tico |
| some aspirin | **dell'aspirina** |
| | del-laspireena |
| some baby food | **cibi per bambini** |
| | cheebee pair bambeenee |
| some contraceptives | **contraccettivi** |
| | contrat-chet-teevee |

| | |
|---|---|
| some cotton wool | **del cotone**<br>del cotoneh |
| some disposable nappies | **pannolini per bambini**<br>pan-noleenee pair bambeenee |
| some eye drops | **del collirio**<br>del col-lee-reeo |
| some inhalant | **dell'inalante**<br>del-linalanteh |
| some insect repellent | **della crema anti-insetti**<br>del-la crem-ah anti-inset-tee |
| some paper tissues | **fazzoletti di carta**<br>fat-tzolet-tee dee carta |
| some sanitary towels | **assorbenti igienici**<br>as-sorbenti eejen-eechi |
| some sticking plaster | **del cerotto**<br>del chairot-to |
| some suntan lotion/oil | **crema/olio solare**<br>crem-ah/olyo solar-eh |
| some Tampax | **Tampax**<br>tampax |
| some throat pastilles | **delle pastiglie per la gola**<br>del-leh pasteel-yeh pair la gola |
| some toilet paper | **carta igienica**<br>carta eejen-eeca |
| **I'd like something for . . .** | **Vorrei qualcosa per . . .**<br>vorray qualcoza pair . . . |
| bites | **morsicature**<br>mor-seecatooreh |
| burns | **bruciature**<br>broo-chatooreh |
| a cold | **il raffreddore**<br>il raf-fred-doreh |
| constipation | **stitichezza**<br>stitiket-tza |
| a cough | **la tosse**<br>la tos-seh |
| diarrhoea | **diarrea**<br>dee-arreh-ah |
| ear-ache | **mal d'orecchie**<br>mal dorrek-kee-eh |
| flu | **influenza**<br>influentza |

| | |
|---|---|
| **I'd like something for . . .** | **Vorrei qualcosa per . . .** |
| | vorray qualcoza pair . . . |
| scalds | **scottature** |
| | scot-tatooreh |
| sore gums | **mal di gengive** |
| | mal dee jenjeeveh |
| stings | **punture** |
| | poontooreh |
| sunburn | **scottature da sole** |
| | scot-tatooreh da sol-eh |
| car (sea/air) sickness | **mal d'auto (di mare/d'aereo)** |
| | mal da-ooto (dee mareh/da-eh- |
| | reho) |

[*For other essential expressions see 'Shop talk' opposite.*]

# Holiday items

**ESSENTIAL INFORMATION**

- Places to shop at and signs to look for:

| | |
|---|---|
| **LIBRERIA-CARTOLERIA** | (stationery) |
| **TABACCHERIA** | (tobacconist's) |
| **ARTICOLI DA REGALO** | (presents) |
| **FOTO-OTTICO** | (photographer-optician) |
| **ARTICOLI FOTOGRAFICI** | (photographical items) |

- and the main department stores:
  **UPIM, STANDA, RINASCENTE**

**WHAT TO SAY**

| | |
|---|---|
| **I'd like . . .** | **Vorrei . . .** |
| | vorray . . . |
| a bag | **una borsa** |
| | oona borsa |
| a beach ball | **un pallone da spiaggia** |
| | oon pal-loneh da speead-ja |
| a bucket | **un secchiello** |
| | oon sec-kee-ello |

| an English newspaper | un giornale inglese |
| | oon jornal-eh inglaizeh |
| some envelopes | delle buste |
| | del-leh boosteh |
| some postcards | delle cartoline |
| | del-leh cartoleeneh |
| a spade | una paletta |
| | oona palet-ta |
| a straw hat | un cappello di paglia |
| | oon cap-pel-lo dee pal-ya |
| some sunglasses | degli occhiali da sole |
| | del-yee oc-kee-al-ee da soleh |
| some writing paper | della carta da lettere |
| | del-la carta da let-tereh |
| a colour film [*show the* *camera*] | una pellicola a colori |
| | oona pel-leecola ah coloree |
| a black and white film | una pellicola in bianco e nero |
| | oona pel-leecola in bee-anco eh nairo |

# Shop talk

## ESSENTIAL INFORMATION

- Know how to say the important weights and measures:

| 50 grams | cinquanta grammi |
| | chinquanta gram-mee |
| 100 grams | cento grammi |
| | chento gram-mee |
| 200 grams | duecento grammi |
| | dooeh-chento gram-mee |
| ½ kilo | mezzo chilo |
| | med-dzo keelo |
| 1 kilo | un chilo |
| | oon keelo |
| 2 kilos | due chili |
| | dooeh keelee |
| ½ litre | mezzo litro |
| | med-dzo leetro |

| | |
|---|---|
| 1 litre | **un litro** |
| | oon leetro |
| 2 litres | **due litri** |
| | dooeh leetree |

[*For numbers see p. 264*]

- You may see the words **etto** (100 grams) or **all'etto** (per 100 grams) on price tickets. This is a colloquial expression for 100 grams.

## CUSTOMER

| | |
|---|---|
| I'm just looking | **Guardo soltanto** |
| | gwardo soltanto |
| How much is this/that? | **Quanto costa questo/quello?** |
| | quanto costa questo/qwel-lo |
| What's that? | **Che cos' è quello?** |
| | keh coz-eh quel-lo |
| What are those? | **Che cosa sono quelli?** |
| | keh coza sonno quel-lee |
| Is there a discount? | **C'è uno sconto?** |
| | cheh oono sconto |
| I'd like that, please | **Vorrei quello, per favore** |
| | vorray quel-lo pair fav-oreh |
| Not that | **Non quello** |
| | non quel-lo |
| Like that | **Come quello** |
| | com-eh quel-lo |
| That's enough, thank you | **Basta così grazie** |
| | basta cozee gratzee-eh |
| More, please | **Ancora, per favore** |
| | ancora pair fav-oreh |
| Less than that | **Meno di così** |
| | men-o dee cozee |
| That's fine ⎤<br>OK ⎦ | **Va bene** |
| | va ben-eh |
| I won't take it, thank you | **Non lo prendo, grazie** |
| | non lo prendo gratzee-eh |
| It's not right | **Non va bene** |
| | non va ben-eh |
| **Have you got something . . .** | **Avete qualcosa . . .** |
| | aveteh qualcoza . . . |

| | |
|---|---|
| better? | **di meglio?** |
| | dee mel-yo |
| cheaper? | **di meno caro?** |
| | dee men-o car-o |
| different? | **di diverso?** |
| | dee deevairso |
| larger?/smaller? | **di piú grande?/piccolo** |
| | dee pew grandeh/pee-colo |
| Can I have a bag, please? | **Posso avere una borsa, per favore?** |
| | pos-so avaireh oona borsa pair fav-oreh |
| Can I have a receipt? | **Posso avere la ricevuta?** |
| | pos-so avaireh la reechevoota |
| **Do you take . . .** | **Accettate . . .** |
| | at-chet-tat-eh . . . |
| English/American money? | **soldi inglesi/americani?** |
| | soldee inglaizee/american-ee |
| travellers' cheques? | **travellers' cheques?** |
| | travellairs sheck |
| credit cards? | **carte di credito?** |
| | carteh dee cred-eeto |

## SHOP ASSISTANT

| | |
|---|---|
| Can I help you? | **È da servire?** |
| | eh da sairveereh |
| What would you like? | **Che cosa desidera?** |
| | keh coza dezeedera |
| Will that be all? | **È tutto?** |
| | eh toot-to |
| Is that all? | **Basta cosí?** |
| | basta cozee |
| Anything else? | **Nient'altro?** |
| | nee-entaltro |
| Would you like it wrapped? | **Glielo incarto?** |
| | lee-el-o incarto |
| Sorry, none left | **Mi dispiace non ne ho piú** |
| | mee dispi-ah-cheh non neh o pew |
| I haven't got any | **Non ne abbiamo** |
| | non neh ab-bee-am-o |
| I haven't got any more | **Non ne abbiamo piú** |
| | non neh ab-bee-am-o pew |

| | |
|---|---|
| How many do you want? | **Quanti ne desidera?** |
| | quantee neh dezeedera |
| How much do you want? | **Quanto ne vuole?** |
| | quanto neh vwoleh |
| Is that enough? | **È abbastanza?** |
| | eh ab-bastantza |

# Shopping for food

## Bread

### ESSENTIAL INFORMATION

- Key words to look for:
  **PANETTERIA** (baker's)
  **PANIFICIO** (baker's bread usually baked on premises)
  **PANETTIERE** (baker)
  **PANE** (bread)
- Opening times vary slightly from place to place but are generally 9–1 and 3.30–8. Most bakers open earlier than other shops and are closed one day a week – the day varies from town to town.
- Although large and small loaves can be bought, rolls are very popular and it is important to note that bread is usually bought by *weight*.
- Bakers often stock other groceries, particularly milk. There is no milk delivery service and the dairy (**LATTERIA**) is fast disappearing.

### WHAT TO SAY

| | |
|---|---|
| A loaf (like that) | **Una pagnotta (così)** |
| | oona pan-yot-ta (cozee) |
| A large one | **Una grande** |
| | oona grandeh |
| A small one | **Una piccola** |
| | oona peec-cola |

| | |
|---|---|
| A bread roll | **Un panino** |
| | oon pan*ee*no |
| 250 grams of . . . | **Duecentocinquanta grammi di . . .** |
| | dooeh-c*h*ento-chinqu*a*nta gram-mee dee . . . |
| bread | **pane** |
| | p*a*n-eh |
| white bread | **pane bianco** |
| | p*a*n-eh bee-*a*nco |
| wholemeal bread | **pane integrale** |
| | p*a*n-eh integr*a*l-eh |
| bread rolls | **panini** |
| | pan*ee*nee |
| crispy bread sticks | **grissini** |
| | gris-s*ee*nee |

[*For other essential expressions see 'Shop talk', p. 231.*]

# Cakes and ice-creams

## ESSENTIAL INFORMATION

- Key words to look for:

| | |
|---|---|
| PASTICCERIA | (cake shop) |
| PASTICCIERE | (pastry maker) |
| PASTE/DOLCI | (cakes, pastries, sweets) |
| GELATI | (ice-creams) |
| GELATERIA ⎤ | (ice-cream parlour) |
| CREMERIA ⎦ | |

- **BAR-PASTICCERIA**: a place to buy cakes and have a drink. Italians often go to a bar for a snack mid-morning as they eat very little for breakfast.
- Most bars only have a few tables and charge more for waiter service. See p. 244, 'Ordering a drink and a snack'.

## WHAT TO SAY

The type of cakes in the shops varies from region to region, but it is usual to find a variety of biscuits and small cream-filled pastries called **paste fresche**. These are bought by weight and it is best to point to the selection you prefer.

| | |
|---|---|
| **200 grams of . . .** | **Duecento grammi di . . .** |
| | dooeh-chento gram-mee dee . . . |
| cream pastries | **paste fresche** |
| | pasteh freskeh |
| biscuits | **biscotti** |
| | biscot-tee |
| A selection, please | **Misto, per favore** |
| | meesto pair fav-oreh |

You may want to buy larger pastries and cakes individually:

| | |
|---|---|
| A cake (like that), please | **Una torta (così), per favore** |
| | oona tor-ta cozee pair fav-oreh |
| An (apple) tart | **Una crostata (di mela)** |
| | oona crostat-a dee mel-a |
| A doughnut | **Un bombolone** |
| | oon bomboloneh |
| A brioche | **Una brioche** |
| | oona bree-osh |
| A . . . ice, please | **Per favore, un gelato . . .** |
| | pair fav-oreh oon jelat-o . . . |
| chocolate | **al cioccolato** |
| | al choc-colat-o |
| lemon | **al limone** |
| | al leemoneh |
| nougat | **al torroncino** |
| | al torroncheeno |
| peach | **alla pesca** |
| | al-la pesca |
| pistachio | **al pistacchio** |
| | al peestac-keeo |
| strawberry | **alla fragola** |
| | al-la fragola |
| vanilla | **alla crema** |
| | al-la crem-ah |
| (1,000) lira's worth | **Da (mille) lire** |
| | da (meeleh) leereh |
| A single cone [*specify flavour, as above*] | **Un cono** |
| | oon cono |

# Picnic food

## ESSENTIAL INFORMATION

- Key words to look for:
  SALUMERIA
  SALUMI ⎫
  GASTRONOMIA ⎭ (delicatessen)
- In these shops you can buy a wide variety of food such as ham,
  salami, cheese, olives, appetizers, sausages, and freshly made
  take-away dishes. Specialities differ from region to region.

## WHAT TO SAY

| Two slices of . . . | Due fette di . . . |
|---|---|
| | dooeh fet-teh dee . . . |
| roast beef | arrosto |
| | arrosto |
| roast pork | arrosto di maiale |
| | arrosto dee mah-yal-eh |
| tongue | lingua |
| | lin-gwa |
| veal with mayonnaise | vitello tonnato |
| | veetel-lo ton-nat-o |
| bacon | pancetta |
| | panchet-ta |
| salami (raw/cooked) | salame (crudo/cotto) |
| | salam-eh (croodo/cot-to) |
| ham (raw/cooked) | prosciutto (crudo/cotto) |
| | proshoot-to (croodo/cot-to) |
| meat loaf | polpettone arrosto |
| | polpet-toneh arrosto |

You might also like to try some of these:

| | |
|---|---|
| **olive verdi** | green olives |
| oleeveh vairdee | |
| **olive nere** | black olives |
| oleeveh naireh | |
| **olive nere al forno** | baked black olives |
| oleeveh naireh al forno | |

| | |
|---|---|
| **olive verdi ripiene** | stuffed green olives |
| ol*ee*veh v*air*dee rip-yen-eh | |
| **funghetti sott'olio** | mushrooms preserved in oil |
| foongh*et*-tee sot-t*ol*-yo | |
| **peperoni sott'olio** | peppers preserved in oil |
| peper*o*nee sot-t*ol*-yo | |
| **peperoni arrosto** | roasted peppers |
| peper*o*nee arr*o*sto | |
| **peperoni ripieni** | stuffed peppers |
| peper*o*nee rip-yen-ee | |
| **pomodori ripieni** | stuffed tomatoes |
| pomod*o*ree rip-yen-ee | |
| **cipolle ripiene** | stuffed onions |
| chip*ol*-leh rip-yen-eh | |
| **melanzane in parmigiana** | aubergines cooked in tomato sauce |
| melandz*a*n-eh in parmij*a*n-ah | and parmesan cheese |
| **zucchini in carpione** | courgettes cooked in oil and |
| zooc-k*ee*nee in carp-y*o*neh | vinegar, sage and garlic |
| **zucchini ripieni** | stuffed courgettes |
| zuc-k*ee*nee rip-yen-ee | |
| **patatine fritte** | crisps, freshly made daily |
| patat*ee*neh fr*ee*t-teh | |
| **lasagne al forno** | wide, flat noodles baked in a sauce |
| laz*a*n-yeh al f*o*rno | of meat and bechamel |
| **gnocchi alla romana** | small, flat semolina 'dumplings' |
| n-y*oc*-kee al-la rom*a*n-ah | with butter and parmesan cheese |
| **cannelloni ripieni** | large tubular pasta stuffed with |
| can-nel-l*o*nee rip-yen-ee | meat, or spinach and cheese |
| **gnocchi alla fontina** | potato 'dumplings' with melted |
| n-y*oc*-kee al-la font*ee*na | fontina cheese |
| **torta di verdura** | vegetable pie |
| t*o*rta dee vaird*oo*-ra | |
| **torta pasqualina** | spinach, eggs and herbs in a puff |
| t*o*rta pasqwal*ee*na | pastry pie |
| **parmigiano** | parmesan, a hard, strong cheese |
| parmij*a*n-o | used in cooking, usually grated |
| **robiola** | a mild fresh white cheese made |
| rob-y*o*la | from ewe's milk |
| **pecorino** | a strong hard cheese, eaten fresh |
| pecor*ee*no | or grated when mature |
| **ricotta** | a soft white, very bland curd |
| ric*o*t-ta | cheese made from ewe's milk |

| | |
|---|---|
| **fontina** | a rich Alpine cheese usually |
| font*eena* | melted in cooking |
| **provolone** | a hard yellow cow's milk cheese |
| provolon*eh* | displayed hanging up |
| **gorgonzola** | a blue-veined cheese with a rich |
| gorgon-tz*o*la | soft texture |
| **mozzarella** | a white flavourless curd cheese, |
| mot-tzar-*e*l-la | should be eaten very fresh |

# Fruit and vegetables

## ESSENTIAL INFORMATION

- Key words to look for:

  | | |
  |---|---|
  | FRUTTA | (fruit) |
  | VERDURA | (vegetables) |
  | PRIMIZIE | (an indication of freshness) |
  | ALIMENTARI | (grocer's and greengrocer's) |
  | MERCATO | (market) |

- It is customary for you to choose your own fruit and vegetables at the market (and in some shops) and for the stallholder to weigh them and price them. You must take your own shopping bag: paper and plastic bags are not normally provided.

## WHAT TO SAY

| 1 kilo of . . . | **Un chilo di . . .** |
|---|---|
| | oon k*ee*lo dee . . . |
| apples | **mele** |
| | m*el*-eh |
| bananas | **banane** |
| | ban*an*-eh |
| cherries | **ciliegie** |
| | chil-y*eh*-jeh |
| grapes (white/black) | **uva (bianca/nera)** |
| | *oo*va (bee-*a*nca/n*ai*ra) |

| | |
|---|---|
| **1 kilo of . . .** | **Un chilo di . . .** |
| | oon k*ee*lo dee . . . |
| oranges | **arance** |
| | ar*a*ncheh |
| pears | **pere** |
| | p*ai*reh |
| peaches | **pesche** |
| | p*e*skeh |
| plums | **prugne** |
| | pr*oo*n-yeh |
| strawberries | **fragole** |
| | fr*a*goleh |
| A pineapple, please | **Un ananas, per favore** |
| | oon *a*nanas pair fav-*o*reh |
| A grapefruit | **Un pompelmo** |
| | oon pomp*e*lmo |
| A melon | **Un melone** |
| | oon mel*o*neh |
| A water melon | **Un'anguria** |
| | oon-ang*oo*-ria |
| **½ kilo of . . .** | **Mezzo chilo di . . .** |
| | m*e*d-dzo k*ee*lo dee . . . |
| artichokes | **carciofi** |
| | carch*o*f-ee |
| aubergines | **melanzane** |
| | melandz*a*n-eh |
| carrots | **carote** |
| | car*o*t-eh |
| courgettes | **zucchini** |
| | tzooc-k*ee*nee |
| green beans | **fagiolini** |
| | fad-jol*ee*nee |
| leeks | **porri** |
| | p*o*rree |
| mushrooms | **funghi** |
| | f*oo*nghee |
| onions | **cipolle** |
| | chip*o*l-leh |
| peas | **piselli** |
| | peez*e*l-lee |
| peppers (green/red) | **peperoni (verdi/rossi)** |
| | peper*o*neh (v*ai*rdee/r*o*s-see) |

| potatoes | **patate** |
| | patat-eh |
| spinach | **spinaci** |
| | speenachee |
| tomatoes | **pomodori** |
| | pomodoree |
| A bunch of . . . | **Un mazzetto di . . .** |
| | oon mat-tzet-to dee . . . |
| parsley | **prezzemolo** |
| | pret-tzem-olo |
| radishes | **rapanelli** |
| | rapanel-lee |
| A head of garlic | **Una testa d'aglio** |
| | oona testa dal-yo |
| Some lettuce | **Dell'insalata** |
| | del-linsalat-ah |
| A stick of celery | **Un sedano** |
| | oon sedan-o |
| A cucumber | **Un cetriolo** |
| | oon chetree-olo |
| Like that, please | **Come quello, per favore** |
| | com-eh quel-lo pair fav-oreh |

# Meat and fish

## ESSENTIAL INFORMATION

- Key words to look for:
  | **MACELLAIO** | (butcher) |
  | **MACELLERIA** | (butcher's) |
  | **PESCHERIA** | (fishmonger's) |
  | **FRUTTI DI MARE** | (shellfish) |
  | **MERCATO DEL PESCE** | (fish market) |
- Butchers, especially in small towns and villages, often use a white sheet hung outside the shop as a sign.
- Mutton and lamb are only sold and eaten during the Easter period.
- Large supermarkets usually have a fresh fish counter.

## WHAT TO SAY

For a joint, choose the type of meat and then say how many people it is for:

| | |
|---|---|
| Some beef, please | **Del manzo, per favore**<br>del man-zo pair fav-oreh |
| Some lamb | **Dell'agnello**<br>del-lan-yel-lo |
| Some pork | **Del maiale**<br>del mah-yal-eh |
| Some veal | **Del vitello**<br>del veetel-lo |
| A joint . . . | **Un arrosto . . .**<br>oon arrosto . . . |
|   for two people | **per due persone**<br>pair dooeh pairsoneh |
|   for four people | **per quattro persone**<br>pair quat-tro pairsoneh |
|   for six people | **per sei persone**<br>pair say pairsoneh |
| Some steak, please | **Della bistecca, per favore**<br>del-la beestec-ca pair fav-oreh |
| Some liver | **Del fegato**<br>del feh-gat-o |
| Some kidneys | **Dei rognoni**<br>day ron-yonee |
| Some heart | **Del cuore**<br>del cworeh |
| Some sausages | **Delle salsiccie**<br>del-leh salseet-cheh |
| Some mince | **Della carne tritata**<br>del-la carneh treetat-ah |
| Two veal escalopes | **Due fettine di vitello**<br>dooeh fet-teeneh dee-veetel-lo |
| Three pork chops | **Tre braciole di maiale**<br>treh bracholeh dee mayal-eh |
| Four lamb chops | **Quattro costolette d'agnello**<br>quat-tro costolet-teh dan-yel-lo |
| Five beef chops | **Cinque fettine di manzo**<br>chinqueh fet-teeneh dee mandzo |

| | |
|---|---|
| A chicken | **Un pollo** |
| | oon pol-lo |
| A rabbit | **Un coniglio** |
| | oon coneel-yo |
| A tongue | **Una lingua** |
| | oona leengwa |

Purchase large fish and small shellfish by the weight:

| | |
|---|---|
| ½ kilo of . . . | **Mezzo chilo di . . .** |
| | med-dzo keelo dee . . . |
| anchovies | **acciughe** |
| | at-choogeh |
| cod | **merluzzo** |
| | merloot-tzo |
| dogfish | **palombo** |
| | palombo |
| eel | **anguilla** |
| | angweel-la |
| fresh tuna | **tonno fresco** |
| | ton-no fresco |
| mussels (two names) | **muscoli/cozze** |
| | moos-colee/cot-tzeh |
| octopus | **polipo** |
| | poleepo |
| oysters | **ostriche** |
| | ostreekeh |
| prawns | **gamberi** |
| | gamberee |
| red mullet | **triglie** |
| | treel-yeh |
| sardines | **sardine** |
| | sardeeneh |
| scampi | **scampi** |
| | scampee |
| shrimps | **gamberetti** |
| | gamberet-tee |
| small squid | **calamaretti** |
| | calamaret-tee |
| squid | **calamari** |
| | calamaree |
| swordfish | **pescespada** |
| | pesheh-spad-ah |

For some shellfish and 'frying pan' fish, specify the number you want:

| | |
|---|---|
| A crab, please | **Un granchio, per favore** |
| | oon gran*keeo* pair fav-*oreh* |
| A lobster | **Un'aragosta** |
| | oonarag*osta* |
| A trout | **Una trota** |
| | oona tr*ot*-a |
| A sole | **Una sogliola** |
| | oona s*ol*-yola |
| A dory [*expensive*] | **Un'orata** |
| | oonor*at*-ah |
| A bass [*expensive*] | **Un branzino** |
| | oon brandz*eeno* |
| A mullet | **Un cefalo** |
| | oon ch*efalo* |

# Eating and drinking out

## Ordering a drink and a snack

### ESSENTIAL INFORMATION

- The places to ask for:
  - BAR
  - BAR-PASTICCERIA       (drinks and cakes)
  - CAFFÈ
  - BIRRERIA               (beer and snacks)
- By law, the price list of drinks (**LISTINO PREZZI**) must be displayed somewhere in the bar.
- There is waiter service in some cafés, but you can drink at the bar or counter if you wish (cheaper). In this case you should first pay at the cash desk (**CASSA**) and then take the receipt (**scontrino**) to the bar and give your order.
- Service is normally included in the bill (**servizio compreso**) but if not should be 10% to 15%.

- Bars and cafés serve both non-alcoholic and alcoholic drinks. There are no licensing hours, and children are allowed in.
- Italians drink a range of aperitifs (**aperitivi**) and digestives (**digestivi**). Their names vary from region to region. Most of the aperitifs are types of vermouth – red or white, sweet or dry – made by different firms such as Campari, Punt e Mes and Martini. The digestives can be made from almonds, fruit, or herbs and are often thick and syrupy.

## WHAT TO SAY

| | |
|---|---|
| I'll have . . . please | **Prendo per favore . . .** |
| | prendo pair fav-*o*reh . . . |
| a black coffee (small and strong) | **un caffè** |
| | oon caf-*f*eh |
| a black coffee (less strong) | **un caffè lungo** |
| | oon caf-*f*eh l*o*ong-go |
| a coffee with a dash of cream | **un caffè macchiato** |
| | oon caf-*f*eh mac-kee-*a*t-o |
| a milky coffee (breakfast) | **un caffelatte** |
| | oon caf-eh-l*a*t-teh |
| a frothy white coffee | **un capuccino** |
| | oon capooch*e*eno |
| a tea | **un tè** |
| | oon teh |
| with milk | **al latte** |
| | al l*a*t-teh |
| with lemon | **al limone** |
| | al leem*o*neh |
| a glass of milk | **un bicchiere di latte** |
| | oon beec-kee-*a*ireh dee l*a*t-teh |
| a hot chocolate | **una cioccolata calda** |
| | oona choc-col*a*t-ah c*a*lda |
| a mineral water | **una minerale** |
| | oona miner*a*l-eh |
| an iced coffee | **una granita di caffè** |
| | oona gran*e*eta dee caf-*f*eh |
| a lemonade | **una limonata** |
| | oona leemon*a*t-a |
| a fresh lemon juice | **una spremuta di limone** |
| | oona sprem*o*ota dee leem*o*neh |

| I'll have . . . please | **Prendo per favore . . .** |
| | prendo pair fav-*oreh* . . . |
| an orangeade | **un'aranciata** |
| | oonaranch*a*t-a |
| a fresh orange juice | **una spremuta d'arancia** |
| | oona sprem*oo*ta dar*a*ncha |
| a fresh grapefruit juice | **una spremuta di pompelmo** |
| | oona sprem*oo*ta dee pomp*e*lmo |
| a pineapple juice | **un succo di frutta all'ananas** |
| | oon s*oo*c-co dee fr*oo*t-ta al-la p*e*sca |
| a lager | **una birra** |
| | oona b*ee*ra |
| a dark beer | **una birra scura** |
| | oona b*ee*ra sc*oo*-ra |
| I'll have . . . please | **Prendo, per favore . . .** |
| | prendo pair fav-*oreh* . . . |
| a cheese roll | **un panino al formaggio** |
| | oon pan*ee*no al form*a*d-jo |
| a ham roll | **un panino al prosciutto** |
| | oon pan*ee*no al prosh*oo*t-to |
| a salami roll | **un panino al salame** |
| | oon pan*ee*no al sal*a*m-eh |
| a sandwich (like that) | **un tramezzino (così)** |
| | oon tramed-dz*ee*no (coz*ee*) |
| a pizza | **una pizza** |
| | oona p*ee*t-tza |

These are some other snacks you may like to try:

| **una pizzetta al pomodoro** | small tomato pizza, usually eaten |
| oona pit-tz*e*t-ta al pomodoro | cold |
| **una focaccia** | a savoury bread, similar to pizza |
| cona foc*a*t-cha | but without tomato spread |
| **una focaccina al prosciutto** | a ham sandwich made with |
| cona focat-ch*ee*na al | **focaccia** bread |
| prosh*oo*t-to | |
| **un toast (al prosciutto e** | a toasted sandwich, normally made |
| **formaggio)** | with ham and cheese |
| oon tost (al prosh*oo*t-to eh | |
| form*a*d-djo) | |

# In a restaurant

## ESSENTIAL INFORMATION

- You can eat at all these places:
  **RISTORANTE**
  **TRATTORIA** (cheaper)
  **ALBERGO** (hotel – often a fixed menu)
  **PENSIONE** (mainly residents – fixed menu)
  **ROSTICCERIA**
  **PIZZERIA** (hot snacks)
  **BIRRERIA**
  **TAVOLA CALDA**
- Menus are always displayed outside the larger restaurants and that is the *only* way to judge if a place is right for your needs.
- Some smaller restaurants do not have a written menu and you must ask the waiter what is available.
- Self-service restaurants are rare.
- Service (of 10% to 15%) is always included on the bill, but an extra tip is usually welcome.
- Restaurants are now obliged, by law, to give receipts, and you should insist on this.
- In the south of Italy the lunch break is longer than in the north, and dinner is eaten later in the evening.

## WHAT TO SAY

| | |
|---|---|
| May I book a table? | **Potrei prenotare un tavolo?** |
| | potr*ay* prenot*ar*-eh oon t*a*volo |
| I've booked a table | **Ho prenotato un tavolo** |
| | o prenot*at*-o oon t*a*volo |
| **A table . . .** | **Un tavolo . . .** |
| | oon t*a*volo . . . |
| for one | **per una persona** |
| | pair *oo*na pairs*o*na |
| for three | **per tre persone** |
| | pair treh pairs*o*neh |
| The à la carte menu, please | **Il menú alla carta, per favore** |
| | il men*oo* al-la c*a*rta pair fav-*o*reh |

| | |
|---|---|
| The fixed price menu | **Il menú a prezzo fisso** |
| | il men*oo* ah pret-tzo f*i*s-so |
| The (8,000) lira menu | **Il menú da (ottomila) lire** |
| | il men*oo* da (*o*t-tome*e*la) l*ee*reh |
| The tourist menu | **Il menú turistico** |
| | il men*oo* toor*i*stico |
| Today's special menu | **I piatti del giorno** |
| | ee pee-*a*t-tee del j*o*rno |
| What's this, please? [*point to menu*] | **Che cos'è questo, per favore?** |
| | keh coz-*e*h questo pair fav-*o*reh |
| A carafe of wine, please | **Una caraffa di vino, per favore** |
| | oona car*a*f-fa dee v*ee*no pair fav-*o*reh |
| A quarter (25 cc) | **Un quarto** |
| | oon qu*a*arto |
| A half (50 cc) | **Un mezzo litro** |
| | oon med-dzo l*ee*tro |
| A glass | **Un bicchiere** |
| | oon beec-kee-*ai*reh |
| A (half) bottle | **Una (mezza) bottiglia** |
| | oona (med-dza) bot-t*ee*l-ya |
| A litre | **Un litro** |
| | oon l*ee*tro |
| Red/white/rosé/house wine | **Vino rosso/bianco/rosé/della casa** |
| | v*ee*no ros-so/bee-*a*nco/rozeh/del-la c*a*za |
| Some more bread, please | **Ancora del pane, per favore** |
| | anc*o*ra del p*a*n-eh pair fav-*o*reh |
| Some more wine | **Ancora del vino** |
| | anc*o*ra del v*ee*no |
| Some oil | **Dell'olio** |
| | del-l*o*l-yo |
| Some vinegar | **Dell'aceto** |
| | del-lach*e*to |
| Some salt/pepper | **Del sale/pepe** |
| | del s*a*l-eh/p*e*h-peh |
| With/without (garlic) | **Con/senza (aglio)** |
| | con/sentza (*a*l-yo) |
| Some water | **Dell'acqua** |
| | del-l*a*cqua |
| How much does that come to? | **Quanto fa?** |
| | qu*a*nto fa |

| | |
|---|---|
| Is service included? | **Il servizio è compreso?** |
| | il sairvitzio eh compraiz-o |
| Where is the toilet, please? | **Dov'è il bagno, per favore?** |
| | dov-eh il ban-yo pair fav-oreh |
| Miss! [*this does not sound abrupt in Italian*] | **Signorina!** |
| | seen-yoreena |
| Waiter! | **Cameriere!** |
| | cameree-aireh |
| The bill, please | **Il conto, per favore** |
| | il conto pair fav-oreh |
| May I have a receipt? | **Potrei avere una ricevuta?** |
| | potray avaireh oona reechevoota |

**Key words for courses, as seen on some menus**

[*Only ask this question if you want the waiter to remind you of the choice.*]

| | |
|---|---|
| **What have you got in the way of . . .** | **Che cosa avete come . . .** |
| | keh coza avet-eh com-eh . . . |
| starters? | **antipasti?** |
| | antipastee |
| soup? | **minestre?** |
| | minestreh |
| egg dishes? | **uova?** |
| | wova |
| fish? | **pesce?** |
| | pesheh |
| meat? | **carne?** |
| | carneh |
| game? | **selvaggina?** |
| | selvad-jeena |
| fowl? | **pollame?** |
| | pol-lam-eh |
| vegetables? | **contorno?** |
| | contorno |
| cheese? | **formaggi?** |
| | formad-jee |
| fruit? | **frutta?** |
| | froot-ta |
| ice-cream? | **gelati?** |
| | jelat-ee |

dessert?                                          **dolci?**
                                                  dolchee

[*'Pasta', spaghetti, etc., are part of the MINESTRE course, see p. 254*]

## UNDERSTANDING THE MENU

- You will find the names of the principal ingredients of most dishes on these pages:

  Starters p. 237            Fruit p. 239
  Meat p. 242                Cheese p. 238
  Fish p. 243                Ice-cream p. 236
  Vegetables p. 240          Dessert p. 236

  Used together with the following lists of cooking and menu terms, they should help you to decode the menu.

- *Remember*, dishes vary considerably from region to region in Italy: a dish with the same name, e.g. **gnocchi alla Romana** (pasta 'dumplings' Roman style), might be cooked in a different way in Rome from Milan – or even from one restaurant to another in the same city. Also, the same dish might appear on menus all over Italy with a different name in each region! If in doubt, always ask the waiter.

- These cooking and menu terms are for understanding only – not for speaking.

### Cooking and menu terms

| | |
|---|---|
| **affumicato** | smoked |
| **all'aglio e olio** | with oil and garlic |
| **agrodolce** | sweet-sour |
| **arrosto** | roast |
| **al basilico** | with basil |
| **ben cotto** | well cooked |
| **con besciamella** | with bechamel sauce |
| **in bianco** | boiled, with no sauce |
| **bollito** | boiled/stewed |
| **alla bolognese** | Bolognese style |
| **brasato** | cooked in wine |
| **al burro** | cooked in butter |
| **alla cacciatora** | cooked in tomato sauce |
| **al cartoccio** | baked wrapped in foil |
| **alla casalinga** | homely style |
| **al civet** | marinated and cooked in wine |

| | |
|---|---|
| cotto | cooked (as opposed to raw) |
| crudo | raw |
| al dente | not overcooked, firm texture |
| dorato | slightly fried (golden) |
| alle erbe | with herbs |
| da farsi | to be prepared |
| ai ferri | grilled without oil |
| alla fiorentina | Florentine style |
| alla fonduta | with fondue |
| al forno | baked |
| fritto | fried |
| in gelatina | in savoury jelly |
| grattuggiato | grated; baked in cheese sauce |
| alla griglia | grilled on the fire |
| imbottiti | stuffed |
| lesso | boiled |
| in maionese | in/with mayonnaise |
| alle mandorle | with almonds |
| alla marinara | with seafood |
| al marsala | with Marsala wine |
| alla milanese | fried in egg and breadcrumbs |
| alla napoletana | Neopolitan style |
| all'origano | with oregano (herb) |
| in padella | cooked and served in a frying pan |
| al pangrattato | with breadcrumbs |
| alla panna | cooked in cream |
| al parmigiano | with parmesan cheese |
| al pecorino | with pecorino cheese |
| al pesto | with basil and garlic sauce |
| alla pizzaiola | with tomato sauce and cheese |
| al prezzemolo | with parsley |
| ragù | rich tomato and meat sauce for pasta |
| alla ricotta | with ricotta cheese |
| ripieno | stuffed |
| alla romana | Roman style |
| al rosmarino | with rosemary |
| salsa | sauce |
| salsa verde | parsley and garlic sauce |
| in salmí | cooked in oil, vinegar and herbs |
| al sangue | rare (steak, etc.) |
| alla siciliana | Sicilian style |

| | |
|---|---|
| spiedini | skewers |
| allo spiedo | on the spit |
| stufato | stew |
| al sugo | cooked in sauce |
| trifolato | cooked with tomato and parsley |
| in umido | steamed; stewed |
| alla veneziana | Venetian style |
| alle vongole | with clam (shellfish) sauce |
| allo zabaglione | with eggs, sugar and Marsala wine |
| zuppa | soup |

**Further words to help you to understand the menu:**

| | |
|---|---|
| abbacchio | young, spring lamb |
| amaretti | macaroons |
| anguilla | eel |
| animelle | sweetbreads |
| anitra | duck |
| baccalà | dried cod |
| bagna cauda | raw vegetables dipped in sauce of hot oil, garlic, anchovies and cream |
| bistecca alla fiorentina | T-bone steak |
| braciole | chops |
| brodo | broth |
| budino | like crème caramel; pudding |
| cacciagione | game |
| capperi | capers |
| capretto | kid |
| capriolo | deer |
| cassata | ice-cream cake with dried fruit |
| cervella | brains |
| cinghiale | boar |
| coppa | very lean bacon; cup (of ice-cream) |
| costate | large chops |
| costolette | small chops |
| cotechino | large pork sausage |
| crema | custard cream; cream soup |
| crostata | fruit or jam tart |
| crostini | small pieces of fried bread |
| fagiano | pheasant |

| | |
|---|---|
| fagioli | fresh or dried beans |
| fave | broad or butter beans |
| fegatini | chicken livers |
| fettine | small tender steaks |
| filetti | fillets |
| fragole di bosco | wild strawberries |
| frittata | omelette |
| frittelle | fritters |
| fritto misto | mixed fried meats |
| fritto di pesce | mixed fried fish |
| frutti di mare | shellfish |
| gelati | ice-cream |
| granita | water ice |
| grissini | crispy bread sticks |
| involtini | slices of meat, stuffed and rolled |
| lepre | hare |
| limone | lemon |
| lombata | sirloin |
| macedonia | fruit salad |
| mandorle | almonds |
| minestrone | vegetable soup |
| mortadella | large mild salami |
| ossibuchi | dish of shin of veal |
| pancetta | bacon |
| panna | cream |
| pasta asciutta | general name of cooked pasta |
| pasta frolla | rich shortcrust pastry |
| pasta sfogliata | puff pastry |
| peperonata | stew of green and red peppers |
| peperoncini | chili peppers |
| pernice | partridge |
| petti di pollo/tacchino | chicken/turkey breasts |
| piccata | small veal slices |
| pignoli | pine nuts |
| pinzimonio | raw vegetables to dip in oil |
| polpette | meatballs |
| prosciutto di Parma | raw ham from Parma |
| quaglia | quail |
| riso | rice |
| risotto | rice cooked in sauce |
| rolata | meat loaf stuffed with herbs |
| salame all'aglio | garlic sausage |

| | |
|---|---|
| salsiccia | sausage |
| saltimbocca alla romana | fried veal with ham and rosemary |
| scaloppine | small veal slices |
| semifreddo | ice-cream with biscuits |
| seppie | cuttle-fish |
| spezzatino | stew |
| stracciatella | hot broth with beaten egg |
| stracotto | beef stew with vegetables |
| tacchino | turkey |
| tartuffi | truffles |
| torta | cake |
| trippa | tripe |
| uccelli | small birds (e.g. thrushes) |
| uova | eggs |
| vongole | clams, cockles |
| zampone | pig's trotter stuffed with chopped, seasoned meat |
| zuppa inglese | chocolate trifle |
| zuppa pavese | broth, lightly boiled egg and cheese |

## Types of pasta

| | |
|---|---|
| agnolini/agnolotti | like ravioli |
| cannelloni | large tubular pasta, often stuffed |
| cappelletti | stuffed pasta rings |
| conchiglie | shell-shaped pasta |
| ditali | short tubular pasta |
| farfalle | butterfly-shaped pasta |
| fettuccine | narrow ribbons of pasta |
| gnocchi | small potato or semolina 'dumplings' |
| lasagne | wide flat pasta |
| maccheroni | large spaghetti with hole in middle |
| pasta asciutta | general term for cooked pasta |
| pasta in brodo | small shapes of pasta in broth |
| pizza | flat 'bread' spread with tomato |
| polenta | porridge of maize flour |
| ravioli | stuffed square-shaped pasta |
| rigatoni | large-grooved tubular pasta |
| spaghetti | long, thin, round pasta |
| tagliatelle | narrow ribbon pasta |

| tortellini | stuffed pasta rings |
| vermicelli | very thin spaghetti, 'little worms' |
| ziti | tubular-shaped pasta |

# Health

## ESSENTIAL INFORMATION

- For details of reciprocal health agreements between the UK and Italy, ask for leaflet SA 30 at your local Department of Health and Social Security a month before leaving, or ask your travel agent.
- The Italian state medical insurance is called **INAM**.
- For minor disorders and treatment at a chemist's see p. 228.
- For asking the way to a doctor, dentist, chemist's or Health and Social Security Office (for reimbursement) see p. 221.
- To find a doctor in an emergency, look for:
  **medici** (in the Yellow Pages of the telephone directory)
  
  | **AMBULATORIO** | (surgery)) |
  | **PRONTO SOCCORSO** | (casualty department, first aid) |
  | **H** ⎤ | (hospital) |
  | **OSPEDALE** ⎦ | |
- Dial 113 for an emergency ambulance service.

### What's the matter?

| I have a pain here [*point*] | **Ho un dolore qui** |
| | o oon do*lore*h quee |
| I have toothache | **Ho male a un dente** |
| | o m*a*l-eh ah oon d*e*nteh |
| **I have broken . . .** | **Ho rotto . . .** |
| | o r*o*t-to . . . |
| my dentures | **la dentiera** |
| | la dentee-*ai*ra |
| my glasses | **gli occhiali** |
| | l-y*ee* oc-kee-*a*l-ee |

| I have lost . . . | **Ho perso . . .** |
| | o p*a*irso . . . |
| my contact lenses | **le lenti a contatto** |
| | leh l*e*ntee ah cont*a*t-to |
| a filling | **un'otturazione** |
| | oonot-too-ratzioneh |
| My child is ill | **Mio/a figlio/a è ammalato/a\*** |
| | mee-o/ah f*ee*l-yo/ah eh am-mal*a*t-o/ah |

**Already under treatment for something else?**

| I take . . . regularly [*show*] | **Prendo regolarmente . . .** |
| | pr*e*ndo regolarm*e*nteh . . . |
| this medicine | **questa medicina** |
| | qu*e*sta medich*ee*na |
| these pills | **queste pillole** |
| | qu*e*steh p*ee*l-loleh |
| I have . . . | **Ho . . .** |
| | o . . . |
| a heart condition | **mal di cuore** |
| | mal dee cw*o*reh |
| haemorrhoids | **le emorroidi** |
| | leh em-orr*o*ydee |
| rheumatism | **i reumatismi** |
| | ee reh-oomat*i*smee |
| I'm . . . | **Sono . . .** |
| | s*o*nno . . . |
| diabetic | **diabetico/a\*** |
| | dee-ab*e*t-eeco/a |
| asthmatic | **asmatico/a\*** |
| | azm*a*t-eeco/a |
| pregnant | **incinta** |
| | eench*ee*nta |
| allergic to (penicillin) | **allergico/a\* alla (penicillina)** |
| | al-l*ai*rjeeco/ah al-la (penicheel-l*ee*na) |

\*For men and boys use 'o', for women and girls use 'a'.

# Problems: loss, theft

## ESSENTIAL INFORMATION

- If the worst comes to the worst, find the police station. To ask the way, see p. 219.
- Look for:

  CARABINIERI ⎤ (police)
  POLIZIA ⎦
  VIGILI URBANI (traffic wardens)
  QUESTURA (police station)

- If you lose your passport go to the nearest British Consulate.
- In an emergency, dial 113 for fire and police.

## LOSS

[See also 'Theft' below; the lists are interchangeable]

| I have lost . . . | Ho perso . . . |
| --- | --- |
| | o pairso . . . |
| my camera | la macchina fotografica |
| | la mac-keena fotograf-eeca |
| my car keys | le chiavi della macchina |
| | leh kee-ahv-ee del-la mac-keena |
| my car logbook | il libretto della macchina |
| | il libret-to del-la mac-keena |
| my driving licence | la patente |
| | la patenteh |
| my insurance certificate | il certificato dell'assicurazione |
| | il chairtee-ficat-o del-las-sicoo-ratzioneh |

## THEFT

| Someone has stolen . . . | Qualcuno mi ha rubato . . . |
| --- | --- |
| | qualcoono mee ah roobat-o . . . |
| my car | la macchina |
| | la mac-keena |
| my money | i soldi |
| | ee soldee |

| | |
|---|---|
| Someone has stolen . . . | **Qualcuno mi ha rubato . . .** |
| | qualcoono mee ah roobat-o . . . |
| my tickets | **i biglietti** |
| | ee beel-yet-tee |
| my travellers' cheques | **i travellers cheques** |
| | ee travellairs sheck |
| my wallet | **il portafoglio** |
| | il portafol-yo |
| my luggage | **i bagagli** |
| | ee bagal-yee |

---

# The post office and phoning home

## ESSENTIAL INFORMATION

- Key words to look for:
  **POSTA**
  **POSTE E TELEGRAFI (PT)**
  **POSTE-TELECOMUNICAZIONI (PTT)**
- It is best to buy stamps at the tobacconist's. Only go to the post office for more complicated transactions, like telegrams.
- Unless you read and speak Italian well, it's best not to make telephone calls by yourself. Go to the main post office and write the town and number you want on a piece of paper.
- To call the UK using STD (**TELESELEZIONE**) dial the code 0044 then the number (less any initial 0).
- For the USA dial the international operator (**ITALCABLE**), on 170.

## WHAT TO SAY

| | |
|---|---|
| To England, please | **Per l'Inghilterra, per favore** |
| | pair ling-eeltairra pair fav-oreh |
| [*Hand letters, cards or parcels over the counter*] | |
| To Australia | **Per l'Australia** |
| | pair la-oostral-ya |
| To the United States | **Per gli Stati Uniti** |
| | pair l-yee stat-ee ooneetee |

| I'd like to send a telegram | **Vorrei spedire un telegramma** |
| | vorr*ay* sped-*eer*eh oon telegr*am*-ma |
| **I'd like this number . . .** | **Vorrei questo numero . . .** |
| [*show number*] | vorr*ay* questo n*oo*mero . . . |
| in England | **in Inghilterra** |
| | in ing-eelt*air*ra |
| in Canada | **in Canada** |
| | in c*a*nada |
| Can you dial it for me, please? | **Può farmi il numero, per favore?** |
| | poo-*o* f*ar*mee il n*oo*mero pair fav-*oreh* |

# Changing cheques and money

## ESSENTIAL INFORMATION

- Look for these words on buildings:
  BANCA
  BANCO
  ISTITUTO BANCARIO } (bank)
  CASSA DI RISPARMIO
  CAMBIO-VALUTE (change bureau)
- To cash your normal cheques, exactly as at home use your banker's card where you see the Eurocheque sign. Write in English, in pounds.
- Exchange rate information might show the pound as:
  £, L, Lira Sterlina L St or even GB.
- Have your passport handy.

## WHAT TO SAY

| I'd like to cash . . . | **Vorrei incassare . . .** |
| | vorr*ay* incas-s*ar*-eh . . . |
| these travellers' cheques | **questi travellers cheques** |
| | qu*e*stee travell*air*s sh*e*ck |
| this cheque | **questo assegno** |
| | questo as-s*en*-yo |

| I'd like to change this . . . | **Vorrei cambiare questi soldi . . .** |
| | vor*ray* cambi-*a*r-eh qu*e*stee s*o*ldee . . . |
| into Italian lira | **in lire italiane** |
| | in l*ee*reh itali*a*n-eh |
| into Austrian schillings | **in scellini austriaci** |
| | in shel-l*ee*nee ah-oostr*ee*-achee |
| into French francs | **in franchi francesi** |
| | in fr*a*nkee franch*e*z-ee |
| into Swiss francs | **in franchi svizzeri** |
| | in fr*a*nkee zv*ee*t-tzeree |

# Car travel

## ESSENTIAL INFORMATION

- Is it a self-service station? Look out for **SELF SERVICE**.
- Grades of petrol:

  **BENZINA NORMALE**  (2 star, standard)
  **BENZINA SUPER**  (3 star and above, premium)
  **GASOLIO**  (diesel)
- 1 gallon is about 4½ litres (accurate enough up to 6 gallons).
- For car repairs, look for:

  **AUTORIPARAZIONI**  (repairs)
  **AUTORIMESSA**  (garage)
  **MECCANICO**  (mechanic)
  **ELETTRAUTO**  (for electrical faults)
  **CARROZZERIA**  (for bodywork)
- Petrol stations are usually closed from 12 to 3, and very few offer a 24 hour service (except on motorways).
- In case of a breakdown or an emergency look for the **ACI** (Italian Automobile Club) sign, or dial 116 from any telephone box.

## WHAT TO SAY

[*For numbers see p. 264*]

| | |
|---|---|
| (Nine) litres of . . . | **(Nove) litri di . . .**<br>(nov-eh) leetree dee . . . |
| (2000) lira of . . . | **(Duemila) lire di . . .**<br>(dooeh meela) leereh dee . . . |
| standard/premium/diesel | **normale/super/gasolio**<br>normal-eh/sooper/gazol-yo |
| Full, please | **Pieno, per favore**<br>pee-ehno, pair fav-oreh |
| Will you check . . . | **Può controllare . . .**<br>poo-o control-lar-eh . . . |
| the oil? | **l'olio?**<br>lol-yo |
| the battery? | **la batteria?**<br>la bat-teree-ah |
| the radiator? | **il radiatore?**<br>il rad-yatoreh |
| the tyres? | **le gomme?**<br>leh gom-meh |
| I've run out of petrol | **Sono rimasta senza benzina**<br>sonno reemas-ta sentza bendzeena |
| Can you help me, please? | **Mi può aiutare, per favore?**<br>mee poo-o ayootar-eh pair fav-oreh |
| Do you do repairs? | **Ripara le macchine?**<br>reepar-ah leh mac-keeneh |
| I have a puncture | **Ho una gomma a terra**<br>o oona gom-ma ah terra |
| I have a broken windscreen | **Ho rotto il parabrezza**<br>o rot-to il parabret-tza |
| I think the problem is<br>here . . . [*point*] | **Penso che il guasto sia qui . . .**<br>penso keh il goo-asto see-ah<br>quee . . . |

## LIKELY REACTIONS

| | |
|---|---|
| I don't do repairs | **Non riparo auto**<br>non reepar-o ah-ooto |

| | |
|---|---|
| Where's your car? | **Dov'è la sua macchina?** |
| | dov-*eh* la soo-ah m*a*c-keena |
| What make is it? | **Che tipo di macchina è?** |
| | keh t*ee*po dee m*a*c-keena eh |
| Come back tomorrow/on Monday | **Ritorni domani/lunedí** |
| | reetornee doman-ee/loon-ed*ee* |

[*For days of the week see p. 266*]

# Public transport

## ESSENTIAL INFORMATION

- Key words on signs

| | |
|---|---|
| **BIGLIETTI** | (tickets) |
| **BINARIO** | (platform) |
| **DEPOSITO BAGAGLI** | (left luggage) |
| **ENTRATA** | (entrance) |
| **FERMATA AUTOBUS** | (bus stop) |
| **FS, FERROVIE DELLO STATO** | (Italian railways) |
| **INFORMAZIONI** | (information) |
| **ORARIO** | (timetable) |
| **PROIBITO-VIETATO** | (forbidden) |
| **SALITA** | (entrance for buses and trams) |
| **USCITA** | (exit) |

- In the main cities automatic ticket systems are in operation on buses, trams and the underground. Tickets must be bought in advance from bars and tobacconists. Ask for details at the local tourist information offices.

## WHAT TO SAY

| | |
|---|---|
| Where does the train for (Rome) leave from? | **Da dove parte il treno per (Roma)?** |
| | da d*o*v-eh p*a*rteh il tren-o pair (roma) |
| Is this the train for (Rome)? | **È questo il treno per (Roma)?** |
| | eh questo il tren-o pair (roma) |

| | |
|---|---|
| Where does the bus for (Florence) leave from? | **Da dove parte l'autobus per (Firenze)?** |
| | da dov-eh parteh la-ootoboos pair (feerentzeh) |
| Is this the bus for (Florence)? | **È questo l'autobus per (Firenze)?** |
| | eh questo la-ootoboos pair (feerentzeh) |
| Do I have to change? | **Devo cambiare?** |
| | dev-o cambee-ar-eh |
| Can you put me off at the right stop, please? | **Può farmi scendere alla fermata giusta, per favore?** |
| | poo-o farmee shendereh al-la fairmat-ah joosta pair fav-oreh |
| Where can I get a taxi? | **Dove posso trovare un taxi?** |
| | dov-eh pos-so trovar-eh oon taxi |
| Can I book a seat? | **Posso prenotare un posto?** |
| | pos-so prenotar-eh oon posto |
| A single | **Solo andata** |
| | solo andat-ah |
| A return | **Andata e ritorno** |
| | andat-ah eh reetorno |
| First class | **Prima classe** |
| | preema clas-seh |
| Second class | **Seconda classe** |
| | seconda clas-seh |
| One adult | **Un adulto** |
| | oon adoolto |
| Two adults | **Due adulti** |
| | dooeh adooltee |
| and one child | **e un bambino** |
| | eh oon bambeeno |
| and two children | **e due bambini** |
| | eh dooeh bambeenee |
| How much is it? | **Quanto costa?** |
| | quanto costa |

# Reference

## NUMBERS

| | | |
|---|---|---|
| 0 | **zero** | dz*ai*ro |
| 1 | **uno** | *oo*no |
| 2 | **due** | d*oo*eh |
| 3 | **tre** | treh |
| 4 | **quattro** | qu*aa*t-tro |
| 5 | **cinque** | ch*i*nqueh |
| 6 | **sei** | say |
| 7 | **sette** | s*et*-teh |
| 8 | **otto** | *ot*-to |
| 9 | **nove** | n*o*veh |
| 10 | **dieci** | dee-*e*chee |
| 11 | **undici** | *oo*ndeechee |
| 12 | **dodici** | d*o*deechee |
| 13 | **tredici** | tr*e*hdeechee |
| 14 | **quattordici** | quat-t*o*rdeechee |
| 15 | **quindici** | qu*i*ndeechee |
| 16 | **sedici** | s*e*hdeechee |
| 17 | **diciassette** | deechas-s*et*-teh |
| 18 | **diciotto** | deech*ot*-to |
| 19 | **diciannove** | deechan-n*o*veh |
| 20 | **venti** | v*e*ntee |
| 21 | **ventuno** | ven-t*oo*no |
| 22 | **ventidue** | ventee-d*oo*eh |
| 23 | **ventitré** | ventee-treh |
| 24 | **ventiquattro** | ventee-qu*a*t-tro |
| 25 | **venticinque** | ventee-ch*i*nqueh |
| 26 | **ventisei** | ventee-s*ay* |
| 27 | **ventisette** | ventee-s*et*-teh |
| 28 | **ventotto** | vent*ot*-to |
| 29 | **ventinove** | ventee-n*o*veh |
| 30 | **trenta** | trenta |

*For numbers beyond 20 follow the pattern of* **venti**: *keep the final vowel except with one and eight.*

| | | |
|---|---|---|
| 31 | **trentuno** | tren-t*oo*no |
| 35 | **trentacinque** | trenta-ch*i*nqueh |

| 38 | **trentotto** | trentot-to |
| 40 | **quaranta** | quaranta |
| 41 | **quarantuno** | quarant-oono |
| 45 | **quarantacinque** | quaranta-chinqueh |
| 48 | **quarantotto** | quarantot-to |
| 50 | **cinquanta** | chinquanta |
| 55 | **cinquantacinque** | chinquanta-chinqueh |
| 60 | **sessanta** | ses-santa |
| 65 | **sessantacinque** | ses-santa-chinqueh |
| 70 | **settanta** | set-tanta |
| 80 | **ottanta** | ot-tanta |
| 90 | **novanta** | novanta |
| 100 | **cento** | chento |
| 101 | **centouno** | chento-oono |
| 102 | **centodue** | chento-dooeh |
| 125 | **centoventicinque** | chentoventee-chinqueh |
| 150 | **centocinquanta** | chento-chin-quanta |
| 175 | **centosettantacinque** | chentoset-tanta-chinqueh |
| 200 | **duecento** | dooeh-chento |
| 300 | **trecento** | treh-chento |
| 400 | **quattrocento** | quat-tro-chento |
| 500 | **cinquecento** | chinqueh-chento |
| 1000 | **mille** | meel-leh |
| 1500 | **millecinquecento** | meel-leh-chinqueh-chento |
| 2000 | **duemila** | dooeh-meela |
| 5000 | **cinquemila** | chinqueh-meela |
| 10,000 | **diecimila** | dee-echee-meela |
| 100,000 | **centomila** | chento-meela |
| 1,000,000 | **un milione** | oon meel-yoneh |

## TIME

| **What time is it?** | **Che ora è?** |
| | keh ora eh |
| It's one o'clock | **È l'una** |
| | eh loona |
| **It's . . .** | **Sono . . .** |
| | sonno . . . |
| two o'clock | **le due** |
| | leh dooeh |
| three o'clock | **le tre** |
| | leh treh |

| It's . . . | Sono . . . |
| --- | --- |
| | sonno . . . |
| a quarter past five | **le cinque e un quarto** |
| | leh chinqueh eh oon quaarto |
| half past five | **le cinque e mezza** |
| | keh chinqueh eh med-dza |
| a quarter to six | **le sei meno un quarto** |
| | leh say men-o oon quaarto |
| It's . . . | È . . . |
| | eh . . . |
| noon | **mezzogiorno** |
| | med-dzojorno |
| midnight | **mezzanotte** |
| | med-dzanot-teh |

## DAYS AND MONTHS

| Monday | **lunedí** |
| --- | --- |
| | loon-edee |
| Tuesday | **martedí** |
| | mart-edee |
| Wednesday | **mercoledí** |
| | maircol-edee |
| Thursday | **giovedí** |
| | jov-edee |
| Friday | **venerdí** |
| | venairdee |
| Saturday | **sabato** |
| | sabato |
| Sunday | **domenica** |
| | domen-eecca |
| January | **gennaio** |
| | jen-nah-yo |
| February | **febbraio** |
| | feb-brah-yo |
| March | **marzo** |
| | martzo |
| April | **aprile** |
| | apreeleh |
| May | **maggio** |
| | mad-jo |

| June | **giugno** |
| | j*oon*-yo |
| July | **luglio** |
| | l*ool*-yo |
| August | **agosto** |
| | ag*o*sto |
| September | **settembre** |
| | set-t*e*mbreh |
| October | **ottobre** |
| | ot-t*o*breh |
| November | **novembre** |
| | nov*e*mbreh |
| December | **dicembre** |
| | deech*e*mbreh |

## Public holidays

● On these holidays offices, shops and schools are closed.

| 1 January | ⎡ **Primo dell'anno** | New Year's Day |
| | ⎣ **Capodanno** | |
| . . . | **Lunedí dell'Angelo** | Easter Monday |
| 25 April | **Anniversario della** | Liberation Day |
| | **Liberazione** | |
| 1 May | **Festa dei Lavoratori** | Labour Day |
| 15 August | **Assunzione** | Assumption |
| 1 November | ⎡ **Tutti i Santi** | All Saints Day |
| | ⎣ **I Morti** | |
| 8 December | **Immacolata** | Immaculate |
| | **Concezione** | Conception |
| 25 December | **Natale** | Christmas |
| 26 December | **Santo Stefano** | Boxing Day |

# Index

# Travellers' Portuguese

**D. L. Ellis, K. Sandeman McLaughlin**

Pronunciation **Dr J. Baldwin**

*Useful address*
Portuguese National Tourist Office
New Bond Street House
1/5 New Bond Street
London W1Y 0BD

# Contents

**Reference**

# Pronunciation hints

In Portuguese, it is important to stress or emphasize the syllables in *italics*, just as you would if we were to take as an English example: Little Jack H*o*rner s*a*t in the c*o*rner. Here we have ten syllables but only four stresses.
**Boa sorte!**

# Everyday expressions

*[See also 'Shop talk', p. 287]*

| | |
|---|---|
| Hello | **Olá** |
| | ol*a*h |
| Good morning ⎤ | **Bom dia** |
| Good day ⎦ | bom d*ee*-a |
| Good afternoon | **Boa tarde** |
| | b*o*a tard |
| Good night | **Boa noite** |
| | b*o*a noyt |
| Goodbye | **Adeus** |
| | ad*eh*-oosh |
| Yes | **Sim** |
| | seem |
| Please | **Por favor** |
| | poor fav*o*r |
| Yes, please | **Sim, por favor** |
| | seem poor fav*o*r |
| Thank you | **Obrigado/a\*** |
| | obreeg*a*h-doo/a |
| Thank you very much | **Muito obrigado/a\*** |
| | moo-*ee*too obreeg*a*h-doo/a |
| That's right | **Exactamente** |
| | eez*a*tament |
| No | **Não** |
| | nown |
| No thanks | **Não obrigado/a\*** |
| | nown obreeg*a*h-doo/a |
| I disagree | **Não concordo** |
| | nown concordoo |
| Excuse me ⎤ | **Desculpe** |
| Sorry ⎦ | deshc*oo*lp |
| It doesn't matter | **Não faz mal** |
| | nown f*a*sh mal |
| Where's the toilet, please? | **Onde é a casa de banho, por favor?** |
| | awnd *e*h ah c*a*h-za der b*a*in-yoo poor fav*o*r |

\*First alternative for men, second for women

| Do you speak English? | **Fala inglês?** |
| | fah-la eenglesh |
| What is your name? | **Como se chama?** |
| | comoo ser shah-ma |
| My name is . . . | **Chamo-me . . .** |
| | shamoo-meh . . . |

# Asking the way

## ESSENTIAL INFORMATION

- Keep a look out for all these place names as you will find them on shops, maps and notices.

## WHAT TO SAY

| Excuse me, please | **Com licença, por favor** |
| | com leesen-sa poor favor |
| How do I get . . . | **Para ir . . .** |
| | para eer . . . |
| to Lisbon? | **a Lisboa?** |
| | ah leeshboo-a |
| to Rua Augusta? | **à Rua Augusta?** |
| | ah roo-a ah-oogooshta |
| to the (hotel) Ritz? | **ao (hotel) Ritz?** |
| | ah-oo (otel) reetz |
| to the airport? | **ao aeroporto?** |
| | ah-oo airoh-portoo |
| to the beach? | **à praia?** |
| | ah prah-ya |
| to the bus station? | **à estação de camionetas?** |
| | ah shtassown der cam-yoonet-ash |
| to the market? | **ao mercado?** |
| | ah-oo maircah-doo |
| to the police station? | **à esquadra?** |
| | ah shkwah-dra |
| to the port? | **ao porto?** |
| | ah-oo portoo |

| | |
|---|---|
| to the post office? | **aos correios?** |
| | *ah*-oosh coor*ay*-oosh |
| to the railway station? | **à estação (de comboios)?** |
| | *ah* shtass*own* (der comb*oy*-oosh) |
| to the sports stadium? | **ao estádio desportivo?** |
| | *ah*-oo sht*ah*-dee-oo deshpoort*ee*voo |
| to the tourist information office? | **ao centro de informações turísticas?** |
| | *ah*-oo s*e*ntroo der eenfoor-mass*oy*nsh toor*ee*sh-teecash |
| to the town centre? | **ao centro (da cidade)?** |
| | *ah*-oo s*e*ntroo da seed*a*d |
| to the town hall? | **à câmara municipal?** |
| | ah c*a*mera mooneeseep*a*l |
| **Is there . . . near by?** | **Há . . . aqui perto?** |
| | ah . . . ak*ee* p*ai*rtoo |
| a baker's | **uma padaria** |
| | *oo*ma padayr*ee*-a |
| a bank | **um banco** |
| | oom b*a*ncoo |
| a bar | **um bar** |
| | oom b*a*r |
| a bus stop | **uma paragem de autocarros** |
| | *oo*ma paraj*ai*m der ah-ootoh-c*a*rroosh |
| a butcher's | **um talho** |
| | oom t*a*l-yoo |
| a café | **um café** |
| | oom caf*eh* |
| a cake shop | **uma pastelaria** |
| | *oo*ma pashtelar*ee*-a |
| a campsite | **um parque de campismo** |
| | oom park der camp*ee*j-moo |
| a car park | **um parking** |
| | oom p*a*rking |
| a change bureau | **um banco com câmbio** |
| | oom b*a*ncoo com c*a*mbee-oo |
| a chemist's | **uma farmácia** |
| | *oo*ma farm*ah*-see-a |
| a delicatessen | **uma charcutaria** |
| | *oo*ma sharcootar*ee*-a |
| a dentist's | **um dentista** |
| | oom dent*ee*shta |

**Is there . . . near by?**   **Há . . . aqui perto?**
ah . . . ak*ee* p*ai*rtoo

a department store   **um armazém**
oom armaz*ai*m

a disco   **uma discoteca**
*oo*ma deesh-cooteh-ca

a doctor's surgery   **um consultório médico**
oom consooltoree-oo medicoo

a dry-cleaner's   **uma tinturaria**
*oo*ma teentooraree-a

a fishmonger's   **uma peixaria**
*oo*ma paysharee-a

a garage (for repairs)   **uma garagem**
*oo*ma garajaim

a greengrocer's   **uma frutaria**
*oo*ma frootaree-a

a grocer's   **uma mercearia**
*oo*ma mersee-aree-a

a hairdresser's   **um cabeleireiro**
oom cab-el-ay-r*a*yroo

a hospital   **um hospital**
oom oshpeet*a*l

a hotel   **um hotel**
oom otel

an ice-cream parlour   **uma gelataria**
*oo*ma jelataree-a

a laundry   **uma lavandaria**
*oo*ma lavandaree-a

a newsagent's   **uma papelaria**
*oo*ma papelaree-a

a night club   **uma 'boîte'**
*oo*ma boo-*a*t

a park   **um parque**
oom p*a*rk

a petrol station   **uma bomba de gasolina**
*oo*ma b*o*mba der gazool*ee*na

a post box   **uma caixa do correio**
*oo*ma k*a*h-eesha doo coor*a*yoo

a public toilet   **uma casa de banho pública**
*oo*ma c*a*h-za der b*ai*n-yoo p*oo*blica

a restaurant   **um restaurante**
oom resht*a*h-oorant

| a supermarket | **um supermercado** |
| | oom supermair*cah*-doo |
| a taxi stand | **um parque de taxis** |
| | oom park der *ta*xeesh |
| a telephone | **uma cabine telefónica** |
| | ooma *cah*-been telef*onee*ca |
| a tobacconist's | **uma tabacaria** |
| | *oo*ma tabacar*ee*-a |
| a travel agent's | **uma agência de viagens** |
| | *oo*ma aj*ensia der vee-a*jainsh |
| a youth hostel | **uma pousada de juventude** |
| | *oo*ma pawss*ah*-da der jooven*too*d |

## DIRECTIONS

| Left/right | **Esquerda/direita** |
| | shk*air*da/d*err*ayta |
| Straight on | **Sempre em frente** |
| | sempr aim fr*en*t |
| There | **Ali** |
| | al*ee* |
| First left/right | **Primeira à esquerda/direita** |
| | preem*ay*ra ah shk*air*da/deer*ay*ta |
| Second left/right | **Segunda à esquerda/direita** |
| | seg*oo*nda ah shk*air*da/deer*ay*ta |

# Accommodation

## ESSENTIAL INFORMATION

### Hotel

- If you want hotel-type accommodation, all the following words
  in capital letters are worth looking for on name boards:
  HOTEL
  MOTEL
  PENSÃO (boarding house)
  ESTALAGEM (quality inn)
  POUSADA (state-owned inns often housed in historic buildings)

Remember that:

- A list of hotels in the town or district can usually be obtained from the local tourist information office.
- Unlisted hotels are usually cheaper and probably almost as good as listed hotels.
- Not all hotels provide meals, apart from breakfast. (**A PENSÃO** always provides meals.)
- The cost is displayed in the room itself, so you can check it when having a look around before agreeing to stay.
- The displayed cost is for the room itself, per night and not per person.
- Breakfast usually consists of strong coffee with milk, or tea with no milk unless otherwise requested, fresh bread or croissants, butter and jam.
- On arrival, you will be asked to complete a registration document and the receptionist will want to see your passport.
- Tip porters, waiters and chambermaids.
- The Directorate-General for Tourism publishes a *Tourist Accommodation Guide* which contains all the basic information on hotel establishments and tourist developments and apartments.

## WHAT TO SAY

| | |
|---|---|
| I have a booking | **Tenho uma reserva** |
| | tain-yoo *oo*ma rez*ai*rva |
| Have you any vacancies, please? | **Tem quartos livres, por favor?** |
| | taim kw*a*rtoosh l*ee*vresh poor fav*o*r |
| Can I book a room? | **Posso reservar um quarto?** |
| | possoo rezair*va*r oom kw*a*rtoo |
| It's for . . . | **É para . . .** |
| | eh p*a*ra . . . |
| one adult/one person | **um adulto/uma pessoa** |
| | oom ad*oo*ltoo/*oo*ma ps*aw*-a |
| two adults/two people | **dois adultos/duas pessoas** |
| | doysh ad*oo*ltoosh/d*oo*-ash ps*aw*-ash |
| and one child | **e uma criança** |
| | ee *oo*ma cree-*a*nssa |
| and two children | **e duas crianças** |
| | ee d*oo*-ash cree-*a*nssash |

| | |
|---|---|
| It's for . . . | **É para . . .**<br>eh para . . . |
| one night | **uma noite**<br>*oo*ma noyt |
| two nights | **duas noites**<br>d*oo*-ash n*o*ytsh |
| one week | **uma semana**<br>*oo*ma sem*ah*-na |
| two weeks | **duas semanas**<br>d*oo*-ash sem*ah*-nash |
| I would like . . . | **Queria . . .**<br>ker*ee*-a . . . |
| a room | **um quarto**<br>oom kw*a*rtoo |
| two rooms | **dois quartos**<br>doysh kw*a*rtoosh |
| with a single bed | **com uma cama singela**<br>com *oo*ma c*ah*-ma seenj*e*la |
| with two single beds | **com duas camas separadas**<br>com d*oo*-ash c*ah*-mash separ*ah*-dash |
| with a double bed | **com uma cama de casal**<br>com *oo*ma c*ah*-ma der caz*a*l |
| with a toilet | **com retrete**<br>com retr*e*t |
| with a bathroom | **com casa de banho**<br>com c*ah*-za der b*ai*n-yoo |
| with a shower | **com duche**<br>com d*oo*sh |
| with a cot | **com uma cama de bébé**<br>com *oo*ma c*ah*-ma der beh-beh |
| with a balcony | **com varanda**<br>com var*a*nda |
| I would like . . . | **Queria . . .**<br>ker*ee*-a . . . |
| full board | **pensão completa**<br>pens*ow*n compl*e*ta |
| half board | **meia pensão**<br>m*ay*-a pens*ow*n |
| bed and breakfast | **dormida e pequeno almoço**<br>doorm*ee*da ee pek*e*noo alm*a*wssoo |

| | |
|---|---|
| Do you serve meals? | **Servem refeições?**<br>s*a*irvaim refay-soynsh |
| Can I look at the room? | **Posso ver o quarto?**<br>p*o*ssoo vair oo kw*a*rtoo |
| OK. I'll take it | **Está bem. Fico com ele**<br>sht*a*h baim f*ee*coo com el |
| No thanks, I won't take it | **Não obrigado/a, não o quero***<br>nown obreeg*a*h-doo/a nown o k*e*h-roo |
| The bill, please | **A conta, por favor**<br>a c*o*nta poor fav*o*r |
| Is service included? | **O serviço está incluído?**<br>oo serv*ee*ssoo sht*a*h eencloo-*ee*doo |
| I think this is wrong | **Acho que isto está errado**<br>*a*shoo ker *ee*shtoo sht*a*h err*a*h-doo |
| Can you give me a receipt? | **Pode-me dar um recibo?**<br>pod-meh d*a*r oom res*ee*boo |

## Camping

- Be prepared to have to pay:
  per person
  for the car (if applicable)
  for the tent or caravan plot
  for electricity
  for hot showers

- You must provide proof of identity, such as your passport. In some parks it is necessary to show a camper's card or licence, issued by a national or international organization that is officially recognized.
- Municipal-run sites are recommended.
- There are a number of limitations regarding camping off-site – check with the tourist office in London before departure.
- There are also a series of campsites with the **ORBITUR** sign – these provide bath, camping and bungalow facilities.
- Most of Portugal's campsites are situated along the coast – those inland are few and far between.

*First alternative for men, second for women

## Youth hostels

- Look for the sign:
  **POUSADA DE JUVENTUDE**
- You must provide your own sleeping bag.
- You must have a YHA card.
- The charge for the night is the same for all ages, but some hostels are dearer than others.
- There are very few youth hostels in Portugal, and those that do exist provide dormitory accommodation. Few provide accommodation for girls. Cooking facilities are limited.

## WHAT TO SAY

Have you any vacancies?

**Tem espaço?**
taim shpassoo

How much is it . . .

**Quanto custa . . .**
kwantoo cooshta . . .

for the tent?

**pela tenda?**
pla tenda

for the caravan?

**pela roulotte?**
pla roolot

for the car?

**pelo carro?**
ploo carroo

for the electricity?

**pela electricidade?**
pla eletreeseedad

per person?

**por pessoa?**
poor psaw-a

per day/night?

**por dia/noite?**
poor dee-a/noyt

May I look round?

**Posso ver?**
posso vair

Do you provide anything . . .

**Fornecem alguma coisa . . .**
foornessaim algooma coyza . . .

to eat?

**para comer?**
para coomair

to drink?

**para beber?**
para bebair

Do you have . . .

**Têm . . .**
tay-aim . . .

a bar?

**um bar?**
oom bar

**Do you have . . .**      **Têm . . .**
         t*a*y-aim . . .

     hot showers?      **duches quentes?**
         d*oo*shesh kentsh

     a kitchen?      **uma cozinha?**
         *oo*ma coozeen-ya

     a laundry?      **uma lavandaria?**
         *oo*ma lavandar*ee*-a

     a restaurant?      **um restaurante?**
         oom resht*a*h-oorant

     a shop?      **uma loja?**
         *oo*ma loja

     a swimming pool?      **uma piscina?**
         *oo*ma peesh-s*ee*na

     a takeaway?      **comida preparada?**
         coom*ee*da prepar*a*hda

[*For food shopping, see p. 289, and for eating and drinking out, see
p. 299*]

## Problems

The toilet      **A retrete**
     a retret

The shower      **O duche**
     oo d*oo*sh

The tap      **A torneira**
     a toorn*a*yra

The razor point      **A ficha de barbear**
     a f*ee*sha der barbee-*a*r

The light      **A luz**
     a l*oo*sh

**. . . is not working**      **. . . não funciona**
     . . . nown foonsee-*a*wna

My camping gas has run out      **O gaz do meu fogão gastou-se**
     oo gash doo m*e*h-oo foog*o*wn
     gasht*a*w-ser

## LIKELY REACTIONS

Have you an identity
     document?      **Tem um documento de
     identificação?**
     taim oom doocoomentoo der
     eedenteefeeca-s*o*wn

| | |
|---|---|
| Your membership card, please | **O seu cartão de membro, por favor** |
| | oo seh-oo cartown der mehm-broo poor favor |
| What's your name? [see *p. 274*] | **Como se chama?** |
| | comoo ser shah-ma |
| Sorry, we're full | **Desculpe, estamos cheios** |
| | deshcoolp shtamoosh shay-oosh |
| How many people is it for? | **Para quantas pessoas é?** |
| | para kwantash psaw-ash eh |
| How many nights is it for? | **Para quantas noites é?** |
| | para kwantash noytsh eh |
| It's (50) escudos . . . | **São (cinquenta) escudos . . .** |
| | sown (seenkwenta) shkoodoosh . . . |
| per day/per night | **por dia/por noite** |
| | poor dee-a/poor noyt |
| I haven't any rooms left | **Não tenho mais quartos** |
| | nown tain-yoo mah-eesh kwartoosh |
| Do you want to have a look? | **Quer ver?** |
| | kair vair |

# General shopping

# The chemist's

## ESSENTIAL INFORMATION

- Look for the word **FARMÁCIA** (chemist) or these signs: a cross or an 'H'.
- Medicines (drugs) are available only at a chemist's.
- Some non-drugs can be bought at a supermarket or department store.
- Normal opening times are 9.00 a.m. to 1.00 p.m. and 3.00 p.m. to 7.00 p.m. From January to November, shops close at 1.00 p.m. on Saturday.

- If the chemist is shut the address of a nearby chemist on duty should be pinned on the door; if not, ask for the nearest **PRIMEIROS SOCORROS** (first aid centre). There may be an extra charge if after midnight (approx. 20%).
- Try the chemist before going to the doctor's as they are usually qualified to treat minor ailments.
- If you don't have insurance you'll have to pay the full rate. Keep receipts and packaging for the insurance claims.
- Some toiletries can also be bought at a **DROGARIA**.

## WHAT TO SAY

| | |
|---|---|
| I'd like . . . please | **Queria . . . por favor**<br>ker*ee*-a . . .poor fav*o*r |
| some Alka Seltzer | **Alka Seltzer**<br>alka seltzer |
| some antiseptic | **antiséptico**<br>antees*e*ticoo |
| some aspirin | **aspirinas**<br>aspeer*ee*nash |
| some baby food | **comida para bébé**<br>coom*ee*da para beh-beh |
| some contraceptives | **contraceptivos**<br>contrasept*ee*voosh |
| some cotton wool | **algodão**<br>algood*ow*n |
| some disposable nappies | **fraldas de papel**<br>fr*a*l-dash der pap*e*l |
| some eye drops | **pingos para os olhos**<br>p*ee*ngoosh para oosh *o*l-yoosh |
| some inhalant | **inalador**<br>eenalad*o*r |
| some insect repellent | **repelente de insectos**<br>repel*e*nt der eens*e*toosh |
| some paper tissues | **lenços de papel**<br>l*e*nsoosh der pap*e*l |
| some sanitary towels | **pensos higiénicos**<br>p*e*nssoosh eegee-*e*n-eecoosh |
| some sticking plaster | **adesivo**<br>ad-es*ee*voo |
| some suntan lotion/oil | **loção/óleo para bronzear**<br>loss*o*wn/*o*lee-oo para brawnzee-*a*r |

| | |
|---|---|
| some Tampax | **Tampax** |
| | tampax |
| some throat pastilles | **pastilhas para a garganta** |
| | pashteel-yash para ah garganta |
| some toilet paper | **papel higiénico** |
| | papel eegee-en-eecoo |
| **I'd like something for . . .** | **Queria alguma coisa para . . .** |
| | keree-a algooma coyza para . . . |
| bites/stings | **mordidelas** |
| | moordeedel-ash |
| burns/scalds | **queimaduras** |
| | cay-madoorash |
| a cold | **constipação** |
| | consh-teepassown |
| constipation | **prisão de ventre** |
| | preezown der ventr |
| a cough | **tosse** |
| | toss |
| diarrhoea | **diarreia** |
| | dee-array-a |
| earache | **dor de ouvidos** |
| | dor der awveedoosh |
| flu | **gripe** |
| | greep |
| sore gums | **gengivas doridas** |
| | janjeevash dooreedash |
| sunburn | **queimadura do sol** |
| | cay-madoora doo sol |
| toothache | **dor de dentes** |
| | dor der dentsh |
| travel sickness | **enjoo de viagem** |
| | enjaw-oo der vee-ajaim |

*[For other essential expressions, see 'Shop talk', p. 287]*

# Holiday items

## ESSENTIAL INFORMATION

- Places to shop at and signs to look for:
  **PAPELARIA-LIVRARIA** (stationery-bookshop)
  **FOTOGRAFIA** (films)
  and of course the main department stores:
  **GRANDELLA**
  **ARMAZÉNS DO CHIADO**

## WHAT TO SAY

| I'd like . . . | Queria . . . |
| --- | --- |
| | ker*ee*-a . . . |
| a bag | **um saco** |
| | oom s*a*c-oo |
| a beach ball | **uma bola de praia** |
| | *oo*ma bol-a der pr*a*h-ya |
| a bucket | **um balde** |
| | oom b*a*hld |
| an English newspaper | **um jornal inglês** |
| | oom joorn*a*l eenglesh |
| some envelopes | **envelopes** |
| | ainvel*o*psh |
| some postcards | **postais** |
| | pooshtah-eesh |
| a spade | **uma pá** |
| | *oo*ma p*a* |
| a straw hat | **um chapéu de palha** |
| | oom shap*e*h-oo der p*a*l-ya |
| some sunglasses | **óculos de sol** |
| | *o*cooloosh der sol |
| some writing paper | **pepel de escrever** |
| | pap*e*l der shkrev*ai*r |
| a colour film [*show the camera*] | **um filme a côres** |
| | oom feelm ah c*a*wresh |
| a black and white film | **um filme a preto e branco** |
| | oom feelm ah pret-oo ee brancoo |

# Shop talk

## ESSENTIAL INFORMATION

- Know how to say the important weights and measures:

| | |
|---|---|
| 50 grams | **cinquenta gramas** |
| | seenkwenta gram-ash |
| 100 grams | **cem gramas** |
| | saim gram-ash |
| 200 grams | **duzentas gramas** |
| | doozent-ash gram-ash |
| ½ kilo | **meio quilo** |
| | may-oo keeloo |
| 1 kilo | **um quilo** |
| | oom keeloo |
| 2 kilos | **dois quilos** |
| | doysh keeloosh |
| ½ litre | **meio litro** |
| | may-oo leetroo |
| 1 litre | **um litro** |
| | oom leetroo |
| 2 litres | **dois litros** |
| | doysh leetroosh |

[*For numbers, see p. 316*]

## CUSTOMER

| | |
|---|---|
| I'm just looking | **Estou só a ver** |
| | shtaw soh ah vair |
| How much is this/that? | **Quanto custa isto/aquilo?** |
| | kwantoo cooshta eeshtoo/akeeloo |
| What is that? | **O que é aquilo?** |
| | oo ker eh akeeloo |
| What are those? | **O que são aqueles?** |
| | oo ker sown akel-esh |
| Is there a discount? | **Faz desconto?** |
| | fash desh-cawntoo |
| I'd like that, please | **Queria aquilo, por favor** |
| | keree-a akeeloo poor favor |

| | |
|---|---|
| Not that | **Esse não** |
| | *ehsse nown* |
| Like that | **Como aquele** |
| | *comoo akel* |
| That's enough, thank you | **Chega obrigado/a\*** |
| | *sheg-a obreegah-doo/a* |
| More, please | **Mais, por favor** |
| | *mah-eesh poor favor* |
| Less | **Menos** |
| | *men-oosh* |
| That's fine | **Está bem** |
| | *shtah baim* |
| OK | **OK** |
| | *oh kay* |
| I won't take it, thank you | **Não quero, obrigado/a\*** |
| | *nown keroo obreegah-doo/a* |
| It's not right | **Não está certo** |
| | *nown shtah sairtoo* |
| **Have you got something . . .** | **Tem alguma coisa . . .** |
| | *taim algooma coyza . . .* |
| better? | **melhor?** |
| | *mel-yor* |
| cheaper? | **mais barata?** |
| | *mah-eesh barata* |
| different? | **diferente?** |
| | *deeferent* |
| larger?/smaller? | **maior?/mais pequena?** |
| | *ma-yor/mah-eesh pekena* |
| Can I have a bag, please? | **Posso ter um saco, por favor?** |
| | *posso tair oom sac-oo poor favor* |
| Can I have a receipt? | **Posso ter um recibo, por favor?** |
| | *posso tair oom reseeboo poor favor* |
| **Do you take . . .** | **Aceita . . .** |
| | *asayta . . .* |
| English/American money? | **dinheiro inglês/americano?** |
| | *deen-yayroo eenglesh/americanoo* |
| travellers' cheques? | **cheques de viagem?** |
| | *sheh-ksh der vee-ajaim* |
| credit cards? | **cartões de crédito?** |
| | *cartoynsh der credeetoo* |

\*First alternative for men, second for women.

## SHOP ASSISTANT

| | |
|---|---|
| Can I help you? | **Deseja alguma coisa?** |
| | dezay-ja algooma coyza |
| What would you like? | **Que quer?** |
| | ker kair |
| Will that be all? | **Não é mais nada?** |
| | nown eh mah-eesh nah-da |
| Is that all? | **É tudo?** |
| | eh toodoo |
| Anything else? | **Mais alguma coisa?** |
| | mah-eesh algooma coyza |
| Would you like it wrapped? | **Quer embrulhado?** |
| | kair embrool-yah-doo |
| Sorry, none left | **Desculpe, está esgotado** |
| | deshcoolp shtah esh-gootah-doo |
| I haven't got any | **Não tenho** |
| | nown tain-yoo |
| I haven't got any more | **Não tenho mais** |
| | nown tain-yoo mah-eesh |
| How many do you want? | **Quantos quer?** |
| | kwantoosh kair |
| How much do you want? | **Quanto quer?** |
| | kwantoo kair |
| Is that enough? | **Chega?** |
| | sheg-a |

# Shopping for food

# Bread

## ESSENTIAL INFORMATION

- Key words to look for: **PADARIA** (baker's) **PADEIRO** (baker)
  **PÃO** (bread)
- Bakeries will open weekdays from 7.30 a.m. – 12.30 p.m. and
  from 5.30 p.m. – 8.00 p.m. They also open on Saturday mornings.

- The most characteristic bread is a small individual bread roll called **papo seco** which is sold by item.
- For any other type of loaf, say **um pão** (oom pown), and point.

## WHAT TO SAY

| | |
|---|---|
| A loaf (like that) | **Um pão de forma (assim)** |
| | oom pown deh forma (asseem) |
| A home-made loaf | **Um pão caseiro** |
| | oom pown cazay-roo |
| A French loaf | **Um cacete** |
| | oom cah-set |
| A bread roll | **Um papo seco** |
| | oom pap-oo sec-oo |
| A crescent roll | **Um croissant** |
| | oom croo-ahssan |
| Two loaves | **Dois pães de forma** |
| | doysh pa-eensh der forma |
| A sliced loaf | **Um pão às fatias** |
| | oom pown ash fatee-ash |
| A wholemeal loaf | **Um pão integral** |
| | oom pown eenteh-gral |

[*For other essential expressions, see 'Shop talk' p. 287*]

# Cakes and ice-creams

## ESSENTIAL INFORMATION

- Key words to look for:
  **PASTELARIA** (cake shop)
  **CAFÉ** (a place where cakes and sandwiches can be bought to be eaten on the premises or taken away – alcoholic drinks are also served)
  **PADEIRO** (baker – some also sell fresh cakes)
  **GELADOS** (ice-cream)
  **GELATARIA** (ice-cream parlour)
  **CONFEITARIA** (sweet shop)
  **PASTELARIA** (cake shop)

● **CASA DE CHÁ** (a tea shop usually open during the afternoon)

## WHAT TO SAY

The types of cakes you find in shops vary from region to region but the following are the most common:

| | |
|---|---|
| **bola de Berlim** | doughnut |
| bol-a der berleen | |
| **duchesse** | cream-filled choux pastry |
| dooshez | |
| **pastel de nata** | custard tart |
| pashtel der nah-ta | |
| **bolo de côco** | coconut tart |
| bawloo der cawcoo | |
| **pão de ló** | sponge |
| pown der loh | |
| **queque** | cupcake |
| kek | |
| **palmier** | flat, crispy pastry biscuit |
| palmee-eh | |
| **mil folhas** | crispy pastry with fresh cream |
| meel fawl-yash | filling – mille feuilles |
| **suspiro** | meringue (bought by weight) |
| soospeeroo | |
| **tarte de amêndoa** | almond tart |
| tart der amaindoo-a | |
| **bolo de noz** | walnut cake |
| bawloo der noj | |
| **petits fours** | petits fours (bought by weight) |
| petee foor | |
| **queijadas de sintra** | individual cheesecakes |
| cay-ja-dash der shintra | |
| **fios de ovos** | |
| fee-oosh der ovoosh | very sweet, egg-based |
| **ovos moles** | confectionery |
| ovoosh molesh | |

| | |
|---|---|
| A . . . ice, please | **Um gelado . . . por favor** |
| | oom gelah-doo . . . poor favor |
| almond | **de amêndoa** |
| | der amaindoo-a |

| | |
|---|---|
| A . . . ice, please | **Um gelado . . . por favor** |
| | oom gel*ah*-doo . . . poor fav*o*r |
| banana | **de banana** |
| | der ban*a*na |
| chocolate | **de chocolate** |
| | der shookool*a*t |
| strawberry | **de morango** |
| | der moor*a*ngoo |
| vanilla | **de baunilha** |
| | der bah-oon*ee*l-ya |
| A (ten-escudo) cone | **Um cone de (dez escudos)** |
| | oom con der (desh shk*oo*doosh) |

# Picnic food

## ESSENTIAL INFORMATION

- Key words to look for:
  **CHARCUTARIA** (pork butcher's, delicatessen)
  **MERCEARIA** (grocer's)

## WHAT TO SAY

| | |
|---|---|
| Two slices of . . . | **Duas fatias de . . .** |
| | d*oo*-ash fat*ee*-ash der . . . |
| ham | **fiambre** |
| | fee-*a*mbr |
| roast pork | **carne de porco assada** |
| | carn der p*o*rcoo ass*ah*-da |
| spam | **mortadela** |
| | moortad*e*la |
| salami | **salame** |
| | sal*a*mee |
| meaty garlic sausage | **paio** |
| | pah-*ee*-oo |
| (parma) ham | **presunto** |
| | prez*oo*ntoo |

| | |
|---|---|
| tongue | **língua**<br>leengwa |

You might also like to try some of these:

| | |
|---|---|
| **salada de feijão frade**<br>salah-da der fay-jown frad | black-eyed bean salad |
| **croquetes**<br>croketsh | tiny meat rolls |
| **pastéis de bacalhau**<br>pashtaysh der bacal-yah-oo | cod in batter |
| **rissóis de camarão**<br>rissoysh der camarown | shrimp rissoles |
| **chouriço**<br>shawreesso | garlic sausage |
| **chouriço de carne**<br>shawreessoo der carn | beefy garlic sausage |
| **pastéis de massa folhada/de carne/de peixe**<br>pashtaysh der massa fool-yah-da/der carn/der paysh | meat/fish vol-au-vent |
| **panados de galinha**<br>panah-dosh der galeen-ya | chicken pieces in breadcrumbs |
| **salsichas**<br>salseeshash | sausages |
| **linguiça**<br>leengoo-eessa | very thin sausage |
| **farinheira**<br>fareen-yay-ra | floury pork sausage |
| **tremoços**<br>tremossosh | lupin seeds (served with beer in **cervejarias**) |
| **pevides**<br>peveedsh | dried and salted pumpkin seeds |
| **castanhas assadas**<br>cashtan-yash assah-dash | roast chestnuts |
| **favas fritas**<br>favash freetash | fried broad beans (served up as cocktail 'nibbles') |
| **queijo fresco**<br>cay-joo freshcoo | fresh goat's cheese (unsalted) |
| **requeijão**<br>recay-jown | fresh sheep's cheese |
| **queijo da serra**<br>cay-joo da serra | tasty full-fat cheese |

**queijo das Ilhas**
cay-joo dash eel-yash

**queijo de Serpa**
cay-joo der sairpa

**queijo de Évora**
cay-joo der evoora

**ovos cozidos**
ovoosh coozeedoosh

**almôndegas**
almawndeegash

**empadas de galinha/marisco**
aimpah-dash der galeen-ya/
 mareesh-coo

**frango no churrasco**
frangoo noo shoorrash-coo

**ovos verdes**
ovoosh vairdesh

**arroz doce**
arrawsh daws

**pudim molotoff**
poodim molotof

strong hard cheese (like Cheddar)

melting cheese (delicacy of the
 town of Serpa)

small, round, very hard, dried
 cheese

hard boiled eggs

meatballs

chicken/shellfish pies

chicken on the spit (spicy)

hard-boiled eggs with yolks
 mashed with parsley

sweet rice with lemon peel and
 cinnamon

egg-white pudding with caramel
 sauce

[*For other essential expressions, see 'Shop talk', p. 287*]

# Fruit and vegetables

## ESSENTIAL INFORMATION

● Key words to look for:
 **FRUTA** (fruit)
 **FRUTARIA** (greengrocer's)
 **LEGUMES** (vegetables)
 **FRESCO** (an indication of freshness)

## WHAT TO SAY

1 kilo of . . .

 apples

**Um quilo de . . .**
oom keeloo der . . .
**maçãs**
masansh

| | |
|---|---|
| apricots | **alperces** |
| | alp*ai*rsssesh |
| bananas | **bananas** |
| | ban*a*nash |
| cherries | **cerejas** |
| | ser*ay*-jash |
| grapes (white/black) | **uvas (brancas/pretas)** |
| | *oo*vash (br*a*ncash/pr*e*tash) |
| greengages | **rainhas cláudias** |
| | ra-*een*-yash cl*ou*d-ee-ash |
| oranges | **laranjas** |
| | lar*a*njash |
| peaches | **pêssegos** |
| | p*e*h-segoosh |
| pears | **pêras** |
| | p*e*rash |
| plums | **ameixas** |
| | am*ay*-shash |
| strawberries | **morangos** |
| | moor*a*ngoosh |
| A pineapple, please | **Um ananás . . . por favor** |
| | oom anan*a*sh poor fav*o*r |
| A grapefruit | **Uma toranja** |
| | *oo*ma toor*a*nja |
| A melon | **Um melão** |
| | oom mel*ow*n |
| A water melon | **Uma melancia** |
| | *oo*ma melans*ee*-a |
| ½ kilo of . . . | **Meio quilo de . . .** |
| | m*ay*-oo k*ee*loo der . . . |
| artichokes | **alcahofras** |
| | alkash*oh*-frash |
| broad beans | **favas** |
| | f*a*v-ash |
| carrots | **cenouras** |
| | sen*a*wrash |
| green beans | **feijão verde** |
| | fay-j*ow*n vaird |
| leeks | **alhos franceses** |
| | *a*l-yoosh frans*e*s-esh |
| mushrooms | **cogumelos** |
| | coogoom*e*l-oosh |

| ½ kilo of . . . | **Meio quilo de . . .** |
| | may-oo keeloo der . . . |
| onions | **cebolas** |
| | sebawlash |
| peas | **ervilhas** |
| | airveel-yash |
| potatoes | **batatas** |
| | batatash |
| shallots | **chalotas** |
| | shalo-tash |
| spinach | **espinafre** |
| | shpeenafr |
| tomatoes | **tomates** |
| | toomatsh |
| A bunch of . . . | **Um molho de . . .** |
| | oom mawl-yoo der . . . |
| parsley | **salsa** |
| | salsa |
| radishes | **rabanetes** |
| | rabanetsh |
| A head of garlic | **Uma cabeça de alho** |
| | ooma cabeh-sa der al-yoo |
| A lettuce | **Uma alface** |
| | ooma alfass |
| A cucumber | **Um pepino** |
| | oom pepeenoo |
| A turnip | **Um nabo** |
| | oom naboo |
| Like that, please | **Assim, por favor** |
| | asseem poor favor |

---

# Meat and fish

---

**ESSENTIAL INFORMATION**

- Key words to look for:
  **TALHO** (butcher's)
  **PEIXARIA** (fishmonger's)
  **PEIXE** (fish)

● Fresh fish can be bought at the market or at the fish auctions (**lotas**) held on the fishing beaches. It can occasionally be found in the larger supermarkets too.

## WHAT TO SAY

For a joint, choose the type of meat and then say how many people it is for:

| | |
|---|---|
| Some beef, please | **Carne de vaca, por favor**<br>carn der vac-a poor favor |
| Some lamb | **Carne de cordeiro**<br>carn der coorday-roo |
| Some mutton | **Carne de carneiro**<br>carn der carnay-roo |
| Some pork | **Carne de porco**<br>carn der porcoo |
| Some veal | **Carne de vitela**<br>carn der veetel-a |
| A joint . . . | **Uma peça . . .**<br>ooma pehsa . . . |
| for two people | **para duas pessoas**<br>para doo-ash psaw-ash |
| for four people | **para quatro pessoas**<br>para kwatroo psaw-ash |
| for six people | **para seis pessoas**<br>para saysh psaw-ash |
| Some steak, please | **Bifes, por favor**<br>beefsh poor favor |
| Some liver | **Fígado**<br>feegadoo |
| Some kidneys | **Rins**<br>reensh |
| Some sausages | **Salsichas**<br>salseeshash |
| for three people | **para três pessoas**<br>para tresh psaw-ash |
| for five people | **para cinco pessoas**<br>para seencoo psaw-ash |
| Two veal escalopes, please | **Dois escalopes de vitela, por favor**<br>doysh shcalopsh der veetel-a poor favor |

| | |
|---|---|
| Three pork chops | **Três costoletas de porco** |
| | tresh cooshtoolet-ash der porcoo |
| Four mutton chops | **Quatro costoletas de carneiro** |
| | kwatroo cooshtoolet-ash der carnay-roo |
| Five lamb chops | **Cinco costoletas de cordeiro** |
| | seencoo cooshtoolet-ash der coorday-roo |
| A chicken | **Um frango** |
| | oom frangoo |
| A rabbit | **Um coelho** |
| | oom co-ayl-yoo |
| A tongue | **Uma língua** |
| | ooma leengwa |

Purchase large fish and small shellfish by the weight:

| ½ kilo of . . . | **Meio quilo de . . .** |
|---|---|
| | may-oo keeloo der . . . |
| cod | **bacalhau** |
| | bacal-yah-oo |
| whiting | **pescada** |
| | pshcah-da |
| dover sole | **linguado** |
| | leengwah-doo |
| sea-bream | **pargo** |
| | pargoo |
| shrimps | **camarões** |
| | camarownsh |
| prawns | **gambas** |
| | gambash |
| mussels | **mexilhões** |
| | mesheel-yownsh |
| sardines | **sardinhas** |
| | sardeen-yash |
| squid | **lulas** |
| | loolash |
| small saurel | **carapau** |
| | carapah-oo |
| salmon | **salmão** |
| | salmown |

| | |
|---|---|
| halibut | **alibute** |
| | aleeb*oo*t |
| fresh tuna | **atum** |
| | at*oo*m |

For some shellfish and 'frying pan' fish, specify the number:

| | |
|---|---|
| A crab, please | **Um caranguejo, por favor** |
| | oom carang*ay*-joo poor fav*o*r |
| A lobster | **Uma lagosta** |
| | *oo*ma lag*a*wshta |
| A female crab | **Uma santola** |
| | *oo*ma santol-a |
| A big lobster | **Um lavagante** |
| | oom lavag*a*nt |
| A trout | **Uma truta** |
| | *oo*ma tr*oo*ta |
| A mackerel | **Uma cavala** |
| | *oo*ma cav*a*l-a |
| A hake | **Uma garoupa** |
| | *oo*ma gar*a*wpa |

# Eating and drinking out

## Ordering a drink and a snack

### ESSENTIAL INFORMATION

- By law, the price list of drinks (**TARIFAS DE CONSUMO**) must be displayed outside or in the window.
- There is waiter service in all cafés, but you can drink at the bar or counter if you wish – same price, but no service charge.
- Always leave a tip of 10% to 15% unless you see **SERVICO INCLUÍDO** (service included) printed on the bill or on a notice.
- Cafés serve non-alcoholic drinks and alcoholic drinks, and are normally open all day.

- Most cafés and 'beer houses' (**CERVEJARIAS**) also serve reasonably priced snacks and some also have a good à la carte service.
- A number of popular local 'nibbles' are often served free with beer/lager: **tremoços** (lupin seeds), **pevides** (salted and dried pumpkin seeds) and **favas ricas** (salted and fried broad beans).
- It is best to drink Portuguese tea on its own as milk impairs its flavour.

## WHAT TO SAY

| I'll have . . . please | Queria . . . por favor |
|---|---|
| | keree-a . . . poor favor |
| a small espresso black coffee | **uma bica** |
| | ooma beeca |
| a small milky coffee | **um garoto** |
| | oom garawtoo |
| a diluted black coffee | **um carioca** |
| | oom caree-oca |
| a large milky coffee | **um galão** |
| | oom galown |
| a tea | **um chá** |
| | oom shah |
| with milk | **com leite** |
| | com late |
| with lemon | **com limão** |
| | com leemown |
| a glass of milk | **um copo de leite** |
| | oom kopoo der late |
| two glasses of milk | **dois copos de leite** |
| | doysh kopoosh der late |
| a hot chocolate | **um chocolate quente** |
| | oom shookoolat kent |
| a mineral water | **uma água mineral** |
| | ooma ah-gwa meeneral |
| a lemonade (fizzy) | **uma limonada (com gás)** |
| | ooma leemoonada (com gash) |
| an orangeade (fizzy) | **uma laranjada (com gás)** |
| | ooma laranjada (com gash) |
| an orange juice | **um sumo de laranja** |
| | oom soomoo der laranja |

| | |
|---|---|
| a grape juice | **um sumo de uva** |
| | oom soomoo der oova |
| a pineapple juice | **um sumo de ananás** |
| | oom soomoo der ananash |
| a fruit milkshake | **um batido de fruta** |
| | oom bateedoo der froota |
| a lager | **uma cerveja** |
| | ooma servay-ja |
| a glass of draught lager | **uma imperial** |
| | ooma eemperee-al |
| a pint of draught lager | **uma caneca** |
| | ooma kaneka |
| a brown ale | **uma cerveja preta** |
| | ooma servay-ja preta |
| **I'll have . . . please** | **Queria . . . por favor** |
| | keree-a . . . poor favor |
| a cheese sandwich | **uma sandes de queijo** |
| | ooma sandsh der cay-joo |
| a ham sandwich | **uma sandes de fiambre** |
| | ooma sandsh der fee-ambr |
| a cheese and ham sandwich | **uma sandes mista** |
| | ooma sandsh meeshta |

These are some other snacks you may like to try:

| | |
|---|---|
| **uma sandes de paio** | a garlic sausage sandwich |
| ooma sandsh der pah-ee-oo | |
| **um cachorro** | a hot dog |
| oom cashaw-rroo | |
| **um prego** | a hot beefsteak roll |
| oom preg-oo | |
| **uma bifana** | a hot pork steak roll |
| ooma beefana | |
| **uma sandes de presunto** | a local parma-type ham sandwich |
| ooma sandsh der prezoontoo | |
| **um bitoque** | a small steak with fried egg and |
| oom beetoc | chips |
| **um pacote de batatas fritas** | a packet of crisps |
| oom pacot der batatash freetash | |
| **uma tosta** | a toasted sandwich |
| ooma tosh-ta | |

| | |
|---|---|
| **uma tosta mista** | cheese and ham toasted sandwich |
| *oo*ma t*o*sh-ta m*ee*shta | |
| **um chourico assado** | a roasted garlic sausage |
| oom shawr*ee*ssoo ass*ah*-doo | |
| **uma dose de mariscos** | a portion of shellfish |
| *oo*ma d*o*z deh mar*ee*sh-coosh | |

# In a restaurant

## ESSENTIAL INFORMATION

- You can eat at these places:
  RESTAURANTE
  CAFÉ
  CERVEJARIA (beer house)
  SNACK BAR
  SELF-SERVICE
  ESTALAGEM (quality inn)
  POUSADA (state owned inn)
- By law, the menus must be displayed outside or in the window
  – and that is the *only* way to judge if a place is right for your
  needs.
- Self-service exists, but most places have waiter service.
- Tip approximately 10% unless service is included.
- Half portions (**meia dose**) can be ordered for adults as well as
  children.
- Eating times are flexible – approximately 12.00 p.m. to 3.00 p.m.
  and 7.00 p.m. to 11.00 p.m.

## WHAT TO SAY

| | |
|---|---|
| May I book a table? | **Posso reservar uma mesa?** |
| | p*o*ssoo rezairv*a*r *oo*ma m*e*z-a |
| I've booked a table | **Tenho uma mesa reservada** |
| | t*ai*n-yoo *oo*ma m*e*z-a rezairv*ah*-da |
| A table . . . | **Uma mesa . . .** |
| | *oo*ma m*e*z-a . . . |
| for one | **para uma pessoa** |
| | p*a*ra *oo*ma ps*aw*-a |

| | |
|---|---|
| for three | **para três pessoas** |
| | p*a*ra tresh ps*a*w-ash |
| The à la carte menu, please | **O menu à la carte, por favor** |
| | oo mehn*oo a*h la cart poor fav*o*r |
| The fixed-price menu | **O menu de preço fixo** |
| | oo mehn*oo* der press*o* f*ee*csoo |
| The tourist menu | **O menu turístico** |
| | oo mehn*oo* toor*ee*shtic*oo* |
| Today's special menu | **Os pratos do dia** |
| | oosh pr*a*t-oosh doo d*ee*-a |
| What's this, please? [*point to menu*] | **O que é isto, por favor?** |
| | oo ker eh *ee*shtoo poor fav*o*r |
| The wine list | **A lista das vinhos** |
| | a leeshta doosh v*ee*n-yoosh |
| A carafe of wine, please | **Um jarro de vinho, por favor** |
| | oom j*a*rroo der v*ee*n-yoo poor favor |
| A half | **Meio jarro** |
| | m*a*y-oo j*a*rroo |
| A glass | **Um copo** |
| | oom c*o*p-oo |
| A (half) bottle | **Uma (meia) garrafa** |
| | *oo*ma (m*a*y-a) garr*a*fa |
| A litre | **Um litro** |
| | oom l*ee*troo |
| Red/white/rosé/house wine | **Vinho da casa tinto/branco/rosé** |
| | v*ee*n-yoo da c*a*h-za t*ee*ntoo/ br*a*ncoo/rozeh |
| Some more bread, please | **Mais pão, por favor** |
| | mah-*ee*sh pown poor fav*o*r |
| Some more wine | **Mais vinho** |
| | mah-*ee*sh v*ee*n-yoo |
| Some oil | **Óleo** |
| | ol-*ee*-oo |
| Some olive oil | **Azeite** |
| | az*a*yt |
| Some vinegar | **Vinagre** |
| | veen*a*gr |
| Some salt/pepper | **Sal/pimenta** |
| | sahl/peem*e*nta |
| Some water | **Água** |
| | *a*h-gwa |

| | |
|---|---|
| With/without garlic | **Com/sem alho** |
| | com/saym al-yoo |
| How much does that come to? | **Quanto é tudo?** |
| | kwantoo eh toodoo |
| Is service included? | **Tem serviço incluído?** |
| | taim serveessoo eencloo-eedoo |
| Where is the toilet, please? | **A casa de banho, por favor?** |
| | a cah-za der bain-yoo poor favor |
| The bill, please | **A conta, por favor** |
| | a conta poor favor |

**Key words for courses, as seen on some menus:** [*Only ask the question if you want the waiter to remind you of the choice*]

| | |
|---|---|
| **What have you got in the way of . . .** | **O que tem de . . .** |
| | oo ker taim der . . . |
| starters? | **entradas?** |
| | entrah-dash |
| soup? | **sopa?** |
| | sawpa |
| egg dishes? | **ovos?** |
| | ovoosh |
| fish? | **peixe?** |
| | paysh |
| meat? | **carne?** |
| | carn |
| game? | **caça?** |
| | cassa |
| fowl? | **aves?** |
| | ahvsh |
| vegetables? | **legumes?** |
| | legoomsh |
| cheese? | **queijo?** |
| | cay-joo |
| fruit? | **fruta?** |
| | froota |
| ice-cream? | **gelados?** |
| | gelah-doosh |
| dessert? | **sobremesa?** |
| | sawbr-mehza |

## UNDERSTANDING THE MENU

- You will find the names of the principal ingredients of most dishes on these pages:

  Starters see p. 292     Fruit see p. 294
  Meat see p. 297         Dessert see p. 291
  Fish see p. 298         Cheese see p. 293
  Vegetables see p. 295   Ice-cream see p. 291

- Used together with the following lists of cooking and menu terms, they should help you to decode the menu.

## Cooking and menu terms

| | |
|---|---|
| em açorda | in breadcrumbs (but not fried) |
| à alentejana | with garlic, clams and coriander |
| com alho | with garlic |
| assado | roasted |
| com azeite | with olive oil |
| bem passado | well done |
| na brasa | barbecued |
| à Bráz | with onions and potatoes in egg |
| à Bulhão-Pato | with garlic, olive oil and coriander |
| caldo | broth |
| na cataplana | cooked on a griddle |
| no churrasco | on the spit |
| com coentros | with fresh coriander |
| cozido | boiled |
| cozido a vapor | steamed |
| cru | raw |
| doce | sweet |
| de escabeche | marinated |
| escalfado | poached |
| à espanhola | with onions and tomato |
| no espeto | on the spit |
| estrelado | fried (egg) |
| estufado | cooked in its own juices |
| fervido | boiled |
| no forno | in the oven |
| frio | cold |
| frito | fried |
| fumado | smoked |
| em geleia | in aspic |

| | |
|---|---|
| à Gomes de Sá | with olives, potatoes and egg |
| gratinado | au gratin |
| guisado | stewed |
| com limão | with lemon |
| com Madeira | with Madeira |
| com manteiga | with butter |
| médio | medium done |
| meio cru | rare |
| mexido | scrambled |
| com molho | with sauce |
| com molho da casa | with the house sauce |
| com molho de vinagrete | with vinaigrette sauce |
| com molho picante | with spicy sauce |
| ao natural | plain |
| com ovo a cavalo | with fried egg on top |
| panado | fried in breadcrumbs |
| passado por água | blanched |
| à portuguesa | with tomatoes, onions, olive oil |
| recheado | stuffed |
| com salsa | with parsley |
| salteado | sautéed |
| com tinta | in its own ink (squid) |
| com tomate | with tomato |
| à transmontana | with cabbage |

## Further words to help you understand the menu

| | |
|---|---|
| açorda à alentejana | very rich coriander soup with egg and bread |
| almôndegas | meatballs |
| ameijoas à Bulhão-Pato | clams in garlic sauce |
| arroz à portuguesa | vegetable rice |
| bacalhau | salted dried cod served in numerous ways |
| bife | steak |
| borrego | lamb |
| cabrito | kid |
| caranguejo | crab |
| carne de porco à alentejana | pork with clams |
| carnes frias | cold meats |
| chispalhada | pigs' trotters stew |
| chocos com tinta | squid in their own ink |

| | |
|---|---|
| codorniz | quail |
| coelho guisado | stewed rabbit |
| dobrada | tripe stew |
| empadas de galinha | chicken pies |
| enchidos | garlic sausages |
| ervilhas guisadas | stewed peas |
| favas | broad beans |
| feijoada | bean and sausage stew |
| fígado | liver |
| gambas al iajilho | king prawns fried in olive oil with garlic |
| gaspacho | cold vegetable soup (usually tomato) |
| linguado | dover sole |
| lulas | squid |
| mexilhão | mussels |
| miolas | brains |
| pastéis de massa folhada | vol-au-vents |
| peixe espada | swordfish |
| peixinhos da horta | runner beans in batter |
| perdizes | partridges |
| perna de porco | leg of pork |
| pombo | pigeon |
| rins | kidneys |
| salada de atum | tuna salad |
| salsichas | sausages |
| sopa de marisco | shellfish soup |
| torta | type of Swiss roll sponge with filling |
| tripas | tripe |

# Health

## ESSENTIAL INFORMATION

- At present there are no reciprocal health agreements between the UK and Portugal. It is *essential* therefore to have proper medical insurance. A policy can be bought through a travel agent, a broker or a motoring organization.

- Take your own 'first line' first-aid kit with you.
- For minor disorders, and treatment at a chemist's, see p. 283.
- For finding your way to a doctor, dentist or chemist's, see p. 276.
- In an emergency, dial 115 for the ambulance service.

## What's the matter?

| | |
|---|---|
| I have a pain here [*point*] | **Tenho uma dor aqui** |
| | t*ai*n-yoo *oo*ma dor ak*ee* |
| I have a toothache | **Tenho uma dor de dentes** |
| | t*ai*n-yoo *oo*ma dor der d*e*ntsh |
| **I have broken . . .** | **Parti . . .** |
| | part*ee* . . . |
| my dentures | **a minha dentadura** |
| | ah m*ee*n-ya dentad*oo*ra |
| my glasses | **os meus óculos** |
| | oosh meh-oosh *o*cool*oo*sh |
| **I have lost . . .** | **Perdi . . .** |
| | perd*ee* . . . |
| my contact lenses | **as minhas lentes de contacto** |
| | ash m*ee*n-yash l*e*ntsh der cont*a*ctoo |
| a filling | **um chumbo** |
| | oom sh*oo*mboo |
| My child is ill | **O meu filho/a minha filha está doente** |
| | oo m*e*h-oo f*ee*l-yoo/a m*ee*n-ya f*ee*l-ya shtah doo-*e*nt |

## Already under treatment for something else?

| | |
|---|---|
| **I take . . . regularly** [*show*] | **Tomo . . . regularmente** |
| | t*o*moo . . . regoolarm*e*nt |
| this medicine | **este medicamento** |
| | *e*sht medeecam*e*ntoo |
| these pills | **estes comprimidos** |
| | *e*shtsh compreem*ee*doosh |
| **I have . . .** | **Sofro . . .** |
| | s*a*wfroo . . . |
| a heart condition | **do coração** |
| | doo coorass*ow*n |
| haemorrhoids | **das hemorroidas** |
| | dash em-oorr*oy*dash |

| | |
|---|---|
| rheumatism | **de reumático** |
| | der reh-oomaticoo |
| I am . . . | **Sou . . .** |
| | saw . . . |
| diabetic | **diabético/a*** |
| | dee-abetico/a |
| asthmatic | **asmático/a*** |
| | ash-maticoo/a |
| allergic to penicillin | **alérgico/a à penicilina*** |
| | alairjicoo/a ah pehnee-seeleena |
| I am pregnant | **Estou grávida** |
| | shtaw grav-eeda |

*First alternative for men, second for women.

# Problems: loss, theft

## ESSENTIAL INFORMATION

- If the worst comes to the worst, find the police station. To ask the way, see p. 274.
  Look for:
  **POLÍCIA**
  **GNR** (Guarda Nacional Republicana – National Guard)
- If you lose your passport go to the nearest British Consulate
- In an emergency, dial 322222 (Fire) or 364141/372131 (Police)

## LOSS
[*See also 'Theft' below: the lists are interchangeable*]

| | |
|---|---|
| I have lost . . . | **Perdi . . .** |
| | perdee |
| my camera | **a minha máquina fotográfica** |
| | ah meenya mac-eena footoografeeca |
| my car keys | **as chaves do meu carro** |
| | ash shavsh doo meh-oo carroo |
| my car logbook | **o livrete do meu carro** |
| | oo leevret doo meh-oo carroo |

| I have lost . . .. | **Perdi . . .** |
|---|---|
| | perd*ee* |
| my driving licence | **a minha carta de condução** |
| | ah m*ee*-ya c*a*rta der cawndoos*ow*n |
| my insurance certificate | **o meu certificado de seguro** |
| | oo m*eh*-oo serteefee-c*ah*-do der |
| | seg*oo*roo |

## THEFT

| Someone has stolen . . . | **Roubaram-me . . .** |
|---|---|
| | rawbar*ow*n meh . . . |
| my car | **o meu carro** |
| | oo m*eh*-oo c*a*rroo |
| my luggage | **a minha bagagem** |
| | ah m*ee*-ya bagaj*ai*m |
| my money | **o meu dinheiro** |
| | oo m*eh*-oo deen-y*ay*-roo |
| my purse | **o meu porta-moedas** |
| | oo m*eh*-oo p*o*rta-m*oo*edash |
| my tickets | **os meus bilhetes** |
| | oosh m*eh*-oosh beel-y*e*tsh |
| my travellers' cheques | **os meus travellers' cheques** |
| | oosh m*eh*-oosh travellers' sk*e*h-ksh |
| my wallet | **a minha carteira** |
| | ah m*ee*-ya cart*ay*-ra |

---

# The post office and phoning home

## ESSENTIAL INFORMATION

- Key words to look for:
  **CORREIOS**
  **CTT – CORREIOS, TELEGRAFOS E TELEFONES**
- Look for the letters **CTT** on a blue sign.
- Unless you read and speak Portuguese well, it's best not to make phone calls by yourself. Go to a post office and write the town and number you want on a piece of paper.

- For the UK dial 0744 and the number you require.
- You can ask at your local post office for a brochure on phoning England from abroad.
- Tourist information (in English) is available on this number in Lisbon: 706341.

**WHAT TO SAY**

| | |
|---|---|
| To England, please | **Para Inglaterra, por favor** |
| | p*ara* eenglat*ai*rra poor favor |
| [*Hand letters, cards or parcels over the counter*] | |
| To Australia | **Para a Austrália** |
| | p*ara* a ah-oosh-tr*a*hlia |
| To the United States | **Para os Estados Unidos** |
| | p*ara* oosh sht*a*h-doosh oon*ee*doosh |
| I'd like to send a telegram | **Queria enviar um telegrama** |
| | ker*ee*-a envee-*ar* oom telegr*a*ma |
| I'd like this number . . . | **Queria este número . . .** |
| [*show number*] | ker*ee*-a esht n*oo*meroo . . . |
| in England | **na Inglaterra** |
| | na eenglat*ai*rra |
| in Canada | **no Canadá** |
| | noo canad*a*h |
| Can you dial it for me, please? | **Podia-me marcar por favor?** |
| | pood*ee*-a-meh marc*a*r poor favor |

# Changing cheques and money

**ESSENTIAL INFORMATION**

- Look for these words on buildings:
  **BANCO** (bank)
  **CRÉDITO**
  **CÂMBIO-EXCHANGE** (change bureau)
- To cash your own normal cheques, exactly as at home, use your banker's card where you see the Eurocheque sign.
- Exchange rate information might show the pound as:
  **£, L, LIBRA** or even **GB**
- Have your passport handy.

**WHAT TO SAY**

| | |
|---|---|
| I'd like to cash . . . | Queria trocar . . . |
| | ker*ee*-a troo*car* . . . |
| this travellers' cheque | **este cheque de viagem** |
| | esht shek de vee-*a*jaim |
| I'd like to change this . . . | Queria trocar isto . . . |
| | ker*ee*-a troo*car* *ee*shtoo . . . |
| into Portuguese escudos | **por escudos portugues** |
| | poor shk*oo*doosh poortoogesh |
| into French francs | **por francos franceses** |
| | poor fr*a*ncoosh frans*ez*-esh |
| into Spanish pesetas | **por pesetas espanholas** |
| | poor pez*et*-ash shpan-y*ol*-ash |

# Car travel

**ESSENTIAL INFORMATION**

- Grades of petrol:
  **SUPER**
  **NORMAL** (2 star standard)
  **DOIS TEMPOS** (two stroke)
  **GASÓLEO** (diesel)
- 1 gallon is about 4½ litres (accurate enough up to 6 gallons).
- Types of garages: Often 'all in one' called **GARAGEM**, but sometimes separate under **BATE CHAPAS** (body repairs); **GARAGEM DE SERVIÇO** (mechanical repairs and service); **REPARAÇÕES ELÉCTRICAS** (for electrical faults); and **PNEUS** (tyres).
- Most garages are open 8.00 a.m. to 12.00 p.m. and 2.00 p.m. to 7.00 p.m. but not Saturdays. If driving inland, remember to fill up as petrol stations may be closed or hard to find.

## WHAT TO SAY

[*For numbers, see p. 316*]

| | |
|---|---|
| (9) litres of . . . | (Nove) litros de . . . |
| | (nov) leetroosh der . . . |
| (200) escudos of . . . | (Duzentos) escudos de . . . |
| | (doozentoosh) shkoodoosh der . . . |
| standard/premium/diesel | normal/super/gasóleo |
| | normal/sooper/gazol-ee-oo |
| Fill it up, please | Pode encher, por favor |
| | pod ainchair poor favor |
| Will you check . . . | Pode verificar . . . |
| | pod vereefeecar . . . |
| the oil? | o nível do óleo? |
| | oo neevel doo ol-ee-oo |
| the battery? | a água da bateria? |
| | a ah-gwa da bateree-a |
| the radiator? | a água do radiador? |
| | a ah-gwa doo radee-ador |
| the tyres? · | a pressão dos pneus? |
| | a pressown doosh pneh-oosh |
| I've run out of petrol | Acabou-se a gasolina |
| | acabaw-seh a gazooleena |
| Can you help me, please? | Pode ajudar-me, por favor? |
| | pod ajoodar-meh poor favor |
| Do you do repairs? | Faz reparações? |
| | fash reparasoynsh |
| I have a puncture | Tenho um pneu furado |
| | tain-yoo oom pneh-oo foorah-doo |
| I have a broken windscreen | Tenho o pára-brisas partido |
| | tain-yoo oo para-breezash parteedoo |
| I think the problem is here . . . [*point*] | Penso que o problema está aqui . . . |
| | pensoo ker oo problema shtah akee . . . |

## LIKELY REACTIONS

| | |
|---|---|
| I don't do repairs | Não faço reparações |
| | nown fassoo reparasoynsh |

Where is your car? **Onde está o seu carro?**
awnd shtah oo seh-oo carroo

What make is it? **De que marca é?**
der ker marca eh

Come back tomorrow/on **Volte amanhã/na segunda-feira**
Monday volt aman-yan/na segoonda fayra

[For days of the week, see p. 318]

# Public transport

## ESSENTIAL INFORMATION

- Frequent fast electric trains connect Lisbon with the tourist zones of Sintra and Cascais. The **CP** (Portuguese Railways) keep two steam trains in circulation during the high season for tourists.
- Lisbon is serviced by trams, buses and a small underground network. If you are spending a couple of days in the capital, buy a *tourist ticket* at any of the City Transport Company's information kiosks (they can only be used for surface public transport).
- Queuing in Portugal can be haphazard.
- Booklets of tickets are also available for tube travel – you will have to pay more if you buy each ticket separately.
- Key words on signs:
  **BILHETES** (tickets)
  **ENTRADA** (entrance)
  **PROIBIDO** (forbidden)
  **CAIS** (platform)
  **INFORMAÇÕES** (information)
  **SAÍDA** (exit)
  **DEPÓSITO DE BAGAGEM** (left-luggage)
  **PARAGEM DE AUTOCARRO** (bus stop)
  **HORÁRIO** (timetable)

## WHAT TO SAY

| | |
|---|---|
| Where does the train for (Lisbon) leave from? | **De onde parte o comboio para (Lisboa)?** |
| | der awnd part oo comboy-oo para (leeshboo-a) |
| Is this the train for (Lisbon)? | **É este o comboio para (Lisboa)?** |
| | eh esht oo comboy-oo para (leeshboo-a) |
| Where does the bus for (Coimbra) leave from? | **De onde parte a camioneta para (Coimbra)?** |
| | der awnd part a kam-yoonet-a para (coo-eembra) |
| Is this the bus for (Coimbra)? | **É esta a camioneta para (Coimbra)?** |
| | eh eshta a kam-yoonet-a para (coo-eembra) |
| Do I have to change? | **Tenho que fazer mudança?** |
| | tain-yoo ker fazair moodansa |
| Can you put me off at the right stop, please? | **Pode dizer-me onde devo descer, por favor?** |
| | pod deezair-meh awnd devoo desh-sehr poor favor |
| Where can I get a taxi? | **Onde posso arranjar um taxi?** |
| | awnd possoo arranjar oom taxi |
| Can I book a seat? | **Posso reservar um lugar?** |
| | possoo rezervar oom loogar |
| A single | **Uma ida** |
| | ooma eeda |
| A return | **Uma ida e volta** |
| | ooma eeda ee volta |
| First class | **Em primeira classe** |
| | aim preemay-ra klas |
| Second class | **Em segunda classe** |
| | aim segoonda klas |
| One adult | **Para um adulto** |
| | para oom adooltoo |
| Two adults | **Para dois adultos** |
| | para doysh adooltoosh |
| and one child | **e uma criança** |
| | ee ooma cree-ansa |
| How much is it? | **Quanto custa?** |
| | kwantoo cooshta |

# Reference

## NUMBERS

| 0  | zero            | zeh-roo           |
|----|-----------------|-------------------|
| 1  | um              | oom               |
| 2  | dois            | doysh             |
| 3  | três            | tresh             |
| 4  | quatro          | kwatroo           |
| 5  | cinco           | seencoo           |
| 6  | seis            | saysh             |
| 7  | sete            | set               |
| 8  | oito            | oytoo             |
| 9  | nove            | nov               |
| 10 | dez             | desh              |
| 11 | onze            | awnz              |
| 12 | doze            | dawz              |
| 13 | treze           | trez              |
| 14 | catorze         | catorz            |
| 15 | quinze          | keenz             |
| 16 | dezasseis       | dez-asaysh        |
| 17 | dezassete       | dez-aset          |
| 18 | dezoito         | dez-oytoo         |
| 19 | dezanove        | dez-anov          |
| 20 | vinte           | veent             |
| 21 | vinte e um      | veent ee oom      |
| 22 | vinte e dois    | veent ee doysh    |
| 23 | vinte e três    | veent ee tresh    |
| 24 | vinte e quatro  | veent ee kwatroo  |
| 25 | vinte e cinco   | veent ee seencoo  |
| 26 | vinte e seis    | veent ee saysh    |
| 27 | vinte e sete    | veent ee set      |
| 28 | vinte e oito    | veent ee oytoo    |
| 29 | vinte e nove    | veent ee nov      |
| 30 | trinta          | treenta           |
| 31 | trinta e um     | treenta ee oom    |
| 32 | trinta e dois   | treenta ee doysh  |
| 33 | trinta e três   | treenta ee tresh  |
| 34 | trinta e quatro | treenta ee kwatroo|
| 35 | trinta e cinco  | treenta ee seencoo|

| 40 | **quarenta** | kwarenta |
|----|----------|----------|
| 41 | **quarenta e um** | kwarenta ee oom |
| 45 | **quarenta e cinco** | kwarenta ee seencoo |
| 50 | **cinquenta** | seenkwenta |
| 55 | **cinquenta e cinco** | seenkwenta ee seencoo |
| 60 | **sessenta** | sessenta |
| 66 | **sessenta e seis** | sessenta ee saysh |
| 70 | **setenta** | set-enta |
| 77 | **setenta e sete** | set-enta ee set |
| 80 | **oitenta** | oytenta |
| 88 | **oitenta e oito** | oytenta ee oytoo |
| 90 | **noventa** | nooventa |
| 99 | **noventa e nove** | nooventa ee nov |
| 100 | **cem** | saim |
| 101 | **cento e um** | sentoo ee oom |
| 102 | **cento e dois** | sentoo ee doysh |
| 125 | **cento e vinte cinco** | sentoo ee veent ee seencoo |
| 150 | **cento e cinquenta** | sentoo ee seenkwenta |
| 175 | **cento e setenta e cinco** | sentoo ee set-enta ee seencoo |
| 200 | **duzentos** | doozentoosh |
| 300 | **trezentos** | trez-entoosh |
| 400 | **quatrocentos** | kwatrosentoosh |
| 500 | **quinhentos** | keen-yentoosh |
| 1,000 | **mil** | meel |
| 2,000 | **dois mil** | doysh meel |
| 10,000 | **dez mil** | desh meel |
| 100,000 | **cem mil** | saim meel |
| 1,000,000 | **um milhão** | oom meel-yown |

## TIME

| What time is it? | **Que horas são?** |
|----|----|
| | ker orash sown |
| It's one o'clock | **É uma hora** |
| | eh ooma ora |
| It's . . . | **São . . .** |
| | sown . . . |
| two o'clock | **duas horas** |
| | doo-ash orash |
| three o'clock | **três horas** |
| | tresh orash |

| It's . . . | É . . . |
|---|---|
| | eh . . . |
| noon | **meio-dia** |
| | may-oo dee-a |
| midnight | **meia-noite** |
| | may-a noyt |
| a quarter past five | **cinco e um quarto** |
| | seencoo ee oom kwartoo |
| half past five | **cinco e meia** |
| | seencoo ee may-a |
| a quarter to six | **um quarto para as seis** |
| | oom kwartoo para ash saysh |

## DAYS AND MONTHS

| Monday | **segunda-feira** |
|---|---|
| | segoonda fayra |
| Tuesday | **terça-feira** |
| | tairsa fayra |
| Wednesday | **quarta-feira** |
| | kwarta fayra |
| Thursday | **quinta-feira** |
| | keenta fayra |
| Friday | **sexta-feira** |
| | sayshta fayra |
| Saturday | **sábado** |
| | sab-adoo |
| Sunday | **domingo** |
| | doomeengoo |
| January | **janeiro** |
| | janay-roo |
| February | **fevereiro** |
| | fev-eray-roo |
| March | **março** |
| | marsoo |
| April | **abril** |
| | abreel |
| May | **maio** |
| | mah-ee-oo |
| June | **junho** |
| | joon-yoo |

| | | |
|---|---|---|
| July | **julho** | |
| | jool-yoo | |
| August | **agosto** | |
| | agawshtoo | |
| September | **setembro** | |
| | set-embroo | |
| October | **outubro** | |
| | awtoobroo | |
| November | **novembro** | |
| | noovembroo | |
| December | **dezembro** | |
| | dez-embroo | |

## Public holidays

● Offices, shops and schools are all closed on the following dates.

| 1 January | Ano Novo | New Year's Day |
|---|---|---|
| . . . | Fexta Feira Santa | Good Friday |
| 25 April | Vinte e cinco de Abril | Freedom Day (date of 1974 revolution) |
| 1 May | Dia do Trabalhador | Labour Day |
| . . . | Corpo de Deus | Corpus Christi |
| 10 June | Dia de Portugal | National Day |
| 15 August | Assunção | Assumption Day |
| 5 October | Proclamação da Replubíca | Proclamation of the Republic |
| 1 November | Todos os Santos | All Saints' Day |
| 1 December | Restauração da Independência | Restoration of Independence |
| 8 December | Imaculada Conceição | Immaculate Conception |
| 25 December | Natal | Christmas Day |

# Index

# Travellers' **Serbo-Croat**
for Yugoslavia

**D. L. Ellis, E. Spong**

Pronunciation **Dr J. Baldwin**

*Useful address*
Yugoslav National Tourist Office
143 Regent Street
London W1

# Contents

---

# Pronunciation hints

In Serbo-Croat, it is important to stress or emphasize the syllables in *italics*, just as you would if we were to take as an English example: Little Jack Horner *sat* in the *corner*. Here we have ten syllables but only four stresses.

For interest, you will find below the characters of the Cyrillic alphabet which you will probably not need but which is used throughout Yugoslavia – except in Slovenia and Croatia where the Roman alphabet is in use. The columns on the left show the printed capital and small letters, and the one on the right the corresponding letter in the Roman alphabet (as used in this book).

| А | а | a | Г | г | g | О | о | o |
| Б | б | b | Х | х | h | П | п | p |
| Ц | ц | c | И | и | i | Р | р | r |
| Ч | ч | č | J | ј | j | С | с | s |
| Ћ | ћ | ć | К | к | k | Ш | ш | š |
| Д | д | d | Л | л | l | Т | т | t |
| Џ | џ | dž | Љ | љ | lj | У | у | u |
| Ђ | ђ | dj | М | м | m | В | в | v |
| Е | е | e | Н | н | n | З | з | z |
| Ф | ф | f | Њ | њ | nj | Ж | ж | ž |

**Dobra zabava!**

# Everyday expressions

[*See also 'Shop talk', p. 338*]

| | |
|---|---|
| Hello (informal) | **Zdravo**<br>zdr*a*-fo |
| Good morning | **Dobro jutro**<br>d*o*b-ro y*o*otro |
| Good day (hello) | **Dobar dan**<br>d*o*b-ar d*u*n |
| Good night | **Laku noć**<br>l*a*-koo n*o*ch |
| Goodbye | **Zbogom**<br>zb*o*g-om |
| Yes | **Da**<br>da |
| Please | **Molim**<br>m*o*l-im |
| Yes, please | **Da, Molim**<br>da m*o*l-im |
| Thank you | **Hvala vam**<br>f*a*-la vum |
| Thank you very much | **Puno vam hvala**<br>p*oo*no vum f*a*-la |
| That's right | **Točno**<br>t*o*ch-no |
| No | **Ne**<br>neh |
| I disagree | **Ne slažem se**<br>neh sl*a*-shem seh |
| Excuse me ⎤<br>Sorry  ⎦ | **Oprostite/pardon**<br>aprost-eet-eh/p*a*r-don |
| It doesn't matter | **Ne smeta**<br>neh sm*e*h-ta |
| Where's the toilet, please? | **Gdje je toaleta, molim?**<br>gd-y*e*h tw*a*-leh-ta m*o*l-im |
| Do you speak English? | **Govorite li engleski?**<br>gov-oree-teh lee *e*n-glesky |
| What's your name? | **Kako se zovete?**<br>k*a*-ko seh z*o*v-et-eh |
| My name is . . . | **Ja se zovem . . .**<br>ya seh z*o*v-em . . . |

# Asking the way

## ESSENTIAL INFORMATION

- Keep a look out for all these place names as you will find them on shops, maps and notices.

## WHAT TO SAY

| | |
|---|---|
| Excuse me, please | **Oprostite, molim**<br>oprost-eet-eh mol-im |
| Which is the way . . . | **Koji je put . . .**<br>koyee yeh poot . . . |
| to Belgrade? | **za Beograd?**<br>za beh-ograd |
| to (Republic) street? | **za ulicu (Republike)?**<br>za ooleetsoo (repoob-leekeh) |
| to the Hotel Lapad? | **za Hotel Lapad?**<br>za hotel lap-ad |
| to the airport? | **za aerodrom?**<br>za ah-airodrom |
| to the beach? | **za plažu?**<br>za plash-oo |
| to the bus station? | **za autobusnu stanicu?**<br>za ah-ooto-boosnoo stan-eetsoo |
| to the market? | **za tržnicu?**<br>za ter-shnee-tsoo |
| to the police station? | **za miliciju?**<br>za meel-eets-yoo |
| to the port? | **za luku?**<br>za loo-koo |
| to the post office? | **za poštu?**<br>za posh-too |
| to the railway station? | **za željezničku stanicu?**<br>za shel-yezneech-koo stan-eetsoo |
| to the sports stadium? | **za športski stadion?**<br>za shport-skee stad-ee-on |
| to the tourist information office? | **za turistički ured?**<br>za toorist-eech-kee oo-red |

| | |
|---|---|
| to the town centre? | **za centar grada?** |
| | za tsen-tar gra-da |
| to the town hall? | **za gradsku općinu?** |
| | za grat-skoo op-chee-noo |
| Excuse me, please | **Oprostite, molim** |
| | oprost-eet-eh mol-im |
| **Is there . . . near by?** | **Ima li ovdje blizu . . .?** |
| | eema lee ovd-yeh blee-zoo . . . |
| a baker's | **pekarna** |
| | pek-arna |
| a bank | **banka** |
| | ban-ka |
| a bus stop | **autobusna stanica** |
| | ah-ooto-boosna stan-eetsa |
| a butcher's | **mesarnica** |
| | mesar-neetsa |
| a café | **kavana** |
| | kava-na |
| a cake shop | **slastičarna** |
| | slastee-charna |
| a campsite | **autokamp** |
| | ah-ooto-kamp |
| a car park | **parkiralište** |
| | par-kee-ral-eeshteh |
| a change bureau | **mjenjačnica** |
| | m-hyen-yach-neetsa |
| a chemist's | **apoteka** |
| | apotek-ah |
| a concert hall | **dvorana za koncerte** |
| | dvora-na za kon-tsairteh |
| a delicatessen | **delikatesna radnja** |
| | delikates-na radn-ya |
| a dentist's | **zubar** |
| | zoobar |
| a department store | **robna kuća** |
| | robna koocha |
| a disco | **disko klub** |
| | disko cloob |
| a doctor's surgery | **liječnička ordinacija** |
| | lee-yech-neechka ordeen-atsee-ya |
| a dry cleaner's | **kemijska čistiona** |
| | kem-eeska cheest-yona |

| | |
|---|---|
| **Is there . . . near by?** | **Ima li ovdje blizu . . .?** |
| | *eema lee ovd-yeh blee-zoo . . .* |
| a fishmonger's | **ribarnica** |
| | reebar-neetsa |
| a garage (for repairs) | **garaža** |
| | gara-sha |
| a hairdresser's | **frizer** |
| | friz-air |
| a greengrocer's | **voćarna** |
| | voch-arna |
| a grocer's | **dućan mješovite robe** |
| | doochan m-yesh-oveeteh robeh |
| a hospital | **bolnica** |
| | bol-nitsa |
| a hotel | **hotel** |
| | hotel |
| an ice-cream parlour | **slastičarna** |
| | slasti-charna |
| a laundry | **praonica** |
| | pra-on-eetsa |
| a newsagent's | **prodavaona novina** |
| | prodava-ona novee-na |
| a night club | **noćni lokal** |
| | nochni lok-al |
| a park | **park** |
| | park |
| a petrol station | **benzinska stanica** |
| | benzeen-ska stan-eetsa |
| a post box | **poštanski sandučić** |
| | poshtan-skee sand-oochitch |
| a restaurant | **restoran** |
| | rest-oran |
| a supermarket | **supermarket/robna kuća** |
| | supermarket/robna koocha |
| a taxi stand | **stajalište taksija** |
| | sta-yaleesh-teh tak-see-ya |
| a telephone | **telefon** |
| | telephon |
| a tobacconist's | **trafika** |
| | traf-eeka |
| a toilet | **toaleta** |
| | twa-leh-ta |

| a travel agent's | **putna agencija** |
| | pootna agentsee-ya |
| a youth hostel | **omladinski dom** |
| | omlad-een-skee dom |

## DIRECTIONS

| Left | **Lijevo** |
| | lee-yev-o |
| Right | **Desno** |
| | desno |
| Straight on | **Ravno** |
| | ravno |
| There | **Tamo** |
| | tamo |
| First left/right | **Prva na lijevo/na desno** |
| | perva na lee-yev-o/na desno |
| Second left/right | **Druga na lijevo/na desno** |
| | drooga na lee-yev-o/na desno |

# Accommodation

## ESSENTIAL INFORMATION

### Hotel

- If you want hotel-type accommodation, all the following words in capital letters are worth looking for on name boards:
  HOTEL
  MOTEL
  PANSION (superior boarding house)
- Houses which let rooms privately usually have signs in French, English, German or Italian:
  CHAMBRES/ROOMS/ZIMMER/CAMERE
  Remember that:
- A list of hotels in the town or district can usually be obtained at the local tourist information office.
- Hotels are divided into five classes, pensions into three.

- Not all hotels provide meals, apart from breakfast. (A pension always provides meals). However, for stays of more than three days, hotels and pensions have fixed prices which include accommodation, three meals a day and whatever services are available.
- The cost is displayed in the room itself so you can check it when having a look around before agreeing to stay.
- The displayed cost is for the room itself, per night and not per person.
- Breakfast usually consists of coffee, milk, tea or cocoa with rolls or toast, butter and jam or honey.
- On arrival you will be asked to complete a registration document and the receptionist will want to see your passport and travel documents.
- Tipping is not obligatory but 10% is usual.

## WHAT TO SAY

| | |
|---|---|
| I have a booking | **Imam rezervirano**<br>*eem*-am rezair-*veer*-ano |
| Have you any vacancies, please? | **Imate li praznu sobu, molim?**<br>*eem*at-eh lee pr*az*-noo so-boo m*ol*-im |
| Can I book a room? | **Mogu li rezervirati sobu?**<br>m*og*-oo lee rezair-*veer*-atee so-boo |
| It's for . . . | **To je za . . .**<br>toh yeh za . . . |
| one adult | **jednu osoby**<br>yed-noo os-oboo |
| two adults | **dvije osobu**<br>dvee-yeh os-obeh |
| and one child | **i jedno dijete**<br>ee yedno dee-yet-eh |
| and two children | **i dvoje djece**<br>ee dvo-yeh dee-yetseh |
| It's for . . . | **To je za . . .**<br>toh yeh za . . . |
| one night | **jednu noć**<br>yed-noo noch |
| two nights | **dvije noći**<br>dvee-yeh nochee |
| one week | **jednu sedmicu**<br>yed-noo sedmee-tsoo |

| | |
|---|---|
| two weeks | **dvije sedmice** |
| | d*vee*-yeh sedm*ee*-tseh |
| I would like . . . | **Želio/željela\* bih . . .** |
| | shel-yo/shel-yel-ah beeh . . . |
| one room | **jednu sobu** |
| | yed-noo s*o*-boo |
| two rooms | **dvije sobe** |
| | d*vee*-yeh s*o*-beh |
| with a single bed | **jednokrevetnu** |
| | yed-nokr*ev*-et-noo |
| with two single beds | **dvokrevetnu sa odvojenim krevetima** |
| | dvo-kr*ev*-et-noo sa odv*o*-yen-eem krev-et-eema |
| with a double bed | **dvokrevetnu** |
| | dvo-kr*ev*-et-noo |
| with a toilet | **sa toaletom** |
| | sa tw*a*-leh-tom |
| with a bathroom | **sa kupatilom** |
| | sa koo-p*at*-eelom |
| with a shower | **sa tušom** |
| | sa t*oo*-shom |
| with a cot | **sa dječjim krevetom** |
| | sa dee-y*ech*-eem krev-et-om |
| with a balcony | **sa balkonom** |
| | sa balk*on*-om |
| I would like . . . | **Želio/željela\* bih . . .** |
| | shel-yo/shel-yeh-ah beeh . . . |
| full board | **sa punim pansionom** |
| | sa p*oo*n-eem pans*ee*-onom |
| bed and breakfast | **sobu i doručak** |
| | s*o*-boo ee d*o*roo-chak |
| Do you serve meals? | **Servirate li jela?** |
| | sairv-eerat-eh lee yel-ah |
| Can I look at the room? | **Mogu li da vidim sobu?** |
| | m*o*g-oo lee da v*ee*-deem s*o*-boo |
| OK, I'll take it | **Dobro je, uzeti ću je** |
| | d*o*bro yeh *ooz*-et-ee ch*oo* yeh |
| No thanks, I won't take it | **Ne hvala, neću je uzeti** |
| | neh f*a*-la neh-choo yeh *ooz*-etee |

---

\*Men use the first alternative, women the second

The bill, please **Račun, molim**
rach-oon mol-im

Is service included? **Je li servis uračunat?**
yeh lee sairvis oorach-oonat

I think this is wrong **Mislim da ovo nije točno**
meeslim da o-vo nee-yeh toch-no

May I have a receipt? **Želio/željela\* bih priznanicu**
shel-yo/shel-yeh-ah beeh preeznan-
eetsoo

\*Men use the first alternative, women the second

## Camping

- Look for the words: **KAMPING** or **AUTO-CAMP**.
- Be prepared for the following charges
  per person
  for the car (if applicable)
  for the tent or caravan plot
  for electricity
  for hot showers
- You must provide proof of identity, such as your passport.
- All campsites are state owned and state controlled.
- If you wish to camp off-site, you must obtain a permit from the local tourist office or the municipality.
- On some sites, accommodation is also available in chalets.

## Youth hostels

- Look for the word: **OMLADINSKI DOM**
- You must have a YHA card.
- Accommodation is usually provided in small dormitories and you should take your own sleeping bag lining with you.
- Food and cooking facilities vary from place to place and you may also have to help with the domestic chores.
- Accommodation is also available in the student hotels to be found in larger towns which are run by **FERIJALNI SAVEZ** (Yugoslav Youth School Organization).
- **NAROMTRAVEL** which specializes in travel and holidays for young people and students in Yugoslavia also runs its own international youth centres in Dubrovnik, Rovinj and Bečići (near Budva).

## WHAT TO SAY

| | |
|---|---|
| Have you any vacancies? | **Imate li mjesta?** |
| | *ee*mat-eh lee m-y*e*sta |
| **How much is it . . .** | **Koliko je . . .** |
| | k*o*l-eeko yeh . . . |
| for the tent? | **za šator?** |
| | za sh*a*-tor |
| for the caravan (trailer)? | **za karavanu?** |
| | za karav*a*noo |
| for the car? | **za kola?** |
| | za k*o*la |
| for the electricity? | **za struju?** |
| | za str*oo*-yoo |
| per person? | **po osobi?** |
| | po *o*s-obee |
| per day/night? | **na dan/noć?** |
| | na d*a*n/noch |
| May I look round? | **Mogu li pogledati okolo?** |
| | m*o*g-oo lee p*o*gleh-da-tee *o*kolo |
| Do you provide anything . . . | **Mogu li nabaviti nešto . . .** |
| | m*o*g-oo lee n*a*-bav-eetee n*e*sh-to . . . |
| to eat? | **za jesti?** |
| | za y*e*s-tee |
| to drink? | **za piti?** |
| | za p*ee*tee |
| **Do you have . . .** | **Imate li . . .** |
| | *ee*mat-eh lee . . . |
| a bar? | **bar?** |
| | bar |
| hot showers? | **vrući tuš?** |
| | vr*oo*-chee toosh |
| a kitchen? | **kuhinju?** |
| | k*oo*-heen-yoo |
| a laundry? | **praonicu?** |
| | pra-*o*nee-tsoo |
| a restaurant? | **restoran?** |
| | rest-oran |
| a shop? | **dućan?** |
| | d*oo*ch-an |
| a swimming pool? | **bazen?** |
| | b*a*z-en |

**Do you have . . .**      **Imate li . . .**
                          eemat-eh lee . . .

  a takeaway?      **snak-bar?**
                          snack bar

[For food shopping, see p. 341, and for eating and drinking out, see p. 351]

## Problems

The toilet          **Toaleta**
                    twa-leh-ta

The shower          **Tuš**
                    toosh

The tap             **Slavina**
                    slav-eena

The electric point  **Utikač**
                    ooteek-ach

The light           **Svijetlo**
                    svee-yetlo

. . . is not working  **. . . ne radi**
                    neh ra-dee

My camping gas has run out  **Nestalo mi je plina**
                    neh-stalo mee yeh plee-na

## LIKELY REACTIONS

Have you an identity      **Imate li legitimaciju?**
document?                 eemat-eh lee leg-eetee-matsee-yoo

Your membership card, please  **Vašu člansku kartu, molim**
                          vashoo chlan-skoo kartoo mol-im

What's your name, please?  **Vaše ime molim?**
[see p. 325]              vasheh eemeh mol-im

Sorry, we're full         **Žao mi je ali smo puni**
                          sha-o mee yeh ah-lee smo poonee

How many people is it for?  **Za koliko osoba?**
                          za kol-eeko os-oba

How many nights is it for?  **Za koliko noći?**
                          za kol-eeko nochee

It's . . . dinars         **To je . . . dinara**
                          toh yeh . . . deena-ra

  per day/per night  **na dan/na noć**
[For numbers, see p. 368]  na dun/na noch

| | |
|---|---|
| I haven't any rooms left | **Nemam niti jednu sobu praznu** |
| | n*eh*-mum n*ee*tee y*ed*-noo s*o*-boo |
| | pr*a*z-noo |
| Do you want to have a look? | **Hoćete li da vidite?** |
| | h*o*ch-et-eh lee da v*ee*d-eet-eh |

# General shopping

# The chemist's

## ESSENTIAL INFORMATION

- Look for the words **APOTEKA** or **LJEKARNA**, a large cross or this sign:
- Medicines can also be bought at supermarkets or department stores.
- Try the chemist *before* going to a doctor: they are usually qualified to treat minor injuries.
- Chemists are normally open between 8.00 a.m. and 9.00 p.m. However, some 'duty' chemists are open twenty-four hours, look for **DEŽURNA APOTEKA** on the shop door or in the local newspaper.
- Some toiletries can also be bought at a **PARFUMERIJA** but they will be more expensive.

## WHAT TO SAY

| | |
|---|---|
| I'd like . . . | **Želio/željela\* bih . . .** |
| | shel-yo/shel-yel-ah beeh . . . |
| some Alka Seltzer | **Alku Seltzer** |
| | alkoo seltzer |
| some antiseptic | **antiseptičnu mast** |
| | anti-septeech-noo m*u*st |
| some aspirin | **aspirinu** |
| | asp*ee*-ree-noo |

\*Men use the first alternative, women the second

**I'd like . . .**        **Želio/željela\* bih . . .**
shel-yo/shel-yel-ah beeh . . .

some baby food      **dijećija hrana**
dee-yech-eeya he-rana

some contraceptives      **kontraceptivno sredstvo**
kontra-tsep-teev-no sret-stvo

some cotton wool      **vatu**
va-too

some disposable nappies      **papirne pelene**
pap-eer-neh pel-en-eh

some eye drops      **kapi za oči**
kap-ee za ochee

some inhalant      **nešto za udisanje**
neshto za oodee-san-yeh

some insect repellent      **sredstvo protiv insekata**
sret-stvo prot-eev insek-ata

some paper tissues      **papirne maramice**
pap-eer-neh ma-ram-eetseh

some sanitary towels      **mjesečne uloške**
m-yesech-neh oolosh-keh

some sticking plaster      **flaster**
fluster

some suntan lotion/oil      **losion/ulje za sunčanje**
lotion/ool-yeh za soon-chan-yeh

some Tampax      **Tampax**
tampax

some throat pastilles      **tablete za grlo**
tablet-eh za gher-lo

some (soft) toilet paper      **(mekani) toaletni papir**
(mek-anee) twa-let-nee pap-eer

**I'd like something for . . .**      **Želio/željela\* bih nešto za . . .**
shel-yo/shel-yel-ah beeh neshtoo
za . . .

bites      **ubode**
oobod-eh

burns      **opekotine**
opek-ot-eeneh

a cold      **nahladu**
na-hladoo

constipation      **tvrdu stolicu**
tver-doo stol-eetsoo

*Men use the first alternative, women the second

| | |
|---|---|
| a cough | **kašalj** |
| | k*a*sh-eye |
| diarrhoea | **proljev** |
| | pro*l*-yev |
| earache | **bol uha** |
| | b*o*hl *oo*ha |
| flu | **gripu** |
| | gree-poo |
| scalds | **oparenje** |
| | oparen-yeh |
| sore gums | **upalu desni** |
| | *oo*p-aloo deh-snee |
| stings | **ubode** |
| | *oo*bod-eh |
| sunburn | **opeklinu od sunca** |
| | *o*pek-lee-noo od s*oo*n-tsa |
| travel sickness | **protiv mučnine** |
| | pr*o*t-eev mooch-neen-eh |

[*For other essential expressions, see 'Shop talk' p. 338*]

# Holiday items

## ESSENTIAL INFORMATION

- Places to shop at and signs to look for:
  **PAPIRNICA** (stationery)
  **KNJIŽARA** (bookshop)
  **FOTO STUDIO** (films)
  and main department stores like: **ROBNA KUĆA**
- If you wish to buy local crafts look for the following sign
  **NARODNA RADINOST**. These shops, to be found in larger
  towns and tourist resorts, specialize in hand-made embroidery,
  filigree jewellery and ceramics.

## WHAT TO SAY

| | |
|---|---|
| I'd like . . . | Želio/željela* bih . . . |
| | shel-yo/shel-yel-ah beeh . . . |
| a bag | **torbu** |
| | torboo |
| a beach ball | **loptu za plažu** |
| | lop-too za pla-shoo |
| a bucket | **kantu** |
| | kan-to |
| an English newspaper | **engleske novine** |
| | en-gleskeh nov-eeneh |
| some envelopes | **koverta** |
| | kovair-ta |
| some postcards | **dopisnica** |
| | doh-pees-neetsa |
| a spade | **lopatu** |
| | lop-atoo |
| a straw hat | **slamnat šešir** |
| | slam-nat shesheer |
| some sunglasses | **naočale za sunce** |
| | na-och-al-eh za soon-tseh |
| some writing paper | **papira za pisanje** |
| | papeera za pee-san-yeh |
| a colour film [show the camera] | **film u boji** |
| | film oo boyee |
| a black and white film | **film crno bijeli** |
| | film tser-no beeyeh-lee |

*Men use the first alternative, women the second

---

# Shop talk

## ESSENTIAL INFORMATION

• Know how to say the important weights and measures:
  [For numbers, see p. 368]

| | |
|---|---|
| 50 grams | **Pedeset grama** |
| | peh-deh-set gra-ma |
| 100 grams | **Sto grama** |
| | sto gra-ma |

| | |
|---|---|
| 200 grams | **Dvjesta grama** |
| | dvee-yeh-sta gra-ma |
| ½ kilo | **Pola kila** |
| | pol-a keela |
| 1 kilo | **Kilo** |
| | keelo |
| 2 kilos | **Dva kila** |
| | dva keela |
| ½ litre | **Pola litre** |
| | pol-a leetreh |
| 1 litre | **Litra** |
| | leetra |
| 2 litres | **Dvije litre** |
| | dvee-yeh leetreh |

## CUSTOMER

| | |
|---|---|
| I'm just looking | **Samo gledam** |
| | sa-mo gled-am |
| How much is this/that? | **Koliko košta ovo/to?** |
| | kol-eeko koshta ov-o/toh |
| What is that? | **Što je to?** |
| | shto yeh toh |
| What are those? | **Što su te?** |
| | shto soo teh |
| Is there a discount? | **Ima li popusta?** |
| | eema lee pop-oosta |
| I'd like that, please | **Želio/željela\* bih to, molim** |
| | shel-yo/she-yel-ah beeh toh mol-im |
| Not that | **Ne to** |
| | neh toh |
| Like that | **Onako** |
| | on-a-ko |
| That's enough, thank you | **To je dosta, hvala** |
| | toh yeh dosta fa-la |
| More please | **Više, molim** |
| | veesheh mol-im |
| Less | **Manje od toga** |
| | man-yeh od tog-a |
| That's fine | **To je dobro** |
| | toh yeh dob-ro |

\*Men use the first alternative, women the second

| | |
|---|---|
| OK | **Dobro je** |
| | dob-ro yeh |
| I won't take it, thank you | **Deću to, hvala vam** |
| | nech-oo toh fa-la vum |
| It's not right | **Nije točno** |
| | nee-yeh toch-no |
| **Have you got something . . .** | **Imate li nešto . . .** |
| | eemat-eh lee neshto . . . |
| better? | **bolje?** |
| | bol-yeh |
| cheaper? | **jevtinije?** |
| | yeft-een-yeh |
| different? | **različitije?** |
| | razleech-eet-yeh |
| larger?/smaller? | **veće?/manje?** |
| | veh-cheh/man-yeh |
| Can I have a bag, please? | **Mogu li da dobijem kesicu, molim?** |
| | mog-oo lee da dob-ee-yem |
| | kes-eetsoo mol-im |
| Can I have a receipt? | **Mogu li da dobijem priznanicu?** |
| | mog-oo lee da dob-ee-yem |
| | preeznan-eetsoo |
| **Do you take . . .** | **Primate li . . .** |
| | preemat-eh lee . . . |
| English/American money? | **engleski/amerikanski novac?** |
| | en-gleskee/amerikan-skee nov-ats |
| travellers' cheques? | **putne čekove?** |
| | poot-neh check-oveh |
| credit cards? | **kreditne karte?** |
| | cred-eetneh karteh |

## SHOP ASSISTANT

| | |
|---|---|
| Can I help you? | **Mogu li vam pomoći?** |
| | mog-oo lee vum pom-ochee |
| What would you like? | **Što želite?** |
| | shto shel-eeteh |
| Is that all? | **Je li to sve?** |
| | yeh lee toh sveh |
| Anything else? | **Nešto drugo?** |
| | neshto droogo |
| Would you like it wrapped? | **Želite li da vam zamotam?** |
| | shel-eeteh lee da vum zamot-an |

| | |
|---|---|
| Sorry, none left | **Žao mi je nemamo više** |
| | sha-o mee yeh nem-amo veesheh |
| I haven't got any | **Nemam ni jedan** |
| | nem-am nee yed-an |
| I haven't got any more | **Nemam više** |
| | nem-am veesheh |
| How many do you want? | **Koliko želite?** |
| | kol-eeko shel-eeteh |
| Is that enough? | **Je li to dosta?** |
| | yeh lee toh dosta? |

## *Shopping for food*

# Bread

### ESSENTIAL INFORMATION

- Key words to look for:
  **PRODAVAONICA KRUHA**
  **PEKARNA**
  **TRGOVINA KRUHA**
- Opening times: 7.00/7.30 a.m. – 12.00 p.m. and 5.00 p.m. – 8.00 p.m. Saturday: 7.00/7.30 a.m. to 12.00 p.m.
- The most characteristic type of loaves in Croatia are **pogača** which are large, flat and round. However, the words for the various types of bread differ throughout Yugoslavia and you should be prepared to point to what you want.

### WHAT TO SAY

| | |
|---|---|
| One loaf (like that) | **Jednu pogaču (kao tu)** |
| | yed-noo pog-achoo (kow too) |
| A large one | **Veliku** |
| | vel-eekoo |
| A small one | **Malu** |
| | mal-oo |
| One bread roll | **Jednu rusicu** |
| | yed-noo roo-see-tsoo |

| | |
|---|---|
| ½ kilo of . . . | **Pola kile . . .** |
| | pol-a keeleh . . . |
| 1 kilo of . . . | **Kilo . . .** |
| | keelo . . . |
| white bread | **bijelog kruha** |
| | bee-yel-og krooha |
| wholemeal bread | **crnog kruha** |
| | tser-nog krooha |

[*For other essential expressions, see 'Shop talk', p. 338*]

# Cakes and ice-creams

## ESSENTIAL INFORMATION

- Key words to look for:
  **SLASTIČARNA** (cake shop)
  **SLADOLED** (ice-cream)
- **KAVANA** is a place where cakes can be bought to be eaten on the premises or taken away – alcoholic drinks are also served.
- Ordering a drink and a snack see p. 351.

## WHAT TO SAY

The type of cakes you find in the shops varies from region to region but the following are some of the most common.

| | |
|---|---|
| **doboš torta** | chocolate layer cake with glazed |
| doh-bosh torta | sugar topping |
| **hladna krema** | custard pie |
| ladna krem-a | |
| **krafen** | doughnut |
| kraf-en | |
| **krem pita** | custard cake |
| krem peeta | |
| **išler** | éclair |
| eesh-ler | |

| | |
|---|---|
| **marcapan** | marzipan |
| martsapan | |
| **pita od jabuka** | apple strudel |
| peeta od ya-booka | |
| **pita od sira** | cheese cake |
| peeta od seera | |
| **princes krafne** | cream doughnut |
| princes kraf-neh | |
| **trokut** | mille feuilles |
| trok-oot | |
| **šampita** | tart with whipped cream and |
| shampeeta | meringue mixture |
| | |
| A . . . ice, please | **Sladoled . . . molim** |
| | sla-doh-led . . . mol-im |
| banana | **od banana** |
| | od banana |
| chocolate | **ok čokolade** |
| | od chokola-deh |
| hazelnut | **od lješnjaka** |
| | od l-yeh-shen-yaka |
| raspberry | **od malina** |
| | od ma-leena |
| strawberry | **od jagoda** |
| | od ya-goda |
| vanilla | **od vanilje** |
| | od vaneel-yeh |
| A single | **Jedan** |
| | yed-an |
| Two singles | **Dva** |
| | dva |
| A double | **Jedan dupli** |
| | yed-an doop-lee |
| Two doubles | **Dva dupla** |
| | dvadoopla |
| A cone | **Kornet** |
| | kor-net |

[*For other essential expressions, see 'Shop talk', p. 338*]

# Picnic food

## ESSENTIAL INFORMATION

- Key words to look for:
  **DELIKATESNA RADNJA** (delicatessen)
  **MESARNICA** (butcher's)
  **ŽIVEŽNE NAMIRNICE** (grocer's)

## WHAT TO SAY

| Two slices of . . . | **Dva odreska . . .** |
|---|---|
| | dva od-res-ka . . . |
| roast beef | **govedjeg pečenja** |
| | gov-ed-yeg pech-en-ya |
| roast pork | **svinjskog pečenja** |
| | sveen-skog pech-en-ya |
| tongue | **jezika** |
| | yez-eeka |
| ham | **šunke** |
| | shoonkeh |
| paté | **paštete** |
| | pash-teh-teh |
| garlic sausage | **kobasica** |
| | kobas-eetsah |
| salami | **salame** |
| | salam-eh |

You might also like to try some of these:

| | |
|---|---|
| **dalmatinski pršut** | ham from Dalmatia |
| dalmat-eenskee per-shoot | |
| **dimljeni sir** | smoked cheese |
| diml-yen-ee seer | |
| **domaće kobasice** | homemade sausages |
| domacheh kobas-eetseh | |
| **domaći sir** | local cheese |
| domachee seer | |
| **jastog** | lobster |
| yast-og | |

| | |
|---|---|
| **kajmak**<br>ka-eemuk | rich soft cheese made from scalded milk |
| **kamenice**<br>kamen-eetseh | oysters |
| **kranjske kobasice**<br>kran-yes-keh kobas-eetseh | sausages from Slovenia |
| **kuhana šunka**<br>koohana shoon-ka | cooked ham |
| **marinirana riba**<br>marín-eerana reeba | marinated fish |
| **mliječni sir**<br>mlee-yech-nee seer | milk cheese |
| **pašteta od džigerice**<br>pash-teh-ta od jeeg-eritseh | liver paté |
| **pašteta od mesa**<br>pash-teh-ta od meh-sa | meat paté |
| **paški sir**<br>pash-kee seer | cheese from Pag island |
| **pečena guska**<br>pech-ena gooska | roast goose |
| **pečena patka**<br>pech-ena patka | roast duck |
| **pečeno pile**<br>pech-eno peeleh | roast chicken |
| **pečena teletina**<br>pech-ena teh-leh-teena | roast veal |
| **pohano meso**<br>po-hano meh-soh | fried meat in breadcrumbs |
| **pohano pile**<br>po-hano peeleh | fried chicken in breadcrumbs |
| **punjena jaja**<br>poon-yen-ah ya-ya | stuffed eggs |
| **sardine**<br>sardeeneh | sardines |
| **sir sa vrhnjem**<br>seer sa verhen-yem | curd cheese with sour cream |
| **sušene haringe**<br>sooshen-eh har-een-gheh | smoked herrings |
| **trapist**<br>trap-eest | ewe's milk cheese (firm and mild) |
| **tunjevina**<br>toon-yev-eena | tuna fish |

[*For other essential expressions, see 'Shop talk', p. 338*]

# Fruit and vegetables

## ESSENTIAL INFORMATION

- Key words to look for:
  **VOĆE** (fruit)
  **VOĆARNA** (fruit shop)
  **POVRĆE** (vegetables)
- It is customary for you to choose your own fruit and vegetables at the market (and in some shops) and for the stallholder to weigh and price them. You must take your own shopping bag: paper and plastic bags are not normally provided.

## WHAT TO SAY

| 1 kilo of . . . | Kilo . . . |
|---|---|
| | keelo . . . |
| apples | **jabuka** |
| | ya-booka |
| apricots | **marelica** |
| | mar-el-eetsa |
| bananas | **banana** |
| | banana |
| cherries | **trešanja** |
| | treshan-ya |
| figs | **smokve** |
| | smok-veh |
| grapes (white/black) | **grožđa (bijeloga/crnoga)** |
| | grosh-ja (bee-yeloga/tsernoga) |
| oranges | **naranača** |
| | naran-acha |
| pears | **krušaka** |
| | kroosha-ka |
| peaches | **breskava** |
| | bresk-ava |
| plums | **šljiva** |
| | shl-eeva |
| strawberries | **jagoda** |
| | ya-goda |
| A pineapple, please | **Ananas, molim** |
| | ananas mol-im |

| | |
|---|---|
| A grapefruit | **Grejpfrut** |
| | grapefruit |
| A melon | **Dinju** |
| | deen-yoo |
| A water melon | **Lubenicu** |
| | looben-eetsoo |
| ½ kilo of . . . | **Pola kila . . .** |
| | pol-a keela . . . |
| aubergines | **melancane** |
| | melan-tsaneh |
| beans | **graha** |
| | gra-ha |
| carrots | **mrkve** |
| | merk-veh |
| courgettes | **tikvice** |
| | teek-veetseh |
| green beans | **mahuna** |
| | mahoo-na |
| leeks | **poriluka** |
| | poreel-ooka |
| mushrooms | **gljiva** |
| | gleeva |
| onions | **luka** |
| | looka |
| peas | **graška** |
| | grashka |
| potatoes | **krompira** |
| | kromp-eera |
| spinach | **spanaća** |
| | spanacha |
| tomatoes | **paradajza** |
| | parada-eeza |
| A bunch of . . . | **Kitu . . .** |
| | keetoo . . . |
| parsley | **peršuna** |
| | persh-oona |
| radishes | **rotkvica** |
| | kot-kvee-tsa |
| A head of garlic | **Glava češnjaka** |
| | glava cheshn-ya-ka |
| A lettuce | **Salata** |
| | sal-ata |

| A cucumber | **Krastavac** |
| | kras-tavats |
| A turnip | **Repa** |
| | rep-a |
| Like that, please | **Tako, molim vas** |
| | tak-o mol-im vus |

[*For other essential information, see 'Shop talk' p. 338*]

# Meat and fish

## ESSENTIAL INFORMATION

- Key words to look for:
  **MESARNICA** or **MESNICA** (butcher's)
  **MESAR** (butcher)
  **RIBARNICA** (fishmonger's)
- The meat is not displayed in the same way as in the UK, nor should you expect to find the same cuts. However, you should tell the butcher whether you intend to boil, grill or roast the meat so that he will know what to give you.
- It is not normal practice in Yugoslavia for the fishmonger to fillet fish, and you may also find that some fishmongers will not clean fish, so check beforehand.

## WHAT TO SAY

For a joint, choose the type of meat and then say how many people it is for and how you intend to cook it:

| Some beef, please | **Komad govedine, molim** |
| | kom-ad gov-ed-eeneh mol-im |
| Some lamb | **Komad janjetine** |
| | kom-ad yan-yet-eeneh |
| Some mutton | **Komad ovčetine** |
| | kom-ad ov-chet-eeneh |
| Some pork | **Komad svinjetine** |
| | kom-ad sveen-yet-eeneh |

| | |
|---|---|
| Some veal | **Komad teletine** |
| | kom-ad teh-leh-teeneh |
| A joint . . . | **Komad . . .** |
| | kom-ad . . . |
| for two people | **za dvije osobe** |
| | za dvee-yeh os-obeh |
| for four people | **za četiri osobe** |
| | za chet-eeree os-obeh |
| for six people | **za šest osoba** |
| | za shehst os-oba |
| to boil | **za kuhati** |
| | za koo-hat-ee |
| to grill | **za na roštilju** |
| | za nah rosh-teel-yoo |
| to roast | **za peći** |
| | za pech-ee |

For steak, liver or kidneys, do as above

| | |
|---|---|
| Some steak, please | **Biftek, molim** |
| | beeftek mol-im |
| Some liver | **Jetre** |
| | yet-reh |
| Some kidneys | **Bubrega** |
| | boob-reg-ah |
| Some sausages | **Kobasice** |
| | kobas-eetseh |
| for three people | **za tri osobe** |
| | za tree os-obeh |
| for five people | **za pet osoba** |
| | za pet os-obah |
| Two veal escalopes, please | **Dvije teleće šnicle, molim** |
| | dvee-yeh teh-lech-eh shnits-leh mol-im |
| Three pork chops | **Tri svinjska kotleta** |
| | tree sveen-ska kot-leh-ta |
| Four mutton chops | **Četiri ovčja kotleta** |
| | chet-eeree ov-chee-ya kot-leh-ta |
| Five lamb chops | **Pet janjećih kotleta** |
| | peht yan-yech-eeh kot-leh-ta |
| A chicken | **Pile** |
| | peeleh |

| A rabbit | **Kunić** |
| | koonich |
| A tongue | **Jezik** |
| | yez-eek |

Purchase large fish and small shellfish by weight:

| ½ kilo of . . . | **Pola kila . . .** |
| | pol-a keela . . . |
| bass | **brancina** |
| | bran-tseena |
| carp | **šarana** |
| | shar-ana |
| squid | **liganja** |
| | leegan-ya |
| cod (dried) | **bakalara** |
| | bakalar-ah |
| cod (fresh) | **svježog bakalara** |
| | svye-shog bakalar-ah |
| eels | **jegulja** |
| | yeg-ool-ya |
| grey mullet | **cipola** |
| | tseep-ola |
| lobster | **jastoga** |
| | yas-tog-ah |
| mussels | **mušula** |
| | moosh-oola |
| oysters | **kamenica** |
| | kamen-eetsa |
| prawns | **gambora** |
| | gambora |
| red mullet | **barbuna** |
| | barboona |
| scampi | **škampija** |
| | shkam-peea |
| sole | **listova** |
| | leestova |
| pilchards | **sardela** |
| | sard-ela |
| salmon | **lososa** |
| | los-os-a |
| fresh tuna | **tunjevine** |
| | toon-jev-eeneh |

For some shellfish and 'frying pan' fish, say the name and then specify the number you want [*For numbers, see p. 368*]

| | |
|---|---|
| A crab | **Rak** |
| | rak |
| A lobster | **Jastog** |
| | yastog |
| An ink fish | **Sipa** |
| | seepa |
| An octopus | **Hobotnica** |
| | hob-otneetsah |
| A sole | **List** |
| | leest |
| A trout | **Pastrva** |
| | past-erva |
| A mackerel | **Lokarda** |
| | lok-arda |
| A herring | **Haringa** |
| | har-eenga |
| A pike | **Štuka** |
| | shtooka |
| Please can you . . . | **Molim vas možete li . . .** |
| | mol-im vus mosh-et-eh lee . . . |
| clean them? | **očistiti ih?** |
| | ocheest-eetee |

# Eating and drinking out

## Ordering a drink and a snack

**ESSENTIAL INFORMATION**

- The places to ask for: **KAVANA  BIFE  BAR**
- By law, the price list of drinks must be displayed outside or in the window.
- There is waiter service in all cafés, but you can drink at the bar or counter if you wish (cheaper).
- Always leave a tip of 10%–15% of the bill unless you see **SERVIS UKLJUČEN** (service included) printed on the bill or on a notice.

- Cafés serve non-alcoholic drinks and alcoholic drinks, and are normally open all day. Children may accompany their parents into bars.
- Local mineral water is available.
- The following list of drinks are all local brandies which you may like to try: **kajsjevača** (apricot brandy), **komovica** (brandy made from grape-pressings), **orahovica** (brandy made from grape pressings with green shells of walnuts in it), **rakija** (brandy from fruit pressings), **šljivovica** (plum brandy).

## WHAT TO SAY

| I'll have . . . | Htio/htjela* bih . . . |
|---|---|
| | htee-o/ht-yelah beeh . . . |
| a black coffee | **crnu kavu** |
| | tser-noo ka-voo |
| a coffee with cream | **kavu sa šlagom** |
| | ka-voo sa shlag-om |
| a tea | **čaj** |
| | cha-ee |
| with milk/lemon | **sa mlijekom/limunom** |
| | sa mlee-yek-om/leemoon-om |
| a glass of milk | **čašu mlijeka** |
| | chash-oo mlee-yek-a |
| two glasses of milk | **dvije čaše mlijeka** |
| | dvee-yeh chash-eh mlee-yek-a |
| a hot chocolate | **kakao** |
| | kaka-o |
| a mineral water | **mineralnu vodu** |
| | meenairal-noo vod-oo |
| a lemonade | **limunadu** |
| | leemoona-doo |
| a lemon squash | **sok limuna** |
| | soak leemoona |
| an orangeade | **oranžadu** |
| | oranja-doo |
| an orange juice | **sok od naranče** |
| | soak od naran-cheh |
| a grape juice | **sok od grožđa** |
| | soak od grosh-ja |

*Men use the first alternative, women the second

| | |
|---|---|
| a pineapple juice | **sok od ananasa** |
| | soak od ananasa |
| a small bottle of beer | **malu bocu pive** |
| | ma-loo botsoo peeveh |
| **I'll have . . . please** | **Molim vas htio/htjela\* bih . . .** |
| | mol-im vus htee-o/ht-yelah beeh . . . |
| a cheese sandwich | **sendvič od sira** |
| | send-wich od seera |
| a ham sandwich | **sendvič od šunke** |
| | send-wich od shoonkeh |
| a pancake | **palačinku** |
| | palach-inkoo |
| a packet of crisps | **paketić krispsa** |
| | pack-et-ich krisp-sa |

\*Men use the first alternative, women the second

These are some other snacks you may like to try:

| | |
|---|---|
| **sendvič od budžole** | a pork sausage sandwich – a |
| send-wich od boojol-eh | speciality |
| **sendvič od čajne kobasice** | a sandwich of smoked sausage |
| send-wich od chaee-neh kobas-eetseh | |
| **sendvič od dalmatinske šunke** | a Parma ham sandwich |
| send-wich od dalmat-eenskeh shoonkeh | |
| **sendvič od Gavrilović salame** | a salami sandwich (Gavrilovic is |
| send-wich od gavril-ovich sala-meh | Yugoslavia's best known salami) |
| **sendvič od gušče pastete** | a goose paté sandwich |
| send-wich od goosh-cheh pash-tet-eh | |
| **sendvič od livanskog sira** | a Serbian cheese sandwich |
| send-wich od leevan-skog seera | |
| **sendvič od mortadele** | a mortadella sandwich |
| send-wich od mortadel-eh | |
| **sendvič od piletine** | a chicken sandwich |
| send-wich od peelet-eeneh | |

Chips are not available as snacks. They can only be ordered as part of a meal in a restaurant when you should ask for **'pom frit'**.

# In a restaurant

## ESSENTIAL INFORMATION

- You can eat at these places:
  **RESTORAN**
  **BIFE**
  (light snacks, alcoholic and soft drinks)
  **EKSPRES RESTORAN**
  (self-service, available only in large towns)
  **GOSTIONA**
  (modest restaurant)
  **KAVANA**
  (ice-creams, cakes, tea, coffee and alcoholic drinks)
  **MLIJEČNI RESTORAN**
  (dairy bar)
  **RIBLJI RESTORAN**
  (principally for fish dishes)
- By law, the menus must be displayed outside or in the window: and that is the *only* way to judge if a place is right for your needs.
- Self-service restaurants do exist, but most places have waiter service.
- Tipping is not obligatory but even where service is included, it is customary to tip 10% of the bill.
- Children's portions (**POLA PORCIJE**) are not commonly available, but it may be worth asking.
- Eating times are flexible and vary between 12.00 p.m. to 13.00 p.m. and 7.00 p.m. to 11.00 p.m.

## WHAT TO SAY

| | |
|---|---|
| May I book a table? | **Mogu li rezervirati jedan stol?** |
| | m*o*g-oo lee rezair-v*ee*r-atee yed-an stol |
| I've booked a table | **Imam rezervirani stol** |
| | *ee*m-um rezair-v*ee*r-anee stol |
| A table . . . | **Stol . . .** |
| | stol . . |

| | |
|---|---|
| for one | **za jedno** |
| | za yed-no |
| for three | **za troje** |
| | za troy-eh |
| The menu, please | **Jelovnik, molim** |
| | yelov-neek mol-im |
| The fixed-price menu | **Pansionski jelovnik** |
| | pansion-skee yelov-neek |
| The tourist menu | **Turistički jelovnik** |
| | toorist-ich-kee yelov-neek |
| Today's special menu | **Današnji specijalni jelovnik** |
| | dan-ashn-yee spetsial-nee yelov-neek |
| What's this, please? | **Što je ovo, molim?** |
| [*point to the menu*] | shto yeh ov-o mol-im |
| The wine list | **Vinska karta** |
| | veen-ska karta |
| A carafe of wine, please | **Bocu vina, molim** |
| | botsoo veena mol-im |
| A quarter (25 cc) | **Četvrt litre vina** |
| | chet-vert leetreh veena |
| A half (50 cc) | **Pola litre vina** |
| | pol-a leetreh veena |
| A glass | **Cašu** |
| | cha-shoo |
| A bottle | **Bocu** |
| | botsoo |
| A half-bottle | **Pola boce** |
| | pol-a botseh |
| A litre | **Litru** |
| | leet-roo |
| Red/white/rosé/house wine | **Crnog/bijelog/ružičastog/domaćeg vina** |
| | tser-nog/bee-yel-og/roosh-ichastog/domach-eg veena |
| Some more bread, please | **Malo više kruha, molim** |
| | ma-lo veesheh krooha mol-im |
| Some more wine | **Malo više vina** |
| | ma-lo veesheh veena |
| Some oil | **Malo ulja** |
| | ma-lo ool-ya |

| | |
|---|---|
| Some vinegar | **Malo octa** |
| | ma-lo ots-ta |
| Some salt | **Malo soli** |
| | ma-lo sol-ee |
| Some pepper | **Malo bibera** |
| | ma-lo beeb-era |
| Some water | **Malo vode** |
| | ma-lo vod-eh |
| How much does that come to? | **Koliko to košta?** |
| | kol-eeko to koshta |
| Is service included? | **Da li je servis uračunat?** |
| | da lee yeh sair-vis oorach-oonat |
| Where is the toilet, please? | **Gdje je toaleta, molim?** |
| | gd-yeh yeh twa-leh-ta mol-im |
| Miss!/Waiter! | **Gospodjice!/Konobar!** |
| | gospoj-yeetseh/kon-obar |
| The bill, please | **Račun, molim** |
| | rach-oon mol-im |

**Key words for courses as seen on some menus**

[*Only ask this question if you want the waiter to remind you of the choice*]

| What have you got in the way of . . . | Što imate za . . . |
|---|---|
| | shto eemat-eh za . . . |
| starters? | **predjelo?** |
| | pred-ee-yelo |
| soup? | **juhu?** |
| | yoo-hoo |
| egg dishes? | **jaja?** |
| | ya-ya |
| fish? | **ribu?** |
| | reeboo |
| meat? | **meso?** |
| | meh-so |
| game? | **divljač?** |
| | deev-leeach |
| fowl? | **piletinu?** |
| | peelet-eenoo |
| vegetables? | **povrće?** |
| | pov-ercheh |

| | |
|---|---|
| cheese? | **sir?** |
| | s*ee*r |
| fruit? | **voće?** |
| | voch-eh |
| ice-cream? | **sladoled?** |
| | sl*a*-doh-led |
| dessert? | **dezert?** |
| | dez*ai*rt |

## UNDERSTANDING THE MENU

- You will find that most menus in Yugoslavia are in one or more European languages and the names of the various dishes will differ all over the country.
- You will find the names of the principal ingredients of most dishes on these pages:

  Starters see p. 344       Fruit see p. 346
  Meat see p. 348        Dessert see p. 342
  Fish see p. 350          Cheese see p. 345
  Vegetables see p. 347   Ice-cream see p. 343

- Used together with the following list of cooking and menu terms, they should help you to decode the menu.

### Cooking and menu terms

| | |
|---|---|
| **banjo marija** | bain marie |
| **na dalmatinsku** | Dalmatian |
| **dimljeno** | smoked |
| **dinstovano** | stewed |
| **dobro kuvano** ⎤ | well done |
| **dobro pečeno** ⎦ | |
| **faširano** | minced |
| **filovano** | stuffed |
| **frigano** | fried |
| **garnirano** | garnished |
| **na gradele** | grilled |
| **gusta juha** | thick soup |
| **hladno** | cold |
| **juha** | broth |
| **sa kiselim vrhnjem** | with sour cream |
| **kuvano** | boiled |
| **kuvano u pari** | steamed |

| | |
|---|---|
| na maslu | with butter |
| meso u hladetini | meat in aspic jelly |
| minestrun | vegetable soup |
| mljeveno | ground |
| sa mušulama | with mussels |
| pasirano | creamed |
| u peć | in the oven |
| pečeno | roast |
| pirjano (podušeno) | poached |
| pire | purée |
| polupečeno | rare |
| u prosulju | in the frying pan |
| punjeno | stuffed |
| na puteru | with butter |
| prženo | fried |
| ragu | stew |
| na ražnju | on the spit |
| na roštilju | grilled |
| seckano | diced |
| slatko/kiselo | sweet/sour |
| srednje pečeno | medium done |
| ukiseljeno (meso/riba) | marinated (meat/fish) |
| u umaku | with sauce |
| na žaru | grilled on charcoal |

**Further words to help you understand the menu**

| | |
|---|---|
| bubrezi | kidneys |
| ćevapčići | kebab of minced meat |
| djuveč | a vegetable dish of tomatoes with peppers and aubergines, sometimes part of a meat stew – the menu will specify |
| dvopek u kremi | trifle |
| faširano meso | minced meat |
| fazan | pheasant |
| file steak | fillet steak |
| gavuni | sprats |
| girice | small Adriatic fish (sprats) |
| golub | pigeon |
| govedje pečenje | roast beef |
| janjeće pečenje | roast lamb |

| | |
|---|---|
| jarebica | partridge |
| jetra | liver |
| jezik | tongue |
| juha od paradajza | tomato soup |
| kobasice | sausages |
| kolač | cake |
| krezle | sweetbreads |
| kunić | rabbit |
| marinirane gljive | marinated mushrooms |
| mozak | brain |
| musaka | moussaka: layers of minced meat and sliced aubergines with a topping of eggs and sour milk |
| omleti | omelets |
| palačinke | pancakes |
| patka | duck |
| piletina na ražnju | chicken on the spit |
| piletina pržena | fried chicken |
| piletina pohana | chicken fried in breadcrumbs |
| punjena jaja | stuffed eggs |
| punjeni patlidžan | stuffed aubergines |
| punjeni paradajz | stuffed tomatoes |
| punjene paprike | stuffed peppers in tomato sauce |
| punjene tikvice | stuffed courgettes |
| puran | turkey |
| razne salate | various salads |
| razni sladoledi | various ice-creams |
| ražnjići | pieces of pork/veal on skewers – shish kebab |
| riblja juha | fish soup |
| rižot | risotto |
| salama | salami |
| sarma | stuffed and pickled cabbage leaves in tomato sauce |
| škampi na žaru | scampi grilled on charcoal |
| slanina | bacon |
| srce | heart |
| šunka | ham |
| svinjska glava | pig's head |
| svinjska kiljenica | pig's trotters |
| svinjsko pečenje | roast pork |
| teleće pečenje | roast veal |

| | |
|---|---|
| **zelena menestra** | green leaf soup with ham |
| **zec (divlji)** | hare (wild) |
| **zubatac** | a large delicately flavoured fish (dentex) |

# Health

## ESSENTIAL INFORMATION

- The medical care of British nationals in Yugoslavia is regulated by a convention signed by the two countries. British nationals have the right to free medical care on production of a valid travel document and on payment of a minimal fee.
- For minor disorders and treatment at a chemist's, see. p. 335.
- For finding your way to a doctor, dentist and chemist, see p. 327.

**What's the matter?**

| | |
|---|---|
| I have a pain here [*point*] | **Boli me ovdje**<br>bol-ee meh ovd-yeh |
| I have toothache | **Boli me zub**<br>bol-ee meh zoob |
| I have broken . . . | **Slomio/slomila\* sam . . .**<br>slom-ee-o/slom-eela sum . . . |
| my dentures | **moju protezu**<br>moyoo protez-oo |
| my glasses | **moje naočale**<br>moyeh now-cha-leh |
| I have lost . . . | **Izgubio/izgubila\* sam . . .**<br>eez-goobee-o/eez-goobee-la sum . . . |
| my contact lenses | **moja kontaktna stakla**<br>moya contact-na stak-la |
| a filling | **plombu**<br>plom-boo |
| My child is ill | **Moje je dijete bolesno**<br>moyeh yeh dee-yet-eh bol-esno |

\*Men use the first alternative, women the second

**Already under treatment for something else?**

| | |
|---|---|
| I take . . . regularly [*show*] | **Uzimum redovito . . .**<br>*oo*zee-mum red*o*v-eetoh . . . |
| this medicine | **ovaj lijek**<br>*o*v-oy lee-y*e*k |
| these pills | **ove pilule**<br>*o*v-eh p*ee*lool-eh |
| I have . . . | **Bolujem od . . .**<br>b*o*loo-yem od . . . |
| a heart condition | **srca**<br>s*e*r-tsa |
| haemorrhoids | **hemoroida**<br>hem-oroyda |
| rheumatism | **reumatizma**<br>reh-oomat-*ee*zma |
| I am . . . | **Ja sam . . .**<br>ya sum . . . |
| diabetic | **dijabetičar**<br>dee-*a*-bet-eechar |
| asthmatic | **astmatičar**<br>asm*a*t-eechar |
| pregnant | **očekujem bebu**<br>*o*chek-ooyem b*e*b-oo |
| I'm allergic to penicillin | **Ja sam alergičan/alergična\* na penicilin**<br>ya sum *a*lairg-ichan/*a*lairg-ich-na na penitsil-*ee*noo |

\*Men use the first alternative, women the second

# Problems: loss, theft

## ESSENTIAL INFORMATION

- If the worst comes to the worst, find the police station. To ask the way, see p. 326.
see p. 326.

- Look for:
  **MILICIJA** (police)
  **SAOBRAĆAJNA MILICIJA** (traffic police)
  **POGRANIČNA MILICIJA** (frontier police)
  **LUČKA KAPETANIJA** (port authority)
- If you lose your passport, go to the nearest British Consulate.
- In an emergency dial 94 for an ambulance, 93 for the fire brigade and 92 for the police.

## LOSS

*[See also 'Theft' below: the lists are interchangeable]*

| I have lost . . . | Izgubio/izgubila sam* . . . |
|---|---|
| | *eez*-goobee-o/*eez*-goobee-la sum . . . |
| my camera | **moj fotoaparat** |
| | moy photo-*a*parat |
| my car keys | **ključeve mojih kola** |
| | klee-y*ooch*-eh-veh m*o*yeeh k*o*la |
| my car logbook | **saobraćajnu knjižicu** |
| | sa-*o*bracha-eenoo kn-y*ee*-shee-tsoo |
| my driving licence | **moju vozačku dozvolu** |
| | m*o*y-oo voz*a*ch-koo d*o*z-vol-oo |
| my insurance certificate | **moju potvrdu osiguranja** |
| | m*o*y-oo p*o*t-ver-doo oseegoo-r*a*n-yah |

## THEFT

| Someone has stolen . . . | Ukrali su mi . . . |
|---|---|
| | *oo*kra-lee soo mee . . . |
| my car | **moja kola** |
| | m*o*ya k*o*la |
| my money | **moj novac** |
| | moy n*o*v-ats |
| my tickets | **moje karte** |
| | m*o*y-eh k*a*rteh |
| my travellers' cheques | **moje putne čekove** |
| | m*o*y-eh p*oo*t-neh ch*e*k-oveh |
| my wallet | **moj novčanik** |
| | moy nov-ch*a*n-ik |

*Men use the first alternative, women the second

my luggage                  **moju prtljagu**
                                  m*o*y-oo pertl-*ya*-goo

---

# The post office and phoning home

---

## ESSENTIAL INFORMATION

- Key words to look for **POŠTA, TELEGRAF I TELEFON**
- For stamps look for the word **MARKE** on a post office counter.
- Stamps are also sold at tobacconists, newsagents and stationers.
- Letter boxes are yellow, and fixed to the walls.
- Unless you read and speak Serbo-Croat well, it's best not to make phone calls by yourself. Go to a post office and write the town and number you want on a piece of paper.
- The code for the UK is 9944 followed by the UK subscriber's own telephone number. Calls to the USA have to go through the operator.

## WHAT TO SAY

To England, please           **Za Englesku, molim**
                                  za en-gles-koo m*o*l-im

*[Hand letters, card or parcels over the counter]*

To Australia                **Za Australiju**
                                  za *ah*-oostralee-yoo

To the United States      **Za Ameriku**
                                  za amerik-oo

I'd like to send a telegram  **Želim da pošaljem telegram**
                                  sh*e*l-im da p*o*shal-yem t*e*legram

**I'd like this number . . .**   **Želim ovaj broj . . .**
*[show number]*            sh*e*l-im *o*v-eey broy . . .
  in England              **za Englesku**
                                  za en-gles-koo

  in Canada              **za Kanadu**
                                  za kanadoo

Can you dial it for me, please?  **Možete li vi nazvati za mene, molim?**
                                  m*o*sh-et-eh lee vee n*a*z-va-tee za m*e*h-neh m*o*l-im

# Changing cheques and money

## ESSENTIAL INFORMATION

- Look for these words on buildings:
  **BANKA** (bank)
  **MJENJAČNICA** (money changed)
  **NARODNA BANKA** (national bank)
  **TURISTIČKA AGENCIJA** (most travel agencies will change money)
- Money can also be changed at some post offices. It is illegal to change foreign currency other than in official exchange offices. Avoid all approaches to change money – particularly on trains.
- To cash your own normal cheques, exactly as at home, use you banker's card where you see the Eurocheque sign. Write in English, in pounds.
- Exchange rate information might show the pound as:
  **L, GB, VB**
- Have your passport handy.

## WHAT TO SAY

| | |
|---|---|
| I'd like to cash . . . | **Želim da promjenim . . .**<br>shel-im da prom-yen-im . . . |
| these travellers' cheques | **ove putne čekove**<br>ov-eh poot-neh check-oveh |
| this cheque | **ovaj ček**<br>ov-aee check |
| I'd like to change this . . . | **Želim da promjenim ovo . . .**<br>shel-im da prom-yen-im ov-o . . . |
| into dinars | **u dinare**<br>oo deen-areh |
| into Austrian schillings | **u austrijske šilinge**<br>oo ah-oos-tree-skeh shee-leen-geh |
| into Hungarian forint | **u madžarske forinte**<br>oo mad-jar-skeh foreen-teh |
| into Rumanian leu | **u rumunjske leje**<br>oo roomoon-skeh leh-yeh |
| into Bulgarian lev | **u bugarske leve**<br>oo boogar-skeh lev-eh |

| | |
|---|---|
| into Italian lira | **u talijanske lire** |
| | oo tal*ee*-yan-skeh l*ee*reh |
| into Greek drachma | **u grčke drahme** |
| | oo gerch-keh dra-hmeh |
| into Albanian lek | **u albanske leke** |
| | oo *a*lban-skeh lek-eh |

# Car travel

## ESSENTIAL INFORMATION

- Grades of petrol:
  NORMAL (86 octane)
  MJEŠAVINA (mixed)
  SUPER (98 octane)
  NAFTA/DIZL (gas oil/diesel)
- 1 gallon is about 4½ litres (accurate enough up to 6 gallons).
- For general repairs, look for the sign
  AUTOMEHANIKA
  Other garages with the proprietor's name in front of the sign
  SERVIS undertake general repair work.
- Opening times: 6.00 a.m. – 12.00 p.m.
- You will find 24-hour service stations along the main roads.
- The Yugoslav Automobile Association (AMSJ) runs some 120 assistance/information bases which are manned by mechanics and open between 8.00 a.m. and 8.00 p.m. Some of these stations still have individual telephone numbers, but many of them can be contacted on 987.
- Members of foreign motoring and touring clubs may get free legal advice from lawyers associated with the Yugoslav AA (particularly applicable in larger towns).

## WHAT TO SAY

*[For numbers, see p. 368]*

| | |
|---|---|
| (9) litres of . . . | **(Devet) litara . . .** |
| | d*e*h-vet l*ee*t-ara . . . |

| (150) dinars of . . . | (Sto pedeset) dinara . . . |
| | sto peh-deh-set deen-ara . . . |
| standard/premium | **normala/supera** |
| | normal-ah/sooper-ah |
| diesel | **mješavine/nafte** |
| | mee-yesha-veeneh/nafteh |
| Fill it up, please | **Napunite, molim** |
| | napoo-neeteh mol-im |
| Will you check . . . | **Molim vas provjerite . . .** |
| | mol-im vus prov-yair-eeteh . . . |
| the oil? | **ulje?** |
| | ool-yeh? |
| the battery? | **akumulator?** |
| | akoomoola-tor |
| the radiator? | **radijator?** |
| | rad-ya-tor |
| the tyres? | **gume?** |
| | goomeh |
| I've run out of petrol | **Ostao sam bez benzine** |
| | osta-o sum bez benzeeneh |
| Can you help me, please? | **Možete li mi pomoći, molim vas?** |
| | mosh-et-eh lee mee pom-ochee mol-im vus |
| Do you do repairs? | **Da li pravite popravke?** |
| | da lee pra-veeteh pop-rav-keh |
| I have a puncture | **Imam probušenu gumu** |
| | eem-am pro-booshenoo goomoo |
| I have a broken windscreen | **Imam razbijeno predje staklo** |
| | eem-am raz-bee-yen-o pred-yeh staklo |
| I think the problem is here . . . [point] | **Mislim da je problem ovdje . . .** |
| | meeslim da yeh problem ovd-yeh . . . |

## LIKELY REACTIONS

| I don't do repairs | **Ne vršim popravke** |
| | neh ver-sheem poprav-keh |
| Where is your car? | **Gdje su vaša kola?** |
| | gd-yeh soo vasha kola |
| What make is it? | **Koja je marka Vaših kola?** |
| | koya yeh marka vash-eeh kola |

Come back tomorrow/on
  Monday

**Povratite se sutra/u ponedjeljak**
pov-rat-eeteh seh s*oo*tra/oo
  pon*e*d-yel-yak

[*For days of the week, p. 371*]

# Public transport

## ESSENTIAL INFORMATION

- Key words on signs:
  **ŽELJEZNIČKA STANICA** (railway station)
  **PRODAJA KARTA** (tickets, ticket office)
  **ULAZ** (entrance)
  **ZABRANJENO JE** (forbidden)
  **ULAZ** (entrance, for buses)
  **PERON** (platform)
  **URED ZA INFORMACIJE** (information, information office)
  **ČEKAONICA** (waiting room)
  **ŽTP JŽ** (initials for Yugoslav railways)
  **IZLAZ** (exit)
  **GARDEROBA** (left luggage)
  **AUTOBUSNA STANICA** (bus stop)
  **RED VOŽNJE** (timetable)

## WHAT TO SAY

| | |
|---|---|
| Where does the train for (Belgrade) leave from? | **Odakle polazi vlak za (Beograd)?** *o*d-akleh pol-azee vl*a*k za (beh-ograd) |
| Is this train for (Belgrade)? | **Da li je ovo vlak za (Beograd)?** da lee yeh *ov*-o vl*a*k za (beh-ograd)? |
| Where does the bus for (Split) leave from? | **Odakle polazi autobus za (Split)?** *o*d-akleh pol-azee *a*h-ooto-boos za (spl*ee*t)? |
| Is this the bus for (Split)? | **Da li je ovo autobus za (Split)?** da lee yeh *ov*-o *a*h-ooto-boos za (spl*ee*t)? |

| | |
|---|---|
| Do I have to change? | **Moram li da presjedim?** |
| | mor-am lee da pres-yeh-dim |
| Can you put me off at the right stop, please? | **Hoćete li mi reći kad treba da se iskrcam, molim vas?** |
| | hoch-et-eh lee mee rech-ee kad treb-ah da seh is-ker-tsam mol-im vus |
| Where can I get a taxi? | **Gdje mogu uzeti taksi?** |
| | gd-yeh mog-oo oozet-ee taxi? |
| Can I book a seat? | **Mogu li rezervirati jedno mjesto?** |
| | mog-oo lee rezairv-eer-atee yed-no m-yesto |
| A single | **Jednosmjernu kartu** |
| | yed-no-smee-yair-noo kartoo |
| A return | **Jednu povratnu kartu** |
| | yed-noo povrat-noo kartoo |
| First class | **Prvi razred** |
| | per-vee raz-red |
| Second class | **Drugi razred** |
| | droo-ghee raz-red |
| One adult | **Za jednu osobu** |
| | za dvee-yeh os-obeh |
| and one child | **i jedno dijete** |
| | ee yed-no dee-yet-eh |
| and two children | **i dvoje djece** |
| | ee dvoyeh dee-yetseh |
| How much is it? | **Koliko košta?** |
| | kol-eeko koshta |

# Reference

## NUMBERS

| | | |
|---|---|---|
| 0 | **nula** | noolah |
| 1 | **jedan** | yed-an |
| 2 | **dva** | dva |
| 3 | **tri** | tree |
| 4 | **četiri** | chet-eeree |
| 5 | **pet** | peht |
| 6 | **šest** | shehst |

| | | |
|---|---|---|
| 7 | **sedam** | seh-dam |
| 8 | **osam** | osam |
| 9 | **devet** | deh-vet |
| 10 | **deset** | deh-set |
| 11 | **jedanaest** | yeh-da-na-est |
| 12 | **dvanaest** | dvah-na-est |
| 13 | **trinaest** | tree-na-est |
| 14 | **četrnaest** | chet-er-na-est |
| 15 | **petnaest** | peht-na-est |
| 16 | **šesnaest** | shehst-na-est |
| 17 | **sedamnaest** | seh-dam-na-est |
| 18 | **osamnaest** | o-sam-na-est |
| 19 | **devetnaest** | deh-vet-na-est |
| 20 | **dvadeset** | dva-deh-set |
| 21 | **dvadeset jedan** | dva-deh-set yed-an |
| 22 | **dvadeset dva** | dva-deh-set dva |
| 23 | **dvadeset tri** | dva-deh-set tree |
| 24 | **dvadeset četiri** | dva-deh-set chet-eeree |
| 25 | **dvadeset pet** | dva-deh-set peht |
| 26 | **dvadeset šest** | dva-deh-seh shehst |
| 27 | **dvadeset sedam** | dva-deh-set seh-dam |
| 28 | **dvadeset osam** | dva-deh-set o-sam |
| 29 | **dvadeset devet** | dva-deh-set deh-vet |
| 30 | **trideset** | tree-deh-set |
| 31 | **trideset jedan** | tree-deh-setyed-an |
| 32 | **trideset dva** | tree-des-set dva |
| 40 | **četrdeset** | chet-er-deh-set |
| 41 | **četrdeset jedan** | chet-er-deh-set yed-an |
| 42 | **četrdeset dva** | chet-er-deh-set dva |
| 50 | **pedeset** | peh-deh-set |
| 51 | **pedeset jedan** | peh-deh-set yed-an |
| 52 | **pedeset dva** | peh-deh-set dva |
| 60 | **šezdeset** | shehz-deh-set |
| 61 | **šezdeset jedan** | shehz-deh-set yed-an |
| 62 | **šezdeset dva** | shehz-deh-set dva |
| 70 | **sedamdeset** | seh-dam-deh-set |
| 71 | **sedamdeset jedan** | seh-dam-deh-set yed-an |
| 72 | **sedamdeset dva** | seh-dam-deh-set dva |
| 80 | **osamdeset** | o-sam-deh-set |
| 81 | **osamdeset jedan** | o-sam-deh-set yed-an |
| 82 | **osamdeset dva** | o-sam-deh-set dva |
| 90 | **devedeset** | deh-vet-deh-set |

| 91 | devedeset jedan | deh-vet-deh-set yed-an |
| 92 | devedeset dva | deh-vet-deh-set dva |
| 100 | sto | sto |
| 101 | sto jedan | sto yed-an |
| 110 | sto deset | sto deh-set |
| 120 | sto dvadeset | sto dva-deh-set |
| 200 | dvjesta | dvee-yeh-sta |
| 300 | trista | tree-sta |
| 400 | cetrsto | chet-er-sto |
| 500 | petsto | peht-sto |
| 600 | šesto | sheh-sto |
| 700 | sedamsto | seh-dam-sto |
| 800 | osamsto | o-sam-sto |
| 900 | devetsto | deh-vet-sto |
| 1,000 | hiljada/tisuća | heel-ya-da/tees-oocha |
| 2,000 | dvije hiljade | dvee-yeh heel-ya-deh |
| 3,000 | tri hiljade | tree heel-ya-deh |
| 10,000 | deset hiljada | deh-set heel-yada |
| 100,000 | sto hiljada | sto heel-ya-da |
| 1,000,000 | milijun | meelee-yoon |

## TIME

| What time is it? | **Koliko je sati?** |
| | kol-eeko yeh sa-tee |
| It's . . . (this is not translated in Serbo-Croat) | |
| one o'clock | **jedan sat** |
| | yed-an sat |
| two o'clock | **dva sata** |
| | dva sa-ta |
| three o'clock | **tri sata** |
| | tree sa-ta |
| noon | **podne** |
| | pod-neh |
| midnight | **ponoć** |
| | po-noch |
| . a quarter past five | **pet i petnaest** |
| | peht ee peht-na-est |
| half past five | **pola šest** |
| | po-la shehst |
| a quarter to six | **petnaest do šest** |
| | peht-na-est doh shehst |

# DAYS AND MONTHS

| | |
|---|---|
| Monday | **ponedjeljak** |
| | pon*ed*-yel-yak |
| Tuesday | **utorak** |
| | *oo*to-rak |
| Wednesday | **srijeda** |
| | sree-y*ed*a |
| Thursday | **četvrtak** |
| | chet-ver-tak |
| Friday | **petak** |
| | p*eh*-tak |
| Saturday | **subota** |
| | s*oo*-bota |
| Sunday | **nedjelja** |
| | n*ed*-yel-ya |
| January | **januar** |
| | y*a*-noo-ar |
| February | **februar** |
| | f*eh*-broo-ar |
| March | **mart** |
| | m*a*rt |
| April | **april** |
| | *a*p-reel |
| May | **maj** |
| | m*a*-ee |
| June | **juni** |
| | y*oo*-nee |
| July | **juli** |
| | y*oo*-lee |
| August | **august** |
| | *ah*-oo-goost |
| September | **septembar** |
| | sep-t*em*-bar |
| October | **oktobar** |
| | okt*o*-bar |
| November | **novembar** |
| | novem-bar |
| December | **decembar** |
| | deh-ts*em*-bar |

**Public holidays**

Offices, shops and schools are all closed on the following dates.

| | | |
|---|---|---|
| 1–2 January | **Nova godina** | New Year holiday |
| 1–2 May | **Prvi Maj** | Labour Day |
| 4 July | **Dan borca** | Fighter's Day |
| 29–30 November | **Dan Republike** | Days of the Republic |

Republican national holidays

*Serbia* 7 July
*Montenegro* 13 July
*Slovenia* 22 July
*Croatia, Bosnia and Herzegovina* 27 July
*Macedonia* 2 August and 11 October

# Index

# Travellers' **Spanish**

**D. L. Ellis, R. Ellis**

Pronunciation **Dr J. Baldwin**

*Useful address*
The Spanish National Tourist Office
57 St James's Street, London SW1

# Contents

# Pronunciation hints

In Spanish it is important to stress or emphasize the syllables in italics, just as you would if we were to take as an English example: little Jack Horner sat in the corner. Here we have ten syllables but only four stresses.
¡Suerte!

# Everyday expressions

[*See also 'Shop Talk', p. 392*]

| | |
|---|---|
| Hello | **Hola** |
| | *o*-la |
| Good morning | **Buenos días** |
| | bwen-os d*ee*as |
| Good afternoon | **Buenas tardes** |
| | bwen-as tard-es |
| Goodnight | **Buenas noches** |
| | bwen-as n*o*ch-es |
| Good-bye | **Adiós** |
| | ad-y*o*s |
| Yes | **Sí** |
| | s*ee* |
| Please | **Por favor** |
| | por fab-*o*r |
| Yes, please | **Sí, por favor** |
| | s*ee* por fab-*o*r |
| Thank you | **Gracias** |
| | gr*a*th-yas |
| Thank you very much | **Muchas gracias** |
| | m*oo*chas gr*a*th-yas |
| That's right | **Exacto** |
| | ex*a*cto |
| No | **No** |
| | no |
| No, thank you | **No, gracias** |
| | no gr*a*th-yas |
| I disagree | **No estoy de acuerdo** |
| | no est*o*y deh acw*ai*do |
| Excuse me ⎤ | **Perdone** |
| Sorry ⎦ | pairdon-eh |
| It doesn't matter | **No importa** |
| | no imp*o*rta |
| Where's the toilet, please? | **¿Dónde están los servicios, por favor?** |
| | d*o*ndeh est*a*n los sairb*i*th-yos por fab-*o*r |
| Do you speak English? | **¿Habla usted inglés?** |
| | *a*bla oost*e*d in-gles |

| | |
|---|---|
| What is your name? | **¿Cómo se llama?** |
| | com-o seh yama |
| My name is . . . | **Me llamo . . .** |
| | meh yamo . . . |

---

# Asking the way

---

## ESSENTIAL INFORMATION

- Keep a look out for all these place names as you will find them on shops, maps and notices.

## WHAT TO SAY

| | |
|---|---|
| Excuse me, please | **Perdone, por favor** |
| | pairdon-eh por fab-or |
| How do I get . . . | **¿Para ir . . .** |
| | para eer . . . |
| to Madrid? | **a Madrid?** |
| | ah madreed |
| to Alfonso Primero street? | **a la calle Alfonso Primero?** |
| | ah la ca-yeh alfonso prim-airo |
| to the Hotel Castilla? | **al hotel Castilla?** |
| | al ot-el castee-ya |
| to the airport? | **al aeropuerto?** |
| | al airo-pwairto |
| to the beach? | **a la playa?** |
| | ah la pla-ya |
| to the bus station? | **a la estación de autobuses?** |
| | ah la estath-yon deh |
| | ah-ooto-booses |
| to the market? | **al mercado?** |
| | al maircad-o |
| to the police station? | **a la comisaría de policía?** |
| | ah la comisareea deh politheea |
| to the port? | **al puerto?** |
| | al pwairto |
| to the post office? | **a correos?** |
| | ah cor-reh-os |

| | |
|---|---|
| **Is there . . . near by?** | **¿Hay . . . cerca?** |
| | *ah*-ee . . . th*air*ca |
| to the railway station? | **a la estación de tren?** |
| | ah la estath-yon deh tren |
| to the sports stadium? | **al estadio de deportes?** |
| | al estad-yo deh dep-*ort*-es |
| to the tourist information office? | **a la oficina de información y turismo?** |
| | ah la ofith*ee*na deh informath-yon *ee* too-r*i*smo |
| to the town centre? | **al centro de la ciudad?** |
| | al th*en*tro deh la thee-ood*a*d |
| to the town hall? | **al ayuntamiento?** |
| | al a-yoontam-y*en*to |

| | |
|---|---|
| **Is there . . . near by?** | **¿Hay . . . cerca?** |
| | *ah*-ee . . . th*air*ca |
| a baker's | **una panadería** |
| | *oo*na panad-er*ee*ah |
| a bank | **un banco** |
| | oon b*a*nco |
| a bar | **un bar** |
| | oon b*a*r |
| a bus stop | **una parada de autobús** |
| | *oo*na par*a*d-ah deh ah-ooto-b*oo*s |
| a butcher's | **una carnicería** |
| | *oo*na carnith-er*ee*a |
| a café | **una cafetería** |
| | *oo*na cafet-er*ee*a |
| a cake shop | **una pastelería** |
| | *oo*na pastel-er*ee*a |
| a campsite | **un camping** |
| | oon c*a*mping |
| a car park | **un aparcamiento** |
| | oon aparcam-y*en*to |
| a change bureau | **una oficina de cambio** |
| | *oo*na ofith*ee*na deh c*a*mb-yo |
| a chemist's | **una farmacia** |
| | *oo*na farm*a*th-ya |
| a delicatessen | **una mantequería** |
| | *oo*na mantek-er*ee*a |
| a dentist's | **un dentista** |
| | oon dent*i*sta |

| | |
|---|---|
| a department store | **unos almacenes** |
| | *oo*nos almath-*e*n-es |
| a disco | **una discoteca** |
| | *oo*na discot*e*c-ah |
| a doctor's surgery | **un consultorio médico** |
| | oon consoolt*o*rio m*e*dic-o |
| a dry cleaner's | **una tintorería** |
| | *oo*na tintor-er*ee*a |
| a fishmonger's | **una pescadería** |
| | *oo*na pescad-er*ee*a |
| a garage (for repairs) | **un garaje** |
| | oon ga-r*a*heh |
| a greengrocer's | **una verdulería** |
| | *oo*na berdool-er*ee*a |
| a grocer's | **una tienda de comestibles** |
| | oona tee-*e*nda deh com-est*ee*-bles |
| a hairdresser's | **una peluquería** |
| | *oo*na pelook-er*ee*a |
| a Health and Social Security Office | **una oficina de la Seguridad Social** |
| | *oo*na ofith*ee*na deh la segoo-reed*a*d soth-y*a*l |
| a hospital | **un hospital** |
| | oon ospit*a*l |
| a hotel | **un hotel** |
| | oon ot-*e*l |
| an ice-cream parlour | **una heladería** |
| | *oo*na ellad-er*ee*a |
| a laundry | **una lavandería** |
| | *oo*na laband-er*ee*a |
| a newsagent's | **una tienda de periódicos** |
| | *oo*na tee-*e*nda deh peri-*o*dicos |
| a nightclub | **una sala de fiestas** |
| | *oo*na s*a*l-ah deh fee-*e*stas |
| a petrol station | **una gasolinera** |
| | *oo*na gasolin-*e*rra |
| a post box | **un buzón** |
| | oon booth*o*n |
| a public garden | **un jardín público** |
| | oon hard*ee*n p*oo*blico |
| a public toilet | **unos servicios públicos** |
| | *oo*nos sairb*ee*th-yos p*oo*blicos |
| a restaurant | **un restaurante** |
| | oon resta-oor*a*nteh |

| Is there . . . near by? | ¿Hay . . . cerca? |
|---|---|
| | ah-ee . . . thairca? |
| a supermarket | un supermercado |
| | oon supermaircad-o |
| a taxi stand | una parada de taxis |
| | oona parad-ah deh taxis |
| a telephone | un teléfono |
| | oon telef-ono |
| a tobacconist's | un estanco |
| | oon estanco |
| a travel agent's | una agencia de viajes |
| | oona ahenth-ya deh bee-ah-hes |
| a youth hostel | un albergue juvenil |
| | oon albair-geh hooben-eel |

## DIRECTIONS

| Left | Izquierda |
|---|---|
| | ithk-yairda |
| Right | Derecha |
| | derech-ah |
| Straight on | Todo recto |
| | todo recto |
| There | Allí |
| | ayee |
| First left/right | La primera a la izquierda/derecha |
| | la prim-aira ah la ithk-yairda/ derech-a |
| Second left/right | La segunda a la izquierda/derecha |
| | la seg-oonda ah la ithk-yairda/ derech-a |

# Accommodation

## ESSENTIAL INFORMATION
### Hotel

• If you want hotel-type accommodation, all the following words in capital letters are worth looking for on name boards: **HOTEL** (accommodation with all facilities, the quality depending on the star rating)
**HOTEL-RESIDENCIA** (similar to the above but often for longer stays)

**PENSION** (small, privately run hotel)
**HOSTAL**
**FONDA** (a modest form of **pensión**)
**MOTEL**
**ALBERGUE** (often picturesque type of hotel situated in the countryside)
**PARADOR** (converted palaces and castles in recognized beauty spots – relatively expensive)

- The last two are run by the **Secretaria de Estado de Turismo** (Secretary of State for Tourism).
- In some places, you will find the following: **CAMAS** (beds), **HABITACIONES** (rooms), **CASA** (house) followed by the owner's name or **CASA DE HUESPEDES** (guest house) – these are all alternatives to a **pensión**.
- Hotels are divided into five classes (from luxury to tourist class) and **pensiones** into three.
- A list of hotels and **pensiones** in the town or district can usually be obtained at the local tourist information office.
- The cost is displayed in the room itself, so you can check it when having a look around before agreeing to stay.
- The displayed cost is for the room itself, per night and not per person. Breakfast is extra and therefore optional.
- Service and VAT is always included in the cost of the room, so tipping is voluntary. In Spain, however, it is normal practice to tip porters and waiters.
- Not all hotels provide meals, apart from breakfast. A **pensión** always provides meals. Breakfast is continental style: coffee/tea with rolls and jam.
- When registering you will be asked to leave your passport at the reception desk and to complete a form.

## WHAT TO SAY

| | |
|---|---|
| I have a booking | **Tengo una reserva**<br>tengo _oo_na res-_air_ba |
| Have you any vacancies, please? | **¿Tiene habitaciones libres, por favor?**<br>tee-_en_-eh abeetath-yon-es _lee_-bres por fab-_or_ |
| Can I book a room? | **¿Puedo reservar una habitación?**<br>pwed-o res-airbar _oo_na abeetath-yon |

| It's for . . . | **Es para . . .** |
| | es para . . . |
| one adult/one person | **un adulto/una persona** |
| | oon adoolto/oona pairson-ah |
| two adults/two people | **dos adultos/dos personas** |
| | dos adooltos/dos pairson-as |
| and one child | **y un niño** |
| | ee oon neen-yo |
| and two children | **y dos niños** |
| | ee dos neen-yos |
| It's for . . . | **Es para . . .** |
| | es para . . . |
| one night | **una noche** |
| | oona noch-eh |
| two nights | **dos noches** |
| | dos noch-es |
| one week | **una semana** |
| | oona sem-anna |
| two weeks | **dos semanas** |
| | dos sem-annas |
| I would like . . . | **Quiero . . .** |
| | kee-airo . . . |
| a (quiet) room | **una habitación (tranquila)** |
| | oona abeetath-yon (trankee-ya) |
| two rooms | **dos habitaciones** |
| | dos abeetath-yon-es |
| with a single bed | **con una cama individual** |
| | con oona cam-ah indibid-wal |
| with two single beds | **con dos camas individuales** |
| | con dos cam-as indibid-wal-es |
| with a double bed | **con una cama doble** |
| | con oona cam-ah dobleh |
| with a toilet | **con servicio** |
| | con sairbith-yo |
| with a bathroom | **con baño** |
| | con ban-yo |
| with a shower | **con ducha** |
| | con doocha |
| with a cot | **con una cuna** |
| | con oona coona |
| with a balcony | **con balcón** |
| | con balcon |

| I would like . . . | Quiero . . . |
|---|---|
| | kee-*air*o . . . |
| full board | **pensión completa** |
| | pens-yon complet-ah |
| half board | **media pensión** |
| | med-ya pens-yon |
| bed and breakfast | **desayuno incluido** |
| [*see essential information*] | desa-*yoo*no incloo-*ee*do |
| Do you serve meals? | **¿Sirven comidas?** |
| | seerben com-*ee*das |
| Can I look at the room? | **¿Puedo ver la habitación?** |
| | pwed-o b*air* la abeetath-yon |
| OK, I'll take it | **Está bien, la tomo** |
| | esta bee-*en* la tom-o |
| No thanks, I won't take it | **No gracias, no la tomo** |
| | no grath-yas no la tom-o |
| The bill, please | **La cuenta, por favor** |
| | la cwenta por fab-*or* |
| Is service included? | **¿Está incluido el servicio?** |
| | esta incloo-*ee*do el sairb*ith*-yo |
| I think this is wrong | **Creo que esto está mal** |
| | creh-o keh esto esta mal |
| Can you give me a receipt? | **¿Puede darme un recibo?** |
| | pwed-eh d*ar*meh oon reth*ee*bo |

### Camping

- Look for the word: **CAMPING**
- Be prepared to have to pay:
  per person
  for the car (if applicable)
  for the tent or caravan plot
  for electricity
  for hot showers
- You must provide proof of identity such as your passport.
- In Spain, most campsites are situated along the coast and those inland are few and far between. You can camp off-site with the permission of the authorities and/or the landowner; however, there are a number of regulations governing where you can or cannot camp – the Spanish Tourist Office in London has details so check with them before travelling abroad.

- Camping carnets are no longer essential but advisable as they do provide third-party insurance for those camping off-site.
- During the high season it is advisable to book in advance by writing direct to the campsite.
- Persons under the age of sixteen are not admitted on a site unless accompanied by an adult.

## Youth hostels

- Look for the words: **ALBERGUE JUVENIL.**
- You will be asked for a YHA card and passport on arrival.
- Food and cooking facilities vary from hostel to hostel and you may have to help with the domestic chores.
- You must take your own sleeping bag lining but bedding can sometimes be hired on arrival.
- In the high season it is advisable to book beds in advance, and your stay will be limited to a maximum of three consecutive nights per hostel.
- Apply to the Spanish Tourist office in London or local tourist offices in Spain for lists of youth hostels and details of regulations for hostellers.

## WHAT TO SAY

| | |
|---|---|
| Have you any vacancies? | **¿Tiene plazas libres?**<br>tee-en-eh plathas lee-bres |
| It's for . . . | **Es para . . .**<br>es para . . . |
| one adult/one person | **un adulto/una persona**<br>oon adoolto/oona pairson-ah |
| two adults/two people | **dos adultos/dos personas**<br>dos adooltos/dos pairson-as |
| and one child | **y un niño**<br>ee oon neen-yo |
| and two children | **y dos niños**<br>ee dos neen-yos |
| How much is it . . . | **¿Cuánto es . . .**<br>cwanto es . . . |
| for the tent? | **por la tienda?**<br>por la tee-enda |

| | |
|---|---|
| for the caravan? | **por la caravana?** |
| | por la caraban-ah |
| for the car? | **por el coche?** |
| | por el coch-eh |
| for the electricity? | **por la electricidad** |
| | por la electrithee-dad |
| per person? | **por persona?** |
| | por pairson-ah |
| per day/night? | **por día/noche?** |
| | por deea/noch-eh |
| May I look round? | **¿Puedo mirar?** |
| | pwed-o mee-rar |
| **Do you provide anything . . .** | **¿Dan ustedes algo . . .** |
| | dan oosted-es algo . . . |
| to eat? | **de comer?** |
| | deh com-air |
| to drink? | **de beber?** |
| | deh beb-air |
| **Is there/are there . . .** | **¿Hay . . .** |
| | ah-ee . . . |
| a bar? | **bar?** |
| | bar |
| hot showers? | **duchas calientes?** |
| | doochas cal-yentes |
| a kitchen? | **cocina?** |
| | cotheena |
| a laundry? | **lavandería?** |
| | laband-ereea |
| a restaurant? | **restaurante?** |
| | resta-ooranteh |
| a shop? | **tienda?** |
| | tee-enda |
| a swimming pool? | **piscina?** |
| | pis-theena |
| a takeaway? | **tienda de comidas preparadas?** |
| | tee-enda deh com-eedas |
| | prepa-rad-as |

[*For food shopping, see p. 394, and for eating and drinking out, see p. 405*]

| | |
|---|---|
| I would like a counter for the shower | **Quiero una ficha para la ducha** |
| | kee-airo oona feecha para la doocha |

## Problems

| | |
|---|---|
| The toilet | **El servicio** |
| | el sairb*i*th-yo |
| The shower | **La ducha** |
| | la d*oo*cha |
| The tap | **El grifo** |
| | el gr*ee*fo |
| The razor point | **El enchufe de la maquinilla de afeitar** |
| | el ench*oo*feh deh la makin*ee*-ya deh affayt*a*r |
| The light | **La luz** |
| | la l*oo*th |
| . . . is not working | **. . . está roto/a** |
| | . . . est*a* r*o*t-o/ah |
| My camping gas has run out | **Mi camping gas se ha acabado** |
| | mee c*a*mping g*a*s seh *a*h acab*a*d-o |

## LIKELY REACTIONS

| | |
|---|---|
| Have you an identity document? | **¿Tiene usted un documento de identidad?** |
| | tee-en-eh oost*e*d oon doc*oo*mento deh id-entid*a*d |
| Your membership card, please | **Su carnet, por favor** |
| | soo carn*e*t por fab-*o*r |
| What's your name? [see p. 379] | **¿Cómo se llama?** |
| | c*o*m-o seh y*a*ma |
| Sorry, we're full | **Lo siento, está lleno** |
| | lo see-*e*nto est*a* y*e*n-o |
| How many people is it for? | **¿Para cuántas personas es?** |
| | p*a*ra cw*a*ntas pairs*o*n-as *e*s |
| How many nights is it for? | **¿Para cuántas noches es?** |
| | p*a*ra cw*a*ntas n*o*ch-es *e*s |
| It's (100) pesetas . . . | **Son (cien) pesetas . . .** |
| | son (thee-*e*n) pes-*e*t-as . . . |
| per day/per night | **por día/por noche** |
| | por d*ee*a/por n*o*ch-eh |
| I haven't any rooms left | **No me quedan habitaciones** |
| | n*o* meh ked-an abeetath-y*o*n-es |
| Do you want to have a look? | **¿Quiere ver la habitación?** |
| | kee-*ai*reh b*ai*r la abeetath-y*o*n |

# General shopping

## The chemist's

### ESSENTIAL INFORMATION

- Look for the word **FARMACIA** (chemist's), or these signs.
- Medicines (drugs) are available only at a chemist's.
- Some non-drugs can be bought at a supermarket or department store, of course.
- Try the chemist *before* going to a doctor: they are usually qualified to treat minor injuries.
- Normal opening times are 9 a.m. – 1 p.m. and 4 p.m. – 8 p.m.
- If the chemist's is shut, a notice on the door headed **FARMACIAS DE GUARDIA** gives the address of the nearest chemist on duty.
- Some toiletries can also be bought at a **PERFUMERIA**, but they will probably be more expensive.

### WHAT TO SAY

| I'd like . . . | **Quiero . . .** |
| --- | --- |
| | kee-*airo* . . . |
| some antiseptic | **antiséptico** |
| | antis*e*ptico |
| some aspirin | **aspirinas** |
| | aspir*i*n-as |
| some baby food | **comida para niños** |
| | com-*ee*da para n*e*en-yos |
| some contraceptives | **anticonceptivos** |
| | anti-conthept-*ee*bos |
| some cotton wool | **algodón** |
| | algod-*on* |
| some disposable nappies | **pañales de papel** |
| | pan-*yal*-es deh pap-*el* |
| some eye drops | **gotas para los ojos** |
| | g*ot*-as para los *o*-hos |

| I'd like . . . | Quiero . . . |
|---|---|
| | kee-*airo* . . . |
| some inhalant | **inhalante** |
| | in-al*anteh* |
| some insect repellent | **loción contra los insectos** |
| | loth-yon contra los insectos |
| some paper tissues | **tisús** |
| | tis*oos* |
| some sanitary towels | **compresas** |
| | compres-as |
| some sticking plaster | **esparadrapo** |
| | esparadr*appo* |
| some suntan lotion/oil | **loción/aceite bronceador** |
| | loth-yon/ath*ay*-teh bronteh-ad*or* |
| some Tampax | **Tampax** |
| | tampax |
| some (soft) toilet paper | **papel higiénico (suave)** |
| | pap-*el* eehi-y*ennico* (swa-beh) |
| I'd like something for . . . | Quiero algo para . . . |
| | kee-*airo* algo para . . . |
| bites/stings | **las picaduras** |
| | las pic-ad*ooras* |
| burns | **las quemaduras** |
| | las kem-ad*ooras* |
| a cold | **el catarro** |
| | el cat*arro* |
| constipation | **el estreñimiento** |
| | el estren-yee-mee-*ento* |
| a cough | **la tos** |
| | la to*s* |
| diarrhoea | **la diarrea** |
| | la dee-ah-r*eh*-ah |
| ear-ache | **el dolor de oído** |
| | el dol-*or* deh o-*eedo* |
| flu | **la gripe** |
| | la greep-eh |
| scalds | **las escaldaduras** |
| | las escald-ad*ooras* |
| sunburn | **las quemaduras de sol** |
| | las kem-ad*ooras* deh sol |
| travel sickness | **el mareo** |
| | el ma-r*eyo* |

[*For other essential expressions, see 'Shop talk', p. 392*]

# Holiday items

## ESSENTIAL INFORMATION

- Places to shop at and signs to look for:
  **LIBRERIA-PAPELERIA** (stationery)
  **FOTOGRAFIA** (films)
  **MATERIAL FOTOGRAFICO** (films)
  and the main department stores:
  **GALERIAS PRECIADOS**
  **SEPU**
  **EL CORTE INGLES**

## WHAT TO SAY

| I'd like . . . | **Quiero . . .** |
|---|---|
| | kee-*airo* . . . |
| a bag | **un bolso** |
| | oon b*o*lso |
| a beach ball | **una pelota para la playa** |
| | *oo*na pelota para la pl*a*-ya |
| a bucket | **un cubo** |
| | oon c*oo*bo |
| an English newspaper | **un periódico inglés** |
| | oon peri-*od*-ico in-gles |
| some envelopes | **sobres** |
| | sob-res |
| some postcards | **postales** |
| | post*al*-es |
| a spade | **una pala** |
| | *oo*na p*al*-ah |
| a straw hat | **un sombrero de paja** |
| | oon sombr*air*o deh p*a*-ha |
| some sunglasses | **unas gafas de sol** |
| | *oo*nas g*af*-as deh sol |
| some writing paper | **papel de escribir** |
| | pap-*el* deh escrib-*eer* |
| a colour film [*show the camera*] | **un rollo en color** |
| | oon r*o*-yo en col-*or* |
| a black and white film | **un rollo en blanco y negro** |
| | oon r*o*-yo en bl*a*nco ee n*e*g-ro |

[*For other essential expressions, see 'Shop talk', p. 392*]

# Shop talk

## ESSENTIAL INFORMATION

- Know how to say the important weights and measures

| | | |
|---|---|---|
| 50 grams | **cincuenta gramos** | thin-cwenta gram-os |
| 100 grams | **cien gramos** | thee-en gram-os |
| 200 grams | **doscientos gramos** | dos-thee-entos gram-os |
| ½ kilo | **medio kilo** | med-yo kilo |
| 1 kilo | **un kilo** | oon kilo |
| 2 kilos | **dos kilos** | dos kilos |
| ½ litre | **medio litro** | med-yo litro |
| 1 litre | **un litro** | oon litro |
| 2 litres | **dos litros** | dos litros |

[*For numbers, see p. 424*]

## CUSTOMER

| | | |
|---|---|---|
| I'm just looking | **Sólo estoy mirando** | sol-o estoy mirrando |
| How much is this/that? | **¿Cuánto es esto/eso?** | cwanto es esto/es-o |
| What is that? | **¿Qué es eso?** | keh es es-o |
| What are those? | **¿Qué son esos?** | keh son es-os |
| Is there a discount? | **¿Hay descuento?** | ah-ee des-cwento |
| I'd like that, please | **Quiero eso, por favor** | kee-airo es-o por fab-or |

| | |
|---|---|
| Not that | **Eso no**<br>*es*-o no |
| Like that | **Así**<br>a*see* |
| That's enough, thank you | **Basta, gracias**<br>b*a*sta grath-yas |
| More, please | **Más, por favor**<br>m*a*s por fab-or |
| Less, please | **Menos, por favor**<br>men-os por fab-or |
| That's fine | **Eso está bien**<br>*es*-o está bee-en |
| OK | **Está bien**<br>está bee-en |
| I won't take it, thank you | **No lo tomo, gracias**<br>no lo tom-o grath-yas |
| It's not right | **No está bien**<br>no está bee-en |
| **Have you got something . . .** | **¿Tiene algo . . .**<br>tee-*en*-eh *a*lgo . . . |
| better? | **mejor?**<br>m*eh*-hor |
| cheaper? | **más barato?**<br>m*a*s ba-r*a*t-o |
| different? | **diferente?**<br>diffair-enteh |
| larger?/smaller? | **más grande?/pequeño?**<br>m*a*s grandeh/peken-yo |
| Can I have a bag, please? | **¿Puedo tener una bolsa, por favor?**<br>pwed-o ten-*air* *oo*na bolsa por<br>fab-or |
| Can you give me a receipt? | **¿Puede darme un recibo?**<br>pwed-eh d*a*rmeh oon reth*ee*bo |
| **Do you take . . .** | **¿Toman ustedes . . .**<br>tom-an oosted-es . . . |
| English/American money? | **dinero inglés/americano?**<br>din-*air*o in-gles/americano |
| travellers' cheques? | **cheques de viaje?**<br>chek-es deh bee-*ah*-heh |
| credit cards? | **tarjetas de crédito?**<br>tarhet-as deh credit-o |

**SHOP ASSISTANT**

| | |
|---|---|
| Can I help you? | **¿En qué puedo servirle?** |
| | en keh pwed-o sairbeer-leh |
| What would you like? | **¿Qué desea/quiere?** |
| | keh des-eh-ah/kee-aireh |
| Will that be all? | **¿Será eso todo?** |
| | serra es-o tod-o |
| Is that all? | **¿Eso es todo?** |
| | es-o es tod-o |
| Anything else? | **¿Algo más?** |
| | algo mas |
| Would you like it wrapped? | **¿Quiere que se lo envuelva?** |
| | kee-aireh keh seh lo enbwelba |
| Sorry, none left | **Lo siento, no queda ninguno** |
| | lo see-ento no ked-ah nin-goono |
| I haven't got any | **No tengo** |
| | no tengo |
| I haven't got any more | **No tengo más** |
| | no tengo mas |
| How many do you want? | **¿Cuántos quiere?** |
| | cwantos kee-aireh |
| How much do you want? | **¿Cuánto quiere?** |
| | cwanto kee-aireh |
| Is that enough? | **¿Basta?** |
| | basta |

# Shopping for food

# Bread

**ESSENTIAL INFORMATION**

- Key words to look for:
  **HORNO** (baker's)
  **PANADERIA** (baker's)
  **PANADERO** (baker)
  **PAN** (bread)

- **Panaderías**, as well as other shops, are open from 9 a.m. – 1 p.m. and from 4 p.m. – 8 p.m. closing at lunchtime. In popular resorts, the shops often remain open all day.
- The most characteristic type of loaf is the **barra** which is a wider version of the 'french stick', and comes in different sizes according to the weight.
- For any other type of loaf, say **un pan** (oon p*a*n), and point.
- In some bakeries you can buy milk; look for this sign: **LECHERIA-PANADERIA**. Soft drinks, sweets and ice-creams can also be bought here.
- It's quite usual in Spain to have your bread delivered; if you wish to take advantage of this service, simply have a word with your local baker. You only have to say: **¿Puede traer el pan a casa?** (pwed-eh tra-*air* el p*a*n ah ca*s*-a).

## WHAT TO SAY

| | |
|---|---|
| A loaf (like that) | **Un pan (así)** |
| | oon p*a*n (as*ee*) |
| One long loaf | **Una barra** |
| | *oo*na b*a*rra |
| Three loaves | **Tres panes** |
| | tres p*a*n-es |
| A bread roll | **Un panecillo** |
| | oon panneth*ee*-yo |
| Four crescent rolls | **Cuatro croissants** |
| | cw*a*tro crw*a*ssans |
| **A packet of . . .** | **Un paquete de . . .** |
| | oon pak*e*t-eh deh . . . |
| English bread | **pan de molde** |
| | p*a*n deh m*o*ldeh |
| toasted bread | **pan tostado** |
| | p*a*n tost*a*d-o |
| brown bread | **pan integral** |
| | p*a*n inteh-gr*a*l |

[*For other essential expressions, see 'Shop talk', p. 392*]

# Cakes and ice-creams

## ESSENTIAL INFORMATION

- Key words to look for:
  **PASTELERIA** (cake shop)
  **CONFITERIA** (confectionery, they also sell cakes)
  **PASTELERO** (cake/pastry maker)
  **PASTELES** (cakes)
  **PASTAS** (pastries)
  **HELADOS** (ice-creams)
  **HELADERO** (ice-cream maker/seller)
  **HELADERIA** (ice-cream shop/parlour)
  **HORCHATERIA** (ice-cream shop which also sells soft ice drinks)
- **CHURRERIA**: a place to buy **churros**, a kind of fritter that can be eaten on its own (takeaway) or dipped in hot thick chocolate. You have to ask for: **chocolate con churros**.
- **CAFETERIA**: a place where you can buy cakes, as well as drinks. You can also have chocolate and **churros**. See p. 405 'Ordering a drink and a snack'.

## WHAT TO SAY

The type of cakes you find in the shops varies from region to region but the following are some of the most common.

| | |
|---|---|
| **un churro**<br>oon ch*oo*ro | a finger-size fritter |
| **un buñuelo**<br>oon boon-yoo-*e*l-o | a round fritter |
| **magdalenas**<br>magda-*len*-as | madeleines (small sponge teacakes) |
| **una ensaimada**<br>oona en-sa-ee-m*a*d-ah | a bun made of puff pastry covered with sugar icing and filled with cream |
| **el mantecado**<br>el manteh-c*ad*-o | shortbread |
| **turrón**<br>too-r*o*n | nougat (can be hard or soft) |
| **el mazapán**<br>el matha-p*a*n | marzipan |

| | |
|---|---|
| **una yema** | a candied egg yolk |
| oona yem-ah | |
| **una rosquilla** | a ring-shaped roll (like a |
| oona ros-kee-ya | doughnut) |
| **un merengue** | a meringue |
| oon meh-ren-geh | |

| | |
|---|---|
| A . . . ice, please | **Un helado de . . ., por favor** |
| | oon elad-o deh . . . por fab-or |
| chocolate | **chocolate** |
| | chocolat-eh |
| pistachio | **mantecado** |
| | manteh-cad-o |
| raspberry | **frambuesa** |
| | frambwessa |
| strawberry | **fresa** |
| | fressa |
| vanilla | **vainilla** |
| | banee-ya |
| nougat flavour | **turrón** |
| | too-ron |
| hazelnut | **avellana** |
| | ab-el-yanna |
| mint | **menta** |
| | menta |
| A single | **Uno sencillo** |
| [specify flavour as above] | oono senthee-yo |

---

# Picnic food

## ESSENTIAL INFORMATION

- Key words to look for:
  **CHARCUTERIA** (pork butcher's delicatessen)
  **EMBUTIDOS** (cold meat sausages)
  **FIAMBRES** (cold meat, cold cuts)
  **TIENDA DE ULTRAMARINOS** (grocer's)
  **MANTEQUERIA** (delicatessen)
  **CARNECERIA** (butcher's)

- In these shops you can buy a wide variety of food such as ham, salami, cheese, olives, appetizers, sausages and freshly made takeaway dishes. Specialities differ from region to region.

## WHAT TO SAY

| Two slices of . . . | Dos rodajas de . . . |
| --- | --- |
| | dos rod-*a*has deh . . . |
| salami | **salchichón** |
| | salcheech*o*n |
| spicy hard sausage | **chorizo** |
| | chor-*ee*tho |
| pâté | **paté** |
| | pat*e*h |
| ham | **jamón de york** |
| | ham-*o*n deh york |
| cured ham, thinly sliced | **jamón serrano** |
| | ham-*o*n serr*a*nno |
| pork and beef cold meat | **mortadela** |
| | morta-d*e*lla |
| stuffed turkey | **pavo trufado** |
| | p*a*b-o troofad-o |

You may also like to try some of these:

| **pizza** | pizza |
| --- | --- |
| p*i*zza | |
| **salchicha de frankfurt** | frankfurter |
| salch*e*echa deh fr*a*nkfort | |
| **pollo asado** | roast chicken |
| p*o*l-yo asad-o | |
| **morcilla** | black pudding |
| morth*ee*-ya | |
| **palitos de queso** | cheese sticks |
| pal*ee*tos deh k*e*s-o | |
| **cortezas** | pork crackling/scratchings |
| cort*e*th-as | |
| **puntas de espárragos** | asparagus tips |
| p*oo*ntas deh esp*a*ragos | |
| **salmón ahumado** | smoked salmon |
| sal-m*o*n ah-oomad-o | |
| **butifarra** | spiced sausage |
| boot-if*a*rra | |

**longaniza**
longa-*neetha*

highly-seasoned sausage made with pork and herbs

**olivas rellenas**
oleebas reh-*yen*-as

stuffed olives

**olivas negras**
oleebas neg-ras

black olives

**patatas fritas**
pat*at*-as freetas

crisps

**pepinillos**
peppinee-yos

gherkins

**galletas saladas**
ga-yet-as sal*ad*-as

crackers

**sardinas en aceite**
sard*ee*nas en ath*ay*-teh

sardines in oil

**sardinas rancias**
sard*ee*nas r*anth*-yas

dry salty sardines

**atún**
at*oo*n

tuna

**queso de Burgos**
kes-o deh b*oo*rgos

soft, creamy cheese

**queso manchego**
kes-o mancheg-o

hard cheese from ewe's milk

**queso de roncal**
kes-o deh ronc*al*

salted, smoked cheese made from ewe's milk

**queso de bola**
kes-o deh b*ol*-ah

a round-shaped, mild cheese

**queso de cabra**
kes-o deh c*a*bra

goat cheese

**queso de teta**
kes-o deh teta

a firm, bland cheese made from cow's milk

[*For other essential expressions, see 'Shop talk', p. 392*]

# Fruit and vegetables

### ESSENTIAL INFORMATION

- Key words to look for:
  VERDURA (vegetables)        FRUTA (fruit)
  LEGUMBRES (vegetables)      FRUTERO (fruit seller)
  VERDULERIA (vegetable shop) FRUTERIA (fruit shop)

**FRESCO** (an indication of freshness)
- It is customary for you to choose your own fruit and vegetables in the market (and in some shops) and for the stallholder to weigh and price them. You must take your own shopping bag: paper and plastic bags are not normally provided.

## WHAT TO SAY

| | |
|---|---|
| 1 kilo of . . . | **Un kilo de . . .**<br>oon k*i*lo deh . . . |
| apples | **manzanas**<br>manth*a*nas |
| bananas | **plátanos**<br>pl*a*ttan-os |
| cherries | **cerezas**<br>there*th*-as |
| figs | **higos**<br>*ee*-gos |
| grapes (black/white) | **uvas (blancas/negras)**<br>*oo*bas (bl*a*ncas/neg-ras) |
| oranges | **naranjas**<br>na-r*a*ng-has |
| pears | **peras**<br>p*e*rras |
| peaches | **melocotones**<br>mellocot*o*n-es |
| plums | **ciruelas**<br>theer-rw*e*llas |
| strawberries | **fresas**<br>fr*e*ssas |
| A pineapple, please | **Una piña, por favor**<br>*oo*na p*ee*n-ya por fab-*o*r |
| A grapefruit | **Un pomelo**<br>oon pom*e*llo |
| A melon | **Un melón**<br>oon mel*o*n |
| A water-melon | **Una sandía**<br>*oo*na sand*ee*a |
| ½ kilo of . . . | **Medio kilo de . . .**<br>med-yo k*i*lo deh . . . |
| artichokes | **alcachofas**<br>alkach*o*ffas |

| | |
|---|---|
| asparagus | **esparrago** |
| | esp*a*rrago |
| broad beans | **habas** |
| | *a*bbas |
| carrots | **zanahorias** |
| | thanna-*o*ree-as |
| green beans | **judías verdes** |
| | hood*ee*-as b*ai*r-des |
| leeks | **puerros** |
| | pw*e*rros |
| mushrooms | **champiñones** |
| | champin-*yo*n-es |
| onions | **cebollas** |
| | theb*o*l-yas |
| peas | **guisantes** |
| | ghiss*a*nt-es |
| potatoes | **patatas** |
| | pat*a*t-as |
| shallots | **chalotes** |
| | chall*o*t-es |
| spinach | **espinacas** |
| | espin*a*c-as |
| tomatoes | **tomates** |
| | tom*a*t-es |
| **A bunch of . . .** | **Un puñado de . . .** |
| | oon poon-y*a*d-o deh . . . |
| parsley | **perejil** |
| | perreh*í*l |
| radishes | **rábanos** |
| | r*a*b-annos |
| A head of garlic | **Una cabeza de ajo** |
| | *oo*na cabeth-ah deh *a*h-ho |
| A lettuce | **Una lechuga** |
| | oona lech*oo*ga |
| A cucumber | **Un pepino** |
| | oon pep*ee*no |
| Like that, please | **Así, por favor** |
| | as*ee* por fab-*o*r |

# Meat and fish

## ESSENTIAL INFORMATION

- Key words to look for:
  **CARNECERIA** (butcher's)
  **CARNICERO** (butcher)
  **PESCADERIA** (fishmonger's)
  **MARISCOS** (seafood)
- The diagrams opposite are to help you make sense of labels on counters and supermarket displays, and decide which cut or joint to have. Translations do not help, and you don't need to say the Spanish word involved.
- Markets and large supermarkets usually have a fresh fish stall.

## WHAT TO SAY

For a joint, choose the type of meat and then say how many people it is for:

| | |
|---|---|
| Some beef, please | **Buey, por favor** |
| | bway por faḇ-or |
| Some lamb/young lamb | **Cordero/ternasco** |
| | cordairo/tairnasco |
| Some mutton | **Carnero/oveja** |
| | carnairo/obeh-ha |
| Some pork | **Cerdo** |
| | thairdo |
| Some veal | **Ternera** |
| | tairnaira |
| A joint . . . | **Un asado . . .** |
| | oon asado . . . |
|    for two people | **para dos personas** |
| | para dos pairson-as |
|    for four people | **para cuatro personas** |
| | para cwatro pairson-as |
|    for six people | **para seis personas** |
| | para seys pairson-as |
| Some steak, please | **Bistec, por favor** |
| | bistec por faḇ-or |

| Some liver | **Hígado** |
| | *eega-do* |
| Some kidneys | **Riñones** |
| | *rin-yon-es* |
| Some sausages | **Salchichas** |
| | *salcheechas* |
| Some mince | **Carne picada** |
| | *carneh peecada* |
| Two veal escalopes | **Dos escalopes de ternera** |
| | *dos escalop-es deh tairnaira* |
| Three pork chops | **Tres chuletas de cerdo** |
| | *tres choolettas deh thairdo* |
| Four mutton chops | **Cuatro chuletas de oveja** |
| | *cwatro choolettas deh obeh-ha* |
| Five lamb chops | **Cinco chuletas de cordero** |
| | *thinko choolettas deh cordairo* |
| A chicken | **Un pollo** |
| | *oon pol-yo* |
| A rabbit | **Un conejo** |
| | *oon conneh-ho* |
| A tongue | **Una lengua** |
| | *oona len-gwa* |

Purchase large fish and small shellfish by weight:

| ½ kilo of . . . | **Medio kilo de . . .** |
| | *med-yo kilo deh . . .* |
| clams | **almejas** |
| | *almeh-has* |
| cod | **bacalao** |
| | *bakkala-o* |
| fresh tuna | **bonito** |
| | *boneeto* |
| hake | **merluza** |
| | *mairlootha* |
| mussels | **mejillones** |
| | *mehee-yon-es* |
| prawns | **gambas** |
| | *gambas* |
| salmon | **salmon** |
| | *sal-mon* |

404/Shopping for food: **Meat and fish**

| ½ kilo of . . . | Medio kilo de . . . |
|---|---|
| | med-yo kilo deh . . . |
| sardines | **sardinas** |
| | sardeenas |
| sea bream | **besugo** |
| | besoogo |
| shrimps (two names) | **camarones/quisquillas** |
| | cammaron-es/kiskee-yas |
| sprats | **sardinetas** |
| | sardinettas |
| turbot | **rodaballo** |
| | roddaba-yo |
| whitebait | **boquerones** |
| | bokeh-ron-es |

For some shellfish and 'frying pan' fish, specify the number:

| A crab, please | **Un cangrejo, por favor** |
|---|---|
| | oon cangreh-ho por fab-or |
| A lobster | **Una langosta** |
| | oona lan-gosta |
| A plaice | **Un gallo** |
| | oon gal-yo |
| A whiting | **Una pescadilla** |
| | oona pescadee-ya |
| A trout | **Una trucha** |
| | oona troocha |
| A sole | **Un lenguado** |
| | oon len-gwaddo |
| A mackerel | **Una caballa** |
| | oona cabal-ya |
| A herring | **Un arenque** |
| | oon arrenkeh |
| An octopus | **Un pulpo** |
| | oon poolpo |
| A carp | **Una carpa** |
| | oona carpa |

# Eating and drinking out

## Ordering a drink and a snack

### ESSENTIAL INFORMATION

- The places to ask for:
  **UNA CAFETERIA** (a more luxurious and modern café)
  **UN CAFÉ**
  **UN BAR**
- If you want to try Spanish wine and **tapas** in a typically Spanish
  atmosphere the places to go are: **UNA TASCA, UNA BODEGA,
  UN MESON** or **UNA TABERNA**. Usually you'll find all these
  places in the same area and it is the custom to make a tour of
  several local bars having one or two drinks in each.
- By law, the price list of drinks (**TARIFA** or **LISTA DE PRECIOS**)
  must be displayed outside or in the window.
- There is waiter service in all cafés, but you can drink at the bar
  or counter if you wish (cheaper).
- Always leave a tip of 10% to 15% of the bill unless you see
  **SERVICIO INCLUIDO**, although it is still common practice to
  leave a few pesetas for these bills also.
- Cafés serve non-alcoholic drinks and alcoholic drinks, and are
  normally open all day.
- You will find plates of assorted food, e.g. cheese, fish, olives,
  salads etc. on the bar, usually before lunchtime or dinner time.
  These are called **tapas**, and you can either have a portion (**una
  ración**, rath-*yon*) or food on sticks (**banderillas**, bander*ee*-yas).
  You have them as an apéritif or a snack with your drink. As with
  drinks you pay for **tapas** on leaving the bar, though some offer
  small **tapas** free.

### WHAT TO SAY

| I'd like . . . please | Quiero . . . por favor |
| | kee-*airo* . . . por fab-*or* |
| a black coffee | un café solo |
| | oon caf*eh* sol-o |
| a white coffee | un café con leche |
| | oon caf*eh* con lech-eh |

| | |
|---|---|
| **I'd like . . . please** | **Quiero . . . por favor** |
| | kee-*airo* . . . por fab-*or* |
| a black coffee with a dash of milk | **un cortado** |
| | oon cort*a*d-o |
| a tea | **un té** |
| | oon t*e*h |
| with milk/lemon | **con leche/limón** |
| | con l*e*ch-eh/lim-*on* |
| a glass of milk | **un vaso de leche** |
| | oon b*a*sso deh l*e*ch-eh |
| a hot chocolate (thick) | **un chocolate** |
| | oon chocol*a*t-eh |
| a mineral water | **un agua mineral** |
| | oon *a*gwa miner*a*l |
| a lemonade | **una limonada** |
| | oona lim-onn*a*d-ah |
| an orangeade | **una naranjada** |
| | oona na-rang-h*a*dda |
| an orange juice | **un zumo de naranja** |
| | oon th*oo*mo deh na-r*a*ng-ha |
| a grape juice | **un mosto** |
| | oon m*o*sto |
| a pineapple juice | **un zumo de piña** |
| | oon th*oo*mo deh p*i*n-ya |
| a milkshake | **un batido** |
| | oon bat*ee*do |
| a beer | **una cerveza** |
| | *oo*na thairb*e*th-ah |
| a draught beer | **una caña** |
| | *oo*na c*a*n-ya |
| a cider | **una sidra** |
| | *oo*na s*i*dra |
| **I'd like . . . please** | **Quiero . . . por favor** |
| | kee-*airo* . . . por fab-*or* |
| a cheese sandwich | **un bocadillo de queso** |
| | oon boccad*ee*-yo deh k*e*s-o |
| a ham sandwich | **un bocadillo de jamón de york** |
| | oon boccad*ee*-yo deh ham-*on* deh york |
| a smoked ham sandwich | **un bocadillo de jamón serrano** |
| | oon boccad*ee*-yo deh ham-*on* serr*a*nno |

These are some other snacks you may like to try:

| | |
|---|---|
| **albondigas con tomate** | spiced meatballs in tomato sauce |
| albondeegas con tomat-eh | |
| **banderillas** | savouries on sticks |
| banderee-yas | |
| **berberechos** | cockles in vinegar |
| bairbehrech-os | |
| **callos** | tripe, usually in hot paprika suace |
| ca-yos | |
| **caracoles** | snails |
| carracol-es | |
| **empanadillas** | small pastries with a variety of |
| empannadee-yas | fillings |
| **patatas bravas** | fried potatoes in spicy sauce |
| patat-as brab-as | |
| **pimientos rellenos** | stuffed peppers |
| pim-yentos rel-yenos | |
| **pinchitos** | grilled kidneys or spicy sausages |
| pincheetos | (usually on skewers) |
| **tortilla de patata** | Spanish omelet, made of potatoes |
| tortee-ya deh patat-ah | and onions |

# In a restaurant

## ESSENTIAL INFORMATION

* You can eat at these places:
  RESTAURANTE
  CAFETERIA (luxurious café)
  HOSTERIA ⎤
  MESON ⎥
  PARADOR ⎥ (regional cooking)
  POSADA ⎦
  ALBERGUE DE CARRETERA (roadside inn)
  FONDA (cheap simple food)
  MERENDERO (on the outskirts of a town suitable for meals or
  snacks during the early evening)
  CASA DE COMIDAS (a simple restaurant with typical Spanish
  food)

- You may also find **CASA** plus the name of the owner.
- Tipping is very common in Spain and it is usual to leave 10% of the bill for the waiter.
- By law, the menus must be displayed outside or in the window and that is the only way to judge if a place is right for your needs.
- Self-service restaurants (**AUTOSERVICIO**) are not unknown, but all other places have waiter service.
- Restaurants are usually open from 1 p.m. – 3/3.30 p.m. and from 9 p.m. – 11.30 p.m. but this can vary. It's not difficult to get a meal before 9 p.m. as lots of restaurants, especially **CASAS DE COMIDAS** or **MESONES** provide meals in the early evening (**meriendas**). And if you want to eat before 1 p.m. you can always try some **tapas** which can be a meal in themselves.
- By law, **Hojas de Reclamaciones** (Complaints Forms) must be kept in restaurants as well as in hotels, bars and petrol stations. All complaints are investigated by the Tourist Authority.

## WHAT TO SAY

| | |
|---|---|
| May I book a table? | **¿Puedo reservar una mesa?** |
| | pwed-o res-air*bar* *oo*na mes-ah |
| I've booked a table | **He reservado una mesa** |
| | eh res-air*bad*-o *oo*na mes-ah |
| **A table . . .** | **Una mesa . . .** |
| | *oo*na mes-ah . . . |
| for one | **para uno** |
| | para *oo*no |
| for three | **para tres** |
| | para tres |
| The à la carte menu, please | **El menú a la carta, por favor** |
| | el men*oo* ah la carta por fab-or |
| The fixed-price menu | **El menú de precio fijo** |
| | el men*oo* deh preth-yo fee-ho |
| The (300) pesetas menu | **El menú de (trescientas) pesetas** |
| | el men*oo* deh (tres-thee-*en*tas) pes-et-as |
| The tourist menu | **El menú turístico** |
| | el men*oo* toor*is*tico |
| Today's special menu | **El menú del día** |
| | el men*oo* del de*ea* |
| The wine list | **La lista de vinos** |
| | la le*esta* deh be*enos* |

| | |
|---|---|
| What's this, please? [*point to menu*] | **¿Qué es eso, por favor?** |
| | keh es *es*-o por fab-*or* |
| A carafe of wine, please | **Una jarra de vino, por favor** |
| | *oo*na *h*arra deh *bee*no por fab-*or* |
| A quarter (25cc) | **Un cuarto** |
| | oon cwarto |
| A half (50cc) | **Medio** |
| | med-yo |
| A glass | **Un vaso** |
| | oon *b*asso |
| A (half) bottle | **Una (media) botella** |
| | *oo*na (med-ya) botel-ya |
| A litre | **Un litro** |
| | oon *l*itro |
| Red/white/rosé/house wine | **Tinto/blanco/rosado/vino de la casa** |
| | tinto/blanco/rosad-o/*bee*no deh la *c*as-ah |
| Some more bread, please | **Más pan, por favor** |
| | mas pan por fab-*or* |
| Some more wine | **Más vino** |
| | mas *bee*no |
| Some oil | **Aceite** |
| | ath*ay*-teh |
| Some vinegar | **Vinagre** |
| | been*ag*-reh |
| Some salt/pepper | **Sal/pimienta** |
| | sal/pim-yenta |
| Some water | **Agua** |
| | *a*gwa |
| With/without garlic | **Con/sin ajo** |
| | con/sin a*h*o |
| How much does that come to? | **¿Cuánto es?** |
| | cwanto es |
| Is service included? | **¿Está incluído el servicio?** |
| | esta incloo-*ee*do el sairbith-yo |
| Where is the toilet, please? | **¿Dónde está el servicio, por favor?** |
| | *d*ondeh esta el sairbith-yo por fab-*or* |
| Miss!/Waiter | **¡Señorita!/¡Camarero!** |
| | sen-yor*eeta*/camma-*rair*o |
| The bill, please | **La cuenta, por favor** |
| | la cwenta por fab-*or* |

**Key words for courses, as seen on some menus:**
[*Only ask this question if you want the waiter to remind you of the choice.*]

| What have you got in the way of . . . | ¿Qué tienen de . . . |
|---|---|
| | keh tee-*en*-en deh . . . |
| starters? | **entremeses?** |
| | entreh-m*ess*-es |
| soup? | **sopas?** |
| | s*o*pas |
| egg Dishes? | **huevos?** |
| | w*eb*-os |
| fish? | **pescados?** |
| | pesc*ad*-os |
| meat? | **carnes?** |
| | c*a*rnes |
| game? | **caza?** |
| | c*a*tha |
| fowl? | **aves?** |
| | *a*bes |
| vegetables? | **verduras/legumbres?** |
| | baird*oo*-ras/leh-g*oom*-bres |
| cheese? | **quesos?** |
| | k*es*-os |
| fruit? | **frutas?** |
| | fr*oo*tas |
| ice-cream? | **helados?** |
| | el*add*os |
| dessert? | **postres?** |
| | p*os*-tres |

## UNDERSTANDING THE MENU

- You will find the names of the principal ingredients of most dishes on these pages:

  | | |
  |---|---|
  | Starters p. 398 | Fruit p. 400 |
  | Meat p. 402 | Cheese p. 399 |
  | Fish p. 403 | Ice-cream p. 397 |
  | Vegetables p. 401 | Dessert p. 396 |

- Used together with the following lists of cooking and menu terms, they should help you to decode the menu.

**Cooking and menu terms**

| | |
|---|---|
| con aceite | in oil |
| en adobo | marinated in red wine |
| al ajillo | in garlic sauce |
| con ajolio (allioli) | in garlic mayonnaise |
| ahumado | smoked |
| en almíbar | in syrup |
| asado (al ast) | roasted |
| a la barbacoa | barbecued |
| a la brasa | grilled on an open fire |
| en cacerola | casserole |
| caldo | stock |
| caliente | hot |
| cocido | boiled |
| crudo | raw |
| a la chilindrón | with tomatoes, peppers and onion |
| dulce | sweet |
| en dulce | in sweet sauce |
| duro | hard boiled |
| empanado | fried in breadcrumbs |
| en escabeche | marinated |
| escalfado | poached |
| estofado | braised/stewed |
| flameado | flamed |
| a la francesa | with milk, flour and butter |
| frio | cold |
| frito | fried |
| gratinado | browned with breadcrumbs or cheese |
| guisado | stewed |
| hervido | boiled |
| horneado | baked |
| al horno | baked |
| al jerez | in sherry |
| en su jugo | pot roasted |
| con mantequilla | with butter |
| marinado (a la marinera) | marinated |
| a minuto | prepared in a very short time |
| a la parrilla | grilled |
| pasado por agua | soft boiled |
| con perejil | with parsley |

| | |
|---|---|
| **a la pescadora** | with egg, lemon, wine and vinegar |
| **a la plancha** | grilled |
| **rehogado** | fried in oil with garlic and vinegar |
| **relleno** | stuffed |
| **a la romana** | deep fried |
| **salado** | salted |
| **en salazón** | cured |
| **en salsa** | in a sauce |
| **en salsa blanca** | in a white sauce |
| **salsa mahonesa** | in a mayonnaise sauce |
| **salsa verde** | sauce made from white wine, herbs, onion and flour |
| **salsa vinagreta** | sauce made from salt, vinegar and oil |
| **salteado** | sautéed |
| **tostado** | toasted |
| **trufado** | stuffed with truffles |
| **al vapor** | steamed |
| **a la vasca** | with asparagus, peas, egg, herbs, garlic, onion and flour |
| **en vinagre** | in vinegar |

**Further words to help you understand the menu:**

| | |
|---|---|
| **anguilas** | eels |
| **arroz a la cubana** | rice, fried eggs, bananas and tomato sauce |
| **arroz a la milanesa** | rice with 'chorizo' (spicy sausage), ham, cheese and peas |
| **atún** | tuna |
| **brazo de gitano** | cake filled with cream or marmalade |
| **buñuelos (buñuelitos)** | small fritters with a variety of fillings |
| **cabeza (de cordero)** | lamb's head |
| **caldereta** | fish or lamb stew |
| **callos (a la madrileña)** | tripe in piquant sauce |
| **cocido (madrileño)** | vegetable and meat stew with beans or chick-peas |
| **codorniz** | quail |
| **cochinillo asado** | suckling pig, roasted |
| **congrio** | conger eel |

| | |
|---|---|
| **conejo a la aragonesa** | rabbit cooked with onion, garlic, almonds and herbs |
| **consomé** | clear soup |
| **criadillas** | sweetbreads |
| **cuajada** | coagulated milk, similar to yogurt |
| **empanada gallega** | tenderloin of pork, onions and chilli pepper as filling |
| **fabada** | beans, black pudding, ham, pig's ear, onion and garlic in a stew |
| **flan** | cream caramel |
| **gallina en pepitoria** | chicken casserole with almonds and saffron |
| **ganso** | goose |
| **garbanzos** | chick-peas |
| **gazpacho** | cold spicy soup made of onion, tomatoes, peppers, bread, garlic, oil and vinegar |
| **huevos a la flamenca** | eggs baked with tomato, ham, onion, asparagus and peppers |
| **huevos al plato** | fried eggs |
| **huevos revueltos** | scrambled eggs |
| **lentejas** | lentils |
| **lengua aragonesa** | tongue with vegetables |
| **liebre** | hare |
| **lomo** | loin |
| **magras con tomate** | smoked ham fried with tomatoes |
| **menestra (de verduras, de carne o pollo)** | mixed (vegetable, or meat, or chicken) stew |
| **mero (lubina)** | sea bass |
| **migas** | bits of bread fried with garlic, spicy sausages, bacon and ham |
| **natillas** | custard |
| **paella catalana** | spicy pork sausages, pork, squid, tomato, chilli pepper and peas |
| **paella marinera** | fish and seafood only |
| **paella valenciana** | the classic paella with chicken, mussels, shrimp, prawns, peas, tomato, peppers and garlic |
| **parrillada** | boned and shelled fish, shellfish, chicken and meat, fried |
| **pastel de carne** | meat pie |
| **pato** | duck |

| | |
|---|---|
| **pavo** | turkey |
| **perdiz** | partridge |
| **pimientos a la riojana** | sweet peppers stuffed with minced meat |
| **pisto** | fried mixed vegetables |
| **pollo a la chilindrón** | chicken fried with tomatoes, peppers and smoked ham or bacon |
| **potaje** | vegetable stew |
| **pote gallego** | beans, meat, potatoes and cabbage |
| **puchero de gallina** | stewed chicken |
| **salmonete** | red mullet |
| **sesos** | brains (of lamb) |
| **solomillo** | tenderloin steak (of pork) |
| **sopa Juliana** | shredded vegetable soup |
| **ternasco a la aragonesa** | young lamb roasted with potatoes and garlic |
| **tocino** | bacon |
| **toro de lidia** | beef from the bullring |
| **torrijas** | bread soaked in milk and egg and then fried, sprinkled with sugar (french toast) |
| **tortilla francesa** | plain omelet |
| **tortilla de patatas/española** | typical Spanish omelet made with potatoes |
| **trucha a la navarra** | trout filled with smoked ham |
| **zarzuela** | savoury stew of assorted fish and shellfish |

# Health

### ESSENTIAL INFORMATION

- There are no reciprocal health agreements between the UK and Spain. It's advisable therefore to arrange medical insurance before you travel abroad.
- For minor disorders, and treatment at a chemist's, see p. 389.
- For finding your way to a doctor, dentist or chemist's, see p. 380.

- In case of sudden illness or an accident, you can go to a **CASA DE SOCORRO**. These are emergency first aid centres open to the general public and are free. If you have a serious accident, the same free service is provided by an **equipo quirurgico**. If you are on the road there are **PUESTOS DE SOCORRO** (first aid centres) run by the **CRUZ ROJA** (Red Cross).
- To find a doctor in an emergency, look for:
  Médicos (in the Yellow Pages of the telephone directory)
  Urgencias (casualty department)
  Casas de Socorro ⎤
  Puestos de Socorro ⎦ (first aid centres)
  H ⎤
  Hospital ⎦ (hospital)

## What's the matter?

| | |
|---|---|
| I have a pain here [*point*] | **Me duele aquí**<br>meh dwel-eh ak-*ee* |
| I have a toothache | **Me duelen las muelas**<br>meh dwel-en las mwel-as |
| I have broken . . . | **Me he roto . . .**<br>meh *eh* rot-o . . . |
| my dentures | **la dentadura**<br>la dentad*oo*ra |
| my glasses | **las gafas**<br>las g*af*-as |
| I have lost . . . | **He perdido . . .**<br>eh paird*ee*do . . . |
| my contact lenses | **mis lentes de contacto**<br>mees lent-es deh cont*a*cto |
| a filling | **un empaste**<br>oon emp*a*steh |
| My child is ill | **Mi hijo/a está enfermo/a***<br>mee *ee*ho/ah est*a* enf*air*mo/ah |

*For boys use 'o', for girls use 'a'.

## Already under treatment for something else?

| | |
|---|---|
| I take . . . regularly [*show*] | **Tomo . . . regularmente**<br>tom-o . . . regool*a*rmenteh |
| this medicine | **esta medicina**<br>*e*sta medith*ee*na |

| | |
|---|---|
| **I take . . . regularly** [*show*] | **Tomo . . . regularmente** |
| | tom-o . . . regoolarmenteh |
| these pills | **estas píldoras** |
| | estas píldor-as |
| **I have . . .** | **Tengo . . .** |
| | tengo . . . |
| haemorrhoids | **hemorroides** |
| | emmoro-eed-es |
| rheumatism | **reuma** |
| | reh-ooma |
| **I am . . .** | **Soy . . .** |
| | soy . . . |
| diabetic | **diabético/a\*** |
| | dee-abet-eeco/ah |
| asthmatic | **asmático/a\*** |
| | asmatico/ah |
| I am allergic to (penicillin) | **Soy alérgico/a a (la penicilina)\*** |
| | soy alair-heeco/ah ah (la penni-thileena) |
| I am pregnant | **Estoy embarazada** |
| | estoy embarrathad-ah |
| I have a heart condition | **Estoy del corazón** |
| | estoy del corathon |

\*Men use 'o', women use 'a'.

---

# Problems: loss, theft

---

### ESSENTIAL INFORMATION

- If the worst comes to the worst, find the police station. To ask the way, see p. 379.
- Look for:
  **COMISARIA DE POLICIA** (police station)
  **GUARTEL DE LA GUARDIA CIVIL**
  (Civil Guard – in small towns and villages)
  **OFICINA DE OBJETOS PERDIDOS** (lost property office)
- If you lose your passport, go to the nearest British Consulate

• In an emergency dial 091 for the police. The numbers for Fire and Ambulance differ according to region. Remember, however, that the ambulance service is not free and nor are emergency calls from public phones.

## LOSS
[*See also 'Theft' below, the lists are interchangeable*]

| I have lost . . . | He perdido . . . |
| --- | --- |
| | eh paird*ee*do . . . |
| my camera | mi cámara |
| | mee c*a*mara |
| my car keys | las llaves de mi coche |
| | las y*a*b-es deh mee c*o*ch-eh |
| my car logbook | mi cartilla de propriedad |
| | mee cart*ee*-ya deh prop-yed-*a*d |
| my driving licence | mi carnet de conducir |
| | mee carnet deh condoot*ee*r |
| my insurance certificate | mi certificado del seguro |
| | mee thair-tific*a*d-o del seg*oo*-ro |

## THEFT

| Someone has stolen . . . | Alguien ha robado . . . |
| --- | --- |
| | *a*lg-yen ah robb*a*d-o . . . |
| my car | mi coche |
| | mee c*o*ch-eh |
| my money | mi dinero |
| | mee din-*ai*ro |
| my tickets | mis billetes |
| | mees bee-y*e*t-es |
| my travellers' cheques | mis cheques de viaje |
| | mees ch*e*ck-es deh bee-*a*h-heh |
| my wallet | mi cartera |
| | mee cart*ai*ra |
| my luggage | mi equipaje |
| | mee ek-ee-p*a*-heh |

# The post office and phoning home

## ESSENTIAL INFORMATION

- Key words to look for:
  **CORREOS**
  **CORREOS Y TELEGRAFOS**
  **SERVICIO POSTAL**
- It is best to buy stamps at the tobacconist's. Only go to the post office for more complicated transactions, like telegrams.
- Unless you read and speak Spanish well, it's best not to make phone calls by yourself. Go to **CENTRAL TELEFONICA (CTNE)** which in large towns are open twenty-four hours a day and write the town and number you want on a piece of paper and hand it over to the operator.
- In Spain the telephone network operates independently of the post office, so don't expect to find phones in post offices.

## WHAT TO SAY

| | |
|---|---|
| To England, please | **Para Inglaterra, por favor** |
| | para ingla-terra por fab-or |
| *[Hand letters, cards or parcels over the counter]* | |
| To Australia | **Para Australia** |
| | para ah-oostral-ya |
| To the United States | **Para los Estados Unidos** |
| | para los estad-os ooneedos |
| I'd like to send a telegram | **Quiero enviar un telegrama** |
| | kee-airo embee-ar oon telegramma |
| **I'd like this number . . .** | **Quiero este número . . .** |
| *[show number]* | kee-airo esteh noomairo . . . |
| in England | **en Inglaterra** |
| | en ingla-terra |
| in Canada | **en Canadá** |
| | en canada |
| Can you dial it for me, please? | **¿Puede usted marcar por mí, por favor?** |
| | pwed-eh oosted marcar por mee por fab-or |

# Changing cheques and money

## ESSENTIAL INFORMATION

- Look for these words:
  **BANCO** (bank)
  **CAJA DE AHORROS** (savings bank)
  **CAMBIO** (change)
  **CAJA DE CAMBIO** (cash desk in a bank)
  **OFICINA DE CAMBIO** (bureau de change)
- To cash your normal cheques, exactly as at home, use your banker's card where you see the Eurocheque sign. Write in English, in pounds.
- Exchange rate information might show the pound as:
  **£, L, Libra Esterlina**, or even **GB**.
- Have your passport handy and remember that in Spain banks open at 9 a.m. and close at 2 p.m. and on Saturdays at 1 p.m.

## WHAT TO SAY

| | |
|---|---|
| I'd like to cash . . . | **Quiero cobrar . . .**<br>kee-*air*o cobr*ar* . . . |
| these travellers' cheques | **estos cheques de viaje**<br>*e*stos ch*e*ck-es deh bee-*a*h-heh |
| this cheque | **este cheque**<br>*e*steh ch*e*ck-eh |
| I'd like to change this . . . | **Quiero cambiar esto . . .**<br>kee-*air*o camb-y*ar* esto . . . |
| into pesetas | **en pesetas**<br>en pes-*et*-as |
| into French francs | **en francos franceses**<br>en franc-os franth*e*s-es |
| into lire | **en liras**<br>en *lee*-ras |
| into escudos | **en escudos**<br>en esc*oo*dos |

# Car travel

## ESSENTIAL INFORMATION

- Look for these signs:
  **SOLIN** ∩r)
  **GASOLINERA** (petrol station)
  **ESTACION DE SERVICIO** (petrol station)
- Grades of petrol:
  **NORMAL** (2 star standard)
  **SUPER** (3 star)
  **EXTRA** (4 star)
  **GAS-OIL** (diesel)
  **DOS TIEMPOS** (two stroke)
- 1 gallon is about 4½ litres (accurate enough up to 6 gallons).
- Petrol prices are standardized all over Spain, and a minimum sale of 5 litres is often imposed.
- For car repairs, look for signs with red, blue and white stripes or **GARAJE**
  **TALLER DE REPARACIONES**
- Most petrol stations operate a 24-hour service, though some close late at night. Take care, however, as the stations themselves are few and far between.
- Garages will open at 8 or 9 a.m. and close between 7.30 and 8 p.m. Most will close lunchtime.

## WHAT TO SAY

[*For numbers, see p. 424*]

| | |
|---|---|
| **(Nine) litres of . . .** | **(Nueve) litros de . . .** |
| | (nweb-eh) litros deh . . . |
| **(Five hundred) pesetas of . . .** | **(Quinientas) pesetas de . . .** |
| | (kin-yentas) pes-et-as deh . . . |
| standard/premium/diesel | **normal/super/gas-oil** |
| | normal/soopair/gas-oil |
| Fill it up, please | **Lleno, por favor** |
| | yeno por fab-or |

| Can you check . . . | ¿Puede mirar . . . |
| | pwed-eh mee-rar . . . |
| the oil? | **el aceite?** |
| | el athay-teh |
| the battery? | **la batería?** |
| | la batteh-reea |
| the radiator? | **el radiador?** |
| | el rad-yad-or |
| the tyres? | **los neumáticos?** |
| | los neh-oomatticos |
| I've run out of petrol | **Me he quedado sin gasolina** |
| | meh eh ked-ad-o sin gasoleena |
| Can you help me, please? | **¿Puede ayudarme, por favor** |
| | pwed-eh a-yoodarmeh por fab-or |
| Do you do repairs? | **¿Hacen reparaciones?** |
| | ath-en reparath-yon-es |
| I have a puncture | **Tengo un neumático pinchado** |
| | tengo oon neh-oomattico pinchad-o |
| I have a broken windscreen | **Tengo el parabrisas roto** |
| | tengo el parabrees-as rot-o |
| I think the problem is here . . . [point] | **Creo que el problema esta aquí . . .** |
| | creh-o keh el problem-ah esta ak-ee . . . |

## LIKELY REACTIONS

| We don't do repairs | **No se hacen reparaciones** |
| | no seh ath-en reparath-yon-es |
| Where is your car? | **¿Dónde está su coche?** |
| | dondeh esta soo coch-eh |
| What make is it? | **¿Qué tipo es?** |
| | keh teepo es |
| Come back tomorrow/on Monday | **Vuelva mañana/el lunes** |
| | bwelba manyan-ah/el loon-es |

[*For days of the week, see p. 426*]

# Public transport

## ESSENTIAL INFORMATION

- Finding the way to a bus station, bus stop, tram stop, railway station and taxi rank, see p. 379.
- Taxis are usually black saloons with a coloured line painted along the side. They display a green light at night and during tne day a sign on the windscreen which says **LIBRE** (free) if they are available.
- These are the different types of trains, graded according to speed (slowest to fastest):
  **TAF/FERROBUS/OMNIBUS**
  **TRANVIAS/AUTOMOTOR** (all short distance local trains, not very reliable)
  **EXPRESO/RAPIDO** (do not be misled by their names; these are both *slow* trains the only difference being the first travels by night, the second by day)
  **ELECTROTREN** (fast and comfortable)
  **TER** (fast and comfortable – supplement payable)
  **TALGO** (luxury train – supplement payable)
- Key words on signs
  **ANDEN** (platform)
  **BILLETES** (tickets, ticket office)
  **CONSIGNA/EQUIPAJES** (left-luggage)
  **DESPACHO DE BILLETES/TAQUILLA** (ticket office)
  **ENTRADA** (entrance)
  **HORARIO** (timetable)
  **LLEGADA** (arrival)
  **OFICINA DE INFORMACION** (information office)
  **PARADA** (bus stop, taxi stop)
  **PROHIBIDO** (forbidden)
  **RENFE** (initials of Spanish railways)
  **SALIDA** (exit)
- Children travel free up to the age of three and pay half-price up to the age of seven. However, if you have an international ticket, children can travel free up to the age of four and travel half-price up to the age of twelve.
- On certain dates throughout the year known as **Días Azules** (Blue Days), numerous reductions are available on train travel;

check with the Spanish Tourist Office for dates and further information.
- On buses and tubes there is a flat rate irrespective of distance and it is cheaper to buy a **taco** (book of tickets) for underground travel. Tubes operate between 6 a.m. and 1 a.m.
- It is worth booking train and coach journeys in advance.

## WHAT TO SAY

| | |
|---|---|
| Where does the train for (Madrid) leave from? | **¿De dónde sale el tren para (Madrid)?** |
| | deh dondeh sal-eh el tren para (madrid) |
| Is this the train for (Madrid)? | **¿Es éste el tren para (Madrid)?** |
| | es esteh el tren para (madrid) |
| Where does the bus for (Barcelona) leave from? | **¿De dónde sale el autobús para (Barcelona)?** |
| | deh dondeh sal-eh el ah-ooto-boos para (barthelona) |
| Is this the bus for (Barcelona)? | **¿Es éste el autobús para (Barcelona)?** |
| | es esteh el ah-ooto-boos para (barthelona) |
| Do I have to change? | **¿Tengo que cambiar?** |
| | tengo keh camb-yar |
| Can you put me off at the right stop, please? | **¿Puede avisarme en mi parada, por favor?** |
| | pwed-eh abee-sarmeh en mee parad-ah por fab-or |
| Can I book a seat? | **¿Puedo reservar un asiento?** |
| | pwed-o res-airbar oon as-yento |
| Where can I get a taxi? | **¿Dónde puedo tomar un taxi?** |
| | dondeh pwed-o tom-ar oon taxi |
| A single | **Un billete de ida solamente** |
| | oon bee-yet-eh deh eeda solamenteh |
| A return | **Un billete de ida y vuelta** |
| | oon bee-yet-eh deh eeda ee bwelta |
| First class | **Primera clase** |
| | prim-aira classeh |
| Second class | **Segunda clase** |
| | seg-oonda classeh |

| One adult | **Un adulto** |
| | oon adoolto |
| Two adults | **Dos adultos** |
| | dos adooltos |
| and one child | **y un niño** |
| | ee oon neen-yo |
| and two children | **y dos niños** |
| | ee dos neen-yos |
| How much is it? | **¿Cuánto es?** |
| | cwanto es |

---

# Reference

---

## NUMBERS

| 0 | **cero** | thairo |
| 1 | **uno** | oono |
| 2 | **dos** | dos |
| 3 | **tres** | tres |
| 4 | **cuatro** | cwatro |
| 5 | **cinco** | thinko |
| 6 | **seis** | seys |
| 7 | **siete** | see-et-eh |
| 8 | **ocho** | ocho |
| 9 | **nueve** | nweb-eh |
| 10 | **diez** | dee-eth |
| 11 | **once** | ontheh |
| 12 | **doce** | doth-eh |
| 13 | **trece** | treth-eh |
| 14 | **catorce** | cat-ortheh |
| 15 | **quince** | kintheh |
| 16 | **dieciséis** | dee-ethee-seys |
| 17 | **diecisiete** | dee-ethee-see-et-eh |
| 18 | **dieciocho** | dee-ethee-ocho |
| 19 | **diecinueve** | dee-ethee-nweb-eh |
| 20 | **veinte** | beynteh |
| 21 | **veintiuno** | beyntee-oono |
| 22 | **veintidós** | beyntee-dos |

| | | |
|---|---|---|
| 23 | **veintitrés** | beyntee-tres |
| 24 | **veinticuatro** | beyntee-cwatro |
| 25 | **veinticinco** | beyntee-thinko |
| 26 | **veintiséis** | beyntee-seys |
| 27 | **veintisiete** | beyntee-see-et-eh |
| 28 | **veintiocho** | beyntee-ocho |
| 29 | **veintinueve** | beyntee-nweb-eh |
| 30 | **treinta** | treynta |
| 31 | **treinta y uno** | treynta ee oono |
| 35 | **treinta y cinco** | treynta ee thinko |
| 38 | **treinta y ocho** | treynta ee ocho |
| 40 | **cuarenta** | cwa-renta |
| 41 | **cuarenta y uno** | cwa-renta ee oono |
| 45 | **cuarenta y cinco** | cwa-renta ee thinko |
| 48 | **cuarenta y ocho** | cwa-renta ee ocho |
| 50 | **cincuenta** | thin-cwenta |
| 55 | **cincuenta y cinco** | thin-cwenta ee thinko |
| 60 | **sesenta** | ses-enta |
| 65 | **sesenta y cinco** | ses-enta ee thinko |
| 70 | **setenta** | set-enta |
| 75 | **setenta y cinco** | set-enta ee thinko |
| 80 | **ochenta** | ochenta |
| 85 | **ochenta y cinco** | ochenta ee thinko |
| 90 | **noventa** | nobenta |
| 95 | **noventa y cinco** | nobenta ee thinko |
| 100 | **cien** | thee-en |
| 101 | **ciento uno** | thee-ento oono |
| 102 | **ciento dos** | thee-ento dos |
| 125 | **ciento veinticinco** | thee-ento beyntee-thinko |
| 150 | **ciento cincuenta** | thee-ento thin-cwenta |
| 175 | **ciento setenta y cinco** | thee-ento set-enta ee thinko |
| 200 | **doscientos** | dos-thee-entos |
| 300 | **trescientos** | tres-thee-entos |
| 400 | **cuatrocientos** | cwatro-thee-entos |
| 500 | **quinientos** | kin-yentos |
| 1000 | **mil** | mil |
| 1500 | **mil quinientos** | mil kin-yentos |
| 2000 | **dos mil** | dos mil |
| 5000 | **cinco mil** | thinko mil |
| 10,000 | **diez mil** | dee-eth mil |
| 100,000 | **cien mil** | thee-en mil |
| 1,000,000 | **un millón** | oon mil-yon |

## TIME

| | |
|---|---|
| **What time is it?** | **¿Qué hora es?** |
| | keh *ora* es |
| It's one o'clock | **Es la una** |
| | es la *oo*na |
| It's . . . | **Son . . .** |
| | son . . . |
| two o'clock | **las dos** |
| | las d*os* |
| three o'clock | **las tres** |
| | las tr*es* |
| a quarter past five | **las cinco y cuarto** |
| | las th*i*nko ee cw*a*rto |
| half past five | **las cinco y media** |
| | las th*i*nko ee m*e*d-ya |
| quarter to six | **las seis menos cuarto** |
| | la s*e*ys men-os cw*a*rto |
| It's . . . | **Es . . .** |
| | es . . . |
| noon | **mediodía** |
| | med-yo-d*ee*a |
| midnight | **medianoche** |
| | med-ya-n*o*ch-eh |

## DAYS AND MONTHS

| | |
|---|---|
| Monday | **lunes** |
| | l*oo*n-es |
| Tuesday | **martes** |
| | m*a*rt-es |
| Wednesday | **miércoles** |
| | mee-*a*ircol-es |
| Thursday | **jueves** |
| | hw*e*b-es |
| Friday | **viernes** |
| | bee-*a*irn-es |
| Saturday | **sábado** |
| | s*a*bad-o |
| Sunday | **domingo** |
| | dom*i*ngo |

| January | **enero** |
| | en-*air*o |
| February | **febrero** |
| | feb-*tair*o |
| March | **marzo** |
| | martho |
| April | **abril** |
| | ab*ril* |
| May | **mayo** |
| | ma-yo |
| June | **junio** |
| | h*oo*n-yo |
| July | **julio** |
| | h*oo*l-yo |
| August | **agosto** |
| | a-*go*sto |
| September | **septiembre** |
| | sept-*y*embreh |
| October | **octubre** |
| | oct*oo*breh |
| November | **noviembre** |
| | nob-*y*embreh |
| December | **diciembre** |
| | dith-*y*embreh |

# Index

## CONVERSION TABLES

Read the centre column of these tables from right to left to convert from metric to imperial and from left to right to convert from imperial to metric e.g. 5 litres = 8.80 pints; 5 pints = 2.84 litres.

| pints | | litres | gallons | | litres |
|---|---|---|---|---|---|
| 1.76 | 1 | 0.57 | 0.22 | 1 | 4.55 |
| 3.52 | 2 | 1.14 | 0.44 | 2 | 9.09 |
| 5.28 | 3 | 1.70 | 0.66 | 3 | 13.64 |
| 7.07 | 4 | 2.27 | 0.88 | 4 | 18.18 |
| 8.80 | 5 | 2.84 | 1.00 | 5 | 22.73 |
| 10.56 | 6 | 3.41 | 1.32 | 6 | 27.28 |
| 12.32 | 7 | 3.98 | 1.54 | 7 | 31.82 |
| 14.08 | 8 | 4.55 | 1.76 | 8 | 36.37 |
| 15.84 | 9 | 5.11 | 1.98 | 9 | 40.91 |

| ounces | | grams | pounds | | kilos |
|---|---|---|---|---|---|
| 0.04 | 1 | 28.35 | 2.20 | 1 | 0.45 |
| 0.07 | 2 | 56.70 | 4.41 | 2 | 0.91 |
| 0.11 | 3 | 85.05 | 6.61 | 3 | 1.36 |
| 0.14 | 4 | 113.40 | 8.82 | 4 | 1.81 |
| 0.18 | 5 | 141.75 | 11.02 | 5 | 2.27 |
| 0.21 | 6 | 170.10 | 13.23 | 6 | 2.72 |
| 0.25 | 7 | 198.45 | 15.43 | 7 | 3.18 |
| 0.28 | 8 | 226.80 | 17.64 | 8 | 3.63 |
| 0.32 | 9 | 255.15 | 19.84 | 9 | 4.08 |

| inches | | centimetres | yards | | metres |
|---|---|---|---|---|---|
| 0.39 | 1 | 2.54 | 1.09 | 1 | 0.91 |
| 0.79 | 2 | 5.08 | 2.19 | 2 | 1.83 |
| 1.18 | 3 | 7.62 | 3.28 | 3 | 2.74 |
| 1.58 | 4 | 10.16 | 4.37 | 4 | 3.66 |
| 1.95 | 5 | 12.70 | 5.47 | 5 | 4.57 |
| 2.36 | 6 | 15.24 | 6.56 | 6 | 5.49 |
| 2.76 | 7 | 17.78 | 7.66 | 7 | 6.40 |
| 3.15 | 8 | 20.32 | 8.65 | 8 | 7.32 |
| 3.54 | 9 | 22.86 | 9.84 | 9 | 8.23 |

| miles |   | kilometres |
|-------|---|------------|
| 0.62 | 1 | 1.61 |
| 1.24 | 2 | 3.22 |
| 1.86 | 3 | 4.83 |
| 2.49 | 4 | 6.44 |
| 3.11 | 5 | 8.05 |
| 3.73 | 6 | 9.66 |
| 4.35 | 7 | 11.27 |
| 4.97 | 8 | 12.87 |
| 5.59 | 9 | 14.48 |

A quick way to convert kilometres to miles: divide by 8 and multiply by 5. To convert miles to kilometres: divide by 5 and multiply by 8.

| fahrenheit (°F) | centigrade (°C) | lbs/ sq in | k/ sq cm |
|-----------------|------------------|------------|----------|
| 212° | 100° boiling point | 18 | 1.3 |
| 100° | 38° | 20 | 1.4 |
| 98.4° | 36.9° body temperature | 22 | 1.5 |
| 86° | 30° | 25 | 1.7 |
| 77° | 25° | 29 | 2.0 |
| 68° | 20° | 32 | 2.3 |
| 59° | 15° | 35 | 2.5 |
| 50° | 10° | 36 | 2.5 |
| 41° | 5° | 39 | 2.7 |
| 32° | 0° freezing point | 40 | 2.8 |
| 14° | −10° | 43 | 3.0 |
| −4° | −20° | 45 | 3.2 |
|  |  | 46 | 3.2 |
|  |  | 50 | 3.5 |
|  |  | 60 | 4.2 |

To convert °C to °F: divide by 5, multiply by 9 and add 32. To convert °F to °C: take away 32, divide by 9 and multiply by 5.

## CLOTHING SIZES

Remember – always try on clothes before buying. Clothing sizes are usually unreliable.

### women's dresses and suits

| Europe | 38 | 40 | 42 | 44 | 46 | 48 |
|--------|----|----|----|----|----|----|
| UK     | 32 | 34 | 36 | 38 | 40 | 42 |
| USA    | 10 | 12 | 14 | 16 | 18 | 20 |

### men's suits and coats

| Europe      | 46 | 48 | 50 | 52 | 54 | 56 |
|-------------|----|----|----|----|----|----|
| UK and USA  | 36 | 38 | 40 | 42 | 44 | 46 |

### men's shirts

| Europe     | 36 | 37   | 38 | 39   | 41 | 42   | 43 |
|------------|----|------|----|------|----|------|----|
| UK and USA | 14 | 14½  | 15 | 15½  | 16 | 16½  | 17 |

### socks

| Europe     | 38–39 | 39–40 | 40–41 | 41–42 | 42–43 |
|------------|-------|-------|-------|-------|-------|
| UK and USA | 9½    | 10    | 10½   | 11    | 11½   |

### shoes

| Europe | 34 | 35½ | 36½ | 38 | 39  | 41  | 42  | 43   | 44   | 45   |
|--------|----|-----|-----|----|-----|-----|-----|------|------|------|
| UK     | 2  | 3   | 4   | 5  | 6   | 7   | 8   | 9    | 10   | 11   |
| USA    | 3½ | 4½  | 5½  | 6½ | 7½  | 8½  | 9½  | 10½  | 11½  | 12½  |